My Tainted Blood

My Tainted Blood

Hubert C. Kueter (signature)

Hubert C. Kueter

With a Foreword by
Peter Arnds

Introduction by
Ferdinand Jones

Polar Bear & Company
Solon, Maine

Polar Bear & Company
P.O. Box 311, Solon, Maine 04979 U.S.A.
207-643-2795 www.polarbearandco.com
First edition 2007
12 11 10 09 08   2 3 4 5 6 7
Cover art & design, Reynard the Fox: E. M. Cornell du Houx.
Illustrations: Kueter-Glaeser family collection, pp 2, 6, 10, 11, 13, 14-19, 25, 27-29, 34,
36, 48, 55, 57, 61, 63, 65, 123, 142, 143, 151, 163, 183, 248, 263, 269, 274, 276, 329,
367, 368, 376; Based on Der Volks-Brockhaus, xx; Matthaeus Merian, 1; Gräfe und
Unzer, 12; Schöning & Co., 52; Dr. P. Wolff & Tritschler, 112; Ramona du Houx, 211,
302, 367; Luftschiffbau Zeppelin, 260; Otto Furter, 282.

Library of Congress Cataloging-in-Publication Data

Kueter, Hubert C, 1930-
My tainted blood : a memoir / by Hubert C. Kueter. -- 1st ed.
p. cm.
Summary: "Professor of German literature recounts surviving the Nazis
and postwar racism. The half-Jewish teenager forages to feed family
and friends. Adventures in school, sports, music, cooking, romance, and
intrigue, involving German, Russian, and African American soldiers, tell
the multifaceted story of the German Jews and their unrequited love of
Germany"--Provided by publisher.
ISBN 978-1-882190-88-1 (alk. paper)
1. Kueter, Hubert C, 1930---Childhood and youth. 2. Jews--Germany--
Breslau--Biography. 3. Mischlinge (Nuremberg Laws of 1935)--Biography.
4. Holocaust, Jewish (1939-1945)--Germany--Breslau--Personal narratives.
5. Holocaust survivors--Biography. I. Title.
DS134.42.K84A3 2007
940.53'18092--dc22
[B]
2007037162

Manufactured in the U.S.A. by Thomson-Shore, Inc., an employee owned
company, using soy ink and acid free, recycled paper of archival quality, at
paper permanence specifications defined by ANSI.NISO standard Z39.48-
992: The ability of paper to last several hundred years without significant
deterioration under normal use and storage conditions in libraries and archives."

TO ALL THOSE WHO MADE IT AND
TO THOSE WHO DIDN'T

Contents

List of Recipes, xii
Author's Note, xiii
Acknowledgments, xv
Foreword, xvii
Introduction, xix
Prologue, 1

Chapter I
Gathering clouds, how we got our Christmas goose,
what my mother told me about being Jewish,
why I dreaded going to school,
and how my grandmother preserved her dignity
Page 8

Chapter II
The Gestapo's offer we couldn't refuse,
the allies tighten the noose,
and how we celebrated our last family Christmas in Breslau
Page 39

Chapter III
Summer pastimes, and how we survived the siege of Breslau
Page 50

Chapter IV
How a Russian bomber provided a fish dinner for hundreds,
how I made friends with a Russian officer who nearly got me killed,
and how I got Antek involved in treasure hunting
Page 59

Chapter V
Why my mother appeared to me like a knight in shinning armor,
and what she meant by "our ticket to America"
Page 77

Chapter VI
How I learned about mushrooms,
and why Antek had to flee
Page 87

Chapter VII
How we fled from Breslau
Page 101

Chapter VIII
Bavarian interlude
Page 118

Chapter IX
How I helped Lindhilda with the pig slaughter
and turned into a Bavarian
Page 133

Chapter X
How we left Munich
Page 141

Chapter XI
How we fared during the train ride,
how refugees and Black troops had
transformed Obergünzburg,
how I learned to jitterbug and fly-fish,
befriended a Black captain,
and met Brigitte
Page 148

Chapter XII
Maternal interrogations,
transition from bombs to
the big band sound
Page 168

Chapter XIII
How I encountered local cuisine,
how and why I fought with my mother,
and how the priest enforced God's will
Page 182

Chapter XIV
How Doktor Zorn could not give up his Nazi habits,
and how we fixed him
Page 195

Chapter XV
How we ended up with a seventy-pound wheel of Emmentaler,
how we prepared for Christmas,
and how Brigitte learned to ski
Page 204

Chapter XVI
How we got our Christmas roast,
and how we had our very own Christmas miracle
Page 217

Chapter XVII
How we were reminded that anti-Semitism is not dead,
and how we dealt with the coal shortage
Page 229

Chapter XVIII
What happened in Munich, and why we visited Misha
Page 238

Chapter XIX
How we used a Picasso as bait,
how Onkel Pippi became an armed guard,
and what we caught in the trap
Page 246

Chapter XX
How we got to visit Switzerland,
how the Swiss were treated to unusual food,
and how they learned American slang and song
Page 257

Chapter XXI
How we almost died on a mountain
Page 280

Chapter XXII
A Chinese banquet in Switzerland
Page 295

Chapter XXIII
How we got our contraband through customs,
and Misha's revelation
Page 311

Chapter XXIV
How I learned to define a fanatic,
how our idyllic existence was terminated,
and how I dealt with my anger
Page 321

Chapter XXV
How Brigitte honored the fourth commandment,
why we had to run,
and how Anja helped us
Page 332

Chapter XXVI
How we celebrated what my mother called "Horst's last hurrah,"
and how Antek's neighbor was
cured of his belief in fences
Page 352

Chapter XXVII
How Antek replaced our "ticket to America,"
and how Brigitte became Anja's sister
Page 360

Chapter XXVIII
How my mother packed up her past
Page 366

The author, 376

Recipes

Rumtopf, 12
Carp, 36
Sauerkraut, 37
Mohnklösse, 38
Sweet and Sour Red Cabbage, 42
Silesian Potato Dumplings, 43
Freshwater Fish, 51
Boiled Beef with Horseradish Sauce, 88
Königsberger Klopse, 89
Sautéed Chanterelles, 98
Rote Grütze, 121
Käsespätzle, 185
Recipe for Cheese Salad and Käseschnitzel, 210
Anis Springerle, 212
Schlesischer Streuselkuchen, 301
Pollo alla Cacciatora, 345
Sauerbraten, parts 1&2, 354

Author's Note

When I was very young, before World War II, my mother used to read me stories of Reynard the Fox. Then one day she said, "When there is trouble, always think: what would Reynard do now? And one more thing: don't ever, even when you are old and gray, tell anyone that we are Jewish. No one must ever suspect that you might have Semitic blood in you."

"You mean that I am a first-degree half-breed?"

"Yes. Which means that to them you have tainted blood."

"Do people all over the world think of us that way?"

There was a long pause.

The impact of this brief conversation has affected me my entire life. True to my mother's orders, as well as my own survival instincts, I avoided any discussion of my origin, and when asked point blank, I would deny, not without fear and torment, any connection with the Jewish race. This book, then, is a departure from a seventy-year-long painful silence. It was time, I felt, to come out of the closet.

Here is my story of survival and adventure, but as Reynard might tell it. It is not my objective to provide a document. Exact data have their vital place in understanding historical events. But on their own they do not always communicate the experience of being there. To deal with the roots and lies of totalitarianism, we sometimes need fiction. For what I hope is just the right amount of fiction, I have created Horst to narrate what is, strictly speaking, almost entirely true. Certain superficial facts have been fictionalized along with some of the characterization, so as to go deeper into the human condition as a whole. As such, this story is true to my experience of an era in which much of the world held its breath in anxious horror. The rise, reign, and end of Hitler, as well as the aftermath of WW II, are the circumstances of the narrative.

I have relived these, my early teens, many times since, pausing at every incident, reevaluating our odds for survival back then, asking myself over and over: What if?— What would have happened had I—

or my mother—or our opponents, the Nazis?— Would I, if the war had ended earlier with Germany's defeat, be living in Breslau now? Or, had the Nazis come out on top, would I and my mother have ended up like so many of us? What if those bombs that landed near me had exploded? The factual data take on universal proportions.

The vivid memories of my youth in Germany have become a living organism, whose roots, branches, and blossoms make up my story, a story that tells not only of pursuit and escape, but one that presents the totality of my existence, every aspect of which—school, friendships, cooking experiences, sports, music, romance, and intrigue—was affected by my "birth flaw." It tells not only of disasters but also of triumphs—our modest victories—in an era of immodest defeats. I realize now that ours was the tragic story of the German Jews and their unrequited love for Germany—Jews who, despite conversion, splendid accomplishments, and boundless love of fatherland, were persecuted, shunned, and driven away.

Seventy years later, Horst disobeys his mother's command of silence, so his story might survive and add some perspective. And while doing so, can't he just sense Reynard's presence, looking over his shoulder, nodding his head, saying over and over, "Keep it up, boy, keep it up!"

Oakland, Maine   H.C.K.
October, 2007

Acknowledgments

My gratitude to all who have contributed with their heart, hand, and head to the successful completion of this book. I am grateful for every added or deleted comma and all critical notes, such as those by Charles Basset who read the manuscript from the English professor's point of view and whose insightful comments gave me a few issues to ponder. Special mention is due to Ingrid Bade for her encouragements; to Sophie Gruhn who supplied me with comments, family history and pictures; to Jane Moss, Michele Brooks, and Jürgen Meyer, my early readers; to Debbie Swart, my last reader; to Gaby Glaeser, and Utte and Bastel Hillebrand, for reading, commenting, and filling in some of the historical facts; and to my publisher/editor Paul Cornell du Houx and his family, who turned the long publishing process into such a pleasant experience, while turning the book into a polished product. Last and most important: thanks to my wife Nancy for her advice, love, and support.

Smarter than all his enemies

Foreword

A Journey Driven by Myth and Memory

"Well, that's how you have to be. Smarter than all the others. When there is trouble, always think: what would Reynard do now?" Horst's mother warns her son so that he may always slip away unnoticed by his potential persecutors, the Nazis. These words are reminiscent of other literary warnings in the face of fascism. Nobel Laureate Günter Grass's mother, for example, used to caution her son to be as smart as Ibsen's Peer Gynt. Indeed, Grass's oeuvre and Hubert Kueter's novel, *My Tainted Blood,* show many parallels. Both have a fascination with recipes and cooking, and as migrants from today's Poland their work is steeped in the picaresque tradition, taking recourse to myths, legends, and the trickster archetype, that timeless wanderer on the margins of society. Yet Kueter's novel is also an important work of memory, and as such a timely undertaking in view of the shadow the Nazis' persecution of the eternal wanderer, the Jews and the Gypsies, still casts on immigration policies today, in view also of religious extremism and the glossing over of truths in the political arena. With its context of war and displacement, its representation through mythological patterns, and its focus on picaresque wandering, this novel can indeed be aligned with the wider tradition of magic realism, not only with Grass's famous *Tin Drum* (1959), but also with key works like Gabriel García Márquez's *One Hundred Years of Solitude* (1967), Salman Rushdie's *Midnight's Children* (1980) and *The Satanic Verses* (1988), Mikhail Bulgakov's *The Master and Margarita* (1967), Michel Tournier's *The Erl-King* (1970), John Irving's *A Prayer for Owen Meany* (1989), or Kurt Vonnegut's *Slaughterhouse V* (1969).

These are texts that relate the central category of the wandering picaro—for that is what Horst or Reynard the Fox are—closely to the notions of memory and even trauma. Texts that reveal that wandering may trigger memory, while sedentariness supports oblivion and the suppression of truths. Like these world-renowned books, Hubert Kueter's autobiography unearths hidden memories. In his recent work, *Peeling the Onion,* which just appeared in translation in the U.S., Grass describes how memory has a tendency to creep away, play hide and seek. To Grass the image of peeling onions is an apt reflection of how one can get to the innermost layers of memory. It is memoirs such as Grass's and Kueter's that manage to lure hidden memories from their hiding places. The importance of this ought not to be underestimated, especially when it comes to the process of acting out and working through trauma, both in its individual and collective contextualization. According to Lewis Hyde, one of the great cultural critics in this country, the artist is, like his or her mythological trickster creations, working with joints, for which Latin has the word *articulus,* the Greek *arthron.* Acting out and working through the traumatic memory of the loss of home, of *Heimat,* during war is an experience shared by writers around the globe. Ultimately, it implies the articulation of a narrative that joins the present to the past. This is precisely what the novels of magic realism and Hubert Kueter's *My Tainted Blood* do to a high degree. They take their readers on wondrous journeys driven by myth and memory.

Peter Arnds, PhD
Professor of German and Italian
Kansas State University

Introduction

Strength of the Human Spirit

Hubert Kueter's account of surviving WWII and its immediate aftermath in Germany as a half-Jewish youth is remarkable in its illustration of several elements of what some resilience scholars are calling "ordinary magic." While prevailing over life-threatening hardships, Kueter also reveals his success in negotiating the psychological intricacies of self-esteem development. In a style that at times reads like an adventure story, he is a precocious and unusually sensitive observer of himself and the people around him. He chronicles his development of extraordinary self-confidence under conditions that would not seem to allow a positive self-view. In fact Kueter, who would as an adult become a chef and a German literature professor, skillfully interweaves stories of inventive food finding and its preparation into his narrative, seeming to exemplify the hardy attitude he attains.

Psychologists have been trying to understand why it is that some individuals survive extreme adversity with minimum disruptions to their development and others are handicapped by the same circumstances. Lately prominent researchers reviewing longitudinal studies of children who were vulnerable to developmental assaults by adverse social, environmental, and physical conditions have been impressed that when certain essential development enhancing foundations are in place children will thrive. Kueter's story is a dramatic demonstration of these protections.

When he is a preschool child in Breslau, Kueter's mother, the Jewish and widowed spouse in a mixed marriage, teaches him two important lessons that later guided him through many actual and psychological minefields. She instructed him that Jews were, especially during that time, a persecuted people. For that reason it was dangerous to reveal the Jewish part of his heritage to anyone. The second message she drilled into him was that he possessed natural gifts of cunning and reasoning, and he should always rely on them to tackle any problems he would encounter in life.

Kueter's mother conveyed her caring for her son in these and in many other examples of solid parenting. She also modeled for him the kind of intelligent social skills that would serve him well. She additionally emphasized to him the importance of being in control of his emotions. These are core qualities of resilient children that have been identified in many studies. They are magical in their common but effective ordinariness.

African American psychologists have been interested in another facet of the resilience question that Kueter's memoir illuminates. How can a child growing up as a member of a denigrated social group attain a positive sense of him- or herself? Why doesn't the bombardment of negative associations to that membership deter self-confidence and prevent maximum individual functioning? We know that these questions touch on what we've learned about the vast complexity of self-identity. For instance, individuals are able to hold many and fluctuating images of themselves all at the same time. We also now appreciate the survival power of the cautionary lessons African American parents and communities teach their children. Like the effective parent in any oppressed group, Kueter's mother affirms his worth and his strengths while arming him with the knowledge that others, especially those in authority, may see him differently and use that different perception to hurt him.

In the austerity of postwar Germany, Kueter and his mother are befriended by a Black American officer in a U.S. military occupation unit. Kueter graphically describes their exchange of goods and culture. He ironically and perhaps unwittingly also depicts a symbolic coming together of racial identity resolution and psychological resilience.

Hubert Kueter's accomplishment in this memoir is a unique literary triumph, but it is as well a vivid account of the strength of the human spirit.

Ferdinand Jones, PhD
Professor Emeritus of Psychology
Brown University

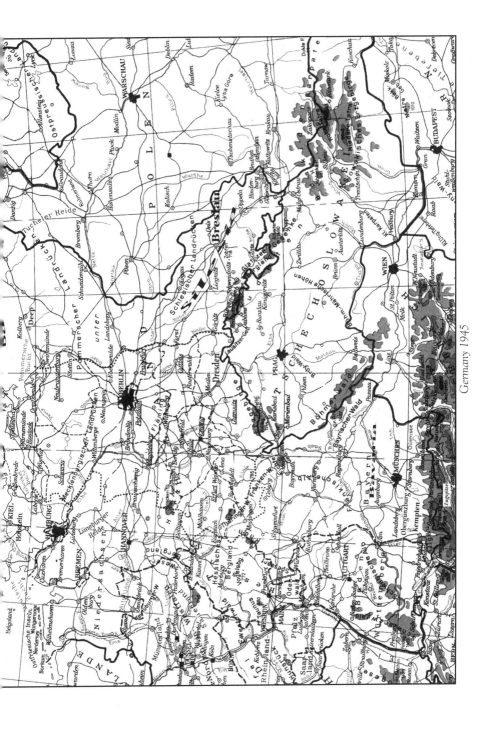

Germany 1945

My Tainted Blood

Prologue

Breslau Etching circa 1650

Ever since the day Adam and Eve were driven from Paradise—or is it ever since the day Cain slew Abel?—they have been on the move; that adds up to millennia. It was a curse, and these events gave rise to the tale of the *eternal Jew* or the *wandering Jew*. Henceforth the Jews were condemned to move from one diaspora to the next, from one pogrom to the next, from one country to the next, from one *shtetl* or ghetto to the next, seldom allowed to rest for more than two or three hundred years in one location. There were always some governments, rulers, and regulations that limited their freedom and kept them at the lowest level of the lowest possible caste. Rarely a liberal monarch would grant them some privileges. Whenever this was the case, many Jews would reach positions of considerable wealth and respectability—great scientists, artists, scholars, musicians, and writers carried Jewish names. But then, without fail, the curse would strike again, sending those of Jewish blood in search of safe havens.

I don't know what events and hopes led my Jewish ancestors to German speaking areas. A few facts, perhaps more than is commonly the case, are known. My mother, Katherina Kueter (1900-1995), née Sachs, thought it would be useful and interesting for younger generations to know a bit of their ancestors' history. So she sat down and wrote what she called, "History of the Immerwahrs." Immerwahr was her mother's maiden name. This, verbatim, is what she wrote.

Katherina Kueter

To start my history, I want to point to Hillel Silberstein from Brieg, a small town in Silesia, through whom, so I have been told, we are all related to one another. Neither the date of his birth nor his profession is known. He died around 1840 in Breslau.

He must have been fairly well-to-do, because he was a financial contributor in the building of the Storchen-Synagoge on Wallstrasse in Breslau. He married Babette Leubuscher, known as Jettel. They had one son, Julius, owner of the agricultural estate, Malkwitz (near Breslau), and five daughters, all of whom married well, two of them in Vienna.

One, Sophie Krohn, had a daughter who became the wife of the editor-in-chief of the Vienna *Freie Presse*. Her cousin, Lina Silberstein, married David Immerwahr, originally from Kreuzburg in Upper Silesia, where he was born around 1790.

As a young man he arrived in Breslau on foot. There he became quite successful. His business—Persian rugs, cigars, and textiles—was located in his home on Ring 19, a house which extended all the way back to the Junkernstrasse, the street running parallel to the Ring. I still remember the entrance with its Gothic columns. My mother used to tell stories about the Friday evenings of her childhood, which she spent in the huge rooms of her grandparents' house.

David Immerwahr's interests certainly were not limited to business. Among other things, he collected musical instruments, which he made available to the Breslau Opera. When the opera house burned down, they were all destroyed. Undaunted, he began his next collection. Some of these instruments remained in the family into the 1930s. My husband played one of his violas. Unforgettable for me is one violin which was entirely inlaid with tortoise shell.

With the conductor of the orchestra, Leopold Damrosch, David had a close friendship. When Damrosch accepted his call to New York, but preferred to initially leave without his family, it was great-grandmother Lina Immerwahr (David's wife) who invited them to stay for the duration of the wait. Thus Mme. Damrosch and her four children moved into the big house on Ring 19.

A grandson of the Immerwahrs, Dr. Rudolf Freund, who had often played with the Damrosch children, later immigrated to the U.S.A. and visited his former playmate, Walter Damrosch, who had succeeded his father as conductor of the New York Metropolitan Opera. The two men celebrated their happy reunion and exchanged fond old memories.

A well-known Silesian portrait artist painted a life-size canvas of David Immerwahr, which showed him surrounded by Persian rugs and cigar boxes—an imposing figure. The painting was destroyed in a bombing raid during World War II. Likewise destroyed was the building on Ring 19. The Poles rebuilt it in its original style.

David must have taken frequent trips to Paris to purchase merchandise. His passport is in the archives of the Baeck Institute, New York. On one of those trips he commissioned a fine Parisian cabinetmaker to make a custom-made living room set for his large living quarters. It consisted of an oversized sofa for at least eight, also a smaller one decorated with woodcarvings, and an enormous table, between the legs of which there was a fruit basket carved in wood. After the death of Philipp Immerwahr, David's son, my mother, Elli, received the larger half of these furnishings, and Clara Immerwahr, her sister, the other half. When we were evicted from our duplex in 1941, my mother was forced to sell these precious pieces, because the apartment which was assigned to us was too small to accommodate them.

One more thing about Lina Immerwahr. She was a *Luisendame*. That means that the German Empire awarded her membership in the Order of Luise for her patriotic activities during the war of 1866.

About three of David Immerwahr's sons I know nothing but their first names: Rudolf, Emil, and Otto. So now I can talk about his fourth son, my grandfather, Dr. Philipp Immerwahr. He was married to his niece, Anna Krohn. Their children were: Paul Immerwahr, who had doctorates in law and philosophy; Lotte, married to Fritz Meffert, a patent lawyer; Dr. Clara Immerwahr, married to Fritz Haber; and Elli, my mother, married to Siegfried Sachs.

Grandfather Philipp was a chemist and, as such, director of the sugar refinery of Trachenberg (Silesia). He also owned the large agricultural estate, Polkendorf, near Neumarkt, and operated the city-owned estates, Oswitz and Ransem. In addition, he was co-owner of the Immerwahr business in Ring 19. While studying at the University of Breslau, he belonged to a fraternity called Raczecks. At that time the fraternities were left-liberal and accepted Jews.

Since I was only eight years old at Grandfather's death in 1908, I got my information about him from the Cramer family who took the lonely man in after his wife's death. The four Cramer children took turns visiting him after school and joined him for dinner, which the Upper Silesian cook invariably turned into gourmet meals. Afterwards he helped the children with homework. My old friend Eva Cramer especially mentioned how good his Latin was and how much he helped her with translating Julius Caesar. He must have been very generous, because people said, "Whoever as much as hits a nail in Dr. Immerwahr's house is eligible for a pension." That applied of course to his cook, Julie, and his man Friday, August, who served as coachman when in the country and as general servant when in the city. About him and Grandfather there exist some characteristic stories which are worth preserving for posterity.

August called Grandfather's attention to the fact that he had been in his service for thirty years now—by way of expecting a gift. Grandfather said to a friend, "I am the one who deserves an award for putting up with him for thirty years."

August was supposed to wake Grandfather at six in the morning; at five o'clock there was a knock on the door, and a voice said, "Sir, you can sleep one more hour. I didn't read the time correctly."

August wasn't feeling well and, on Grandfather's advice, went to see Dr. Cramer. When Grandfather inquired about the examination, August said, "The doctor said my brain is enlarged." Whereupon Grandfather commented, "Well, August, in that case you might become awfully smart one of these days."

Grandfather's son Paul was one of the directors of the well-known Auergesellschaft. Unfortunately, Philipp's relationship to this son suffered in later years, owing to a petty inheritance matter involving a porcelain washbowl and a pitcher.

Paul loved animals. His last will began thus: "It is my last will and testament that all my possessions be left to my dog Feldmann and to my rabbit Hoppel ..." It behooves my generation, however, to remember him with gratitude, because, after the death of his wife, we received a sizeable inheritance; in addition, the Nazis overlooked his family foundation which helped many of us through the postwar years.

Of my grandfather's daughters, my mother, Elli, was the eldest. They always said that Elli was the most distinguished, Lotte the most easygoing, and Clara the most intellectual. My mother, Elli, was married to Siegfried Sachs, who managed the estates Oswitz and Ransem, as well as Masselwitz on the other side of the Oder River. I did not know my father, who died when I was one year old.

The youngest of the sisters, Clara, attended the University of Breslau and was the first woman to receive a doctorate from that university—in chemistry. She married Prof. Fritz Haber who received the Nobel Prize in 1918 for finding a way to synthesize ammonia and nitrogen from air. When Clara and Fritz were married, the newspaper carried the story: FRÄULEIN DOKTOR—FRAU PROFESSOR. In 1915, after her husband, the father of chemical warfare, had invented the deadly chlorine gas in order to aid Germany's war effort, Clara, probably in protest to her husband's work, committed suicide.

Fritz Haber, along with all the German Jewish scientists under Hitler, was removed from his leading position. Despite his poor health, he attempted to continue his career in several countries. Weizmann, who later became the first president of Israel [1949-52], wanted to have him in Israel at the Weizmann

Institute in Rehovot, but he was more inclined to accept an invitation to the University of Cambridge, England—this never came to pass because he died in 1934 in Basel, Switzerland. I

Siegfried Sachs,	Claras Schwester
Schwager von	Elsbeth Rosalie Sachs,
Clara Immerwahr	geb. Immerwahr

often visited Clara's and his grave there.

Now I want to write about my father's family, the Sachses. This will take us back to, as stories have it, the 14th or 15th century. It is said that the Sachs family had lived in Spain, but in the 15th century all Jews were driven from the Iberian Peninsula. How and when the Sachses arrived in Prague is uncertain, but there exist a number of very old gravestones that bear their name. The name itself is a Hebrew acronym meaning as much as "descendant of martyrs."

Even though there were no pogroms in Prague during the 16th century, there were mass expulsions. That is how an Abraham Sachs came to Silesia, where he settled in Glogau. There, a special privilege was granted to his family, protecting them and allowing them to remain. We know of a Mayer Sachs who died in 1775 in Glogau.

Then there was a Süssman Sachs (1747–1827), a textile

merchant, who died in Breslau. His gravestone is in the Jewish cemetery on Clasenstrasse. One of his sons was Moritz, a very prosperous merchant in textiles, furniture, and antiques. He bore the title of *Hoflieferant* (royal court merchant). He was married to Mathilde Schlesinger. His son Leopold Sachs, though still a merchant, branched out into agriculture, later owning and working the Masselwitz estate (Rittergut). His son Leopold Moritz (1832–1879) added two more estates to his possessions. He was my grandfather.

My father, Siegfried (1853 -1901), married an Immerwahr, Elsbeth Rosalie, known as Tante Elli. In 1941, in order to escape deportation, she committed suicide. She, her husband, as well as their children, were baptized. Now there are cousins who bear the name; one of them is Günther Sachs, the general.

All the agricultural estates were first taken over by the Nazis, after 1945 by the Poles. Some of the family properties in Breslau made it through the siege; the others have been rebuilt. Our family received some very modest reparations from the West German government for the losses. The Sachs-Immerwahr gravesites in the Jewish cemetery still exist and are maintained by the Jewish congregation of Breslau. I hope some of you will look at them when you visit Breslau (Wroclaw), the city where your ancestors lived and prospered for about a century and a half.

I

Gathering clouds, what my mother told me about being Jewish, why I dreaded going to school, how my grandmother preserved her dignity, and how we got our Christmas goose

MY MOTHER, HOLDING A blond, curly haired child, entered the open veranda. Inspecting the large oval table, she adjusted a plate here, a cup there, fussed with the flower arrangement, turned her head into the breeze and sniffed the air, which was fragrant with the aroma of freshly brewed coffee. As she contemplated the platters heaped with mountains of Streuselkuchen, an irresistible urge seized her. Unable to overcome the temptation, she extracted a particularly large, buttery streusel from its bed of yeast cake, chewed it slowly and pleasurably, then created another empty space in the dense streusel cover for her child's delight.

Roses and dahlias bloomed in endless flowerbeds. On the lawn, several older children were playing Boccia. Laughter and the sharp cracking sounds of wood on wood added to the summery atmosphere. To make the idyll complete, stringed instruments were playing somewhere inside the house. My father and two of his colleagues, all members of the Silesian Philharmonic, were practicing for their performance later on. My mother's brother-in-law, Onkel Pippi, was glancing at the poem he had composed for the occasion.

My grandmother's 65th birthday was not to be taken lightly. She was an awe-inspiring woman who ran the huge estate as efficiently, strictly, and capably as any general in command of an army. The keys to every door, chest, and cupboard were attached to a ring dangling from her belt. She apparently did not realize that every one of her steps produced a jingling which would alert employees to the approaching danger. No one had ever seen her without it. There were also rumors to the effect that she rationed out toilet paper, not on the generous side, either.

"Emma!" my mother called. "Make sure the maids are ready to receive the guests."

Emma had been with the family for many years. She was the only one my grandmother fully trusted. In her, all the qualities of an indispensable aide were combined: she was cook, educator, governess, and confidante for all the children and grandchildren.

Punctually—no one would have dared to do otherwise—the guests arrived. Since it was such a beautiful day, all the friends and relatives had enjoyed the stroll to Oma's* manor. It was only a fifteen-minute walk from the streetcar stop, Oswitz, the last one on the Number 22 line.

Oswitz, on the outskirts of the city, was a popular destination for Breslau's weekend nature lovers. Numerous meticulously groomed paths along the Oder River attracted a steady stream of visitors from the city. One path led to the famous Schwedenschanze** a remnant of the Thirty Years' War; others meandered from garden café to garden café where guests could enjoy delicious pastries while watching the huge Oder barges passing by in both directions.

After the initial pleasantries, everyone was directed to an assigned chair at the table, Oma's two daughters traditionally to her right and left. Onkel Pippi, accustomed to assuming the role of host, welcomed all who had come to pay homage to the grande dame of the family. As frequently happened, he displayed a certain reluctance to end his address and continued rhapsodically praising his mother-in-law's virtues with a cannonade of words. Soon two maids began serving coffee from large Meissen pots. Of robust Silesian farmers' stock, they appeared dainty beyond reality in black uniforms with white, embroidered cuffs and caps. While this was going on, Onkel Pippi managed to fit in the poem he had composed, a poem reviewing Oma's accomplishments, which culminated in the existence of her five grandchildren. Everyone marveled at the poet's skill of having been able to work the names of all five of them—Otto, Hannes, Sophie, Werner, and Horst—into rhyming verse.

While the mountainous Streuselkuchen platters were losing altitude, my father's string trio performed, and, as if all this were not

*Oma: German for grandmother **Swedish wall fortifications

*My mother, holding
a blond, curly haired child*

enough, the grandchildren treated the party to a skit, written, rehearsed, and directed by Onkel Pippi, in which Oma, played hilariously by Sophie, appeared as some mythological, supernatural Earth mother who bestowed health and wealth throughout the land.

As dessert wines were circulating, conversations turned to politics. It was 1933, after all, and the extreme nationalistic Hitler party was beginning to frighten, not just the birthday celebrants, but the entire world. Onkel Fritz, a wealthy banker and city councilor, announced that he was making plans to leave Germany for good. "Mark my words," he stated. "It's the Nazis' goal to make life miserable for all of us. If you heard that Goebbels speech the other day, you'll know that they will not rest until Germany is free of every last one of us. America, or perhaps England, will be the only safe haven for Jews."

My grandmother sat rigidly, stony faced in her chair. She was a bit paler now than a few minutes ago. "I am not leaving," she announced somewhat haughtily. "I don't think I have to. They all know who I am and what I stand for. I have made large gold donations to the war effort; my brother was a decorated major in the German Army; my sister was the first woman to earn a PhD at the University of Breslau, not to mention the fact that her husband, Onkel Fritz Haber, is a Nobel Prize winner. Besides, I am a Protestant, as was my husband." Her voice was wavering; her hands were shaking.

"Tante* Elli—" Günther, her nephew, interrupted my Oma. He was the black sheep of the family because he had chosen to be fighter pilot during the war, instead of following the traditional intellectual pursuits. Now, miraculously, he was a major in the newly established German Air Force. He and Göring had served in the same squadron

*Tante: German for aunt

during the war—Göring, who was quoted as saying, "I decide who is Jewish and who is not."

"Tante Elli!" Günther continued, "You don't know the Nazis as I do. They will not stop for any reason in their efforts to get rid of us. Possibly your last name alone—Sachs—the same as mine, may be lethal. I have powerful friends in top positions who protect me. But I have to be very careful. And don't think that your conversion to Christianity will protect you. The Nazis believe that Semitic blood is infinitely inferior to Aryan blood. To them we are nothing but a bunch of ugly, cowardly, pushy, cheating, lying, greedy, lecherous degenerates, and they will not have these traits perpetuated in their country. Why can't you, all of you, get it through your heads that, to a Nazi, being Jewish means only one thing: carrying *Semitic* blood! It has nothing to do with any religion."

Trained to be cautious, Günther paused while one of the maids cleared away dishes.

"I can only guess as to what may happen to Jews within the next few years, but I know that German industry is making a huge effort to surpass the air capability of England and France. And once a war breaks out, Germany won't care if other countries condemn its actions against Jews. No! I would advise all racially pure Jews to leave while they can. As for mixed marriages," and he looked at my mother and her sister, "I think you might be safe for a while. But I don't guarantee it. As for myself and all my half-breed cousins here? Who knows? I suppose, as long as we are of some use to them, they'll tolerate us."

It took some time to overcome the silence of depression. Gradually, the party split up into smaller groups which went about pursuing their own interests. Some of the gentlemen withdrew to

Onkel Pippi was glancing at the poem.

distant rooms for cigars, port wine, and billiards; the ladies strolled through the park, pausing at the pond to feed ducks and carp; some of the older cousins sauntered to the stables for horseback riding, others down to the river where a section had been roped off for safe swimming. The general aim was to aid digestion of the Streuselkuchen and to make room for things to come.

Yes, let the truth be known: all these good people had not traveled one or two hours merely to honor an old lady or to get their ears filled with doomsday predictions. No. The secondary, if not the primary reason behind their journeys from afar, was to have their stomachs filled and their cravings satisfied with taste sensations which my grandmother could provide better than anyone else. The delicately handwritten invitations had included the menu for tonight's feast: truffled goose livers on toast, followed by *avgolemono,* a lemony, creamy chicken soup which Oma had come to appreciate during a trip through Greece. Then there would be a course consisting of a regional specialty: crayfish from the Oder, large, meaty crustaceans which were famous throughout Germany, served with melted herbed butter. And anyone who expected to find cold roast beef with Cumberland sauce on the menu was not disappointed. Its absence was as unimaginable as would be the absence of Oma's trademark dessert: *Rumtopf* with whipped cream.

Ah, Rumtopf! Layers of choice, seasonal fruit—raspberries, apricots

Watching the huge Oder barges passing by

quartered, pears quartered, strawberries, cherries, currants, plums, peaches quartered, and pineapple in chunks—marinated in rum and sugar for an entire year. Every pound* of fruit gets a half pound of sugar. At all times, the 80-proof rum should never fall below an inch above the fruit. Each additional fruit is layered in as it comes into season. It is traditionally marinated until Christmas.

She was an awe-inspiring woman.

If anything is capable of restoring hope and faith in humanity it is a stomach filled with exquisite food and strong drink. Even Onkel Günther, the major, suddenly announced, in between spoons heaped with rum cherries and whipped cream, that his view of the Nazis was perhaps not quite as grave as he had expressed earlier. "No, they are mostly quite decent chaps. Göring invited me to his hunting lodge some time ago. Know what he said? 'Only a German is truly capable of loving animals'."

May it be mentioned in my uncle's defense that he said that after several glasses of Madeira.

My mother's diary entry for this day in July 1933 reads:

> Spent two days at Oma's for her birthday. Everyone was there, even Günther. Why did he have to wear his uniform? Food as usual: everything just perfect. Fidi and his colleagues played the first movement of a Haydn string trio. Fidi played beautifully. Why don't they make him concertmaster? His Jewish wife? Pippi, as always, a little long winded. Funny poem, though. Politics, of course: Fritz, Hans, and Eduard have decided to go to America. They think we should, too. Günther, who should know, said that there is no future for Jews in Germany. Horsti was a very good boy. I think he'll turn into a real gourmet. Goose liver seems to

*One German pound (Pfund) is 500 grams.

The black sheep of the family

be his favorite, but he was afraid of the crayfish and started crying when someone came at him with one of the claws. They all love him, though. With his Aryan looks he may be the savior of all of us—or they'll take him away from me.

During the months following this gathering, our circle of friends and relatives grew ever smaller. Fortunately, most of the guests at that 65th birthday celebration had not taken Onkel Günther's drunken pro-Nazi remarks seriously. They had gathered up their belongings, as much as the Nazis permitted them to, and had left the country.

"Why are all these people moving away?" I asked my mother.

Gradually—actually it took a few years to get the full picture—my mother hinted that our family was different from other German families, but for a long time she had avoided mentioning THE WORD. One day, a unit of Hitler Youth was passing our house. I always enjoyed watching them because of their singing. Little did I or, at that time, any German, realize that some of their songs predicted the death of millions and the destruction of Germany:

> Wir werden weiter marschieren,
> Wenn alles in Scherben fällt,
> Denn heute gehört uns Deutschland,
> Und morgen die ganze Welt.

The following translation accurately expresses the sentiment of the song.

> We'll go on marching together,
> May walls crumble and fall.
> Today's prize is Germany,
> Tomorrow's the world and all.

Mother tried to shield me from these songs, but one day I caught some really shocking and scary words: something about "Jew-blood dripping from the knife . . ." That's when the word "Jewish" was, for the first time, brought into direct relationship with me. Up to that point I had had the vague impression that "Jewish" was synonymous with "no good." People were sent to prison because of it, or were beaten up, or thrown out of school, or shunned by other Germans. Now I was one of those? It shook me as badly as the news would that none of my friends would ever play with me again. In fact, that was precisely what I feared. I had no idea what "Jewish" really meant, but it had to be something pretty bad, which meant, as far as I could see, that my life would never be the same again.

As my mother's lectures continued, I gradually learned about the religious, racial, and historical significance of being Jewish.

"But how can we be Jews then?" I wailed. "We are Protestants! Oma is a Protestant, and Papa is—what do you call them? Yes! An Aryan."

So I was introduced to the Nazi's subtle, new, Nuremburg laws, devised to the detriment of Jews, the "Law for the Protection of German Blood and German Honor." I learned that my mother, though baptized, was considered a "racially full Jew," whereas I, the child of a full Jew and an Aryan, was a *Mischling ersten Grades* (first-degree half-breed). My children, if I married an Aryan, would be second-degree half-breeds. Chances for this to happen, however, were remote. There was a free trip to Auschwitz reserved for all first-degree half-breeds who might be foolish enough to want to touch a pureblooded Aryan. My mother, the

Author's parents

fully Jewish Protestant, whose marriage had predated these laws, was not quite as badly off as others like her, because she was married to an Aryan. Moreover, my—the half Aryan's—existence offered a certain amount of protection to her, protection which my grandmother, being the widow of a racially full Jew, was utterly lacking.

After my mother's detailed lecture on Nazi law regarding Jews, her six-year-old son felt as if he had eaten way too much Streuselkuchen, with way too much whipped cream.

"Mama," I groaned, "I think am going to be sick. What are we going to do? Does everyone know? My friends, their parents, our neighbors?"

"No, Horsti, no one knows. And I am going to tell you something that will help you and all of us. Remember that story I read to you? The one you liked so much, about the fox who was smarter than all of his enemies and who came out on top in the end?"

"Sure! Reynard the Fox!"

"Well, that's how you have to be. Smarter than all the others. When there is trouble, always think: what would Reynard do now? And one more thing: don't ever, even when you are old and gray, tell anyone that we are Jewish. No one must ever suspect that you might have Semitic blood in you.

Why don't they make him concertmaster?

"You mean that I am a first-degree half-breed?"

"Yes. Which means that to them you have tainted blood."

"Do people all over the world think of us that way?"

There was a long pause.

"There are good, intelligent people—many I hope—even here in Germany, who don't dislike Jews. And there are bad, ignorant people—not too many I hope—even in America, who do dislike Jews. That is why I told you to never tell anyone, because even in a free country like America anti-Semitism could suddenly flare up. So my answer to your question is yes and no. But right here and right now in Germany, things are about as bad as can be. That is the reason why so many of our friends and relatives have moved to America. At least there, no laws are directed against Jews."

"Why don't we go to America then?"

"I know. I think about this all the time. But this is our home. Papa works here, and there are many smart people who say that the Nazis won't last long and that the rest of the world won't permit the Nazis to hurt us."

My mother's revelations and stern admonitions cast a shadow

With his Aryan looks he may be the savior of all of us.

over me, which accompanied me wherever I went and whatever I did. Never again would I be entirely free of it, always consciously or subconsciously afraid that people would take note.

Journal entry, summer 1935: Finally had that dreaded talk with Horsti. Tried to explain "Jewish" to him and what it means for us. Now he is worried and scared. But I think he needed to know—to get used to the idea. It's on his mind all the time now. Asked me the other day if some dogs or trees could be Jewish. One dog he knows is black and has such a long nose, and that one tree has such crooked ugly branches. Scares me!*

By the time I was six my father had died of a kidney infection, Oma had been forced to sell the estate, and World War II was less than three years away. We now lived in a two-family villa in the suburbs, we in the downstairs apartment, Oma upstairs. Now the protection provided by my Aryan father's existence was gone, and friends and relatives kept urging us to leave the country, the sooner the better, but my mother and Oma, joined by other more or less well-informed friends and relatives, kept insisting that this nightmare would soon be over. My Tante Detta's and Onkel Pippi's family, the Glaesers, were

*This and all subsequent entries are from my mother's journal.

also unwilling to abandon everything. Now they would come to visit us in our new home on Sundays in order to enjoy Oma's still-fabulous dinners.

As my friends and I went on playing cowboys and Indians and engaging in varied sports, my earlier fears gradually subsided to a degree. Yet, every day I encountered so many constant reminders of my precarious status that I learned to move and speak very cautiously.

During these years, food was still plentiful, and I had ample opportunity to observe and help my grandmother in the kitchen. Thus my interest in food and culinary matters developed. It was an enjoyable, useful, non-confrontational pastime.

But no matter how involved I got with measuring, stirring, tasting, and licking, there remained a constant reminder in the back of my mind that something dreadful was relentlessly approaching: my first day of school. If in itself a fearsome event for anyone, how much more so for me with my horrible secret? Or was it a secret?

Journal entry, April 1936: Horsti's first day in school. His best friend, Wolfgang, from across the street, is in his class. "Does Wolfgang know?" he asked. He did not say much else on the way, but he really looked worried and complained about a stomachache. He was in much better spirits when I picked him up again. Said the teacher was very nice. They had sung in class, and he had been the only one who knew all the songs. Really loves to sing.

Now I was one of those?

Whenever I was sick with one of the childhood diseases—I

think I had them all—Oma would sit by my bed, reading to me for hours on end. One day I asked her, "Oma, do you have some books I could read and look at?"

"Well, yes. Of course I have books. What sorts of books do you have in mind?"

"Okay. You know that thick cookbook with all those pictures? I would really like to look at them and read some of the recipes."

"Really? Fine. I'll get it. I hope those pictures with all that food won't make you even sicker."

The first woman to earn a PhD at the University of Breslau

Journal entry, September 1937: I wonder why Horsti has to stay home so often. I think the pressure is affecting his stomach. Dreads the walks back and forth to school. There are ugly posters of Jews everywhere. The worst caricatures one can imagine. By the time he reaches school he has stomach cramps and feels sick. In school he is afraid to go to that dark toilet in the basement. Scared that one of the vile, ugly Jews from the posters might be lurking down there. More cramps as a result. If this propaganda has that much effect on a child with Horsti's background, imagine what it does to the average German? But what can I do? America? A penniless widow with a young child alone in a foreign country? Pastor Konrad said in his sermon that God will not allow this evil much longer. Was promptly arrested and taken to a concentration camp. Such a wonderful man! The new pastor is very young and scared. Looks over his shoulder every time he says Amen.

March 1938: Finally got my courage up to talk to Horst's teacher, Herrn Sanke. He knew already! How? They must really have it down to a system. Assured me he would do all he could to protect Horsti. Said he loves Horsti's musicality and his sense of humor. There are still a few good Germans left.

However, cookbooks were not my only source of inspiration. My father had been an avid naturalist, and among his books was a huge ten-volume encyclopedia on every known living creature, called *Brehms Tierleben.* Of these, the one that captured my interest most was the one on fish, more specifically, edible fish: where they lived, how they lived, what they ate, how they mated, where and when they spawned, and how they could be caught. That was the part I would pore over for hours. Living near a large river and surrounded by lakes, it was mostly freshwater fish I studied: carp, eel, pike, perch.

I don't know if any of the described methods for capture ever worked for anyone; they surely did not work for me. Imagine sliding along the ice of a stream or lake, peering into the depths below, provided there is no snow cover, until you would spot a pike, those creatures that hover motionlessly among aquatic plants until an unsuspecting little fish comes into striking distance. When you spot such a pike, said the directions, you should take your axe and strike hard at the ice above it—with the blunt side, of course. This blow would so stun the pike that it would go belly up, whereupon you would then take the cutting edge of the ax, chop a hole through the ice and gather up your prey. I must have looked pretty silly, stalking along the shore of that lake, carrying an ax raised above my head.

Also, to catch a large eel in winter, you were to proceed as follows: attach a small piece of wood centered at right angles at the top of a long stick and sink long spear-point-like tips—in my case long nails, three of them—into the piece of wood, so you would end up with a forklike three-pronged spear. In winter, eels reportedly burrow into the muddy bottom of lakes and rivers, where they can easily be speared through a hole in the ice. Of course, there was no possibility of visually penetrating the dark depth below, and you had to have some kind of sixth sense that would tell you where to start poking around. Obviously, I was lacking in that respect. One more time I amused the public with my futile efforts. After I had sent two axes to the bottom of the lake and had broken through the ice to my waist a few times, I gave up, much to my mother's relief. Later, I learned a much more productive fishing strategy from Russian soldiers.

Journal entry, autumn 1939: Poland has fallen. Tanks against cavalry. There are horrible stories about what the Nazis are doing to Polish Jews. Exactly as Günther predicted. Now there are endless columns of trucks, men, tanks moving west through Breslau, on to the next victim, France. People are going crazy, throwing flowers and candy at the soldiers. Horsti is one of them. Should he be the only one among his friends not participating in this demonstration? I am sure France won't be as easy.

There are ugly posters of Jews everywhere.

Summer 1940: Horrible rumors are going around—no, not rumors! Reports from very reliable sources about the systematic annihilation of Jewish inmates of concentration camps. Tante Lisbeth and Onkel Herrmann in Auschwitz, Tante Clara in Buchenwald. No news about them.

September 1940: Hurrah! Horsti passed the entrance exam. We were all worried about that. Now he is attending the *Gymnasium.* He and Wolfgang are in the same class. He is very scared that his class advisor may say something. I had a talk with that man who was wearing the Golden Party Pin. Was actually quite decent, but couldn't understand why Horsti is so timid in class, even though he is the best athlete. Felt like asking him how he would act if he were constantly reminded that he was scum.

Everyone knew about my food fascination, which resulted in occasional food-related gifts, not what one might expect—cakes and candy—but the raw materials for creating such items. These were the war years by now, so there was virtually nothing to have fun with, neither cooking fun nor the fun of actually munching down your own creations. We did, however, have friends who had small farms in the country. So, instead of toys or books of literary merit, I would get here a few eggs, there a lump of butter, an occasional bag of flour, or some fruit, even a slaughtered rabbit or chicken, and once, as I remember, a pound of hotdogs. As a result, I could do some actual experimentation with recipes that sounded tempting but not too overwhelming in terms of ingredients like some of the old cookbooks that called for nothing less than a dozen eggs and two pounds of butter.

Unfortunately, my grandmother was prevented from sharing baking and cooking joys with me. The Nazis had a lot to do with this tragic turn of events. Life had become unbearable for her. She was a proud woman, not used to being treated like a subhuman species. There were documents from the German emperor in her possession, thanking her for her generous gold donations to the war effort. GOLD I GAVE FOR IRON, it said on a small, black, oval, iron medallion. Now she was forced to wear the Star of David on all outer garments, making her the object of constant public contempt and harassment. She knew it was only a matter of time until she would receive that dreaded notification: "Report to the *Bahnhof*. One small suitcase per person." When it did arrive, she was ready. Like many in her situation, she had an ample amount of Veronal, enough for a fatal overdose.

Journal entry, November 1941: Very few old friends at the funeral service. Not many left by now. Several star-wearers were present, even though they try to avoid being seen in public. What a horrible way to end! What fiendish cruelty to make them wear the star. Horsti would no longer go for walks with her and would not have friends over anymore. That really hurt her. Then the notification to get ready for "a trip." She knew what that meant. Doktor Hirschberger helped her. Came to the funeral, too. He is wearing the star but said he would go to a camp if they called him, so he could help people. Her grave is in the family plot next to her husband, my brother, and Fidi. Horsti cried and misses her but also seems relieved in a way. What a terrible conflict.

Journal entry, November 20, 1941: What really drove Oma to her death, I think, was not only the prospect of being sent to a KZ* but the realization that her fervently beloved fatherland

---

Konzentrationslager, a common abbreviation for "concentration camp"

had turned her away, had not accepted her and her family's unconditional support. All the attempts to become and be exemplary Germans had failed: conversion to Christianity three generations ago, the rendering of service as decorated officers in the Prussian and German armies, as leaders in science (one had brought Germany a Nobel Prize), and as well-known artists and philanthropists. They had come so close, had done it all—and then how little it had taken to wipe out the past and to make them feel hated, ridiculed, and perhaps worst of all for many, ostracized. Now I understand what went on in Oma's head when she kept on reciting those two lines from the Heine poem:

Denk ich an Deutschland in der Nacht,
So bin ich um den Schlaf gebracht.

If I think of Germany at night,
My sleep is gone.

I only hope Horst will be spared this feeling, but how can he? I think subconsciously he is already experiencing it. Every step he takes must remind him of his precarious and isolated position—and he so craves to belong and be as everyone else.

April 6, 1942: Panic! Summons to report to the Gestapo headquarters—with Horsti! Are they going to take him to put him into one of their party schools? That's what happened to the Lachmann's son. Without Horsti, I would be on my way to Buchenwald or Auschwitz in no time. Now I wish he didn't have that blond, curly hair and Hitler Youth look.

April 8, 1942: It was scary! They acted so decent and concerned. Looked him over from all sides, took photos, asked about school, sports, then his health. Told them he is on a strict diet due to an earlier severe bout with hepatitis. Also mentioned his frequent stomach cramps when under pressure. They sent us home after that. Hope I scared them off.

October 1942: Long talk with our neighbor, Herrn Krause. Still believes that Moses will come to deliver us. "Frau Küter,"

he said, "you should be proud. You are the chosen people."

"I don't feel very proud," I told him.

"Don't weaken!" he admonished, "God is testing you. Remember Job!"

Horsti commented, "Either Herr Krause is right, or he is nuts."

Nuts would be my opinion.

December 1942: They'll never forget the name of that city—Stalingrad. I know hardly anyone who doesn't have a friend or relative there. What a terrible tragedy. All those boys starving and freezing to death. What insanity! What hubris! To think he could succeed where Napoleon had failed. I should rejoice because now Germany is doomed. But I can't.

The war was in full swing now. German armies were fighting in Russia, Africa, and a few other countries. I was fighting too. For our survival. Food was edging more and more out of sight. I had grown older and more sophisticated, no longer willing to meekly await some kindhearted handouts while my friends managed to have access to all kinds of goodies: ham, eggs, butter, smoked fish, fruit and vegetables, oil and coal in winter. How did I know? I could smell it when I visited, and I could see it in their lunches at school. Was that fair, or did they share? How about a ham sandwich, boy? Only in my dreams. Considering the meager government rations, how was such immodest affluence of food possible? Well, one family had a shoe factory. In those days shoes were worth their weight in gold and could easily be traded for anything. Another friend's family owned an immense estate in East Prussia where they produced every imaginable food item. Huge postal packages would arrive regularly. A third friend's father owned a fertilizer business. Farmers would ensure having access to an ample supply of fertilizer by supplying him with ample amounts of all sorts of agricultural products. It was painful for me to see thick slices of sausage hanging over the edges of sandwiches, to see an orange in a friend's hand, or to smell cakes baking. No wonder I grew bitter and vengeful. After such experiences I often read Reynard stories in order to ignite my imagination and reinforce my indignation.

Only at birthday parties for their sons would there be edibles for all the guests: pastries, homemade of course, which even now occasionally play major parts in my dreams.

Despite frequent periods of food envy, the four of us—Dieter, Busso, Wolfgang, and myself—were a closely knit band of friends. We exchanged books, went swimming, played cowboys and Indians, went to the movies, built model railroad

Author, 1942

networks through entire apartments, and talked about girls. My mother never gave me a direct answer when I occasionally asked, "Do the parents know about us?"

How could they not? I told myself. But their sons did not ask why I did not own a *Jungvolk* uniform, or why I did not report for training every Wednesday afternoon. And if asked, what would I answer? I often tortured myself.

Journal entry, December 1943: Horsti is really beginning to worry me. Seems his usual humorous, easygoing self on the surface, but there is so much resentment and anger building up inside of him, especially now, before Christmas. Imagines it's up to him to provide food for our family, food items which seem to be available to every other German family. I am so worried he'll land us all in a concentration camp. Wish I had not told him to be like Reynard. He takes this advice too literally.

I am worried about our safety—no, not the Nazis this time. I think Breslau is the only major city in Germany that is not being bombed. What does that mean? Are the British bombers saving us for something special?

The fertilizer family lived just a few houses away from us in a nice villa with a spacious balcony not too high off the ground. With my binoculars I could easily see what went on over there. When winter came, they would put some of the perishables out on the balcony. I often spent time drooling at the mere sight of some of the things on display. Huge sausages, bags of apples, hams—not all at the same time, of course, but in a continuous stream.

One day, my friend's mother appeared on the balcony. She was obviously carrying something heavy. Well, what could that be? I wondered. It was stuck in a canvas sack, but something white peeked out of a corner. Now, what is heavy, can be transported and concealed in a sack and has something like—wait! Let's have a look at that again— like feathers on it? White feathers? And then it hit me. It was close to Christmas, so—what else could it be but a Christmas goose! One of those heavy Polish ones with the huge liver for goose liver pâté! What a discovery!

"Mama!" I yelled, "Do we have a Christmas goose yet?"

"Now I know you are teasing me, right? What do you think I am, a shoe factory? Christmas goose! Really!"

"So what is happening Christmas Day? Turnips and potato soup?"

"No, no, no, we'll be going to the Glaeser's, and I have heard something about rabbit or chicken."

"For ten people? One rabbit?"

"Oh, come on. Think of the soldiers at the front or of our relatives—well you know where." I knew what she meant and could not get myself to look her in the eyes.

"Yeah, okay," I said, "you are right. But still—" The less said the better, I thought. My mother could get downright firm and nasty under the right circumstances. And this could turn into one of those circumstances. Once she had even slapped me and, the ultimate punishment and humiliation, had made me go to church with her and talk to the pastor. That was after I had proudly brought home a couple of beautiful carp which I had caught in one of the state-operated carp ponds. As she put it, "Imagine the headlines: HALF-JEWISH BOY STEALS CARP FROM THE STARVING GERMAN NATION! And have you forgotten? Reynard the Fox? What would he have done?"

Of course, she was right. I realized it had not so much been the act of stealing that had brought on her violent outburst as the thought of what would happen to her and me if I got caught. And stealing? What did she mean, *stealing?* Oh—did I forget to mention that my mother's food-ration cards, as well as her ID, had the letter *J* printed all over—*J* for Jewish? And that the amount of food allotted her was far less than for Aryans? No, what I had done was merely a desperate though feeble attempt to bring the scales of justice back into balance. As for Reynard? It was fine and laudable to be clever and careful as he, but, if I remembered correctly, he took chances too, when starvation was threatening his family. But he, unlike me, was not so unjustly deprived and persecuted. Thus, to suit my needs, I added a new dimension to Reynard: clever and careful, yes, but also a champion of justice. Besides, these carp were swimming around there by the thousands, snapping at anything that hit the water. Still, I could see old Reynard shaking his head disapprovingly at my lack of circumspection. In general, though, I was delighted with my sound reasoning; here was the banner that would fly high over all of my future food procurement operations: JUSTICE! Get a little back for all the hardships we had to endure. I loved it. This made everything so much simpler. "Hey, I am just adding a little more weight on our side of the scale."

But appropriating my friend's Christmas goose? That was a tough one. On the one hand, he was a good friend; on the other: What about the fact that he was a squad leader in the German Youth, leading kids who sang brutal hate songs against the Jews? The fact that I had seen his father in an SA officer's uniform? The fact that his mother wore the party membership pin? The fact that they never shared any of their

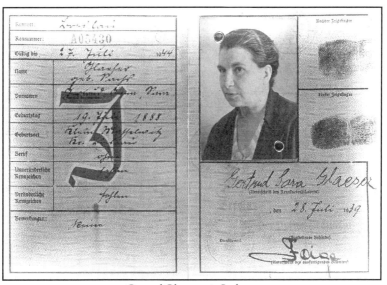

Gertrud Glaeser, née Sachs

surplus with me, even though I spent quite a bit of time at their house? So—did the positive outweigh the negative factors? I think not! And then I thought of this: Wasn't what they did strictly forbidden? It was a black-market transaction, accepting a bribe in return for fertilizer! How did that stack up against the total war effort!

Having my conscience cleared in this precise, logical, and compelling fashion, I now had to tackle a more formidable task: to spirit away an approximately twenty-pound object from a balcony, accessible from the ground to be sure, but still attached to an occupied apartment. Good thing, they don't own a dog, I thought.

> Journal entry, December 1943: No news from Otto or Werner. We are all so worried. Last we knew they were heading for Vienna. Sophie had her child, a girl. Now they are hiding in a tiny village in the Silesian mountains. Must be beautiful there. Horsti loves to visit there, especially in the winter because of the skiing. I just don't dare to get on a train. That *J* on my ID! Horst is going crazy worrying about Christmas. Wants to bake all the traditional cakes and cookies. Where am I to get butter, eggs, nuts, and chocolate. He is developing a really criminal mind.

Of course, I realized instantly that appeasing my conscience would be by far the easiest part of this or any future operation. Right now, the obstacles I faced were truly daunting, almost enough to make one give up. But then again, consider the rewards, I thought. No, I had to give it a try, think the whole thing through, make a step-by-step plan. So, what was I up against?

For starters, I had only three days until Christmas Day, which meant that the goose might be taken to its final destination, the Kohlers' kitchen, anytime now. Not so good. I hated to work under pressure.

They did not own a dog. That was good.

There was no snow. That was good. No footprints in the snow.

There was a low fence around their property. That was not so good, but we

Skating in winters past

had scaled that fence innumerable times in our games.

But then again—doing this while carrying a twenty-pound goose? Not so good, but doable: just throw the sack over first.

And once the bird was safely in my possession—then what? "Hey Mama! Look what just landed in our kitchen!" Not that I was afraid of another slap. But this was Christmas, after all, and I just could not see myself doing this to her.

No! What I had thought of all along was that I would take the bird to my Tante Detta's house. There was no hope that she would react differently from my mother,

Always loved winter sports

but what I counted on was the ingenuity of Emma, who was with the Glaesers now. And how could I hope that a person with such an illustrious past—based on trust, responsibility, and honesty—would stoop to my level? Well, over the years I had come to the realization that whenever food was involved, her generally high moral standards would weaken, if not disappear. In this regard, I considered her my equal and a possible accomplice. Of course, she was well aware of my culinary obsession, having never failed to contribute something appropriate on my birthdays, like a jar of lard, or hotdogs. I knew she would answer the phone if I called now. Sure enough, there she was.

"Emma," I asked, "wouldn't it be great if we could have more than just one rabbit for Christmas dinner?"

"Jaaaa?"

"Okay, Emma. I might be able to get us a goose."

"Jaaaaa?"

"Ja, a big one. I think it would have to be plucked and gutted. Is that okay?"

"Phffff! I have done that hundreds of times."

"So, what do you think? What should I do?"

"Well, if you can get it, I guess you should bring it sometime in the morning when no one is home. I can say I got it from my brother. And boy, be careful."

A chill came over me. So now I had a deadline! My heart started to pound, my forehead felt sweaty. Was I nuts? I forced myself to think of all the steps that had to be taken between my house and the Glaesers' house.

School? No problem. Christmas vacation.

Transportation? One hour by streetcar to the other end of town where the Glaesers lived.

Concealment of the bird at home and on the way? No problem. I had been collecting old newspapers and other wastepaper as part of the war effort and for brownie points in school. I had about ten pounds in a sack in our basement. Time to take it to the collection center in the morning.

It all seemed so simple and logical. What could go wrong? Actually, everything. And there was the pounding heart and the sweaty face again. And why were my teeth rattling together in such a funny way, all of a sudden? But then something took over inside of me, as it always did when I was facing an almost certain disaster. As if somebody else was filling in for me, and that person would be doing everything, would be taking all the risks. So, why worry? This self-deception worked well, although deep down I always knew it was me, after all. But it did give me a sense of indifference and invulnerability. Only once had it failed me completely: when that "something" had flunked a math test for me.

It was dark early that evening in December, quite cold but snowless. There was a gusty wind whipping the branches of the old linden trees that bordered the street. And there was barely a glimmer of light anywhere. These were the days of total blackout.

"Mama!" I called out. "I am going over to visit Wolfgang, okay?"

"Okay, don't stay too long."

Wolfgang lived across the street from us; the goose was on the same side as we, two houses down. I strolled along the street to check what was going on at my friend Dieter Kohler's house. The family seemed to be in a room facing the street, judging by the tiny crack of light that came through the blackout shades.

No lights visible at the back of the house where the balcony was. So far, so good. Back to our house now and silently into our yard. At the far end, hidden by evergreens, I scaled the fence into the neighbor's yard and from there, over the next fence into Dieter's yard, which was filled with all sorts of shrubs and trees. Cautiously and very slowly, I groped my way to the entrance of the balcony, and then, just three steps up, and I was at my destination.

Naturally, I knew exactly where the goose was—could have found it blindfolded. And blindfolded I might as well have been—that's how dark it was. I inched my way to the other side where I knew the bird was lying on a small table. There it was! My hands stroked over it, feeling its height and width. Then I carefully slid my hands under it and gave it a yank. It didn't budge. I listened nervously, then I gave it another yank. Nothing! Lord, how heavy is that bird? Did they nail it to the table? Once more I probed around the bottom of the bird, and then it dawned on me. Some of the body juices of the goose had oozed through the packaging, and now it was frozen to the table! What to do?

I could not remember—was it a wooden table? metal? ceramic tile, perhaps? As I groped around some more, I realized that the table was covered with a cloth, one of those wax cloth coverings, as I now recalled from the summer. Okay, what the heck, I thought, as I carefully gathered up all sides of the cloth to pile them up in the middle of the table, which was also the middle of the goose. And then I heaved the entire package up into my arms, and pressing it against my chest, I slowly retreated. No lights, no sounds, except for the wind. I left the way I had come. Over the fences we went, first the bird, then I. In our yard, I deposited the bird at the back entrance to our cellar. The rest was easy and safe. I slipped into our basement and opened the back door from the inside and pulled my bundle in. Next, I took it to the spot where my paper collection was and lowered it into the sack, making sure there would be plenty of paper on top of the bird. Then I went up to our living quarters.

"Glad to see you back," my mother said. "Did you fight or something? You're all red and out of breath. Did you have a pillow fight? There are a couple of white feathers on your sweater."

"Yeah, we did a bit of wrestling on Wolfgang's bed; perhaps his pillow leaked. Oh, would you please get me up fairly early tomorrow? I want to take the paper to the collection center."

Truth was, I wanted to get going rather early with my large and heavy bundle—preferably before all hell would break loose in our quiet little street.

I don't think I slept much that night. Mama was a little surprised when she saw me up so early on a vacation day.

"Well, I want to be back before noon, because we are going skating."

"Okay, see you soon, then."

It was still a little dark outside as I stepped through the garden gate into the street. What a heavy bird, I thought, as I struggled along for about fifteen minutes to the streetcar stop. Good thing I didn't have to change to another line. Further into town passengers began to crowd in, and I protectively straddled my sack.

"What you got in that sack, kid? You act as if you are guarding a treasure."

Finally, my stop came, and after another ten-minute hike I delivered my burden into Emma's open arms. She was almost as excited as I was.

"*Donnerwetter,* that is one magnificent bird! About the biggest goose I have ever seen. Good work!" She did not ask how or why or anything, and I was grateful for that.

"I'll bet you could use a bite to eat just about now, and I think I have exactly what you like, if I remember correctly," and she got out a crock of lard with crackling, onion, and apple slices. This she spread heavily onto two huge slices of dark rye bread, a dash of salt sprinkled on top.

"Okay, I'll take care of everything. You better run along home now. I'll get rid of the paper. Any need for that wax cloth? Not bad, actually. Think I'll keep it. I could give it to my sister as a Christmas present. Ja, that's what I'll do. Und ja, ja, I promise, I'll put away a crock of goose fat for you, you little *Vielfrass.*"

So, mentally relieved and physically twenty pounds lighter, I was on my way home.

As I had dreaded, utter turmoil and excitement greeted me when I got back to home territory. People were buzzing around in the street, converging in front of Dieter's house where a police car was parked.

"What's going on, Mama? Someone get murdered or something?"

"Can you imagine? The Kohlers were robbed last night."

"Oh yeah? What did they take? A few bags of fertilizer or the tires off Mr. Kohler's car?" At this point I thought my best strategy would be to joke about it and apply some sarcasm. My mother looked sternly at me. Why is she raising her voice? I wondered.

"No, nothing was taken except their Christmas goose."

"So they broke into the cellar?"

Again, the piercing look and the scary voice, as she continued. Horrible suspicions entered my mind. "No, it was not in the basement, it was on the balcony."

"On the balcony? How stupid can they be? Anyone can climb over the fence and get on the balcony. And there are enough people around who know that food is often put out there in winter. Or perhaps a dog got in and dragged if off. Or perhaps a fox."

My mother's vocal volume intensified some more. "Yes, or perhaps a bear or a lion!"

This was definitely turning into something rather awkward. But at this point, what could I do?

"Ha, ha, right! Anyway, any clues or theories so far? Did anyone ask you anything?"

"No, nothing. No one asked and no clues. Must have climbed over the fence and gotten out the same way. But I do feel sorry for them. So close to Christmas!"

"And only two days ago, you were so upset because Mrs. Kohler keeps avoiding you and does not say hello anymore."

Dieter was inconsolable. He lamented his and his family's tragic fate almost hysterically. He had put on his German Youth uniform and had strapped the dagger with the swastika around his waist. He was also carrying a huge stick, the tip of which he had coated with pitch. I never did find out what he thought that would accomplish. About every twenty minutes he would sob uncontrollably.

"Come on, Dieter, you are wearing the uniform and the swastika dagger! You can't cry! If any of the leaders see you like this, your goose will be cooked." That was a cruel joke, but it did the trick, even if he didn't get it. He stopped crying but kept stomping around the neighborhood. A little later his father called him, and they took off in their Mercedes. Late in the afternoon they returned, and I saw them carrying something heavy into their house. When I saw Dieter again he was all smiles.

"So, what's the good news? Did they catch the thief?"

"Oh no, we just went for a ride to take some fertilizer out to one of the farms." He smiled sheepishly.

"And?" I asked.

"Well, they asked my father, if we needed anything—they always do, you know. So my father got us another goose. Even bigger than the stolen one."

And I had begun to feel sorry for them. Really!

"Well, I am glad they'll have their goose after all," said my mother in that creepy tone of voice, when I told her.

Christmas always involved two trips out to the Glaesers. One for the celebration of Christmas Eve and the next one on the 25th, which had not so much to do with presents as with eating. Presents were traditionally exchanged on Christmas Eve, usually before the festive Christmas Eve dinner. But first, all the candles had to be lighted on the huge tree, together with a lot of sparklers. Except by now, this being the fourth year of the war, the Third Reich had to turn everything that burned and crackled into grenades and bombs. Of course nothing edible that could not be grown within Germany was under the tree. But there was an enormous crèche composed of a one-hundred-piece angelic orchestra, plenty of shepherds and sheep, cows and donkeys, and the customary occupants of the stable, every one of them hand carved in the 17th century, as I was told.

Before any presents could be opened, my uncle would play the lute, accompanying us as we sang the old familiar carols. That was very hard on me for two reasons: I could smell mouthwatering things happening in the kitchen where Emma was hard at work, and I was the only one in the family who could carry a tune. Keeping a straight face, with my mother and her sister standing behind me, was absolutely impossible. At first I thought, oh, they are harmonizing, singing in parts. I had some

A closely knit band of friends—60 years later. From left: Dieter, Wolfgang, author, Busso

experience in this, having been drafted into the school choir. I soon realized however, that they were not harmonizing. Once it sounded like a chord, but that must have been just a lucky coincidence. No. I concluded that somehow they had not realized what was being sung. What on earth are they singing? I thought, and listened very carefully to their words. But they did have the right carol—not the right melody, though. By the middle of "Silent Night," I was laughing hysterically, infecting all the others. Only my uncle, stoically and a bit miffed, kept performing to the end, and then we were saved from utter chaos by the appearance of Emma, swinging a little silver bell, the signal to move into the dining room. There, the huge round family table was set for a formal dinner. As before every Christmas dinner, my mother tried to explain to me what each implement and glass was for, and what it was made of and where it came from. This glass for white wine, that for red, the little one for dessert wine, the tiny one for brandy.

Was I able to pay attention or retain any of this when a huge platter with *Karpfen blau** was about to enter the room? Of course not. And it really was blue. Sort of a pale, milky looking blue.

Did I have to ask my mother how they managed to get the carp's skin so blue? Of course not! I had known for years. One pours a boiling vinegar solution over the carp, before submerging it into the special fish poacher, a long narrow pan filled with boiling court bouillon. And if you follow the same procedure with trout, you have *Forelle blau.*** But you must never, ever attempt to scale a fish that you expect to stare at you through pale blue eyes. If you did, you would remove the layer of mucous that covers the skin of these fish, and that's the part that turns blue.

At this point one might well ask, where on earth did all that carp, enough to feed fifteen people, come from at a time when all but a few well-connected people were starving? And why did all eyes turn to me as the platters were carried in? I could not help but blush a little, even though I had not contributed in the least, this time. But my fame as provider was well established, I felt.

Actually, when it came to carp, the Glaesers were well connected. Uncle Pippi was a scholar and writer of pieces on Silesia and the historical and cultural significance of the old Silesian aristocracy. And one of these aristocrats, old Count Schaffgotsch, owned vast tracts of

*Carp au bleu **Truite au bleu

land not far from Breslau, land dotted with numerous lakes which were stocked with carp. In Europe, carp is a very popular freshwater fish, surpassed only by trout and salmon, and when it is raised in carp ponds it does not acquire that muddy flavor of a bottom feeder.

Again I must mention Professor Brehm's work, which describes a very good method for keeping carp from getting mud ridden, fat, and lazy: put a few big pike into a carp pond, and your troubles will be over. This practice became so well established that one not infrequently heard a remark like, "Oh, that fellow—he is like a pike in a carp pond."

All this came back to me a few years later. I was standing on the banks of an American body of water, not far from New York City. Memories always attract me to anglers at the water's edge. And here was an older fellow, just sitting, smoking his pipe while watching the bobber on his line. Suddenly the bobber disappeared. I stepped forward so I would not miss a thing, and I got pretty excited, much more so than the old timer, who began to reel something in, something huge, judging by the curve in his rod. I was nearly overcome by waves of nostalgia when I saw what he had hooked: a carp, a hefty one, perhaps three to four pounds. "Oh, think of the feast in that fellow's home tonight!" What happened next totally stunned me. Mumbling some obscenities, that fellow unhooked the fish and tossed it back into the water.

"What are you doing that for?" I shouted, audibly frustrated and annoyed.

Uncle Pippi (left) was a scholar and writer—visit with Gerhart Hauptmann, German 1912 Nobel laureate in literature (center).

The fellow glanced at me calmly, "Listen, boy, that fish has all the shit of all of New York in its gut. But if you're interested, I'll let you have the next one."

Anyway, the old count was only too happy to supply my uncle generously with carp, my uncle, who, in his articles, had so generously honored that count's countless ancestors and their feats as Prussian generals in the Thirty Years' War, the Seven Years' War, the Napoleonic Wars, the Franco-Prussian War, the Austro-Prussian War, World War I, and now World War II, in which two of his sons had already fallen, highly decorated, of course.

By now, the carp, looking truly handsome in their blue splendor, were being passed around the table. My uncle whom, incidentally, friends and relatives considered to be a bit eccentric, if not weird, had guided onto his plate that piece of the carp he would gladly die for—the head. "Ah yes, the jaw muscles and the eyes are the most exquisite parts of this heavenly creature. Of course, the brain isn't too bad, either; pity it's so small." He paused thoughtfully, then continued, "Not a very pleasant topic these days: small brains. There are so many of them around, and they are so destructive. Imagine, Germany run by a bunch of carp—as it were." Some of the guests exchanged guarded glances. One could never be too careful! Closet Nazis were lurking everywhere.

But man shall not live by carp alone. That is why God created sauerkraut. On the eighth day. He knew something was missing when He reflected on His carp. You've got to have something to offset that mild, sweet taste of the carp. So, let there be SAUERKRAUT! He tasted it and, behold, it was good! Especially with some bacon drippings and a little bit of finely diced raw onion, the Silesian way, to accompany carp, or sausages, or smoked or unsmoked pork roasts. Granted, it may strike you as an unlikely combination: fish and sauerkraut, but those who have tried it—and believe me, I have forced many to do so—agree, there is a certain synergy at work here. Well, actually, there is a third ingredient to create that sensational taste: whipped cream, lightly sweetened, combined with a good portion of grated horseradish, enough to give it some bite. A little salt, of course, perhaps a hint of lemon juice.

Naturally, potatoes, preferably parsleyed, are a must, and over everything, a drizzle of melted butter, lightly browned. Not easy to come by in the winter of the fourth year of the war, when rations for luxury items such as butter scarcely sufficed to cover one slice of bread. Everyone had contributed a little.

After my third helping of carp, my mother cautioned me, "You may want to leave a bit of room for dessert, you know."

"What's for dessert?" As if I did not know! What else could it be? It was Christmas Eve and we were eating carp, and carp on Christmas Eve can only be followed by *Mohnklösse** a superrich combination of various hard-to-come-by ingredients: poppy seeds (one to two pounds, depending on the number of people to be fed), stale white bread, raisins, sugar, and whipped cream. And the finished product did not resemble dumplings in the least. What appeared on the table later was sort of a layered pudding in a crystal bowl. No one knew why this was called "dumplings," but no one had ever called it by any other name.

To create the confection, the seeds have to be ground, then scalded in milk and drained, mixed with sugar, raisins, and a little bit of vanilla; slivered almonds may be tolerated. The sliced bread is softened in milk and squeezed dry; the cream is beaten and sweetened. Then these items are layered into the bowl, about half an inch each of bread, poppy seeds, whipped cream, and so on, and on until the bowl is full. The top layer is always whipped cream. Chill overnight.

Alas, I should have skipped that last piece of carp. After but a small helping of the dessert I had to give up. Looking around, I noticed that all the others had also stopped eating. Contentment or, as the case might have been, the discomfort of having overstuffed oneself, had descended upon the group. Addressing this, my aunt said, "After living on turnips and plain potatoes all year, no wonder, a meal like this—" At this point she suddenly jumped up and ran out of the room.

"She has always had a delicate digestive system," my mother informed me.

And tomorrow another meal like this, I thought. The day of the goose was nigh. But there was no joyful feeling of anticipation for me.

---

*Poppy seed dumplings

II

The Gestapo's offer we couldn't refuse, the allies tighten the noose, and how we celebrated our last family Christmas in Breslau

W AS IT MY STRESSED stomach rebelling against the onslaught of food it was no longer accustomed to—in quality as well as in quantity? I tossed and turned in my bed, trying to settle into a comfortable position, but it was of no use. Carp and goose were facing off against each other, the carp in my stomach against the goose in my head. Yes, indeed, the goose was raising its long ugly neck, the head appearing eerily beyond the footboard of my bed, staring down at me like an exclamation mark with beady little eyes. The longer I thought about this issue, the more I realized that it was not at all the ill-gotten goose that bothered me; after all, not only had it been illegally acquired by the Kohlers, they had already succeeded in replacing it, once more illegally. No, it was the fact that I had so monstrously deceived and betrayed my mother. Oh, what to do now? Heart pounding, sweat on my forehead, I jumped out of bed, ran through the cold hallway and knocked on my mother's door.

"I thought you might come," she said coolly. "So, how does it feel?"

"What do you mean—you mean—my stomach?"

"No, not your stomach. I think you know what I mean, don't you?"

Long pause.

"Well, yes, I guess. How did you know?"

"How dumb do you think I am? Feathers all over the place! Little white feathers. Pillow fight—come on! Some of the feathers had blood on them, as if they had just been plucked right out of a live pillow!"

"Oh. And why didn't you say anything?"

"Well, it was a little late for that, wasn't it? Besides, I thought a goose would be really nice, for a change. And the Kohlers have so much all the time, while we can hardly survive. But don't you ever do anything that foolish again!"

There followed a long lecture on honesty, lying, virtues, vices, and sins, hell and the Ten Commandments. Greatly relieved I fell sound asleep. At one point that night Reynard appeared to me in a dream. He was smoking a cigarette, wearing a German Army cap, the prestigious Knight's Cross around his neck, and I was shocked to see the Nazi party pin on his chest. Every time I tried to discover whether he was also wearing the oak-leaf cluster around the Knight's Cross, he put one of his front paws over it. Baring his teeth in a broad grin, he kept on nodding his head, saying over and over, "Keep it up, boy, keep it up."

On Christmas morning I awoke refreshed, no longer physically or mentally burdened by either carp or goose. In fact, I was pestering my mother to get ready for our trip across town. When we arrived there, I scaled the eight-foot wrought iron fence at the Glaesers, took the key out of the mailbox and let my mother in. Why bother with doorbells? Inside, Emma stuck her head out of the kitchen to greet us. She winked at me. My mother took note.

"Yeah, yeah," said my mother, "I know the whole story. My best regards and a merry Christmas to your brother, and we'll be forever grateful to him."

Emma quickly withdrew. Ten seconds later her head reappeared.

"Horsti," she said, "I could really use a little help here. Think you could come in and do a few things?"

What a question! This was what I had hoped for. By now, I always knew exactly what Emma wanted me to do and how to do it quickly and competently. Off flew my cap, gloves, and overcoat.

"Wash your hands, put an apron on!" my mother shouted as I disappeared into the steaminess of the kitchen.

It was pure magic to me. A large room, heavy wooden counters and cupboards, two pantries, in the middle a huge cast-iron kitchen stove heated entirely with wood and coal. Oh, and the varied smells escaping from pots, pans, and casseroles, intermingled with just the right amount of wood smoke!

Merely looking and sniffing were not the only things I had in mind. No! What I really needed was to get my taste buds involved. Unfortunately, at this point, nothing was close to being done, but a peek into the baking oven couldn't hurt. The typical roast goose smell was all over the house already.

"Wow, that is some bird! Look at all the fat in the roaster! Want me to scoop some out?"

"Yeah, that's a good idea. Let's put it in this crock here. Want a piece of bread to dip into it? You look absolutely starved."

"God, yes! There is nothing like goose fat."

While I was munching away, my nose was busy analyzing other smells.

"And what's the stuffing?" I asked after a few minutes. "There is sort of a fruity smell to it but something else, too. Something unusual."

"Ah, very good," Emma said. "Of course prunes and apples, but I am surprised you could smell the other. Well, it's chestnuts. My cousin brought some when he came on leave from Italy. Perfect with goose."

Chestnuts! My favorites! How I loved the yellow, mealy, sweet, fragrant meat of these nuts. Before the war, in winter, there used to be chestnut roasters at various locations throughout the city, little grills with charcoal fires underneath, chestnuts on top, filling the air with their unique scorched-shell aroma. Those were the big chestnuts that grow in Northern Italy and other warmer places. There were a few chestnut trees in our park, huge trees that produced nuts about the size of a child's fingernail. Tasty, to be sure, but to get to them you had to fight armies of red squirrels—who usually won.

Traditionally, roast goose is served with sweet and sour red cabbage, potato dumplings, and winter vegetables like Brussels sprouts, carrots or kale, and with lots of gravy. As I could smell, the cabbage—two large heads, shredded, together with five to ten apples, peeled, cored, and sliced—was already boiling in a huge pot.

"Why don't you check if the cabbage is ready?"

"Okay—about ten more minutes."

"Well, drain the pot when it's done, please. You remember what to do then, don't you?"

"Sure do."

"Well, let's hear it."

"You add some butter, or better, goose fat—for that much cabbage I would say about half a cup—then sugar, about one cup. Got to keep checking for sweetness—then, vinegar, a cup to a cup and a half, perhaps. Again, you've got to keep checking, so it's good and sweet and good and sour."

"Excellent, my boy, but haven't you forgotten something? Something everybody would miss terribly?"

"Uh—washing my hands first?"

When this did not seem to be the sought-after answer, I thought for a few minutes, sniffed into the boiling cabbage, and then I knew. Oh my God! That without which red cabbage would not be accepted by anyone as the real thing: "Cloves, of course! Either about half a teaspoon of whole cloves or a couple of pinches of ground clove."

"Okay, very good! And what exactly is a pinch?"

Wasn't this getting to be a little unreasonable? It sounded more and more like something from school. I actually had to think about that one. Not that I didn't know what a pinch meant, but how should I express this knowledge in a brief and logical fashion? "Well, the amount of anything ground or grainy or powdery that you can hold between the tips of your thumb and index finger when you pinch them together."

"Right! So, don't forget to do that after you have drained the water off. And to make it really good—and you won't find this in any cookbook—add about half a bottle of good red wine to the finished product and let the whole thing simmer for about an hour. But be careful—nothing is worse than burnt red cabbage."

"Yeah, right, but wait," because at that moment something occurred to me. "Wouldn't it be better perhaps to add the apples later? I mean, for the second cooking, because if they get cooked with the cabbage the first time, and then we drain all the water off, wouldn't we lose much of the apple flavor?"

What happened next was totally unexpected and scared the hell out of me. She threw both arms up in the air and shrieked one of those horrible Upper-Silesian curses, half German, half Polish, which all of us had come to dread.

"That's all right," I stammered. "Forget about the cabbage."

"No, no, no!" she shouted. "Not the cabbage, the goose, the goose! I just got boiling fat all over my arm! Quick, get an icicle from the porch."

After she had soothed her burns and regained her composure, she came back to my idea. "Makes sense what you said about the apples before, ja, let's try that right now. See those apples over there? Why don't you take five good ones and get them ready. You know—peel, core, and slice. You are the boss on that."

The boss? I wondered. Do bosses peel and core and slice? That's what I get for opening my big mouth. But the end result justified my labors and earned raves during dinner. Emma did not hesitate to mention my involvement.

As for the dumplings, almost every region of Germany has its own particular favorite version thereof, featuring boiled potatoes, or raw potatoes, or half-and-half, with flour or without flour, with eggs or without eggs, stuffed with croutons and bits of bacon, baked or boiled. Of course there is also the all-flour variety, with yeast or baking powder. We in Breslau favored the Silesian potato dumpling, a rather primitive variety, composed primarily of potatoes, boiled and peeled the previous day, then riced. As far as I was concerned, dumplings, especially Silesian ones, were only as good as the food surrounding them, particularly the gravy. As I had anticipated, the job of pressing about five pounds of boiled potatoes through the ricer was mine.

"Okay, now about one and a half cups of flour and then knead it all into a firm, smooth dough, and don't forget salt."

Personally, I would have preferred good old mashed potatoes or even just plain boiled potatoes. But who was I to try to prevail over tradition? Nevertheless, and at the risk of provoking another German-Polish outburst, I gently addressed Emma. "Emma," I said ever so softly. Suggesting a culinary innovation to Emma was like walking on black ice. "The other day I came across an old cookbook. Very interesting. You would like it. It had a whole collection of handwritten family-heirloom dumpling recipes. Some from the eighteenth century."

"Sooo?" She eyed me suspiciously, sensing something was on my mind, something controversial.

"Well, yeah, don't you think our dumplings would be a lot better if we added a couple of things to them?"

"Like what?" Her voice was razor sharp now, ready to cut me to ribbons.

"Things like eggs. I didn't find one recipe that didn't call for eggs. And putting a few croutons into each dumpling, you know, little bread cubes browned in butter with a little nutmeg? Boy, wouldn't that be good?"

"Now hold on there. What do you think we are here? The emperor's dumpling factory? No! None of that fancy stuff for me! But, oh well, a few eggs can't hurt. So, okay, four to five eggs, and then you'll need to add some extra flour. But you've got to hurry. Everything else is getting close to done.

"Finish the dough, and keep your hands floured to form the dumplings, each one about two inches in diameter. Then put them into the boiling water here, and let them simmer until they rise to the surface—no lid or they may break up!"

I felt as if I had won a major battle. Triumphantly, I cracked five eggs into the potato mush.

My aunt and mother were summoned to come and help with the last minute tasks, like getting everything onto platters and into bowls and taking it all out to the round table.

"Wash your hands, take that greasy apron off, and comb your hair," my mother admonished.

Again there was a festive table with all the different glasses and silver candlesticks. In addition, there was now some fragrant pine greenery at each setting. Just as I was entering the room, everyone was sniffing the air, commenting how this mixture of pine needles and beeswax candles was conjuring up memories of past Christmases. What was different this year, I noticed, was the absence of some of the regular guests and family members. Two of the Glaeser sons, despite their blood, were German soldiers; some of the older relatives, because of their blood, were elsewhere. And then my uncle started to carve.

"Finest bird I have ever seen," he muttered. "We must do something wonderful for your brother," he addressed Emma who, keeping her eyes glued to the plate, turned beet red.

As always on major occasions, my uncle said grace. This is how he ended: "Oh Lord, bless also those who in their kindness opened their hearts and hands to share with us in their bounty."

My mother joined Emma in her effort to analyze the gold rims of the plates. But not for long. Everything was just too delicious, triggering questions around the table.

"Tell me, what makes these dumplings so different and delicious this time?"

"Yes! And the red cabbage! Why doesn't mine ever taste like that?"

"My God! Is that chestnut stuffing I taste? Where on earth did that come from?"

"Really! But that goose, that goose! An angel must have dropped that off!"

At that, I joined my mother and Emma in the contemplation of the gold rims on the plates. An angel? I thought. Does that mean I will be sprouting wings?

About halfway through dinner, my uncle rose and tapped on his glass: "I think it would be a grave oversight if we did not once more express our gratitude and appreciation to those who so lovingly and generously contributed to our bodily well-being. And so I am proposing a heartfelt toast to our beloved Emma who over the years has truly become one of our family and also to her dear, dear brother who sadly cannot be with us on this festive occasion."

My uncle had obviously more on his mind, having planned to go on and on, but at this point the doorbell rang. Being the youngest and fastest, I jumped up and ran out to the garden gate. Three minutes later I was back, gesturing with jerky head motions for Emma to follow me out. I carefully closed the dining room door behind us and whispered, "Your brother!"

She let go with one of her native curses, the likes of which I had never heard before. Then she vanished into the darkness of the December evening.

Was this an act of divine retribution, the just punishment for my sin? The Ten Commandments my mother had mentioned last night came to mind. Which one or ones applied to me? Certainly none of the first six. But then: "Thou shalt not steal." Yup, that applied. Or, how about this: "Thou shalt not covet thy neighbor's house"? I felt secure enough here, but then: "nor ox, nor ass, nor anything that is thy neighbor's"! That certainly applied. No question—that said it all. No doubt about it. I was doomed!

Emma emerged out of the darkness, followed by a huge, dark hulk—her brother. "This is Antek, and everything will be all right, I hope. I told him, and he will play along, or perhaps he can leave before anyone else comes out."

But too late! My uncle appeared, absolutely delighted when he found out who the stranger was. "Oh, what a delightful surprise! I was just talking about you. You must come in and dine with us and have a taste of the—of YOUR goose. Please, my good man, do us the honor and give us the pleasure of your presence."

There was no turning back. More pulled and pushed than acting of his own volition, Antek entered the dining room.

"We must set a place at the table for this wonderful man!" my uncle shouted. "This is Antek, Emma's saintly brother."

Saintly—wow! I thought.

A huge round of applause greeted Antek. He was visibly embarrassed, making little bows in all directions, while never looking up at anyone. Another person at the table not looking up was my mother. Her facial expression was somewhere between, "Oh, please Lord, take me now!" and, "That will teach you!" Her mouth was tightly closed, her lips a straight, narrow line.

Antek was not what you would call a brilliant conversationalist. In fact, he said as little as possible, just taking little bits of food now and then. Soon Emma announced that Antek had to hurry off to another commitment. He had volunteered to play Santa Claus at some orphanage. Oh, what a saintly man!

Suddenly my uncle jumped up. "Wait, my good man! I have a wonderful idea." He left the room, returning after a few minutes with a medium-size basket filled with six bottles of wine. "This, my most excellent sir, is the very least I can do. May God bless you!"

And me too, please, I thought.

My mother's face had a definitely purplish hue by now. Her eyes shot poisoned darts in my direction.

Journal entry, Christmas, 1943: Pippi should have remembered to mention Oma—I should have reminded him. Everything was perfect, as if she had prepared it. Horsti—I don't know what to do with the boy. What has gotten into him? As if he were possessed. Wants to have everything like his friends. Stealing a goose! "Getting even," he calls it. I can understand his motivation, but I worry: what's going to happen once he reaches puberty?

That was the Christmas dinner of 1943. It was the last time we were all together in Breslau. Food rations became ever smaller now; outside sources dried up more and more. We were no longer living in our beautiful villa in the suburbs. How come? Why, because we were Jewish, of course! Two Gestapo families had simply fallen in love with it. And who can say no to those jolly fellows?

They put us into the attic apartment of a huge 19th century mansion, even letting us take our furniture. Couldn't ask for more than that, could you?

It was not all bad up there, but my mother never overcame the loss of her beloved house. Even after the war, when our entire street was nothing more than rubble, she could not bring herself to go near it.

Journal entry, spring, 1944: If it were not for Horsti I could not endure it any longer. No food, not allowed to travel or go to concerts, not even to movies, and then there is that constant fear of the concentration camp! First, Fidi was gone, then Oma, now our house with my beloved garden and all my flowers. It would break my heart if I ever entered that neighborhood again. All those fools who assured us that the Nazis would not last long! Most of them must be dead by now. I almost envy them. Fortunately Horsti is content enough—as long as he can go around foraging, "appropriating," as he calls it.

Journal entry, June 1944: Hurrah for once! The Allies have landed in Normandy and are not budging. Now there may be hope. Everyone asks, how and why does Germany keep on fighting? No food, and night and daytime bombing are turning Germany into rubble. And all those innocent people! How am I supposed to feel about that?

As for me, there were a few factors regarding our new home which offered some compensation. The house was surrounded by a large park, and in it there were a few very attractive and intriguing bushes and trees: numerous espalier pear trees, several huge hazelnut bushes, two tall walnut trees, and two apricot trees. The kind, partly Jewish old lady, Frau Hopf, who owned the house, graciously gave us full range of the grounds, much to her later regret. It must have seemed to her as if the wrath of the Lord was upon her. She just could not fathom it. Never had there been fewer hazelnuts or walnuts! And why did her fruit trees suddenly produce such small crops after such an abundant bloom?

Journal entry, June 1944: Worried to death! Frau Hopf informed me that "two charming young gentlemen from the Gestapo" had inquired about me, saying they would be back. Is my time up? Horsti has reached that age when they confiscate the child and the mother ends up in a KZ.

That fall I became very popular in school. Could that have been because my pockets were filled with nuts? Kids whose names I did not even know asked me not IF but WHEN they could come over to play. Naturally this popularity was subject to seasonal cycles and, as it turned out, to some other events that disrupted the course of everyone's existence. The Allied invasion forces were rapidly advancing from the west, the Red Army from the east. Breslau would be one of the first major German cities in Russians' path. Families began to pack up and evacuate, attempting to reach areas where the Americans or the British could be expected to arrive ahead of the Russians. Among them were the Glaesers. They even got most of their furniture out and managed to disappear with it in a tiny village in the foothills of the Alps, leaving their house keys with us. My mother had turned down the invitation to join them. She thought that by staying in Breslau we could be out of Nazi reach earlier.

Two Gestapo families had simply fallen in love with it.

Journal entry, June 1944: It was a very difficult decision, but I think it was a wise one to opt to remain in Breslau. The sooner we escape the Nazi regimen, the better. I did not want to scare Horsti by telling him this, but when he turned fourteen he no longer required a mother, according to party directives. In situations like this, mothers are considered superfluous and are usually shipped to a concentration camp.

III

Summer pastimes, and how we survived the siege of Breslau

YET, AMIDST ALL THIS turmoil, fear, and planning, I spent a most memorable summer in a small fishing village on the coast of the Baltic Sea. One of my aunts, Tante Hildegard, with her two small daughters, lived in a farmhouse there, just ten minutes from the beach by rowboat. They had been evacuated from Berlin in order to escape the daily and nightly bombing raids.

I saw an incredible opportunity. "Any chance we might be able to visit them up there? Can't be very far from here: take the train north along the Oder to Stettin and from there to Treptow and on to Deep. Why don't you write to them?"

Mama didn't answer for a few minutes. I knew what she was thinking: "How can I go—with my name and the *J* across my picture ID?" What she finally did say surprised me, "Yes, all right, I'd love to have you spend a summer on the Baltic. I think you are big enough now for a solo trip like this. And the less time you spend in Breslau the better. Everyone says it's just a matter of time now until they'll start bombing us."

Journal entry, June 1944: It can't go on like this much longer. The question is: Who will outlast the other? Who will get to us first, the Allies or the Nazis? They are putting everyone into camps now, so-called labor camps, to build fortifications against the Russians. Many of our friends are among them, including the Hillebrands. No trace of either Hannes, Otto, or Werner. Life in larger cities must be unbearable with day-and-night bombing. Why has Breslau been spared so far? Heard horror stories from Hamburg survivors. "Firestorm bombing" they call it.

Despite my attachment to my Silesian homeland, I had always considered the sea part of my heritage. My father's family came from the shores of the North Sea and the Baltic, and many a summer had been spent among tides, breakers, beaches and dunes. But now this place on the Baltic had an additional appeal. It was located at the mouth of a small river, the Rega. There my aunt's family lived, and if they wanted to go anywhere they had to get into their little rowboat and start pulling: shopping, post office, church, railway station, and to the beach. For me, considering my inclinations and background, this place had all the makings of heaven on earth—nothing better than wading through the tall, dewy grass pastures early in the morning, down to the river where I had laid out my illegal nightlines for eel and pike. Nothing better than being out in the pinewoods, foraging for raspberries, blueberries, and mushrooms. Nothing better than getting into the boat to row down to the beach. Rowing back home, upriver, took a little getting used to, not to mention developing an all-new set of muscles. "Hey, I know how to row! I'll get us home!" One pull later, I was on my back behind my seat. I had to learn how to pull gently and evenly in order to prevent the oars from jumping out of the oarlocks. And nothing better than being in our sandcastle,* warming my wet body after diving into the breakers.

I had always been fond of fishing; now it became my favorite pastime. Not so much for the sport of it as for nourishment. Miraculously, here I actually had a visitor's fishing license. Everyone did. All the fugitives from the bombed-out cities fished in the river, the result being that there were not many fish left and then mostly little ones. But there was one place I discovered, an old branch of the river where no one ever went, the reason for this being that it was well concealed behind willow thickets and that there were signs posted: PRIVATE PROPERTY. NO FISHING. Are they joking? I mused to myself. Do they really think they can intimidate someone with my experience and daring? I think not!

My aunt was delighted with the sudden, almost daily supply of fresh fish. Nothing big, usually, but the numbers were respectable. I cleaned and scaled them myself down by the river, and she cooked them. She

---

*Sandcastle: Direct translation from the German *Sandburg,* which is nothing more than a shallow sandpit about eight to ten feet in diameter surrounded by a sand wall. These castles were often elaborately decorated with pebbles or seashells and jealously defended by their occupants.

fried them in very little oil and somehow got them so crisp that one could eat the whole thing, bones and all. Or, she would boil them in very little water with some onion, carrot, parsley, and salt. When done, she would add some vinegar to make it good and sour. The vinegar would work on the calcium of the bones, and again, you could eat the whole thing. The acidic broth, when cold, would become a little gelatinous and was delicious with fried potatoes. A third possibility was to boil the fish as above with onion, carrot, parsley, and salt, then thicken everything with flour dissolved in water or milk, finishing it off with a lot of chopped mixed herbs, like chives, parsley, and dill. But that was tedious. It was hell to sort out all those tiny bones.

I have mentioned illegal nightlines earlier. That's how I sometimes got a bigger fish. Not huge ones, but up to two pounds. The long lines, with two or three hooks about two feet apart, would be baited with worms. One end had to be secured on the bank; then the line with some weight at the end would be tossed out into the water. Eels, being bottom feeders, as Professor Brehm had taught me, would look for food, find the worm, and I would pull out the bounty in the morning. So it said in the book. Actually, my rate of success was less than I had hoped. But I did catch a few good ones, once more delighting my aunt, because eel was almost as good and popular as carp. Poached eel in dill sauce was a dish every respectable seafood restaurant would offer, not to mention smoked eel, a very costly delicacy, available to this day anywhere in Northern Europe.

For the pike you needed live bait, one of those little fish I caught by the dozen. Attach it to a harness with hooks and that to a short, strong line, perhaps five feet long, and tie the other end to something sturdy on the bank. A big pike can be quite forceful. My aunt's husband was indeed impressed when he was served a major portion of pike one day.

"Where is this coming from?" he asked, glancing around the table from one to the next, until his eyes came to rest on me, while his eyebrows were rising up higher and higher. He had been the one who had introduced me to the finer points of fishing, so it was not difficult to come to the conclusion that I must have had something to do with the appearance of this delectable morsel on his plate. More difficult for him to grasp was the fact that I had succeeded where he had always come home empty handed. Now I had some explaining to do.

"Well, you know that hidden old stagnant water with the No Fishing sign? Well, it's open now. Someone took the sign down. Lots of big ones in there and no one else has been fishing there, so far. I'll take you tomorrow." I don't know if he bought that story, but he enjoyed my pike without further interrogation.

This acquired uncle was a most understanding fellow who had instantly become my favorite person, my idol. Not only had he greatly improved my fishing skills, to me he was a universal genius. He had to be. How else could he be a world-class athlete, a poet, a painter, an actor, and a musician? I had no reason to doubt the validity of his talents because often enough I had heard friends and relatives talk about his accomplishments. Among these gifts, one surpassed all others for me—his athletic ability. He had come in second in the Berlin marathon! He was a lawyer by training and, though in the army, was stationed in Berlin in some armament position. On weekends he came to be with his family.

In the evenings, when swaths of fog crept over the meadows and the fragrance of freshly cut hay hung in the air, he would emerge from the house with his lute. A candle was lit in the little pavilion in the garden. We all gathered there and took our seats on benches or chairs. He tuned his instrument for a few minutes, and then he would begin. He was so good, and he knew so many songs! His wife brought out sheets of cake we had baked, nothing fancy, just a plain yeast dough on a cookie sheet covered heavily with berries we had picked, blueberries and raspberries, with not much sugar, but awfully good, considering the year: 1944.

His songs were mostly old German folksongs, songs I could listen to for hours. Some I already knew and many I learned as the summer went on. I knew the harmonies for the more familiar ones, and for the new ones it was not too difficult to figure out a good harmony line. We were a great duet! Singing like that together gave me the same feeling of bliss that I felt when tasting goose liver, licking butter cream frosting, or when pulling a big fish out of the water. If I had had to choose, I don't know what I would have picked as my favorite pastime—singing or fishing. Fortunately, I did not have to. I was given plenty of opportunity for both.

Journal entry, August 1944: Katinka, the Glaeser's new maid, now living with them in their house in Breslau. One of the thousands the Nazis shipped as slave labor to Germany. Truly beautiful. From the Ukraine, speaks hardly a word of German, so she was easy prey for Werner. She was devastated when he got married to Gaby. That was so mean of him: carrying on with her while marrying another.

Toward the end of the summer, a general unrest and nervousness could be felt everywhere, especially among party members, and somehow, almost magically, as if they had never existed, the fearsome little black, white, and red party member pins with the swastika in the middle vanished. What did not vanish were the endless processions of Allied bombers overhead on their way to unload on some German city, Breslau, with my mother in it, for all I knew. But that did not happen until the very end of the war.

One afternoon, as I was sitting in our rowboat, fishing not too far from shore, my aunt came running, shouting excitedly, "Quick! Come quickly, I have to tell you something wonderful!"

Wow, something wonderful—at this point? The only wonderful thing I could imagine was that someone had given us a couple pounds of butter, or sugar, or meat.

My aunt gestured wildly to come in all the way, really close, and then she whispered, "Hitler is dead! Yes, it was on the radio. They exploded a bomb in his shelter."

But alas! How much grief all of us would have been spared, had it been true.

Journal entry, August 1944: Horsti is gone for three weeks so far, two more to go. Can't wait! I miss him terribly, but he is having such a wonderful time. Hildegard writes that he fishes and swims all day long and sings with Onkel Ernest at night. Seems he really adores this uncle. She also wrote that he has a crush on a girl there. Helga from Hamburg, who sometimes babysits for the girls. Talks about her all the time but won't go near her. Too funny, she writes. I am sorry he missed Cousin Werner's wedding—to Gaby, the only good-looking half-Jewish girl in Breslau, I am sure.

Guess God did not answer our prayers. What a disaster that July 20 attempt on Hitler's life! And now the hunt is on for the conspirators. All those courageous people who tried to save Germany. Hope Günther was not involved.

Summer's end and the Russian Army came closer and closer. Time to return to Breslau. There, a general exodus was taking place. It seemed that anyone who had any sense at all was trying to leave the city as fast as possible. Breslau had been given the status of "fortress," meaning it was to be defended to the last bullet and the last drop of blood. Who would want to be part of that?

The decision to remain in Breslau must have been very difficult for my mother. Once before she had had to face a similar situation and had made the wrong choice, the choice of staying in Germany in the '30s rather than following friends and relatives into foreign countries. Now, one look out of our third-floor window onto the street, a major artery in a westerly direction, must have convinced her that what those people down there were doing was akin to suicide: a steady stream of mostly women and children, pushing or pulling little wagons, bikes, or sleds, was moving along, a millipede with little to feed on and without warmth in this record cold. Did they have a chance? Wouldn't they be overtaken and brutally dealt with by the rapidly advancing Russians? But before that, what would be my mother's fate when confronted by German military police, she with the Nazi-imposed "Sara" in front of her last name and the huge J printed across her picture ID? Well, to my mother, staying in Breslau sounded preferable to a concentration camp any day! And so it happened that my mother and I became part of the

Gaby

heroic few who had decided to brave the onslaught from the east and
to become defenders of Fortress Breslau.

December 1944: Horror stories about the Russians in East
Prussia. Their revenge for what the Germans did to them. Day
and night treks of refugees pass our house: on foot, on skis,
some pulling little wagons, occasionally something larger with
horses, in between mothers with baby carriages. What do they
eat, where do they sleep? And so cold! So many are freezing
to death. A record cold, they say. In the distance we can hear
rumbling like thunder. The front. Horst went out to check on
the Glaeser's house. Suddenly, he told me, there was that man in
the basement, helping himself to a bottle of wine. Turned out it
was Bastel, Gaby's brother who had escaped from a labor camp
and was hoping to make it to the West before the Russians.
Horst helped him to heat up water so he would be able to take a
bath before leaving. Hope he makes it out of the city.

February 14, 1945: Dresden! How can that be? Are the Allies
just as bad as the Nazis? All those refugees in the city and then
the firestorm bombing? Twice? Incomprehensible! Some of our
friends must have been there. That beautiful city gone. More

Pushing or pulling little wagons

than 40,000 dead. Horst rode his bike out to the Glaeser's house. Everything fine there. Found some beautiful riding boots and officer's pants in the upstairs apartment. Way too big, of course. But at this point—who cares.

By February 15, 1945, the Red Army had completely encircled Breslau, but failed in its efforts to take it. Too many German soldiers, munitions, and supplies were in the city, not to mention the fact that the mayor, who had dared to consider capitulation, had already been summarily shot. So the Russians

Anordnung!

Frauen jeden Alters
sowie männliche Jugendliche
unter 16 Jahren und Männer
über 60 Jahre
**haben das Stadtgebiet von
Breslau zu verlassen!**

Um den Abtransport von Kranken und
Gebrechlichen weiter zu ermöglichen,
setzen sich alle Gehfähigen
zu Fuß in Marsch.

Breslau, den 26. Januar 1945

Hanke
Gauleiter und Reichsverteidigungskommissar

*Poster: All women, males under 16 and
over 60 must leave the city.*

resorted to shelling and bombing the city round the clock for three months, while house-to-house combat was going on in the suburbs. However, for me personally, the situation was not without attractive opportunities. Sure, there was the death penalty set for looting, "stealing from the German people," as it were, but with 90 percent of all houses and apartments empty and turning into more and more rubble by the hour, who would worry about a law like that? Even my mother got used to my showing up with bags filled with staples: canned goods with meat, fish, fruit, potatoes, even liquor for bartering purposes. One of my friends, apparently a whiz in his profession, had been apprentice to a locksmith. I firmly believed that there was not a lock in the entire city he couldn't have picked in a few seconds. Soon I was able to keep up with him. Our nimble fingers placed us miles ahead of the competing teenage gangs.

Journal entry, March 7, 1945: Russian infantry across the street. Mortar shelling and machine gun fire all day long. A huge artillery shell came through the wall, rolled up to Horsti's feet, didn't explode. On my birthday German soldiers came and guided us out of the house and away from the front line. Their unit had just lost its cook. A major asked if we would stay so I could cook for them. I think he likes me. If he knew! So here we are. How ironic! A Jewish widow cooking for the German Army. Horsti loves it. He follows the soldiers and brings back stuff from empty houses. Now the major uses him as messenger to other units because he is so fast and knows the neighborhood so well. Russians pick these youngsters off like sparrows. Have to get out of here! If I tell him we are Jewish he may let us go.

March 9, 1945: Thank God! I had a talk with the major, and it worked. He was shocked but very fair. Gave us an escort to a safe place. Now we are in a small cellar apartment in another section of town. Have to report to labor units every morning. Mostly cleanup work and digging up corpses, looking for survivors. Horsti, too. I think he now has a crush on that sexy girl, Marianne, thirteen years old. I think she sleeps around a lot. Heard her mother complain that she is gone every night. Well, the front is coming closer, so we'll soon be moved again, hopefully away from her.

There is a good side to almost everything, even to the most dismal calamities. At least, that was my experience as one house after another was shot to pieces over our heads—thirteen times altogether. Whenever this happened, some party official would appear—no questions asked, for a change—to conduct us to a new domicile. As far as I could figure, they would pick anything unoccupied and open it up to us or other families on the move. This way I became acquainted with parts of the city I had not even known existed. Not only that! Often, these apartments turned out to be veritable treasure troves. Some of the booty shirts I wear to this day! Even more importantly, to me, every new place opened up new territories for our neighborhood expeditions.

IV

How a Russian bomber provided a fish dinner for hundreds, how I made friends with a Russian officer who nearly got me killed, and how I got Antek involved in treasure hunting

UNPERTURBED THE ODER FLOWED silently on through all the shelling, bombing, and fighting. She was and always had been an integral part of my life, and I must not neglect to bring her back into the picture. One of Germany's major arteries for the shipping industry, she was also a very popular choice for various water sports, especially kayaking. On warm summer weekends, hundreds of boats were being paddled up and down stream. Small islands and cozy bays invited the weary to put up their tents. Evenings, if you did not play the guitar or an accordion, then you would cast out a line with a baited hook on it. For years it had been my dream to join those happy people on the river, but every time I broached the subject I met with stiff resistance from my mother. For one thing, kayaks, the elegant, folding kind, were impossible to come by, and then—consider the danger! Every summer careless swimmers succumbed to the treacherous river.

But now I saw my chance. It was a balmy day in early April, and I suggested to my friend that we pay a visit to one of the boathouses on the river where these kayaks were stored. Forsaken by their cowardly owners, they were just aching to be liberated by some enterprising youths.

Apparently a grenade had ripped through the roof and fragments had punctured many of the boats. Sadly we wandered through the storage aisles, lifting a broken paddle here, pushing aside a plank there. Finally, we spotted a fine Klepper two-seater, hopefully unscathed. Wow! Not a scratch on it. So let's get it into the water and go—where?

I had a plan all ready. The Glaesers' house was a five-minute walk from a branch of the Oder. We would simply paddle for about an hour, carry the boat to their house and store it in the shed. They themselves, of course, had left the city long ago.

It was a bit scary, being out on that big river for the first time: choppy waters, swift currents, a dead German soldier jammed up against one of the bridge supports, and neither of us had paddled a kayak before, but we made it. From that day on we paddled whenever and wherever we could. After we had drawn machinegun fire a little bit upstream, we shied away from those parts. But there were other opportunities for paddle adventures. One of them was the Schiller Pond, again not far from the Glaesers' house, famous for skating and infamous for being the pond from which I had extracted my first carp back when I got slapped. Now we paddled on that romantic, willow-framed body of water in a park on the outskirts of the city. To this day I don't know why we failed to fish for carp from our boat. As it turned out, we did not need to.

It was Easter weekend; we were on the pond, trying out a little sail which the former owner had thoughtfully included. The Russians were in the air, trying to get downtown Breslau ready for spring plowing;

Unperturbed the Oder flowed.

some of the houses were still in the way.
Wave after wave of bombers appeared
over the treetops, as we huddled in our
little trenches on shore. These trenches
were running in zigzag patterns amidst and
through flowerbeds. This pattern was not
designed to circumvent precious plants, but
to protect humans from bomb fragments:

A fine Klepper two-seater

if some explosive landed in the trench, the
resulting fragments would fly straight, sparing everyone around the
next corner. I did not know if citizens had dug them for their own
protection or if party work crews had created them in preparation for
future trench warfare. We watched as the bombs tumbled toward the
ground, in the not too distant city.

Somehow, our presence must have been an irritation to one of
the bombardiers up there. Was it our boat on shore, or did he feel
threatened by the white sail? But wasn't white the color of surrender?
Well, not to that fellow! "No more sailing for you, buddy," as he
operated the bomb release.

We could actually see the bombs coming; then we heard them. An
incredible roaring in the air, as we buried our faces in the dirt—then
deafening explosions; everything shook and trembled, and it rained
on us—dirt, sand, and water. A couple of bombs must have hit the
pond.

"Ha, so he did try to get our sail, the bastard!"

Luckily the boat was unharmed, except for being sandy and wet.
And then we looked around, looked at the water, looked at each other,
and started first grinning then shouting. There were hundreds and
hundreds of carp floating belly up on the surface. By now, quite a few
Easter promenaders had emerged from their ditches. They crowded
along the shore, broke off branches to rake fish in close enough so
they could grab them, but most of them had drifted toward the middle
of the pond. Suffice it to say, we were very busy the next couple of
hours. It was incredible. Sort of like the feeding of the biblical five
thousand, I thought in awe. The parallels were indeed striking: both in
Palestine back then, as well as here now, the blessing had come from
above! There was an inexhaustible supply of carp. And this time, I did
not get slapped.

The systematic destruction of the city continued for a few more

weeks. Round-the-clock shelling, bombing and burning turned everything into a vast landscape of rubble with a few remnants of houses
rising above it all, sticking out like broken teeth in an otherwise vacant
mouth. Block after block disappeared, the Russians not being the cul-
prits this time, but Germany's own SS. This was Operation Parched
Earth—nothing of any value was to fall into enemy hands. So street
after street was burned or dynamited.

As is frequently the case with desperate situations, rumors sprouted
like mushrooms after a warm summer rain: Two armored SS divisions
are on their way to liberate the city; the new German miracle weapon is
annihilating the enemy; the United States has signed a peace treaty with
Germany and has declared war on Russia; a deadly epidemic is killing
off the Russian Army. Then: Hitler is dead; Germany has surrendered.
The last two were fact. The bombing, shelling and burning ended, and
the arrival of the victors was awaited with fearful anticipation. Women
disappeared from sight; white or red flags were appearing instead.
Observing the general panic, a passage from the Bible occurred to
me, in which Matthew comments on the behavior of the damned
anticipating the horrors awaiting them in hell. He has them "weeping
and gnashing their teeth." This, I thought, described the behavior of
the German population on that day.

And there they came! Columns and columns of trucks and tanks,
followed by marching soldiers, four abreast, clutching their famous
little submachine guns, affectionately nicknamed "balalaikas." What
really amazed me was the fact that they were singing, and not so much
the "what" as the "how." These guys were not just singing: they were
singing in parts, and in between there were solo voices that sounded
like the voices of opera singers. "It must be a special unit that has been
rehearsing a long time for this occasion," I concluded. "Or perhaps,
they are part of the famous Don Cossacks chorus?" Everything was
orderly and peaceful, unlike in other places that had suffered terribly,
wherever the German population had been overrun by fighting Russian
units. My mother's intention had been to rid ourselves of the Nazis
while not getting brutalized by the Russians. Whenever she had talked
about this plan, it had sounded to me as if I were listening to some
amateur explaining how she would perform a complicated circus act
on a high wire—without a net. But I had to admit it; her gamble had
served us well. We had outlived the Nazis while surviving the fighting.
Even our empty stomachs could detract but little from that feeling of
triumphant relief.

Frontzeitung der Festung Breslau

Schlesische Tageszeitung

AMTLICHES BLATT DER NSDAP. UND SÄMTLICHER BEHÖRDEN

16. Jahrgang / Nr. 118   Festung Breslau, Mittwoch, den 2. Mai 1945

Heldentod des Führers

Großadmiral Dönitz als Nachfolger eingesetzt
Volk und Wehrmacht stehen unter seiner Führung

| Dönitz an das deutsche Volk | Aus dem Führerhauptquartier wird gemeldet, daß unser Führer Adolf Hitler gestern nachmittag in seinem Befehlsstand in der Reichskanzlei, bis zum letzten Atemzuge gegen den Bolschewismus kämpfend, für Deutschland gefallen ist.

Am 30. April hatte der Führer Großadmiral Dönitz zu seinem Nachfolger eingesetzt. Der Großadmiral hat den Oberbefehl über die Wehrmacht und die Führung des deutschen Volkes übernommen. | Wer leben will, der kämpfe also! |

Hitler is dead.

Journal entry, May 1945: Strange! I had always imagined what it would feel like to suddenly be rid of the Nazis. Dancing and partying for days, doing crazy things. Now it is nothing like that at all. Sure we outlasted them, but after three months of constant shelling and bombing, to be harassed by Russians and Poles is no great comfort. Good thing Horsti is so absorbed by his daily survival adventures that he does not feel my disappointment. I wonder every waking minute if any of our friends and relatives in the camps survived. It would be a miracle. How can one find out? Speaking of miracles, the day before the surrender there was one final bombing. Nothing major. Horsti and a friend were in their little shelter across the street. He told me that suddenly he heard a huge roar in the air, then nothing, then everything shook violently but without a sound. Afterwards he examined the surroundings and there, about ten feet from his shelter, was a huge hole in the ground, some fifteen inches in diameter, drilled by the bomb, the end of which must have been located directly beneath his shelter. I saw the hole where the dud was buried. Same thing as back in March when the shell came through the wall, rolled up to his feet and did not explode. Gives me goose bumps.

May 1945: Amusing occurrence. A young captain, Tovarishch Kapitano, (everyone is Tovarishch or "comrade" something, all the way up to general, even Stalin), came into our room. Nice looking and polite. Was carrying a blanket and some bread. Gestured that he wanted to put his blanket next to me. What could I do? So he put the blanket down, gave me some bread. Then he stretched out on the blanket and fell asleep instantly. I got up very early next morning. He was so handsome.

So far so good. But what now? We had lost everything except the few things we had been able to hand carry from house to house. Nor were the prospects for the future in any way promising. We found out that Breslau,* as well as most of Silesia, would become part of Poland, and the Polish Milizia was already beginning to harass and exploit all Germans and, funny thing, us too, although we had been promised special treatment and extra rations. So, to the Germans we had been Jews, and to the Poles we were Germans now. How maddening! The documents identifying us in three languages as victims of Nazi persecution had little value. That was the time when we came to the realization that there was no future for us in Breslau or in Germany. What were the options?

"Okay, the way I see it, there is only one viable choice for you, only one way to go. You've got to get out of here, you've got to get to the American Zone somehow, and from there you've got to get in touch with your friends and relatives in the States. That's the only place where you can hope to find a new life and a future." An old friend gave us that advice. To us, America seemed as remote and inaccessible as the moon.

For the moment, the order of the day was the old familiar SURVIVAL. There really was nothing to eat anymore. The few supplies that were left from Nazi days were rigidly controlled by the Poles who had organized a huge black market in order to force the German population to spend their last money or trade in their jewelry and other valuables for food.

For me, the emergency food situation was the signal for intensified foraging efforts. But where to turn? All the houses and apartments had been picked clean, at least of anything edible. But there still were some

*Now called Wroclaw, since the takeover by the Poles.

Identifying us in three languages

furnishings and knickknacks around that could be used for barter at the black market. Curiously, the Russian soldiers were after the same objects as we, and often we would rummage side by side through closets, dressers, and basements. Never a harsh word or a threatening gesture, though the first time this happened I was paralyzed with fear.

After a few encounters we actually became well acquainted with a couple of groups, and they would greet us enthusiastically whenever we met. A captain with two lieutenants was particularly friendly. We worked well together as a team. My friend and I would scout ahead; the Russians would follow our directions. Whenever there were obstacles, such as locked doors, padlocks, metal cages or boxes, a short blast from the balalaika took care of the problem. Once we discovered a very well concealed cache of liquor buried underneath shrubbery in the garden of a villa. Granted, that would have been a great commodity for the black market, but nothing doing! The captain gave us five wristwatches from his right arm and proceeded to uncork the first bottle. We politely declined when our turn came. Soon thereafter we left. We were not anxious to test the validity of all the stories about drunken Russians and did not want to push our luck. Driven by curiosity, we revisited that house again after a few hours. Loud singing came through the windows: first singing, then a few empty bottles. Hastily, we withdrew. We started running when rapid balalaika fire drowned out the singing. Fearing the worst, we went home, planning to check things out the following morning.

Nothing unusual was noticeable as we approached the house around noon the following day. No vehicles, no military police, no Polish Milizia. Cautiously we entered the room where we had left our friends. There were a few more now. We counted nine, sprawled out all over the place. Industrial strength snoring caused the chandelier to vibrate. Other than that—tranquility, except for a few broken windows, cracked chairs, puddles of liquor on and in the grand piano. The remnants of a campfire on the Oriental rug were still smoldering, and of course there were the inevitable bullet holes in walls and ceilings. Seeing all this and more I could not help but pray, "Please, oh God, send one of your angels down to teach these lost souls the difference between toilet bowls and bathtubs, and let them not defile the sanctity of lace curtains with their bodily waste."

We attempted to revive the captain, he being the highest ranking—if not reeking—officer on the floor. Bleary-eyed, he grunted something unfriendly, finally recognizing us and remembering the preceding events. After a lengthy swig from a rum bottle, he rose, still—or again—swaying a bit, and proceeded to kick the life back into his comrades. Then he thanked us for waking them up, probably preventing their court-martial by doing so, and finally he gave us three more wristwatches. "No good," he muttered contemptuously. "Kaput—German—watch—shit," and he showed us ten more watches on his left arm, none of them running, all of them showing different times. He was amazed and once more thanked us profusely after we had instructed him how to set and wind a watch. Amongst the nine of them, they must have had a bucketful of watches. When we checked that house a bit later, the entire crew was sitting there, peacefully working on their watches while lovingly clutching their balalaikas. And they say there is no hope for mankind!

This looting and drinking activity was happening not far from the house where we lived at that time. It was located near the Oder, in an elegant suburban neighborhood that had remained relatively unharmed by the fighting. For some reason very few houses there were occupied. Thus it was the ideal hunting ground for us and our friends.

A few days later, our Russians, excitedly pacing about and carrying some packages, were already waiting for us as we arrived. They waved us on, to follow them through the garden which ended at the river's edge. "Dawai! dawai!" they kept on shouting.

There, to my surprise and delight, were a rowboat and a kayak. So—something involving us and the boats!

My captain friend must have spent some time with his Russian-German dictionary, because he addressed me in German: "Du—ich—Boot—paddel—boom—Fisch—ja?" He grinned seductively and held up one of the packages: "Boom!"

Aha—I had seen that stuff before: explosives with a few feet of fuse, enough to blow up a good-size bridge.

"Du—ich—paddel—boom!" and he threw up both arms to indicate the magnitude of the anticipated explosion. "Fisch—karascho, dawai," he concluded, while his buddies nodded enthusiastically. Apparently, he wanted me to paddle him around while he tossed the explosives overboard.

But first, he wanted to test the sea worthiness of our craft, the kayak. "Du—warten," another new word, as he took a long swig from his vodka flask, and before I could warn him, he had stepped into the kayak.

Now, you don't step into a kayak! You crouch down and gingerly move your butt over the center of the boat before you sit down. But too late. There was an expression of immense surprise and dumbfoundedness on his face, as the boat tipped, and he went in headfirst.

Was he a good swimmer? The river was deep and swift here.

Yes, he was, and what came out of his mouth, once he stood on firm ground, was not fun to listen to. It sounded a lot like one of Emma's Polish outbursts. But he was a fighter. While his comrades were rolling on the ground with laughter, he pointed imperiously at me: "Du—los—paddel—dawai!"

We had retrieved and emptied the kayak, and I proceeded, very slowly, exaggerating each movement, to demonstrate getting in, casting off, paddling.

It was a fairly warm day, early June, so the wet uniform didn't seem to bother him standing there on the shore. I was having a good time paddling around until he shouted at me, "Du—kommen—boom!"

By now I was aware that I was to do the navigating, he the booming. Everyone helped steady the boat as he got in. And we were off! He motioned toward a cove that somehow appeared promising to him. We arrived there, and he was having a hard time igniting the fuse.

Normally, in a two-seater, both paddlers would be facing the same direction, but for this occasion he was turned around so he was facing me. This way, I could watch what he was doing. I did not like what I was seeing. Over and over his lighter would go out; then the fuse would go out after a second but, of course, in the process getting shorter and shorter. Suddenly, with merely a stub of fuse left, it took off, burning like a sparkler on a Christmas tree. There were shrieks of terror from both of us; he tossed the bundle overboard, and the boat lurched forward—not one second too soon. There was a huge *boom,* and a fountain of water, smoke, and mud shot up. It looked like the explosion of a depth charge in a submarine movie. We were tossed around by the upheaval below. Then, after substantially fortifying himself from his flask, the part we were all waiting for started—looking for belly-up fish. But darn it—nothing, absolutely nothing.

"Scheisse," my captain said. "Deutsch Fluss—Scheisse. Volga—prima, Oder—Scheisse."

So they all went home, leaving us and the boats behind. I, however, knew better! There was that swift current. Didn't it make sense that dead fish would be swept down stream? I paddled a bit and sure enough, in the next few coves were plenty of dead fish. Nothing like the day of the carp-pond bombing but enough for a few good meals.

Now, wasn't that a great learning experience! Goodbye fishing poles, lines, hooks, sinkers, and worms! Hello hand grenades and bazookas! There was no shortage of weapons and ammunition cluttering up the environment. We knew where we could get our hands on anything from bullets to antiaircraft guns. The thing of course was, once more, not to get caught. First the Nazis and now the Poles and the Russians were interfering with my visions.

Obviously, hand grenades were the only logical way to go. Not those big, clumsy ones with the wooden handle, but the small, roundish ones called, "egg-grenades." "Easy to carry and conceal and easy to operate," as the easy-to-follow instructions read—unlike bazookas which were a little tricky to fire and impossible to hide. Feeling we owed it to ourselves to fire one anyway, two of my friends ended up with nasty burns.

No! Definitely, egg-grenades had to be the choice of the day. The question was—where to go? After careful deliberation we decided on a small pond, once our favorite swimming hole, out of the way and owned by the local fishermen's association. That alone would have cinched it. With credentials like that—how could it not be full of fish?

Strange, though, now, without laws and order and police, you'd think that hungry Germans would come out and start fishing everywhere. But no! It seemed that the years of Nazi suppression had brainwashed any inclination toward independent thought or action out of them.

So there was that lake, just begging for someone to come and harvest its fish. How could we refuse? On a warm summer morning, quite early, we packed up the customary swimming paraphernalia of the day: swimming trunks, towels, hand grenades, and some empty bags, just in case. It was about an hour's bike ride, and by the time we arrived we were ready for a cooling bath. Willows, cattails, pond lilies, and a few birds greeted us. Otherwise—not a soul. We headed for the far side, the deep end of the lake. In warm weather fish like to be deep, I had read.

There were five of us, each one carrying a well-hidden grenade. I don't remember what logic there was behind this strategy, but the plan was that we would throw the grenades in such a fashion that they would land in a circle and explode simultaneously. Of course we all knew how to set off a hand grenade! We were fourteen or a little older, after all, and some of us fifteen-year-olds had actually been in the army and had seen some action. During the last days of the war, however, they had been advised by their officers to go home and put on their lederhosen, thus escaping the dismal prospect of becoming POWs and marching off for a prolonged visit to Siberia.

We lined up on the shore, figured out who would throw where, then the oldest and most experienced warrior counted: "One—two—three—throw!" and every grenade landed approximately where it was supposed to. It took a few moments, since we had not counted seconds prior to the throw, then came five simultaneous explosions with the familiar fountains of mud and water, and we were pleased to notice the almost perfect circle in which they occurred.

While we quickly changed into our bathing suits, we kept a sharp eye on the targeted area for fish harvesting. We had no idea what to expect and were enormously excited. Each one of us had already made plans as to what to do with his share of the bounty. Foremost—provide nourishment for family and friends. Some of us were going to construct a smoke barrel, so some of the fish could be preserved for a few days longer. Others were going to take a few fish to the black market to trade them for other things. But what if nothing happened? Suddenly, there was a triumphant shout: "Something white on the surface!"

A few seconds later: "A couple more on the left side!"

Then there was a sighting on the right. At this point, we all dove in, and we instantly knew that all of our dreams and plans would come true. There were dozens of fish on top now, and we formed a relay to get them all out quickly. Every imaginable type of fish was represented, some truly huge: pike, catfish, carp, eel, and some neither I nor Professor Brehm had ever seen. Soon we had collected quite a pile, and still there were more in the water.

"I'll go and get some help," I said, and took off on my bike. It was not far to the nearest street, and soon an eager stream of people appeared, young and old. My friends and I had packed up all we could carry; the rest we just left. It was amusing to watch how most of our "guests" jumped fully dressed into the lake. As they were yelling thank-yous and blessings in our direction, we pedaled homeward. It was a memorable event.

My mother, even though she appreciated my contributions, was not happy with my questionable activities. She often fixed her imploring eyes upon me. I could guess what she was feeling. Her looks said, where will it end?—a sentiment she shared with some of our neighbors. I knew this because I had overheard two ladies agreeing: "I feel so sorry for Käte! That boy of hers is bound to end up a criminal," one of them predicted. Käte was my mother's name.

I was shocked. True, I had done some wild things, but it had never been anything truly criminal, I thought, like stealing money or hurting someone. It had all been done to bring some justice into our existence. I had to make up for the connections which we, in contrast to most others, were lacking. And furthermore, it had always been my practice to share my successes with as many people as possible. Come to think of it, hadn't we read something in English class about a legendary folk hero who took from the rich to help the poor? Robin . . . something . . . was his name, somewhere in medieval England. Got to find out more about that fellow! Yup, Robin would have been proud of me. I mean, there were kids my age who were trading things by the trainload: cigarettes, booze, sugar, butter, gasoline— you name it. Compared to them I was a paragon of virtue, nobility, and chivalry.

My mother nodded a few times when I informed her that I was merely following in the footsteps of my latest idol, Robin Hood.

"Okay, Horsti, I see what you are driving at, and I approve of your motives. But keep it in moderation. Stay away from the big-time gangsters and anything that has to do with firearms or drinking!

Remember, there are just the two of us, that's all we've got on this earth. If anything happened to you!—"

I promised to be good and not to take any chances. But then temptation came one morning when I strolled down to the Oder to check my lines. As I entered the lush meadows between the Oder dikes and the water's edge, I suddenly found myself surrounded by hundreds of sheep. Not far away I spotted the shepherd sitting under a tree, a Russian soldier, smoking, balalaika on his knees, a truly bucolic scene. I kept sauntering along the shore, casually ignoring the sheep who were politely reciprocating. There was quite a bit of bleating all around me, low-pitched alto sounds, but suddenly there was a soprano mixed in. What's this? I thought, an all-sheep chorus? But that soprano is definitely way off key.

I followed the juvenile sound, and there it was: a little lamb, caught in some prickly bush, its mother standing helplessly by. What was I to do? "Why, free the poor critter of course," was my instinctive impulse.

"Now, just a minute, please," another instinctive impulse intruded. "Pass up this unique opportunity, this obvious gift from heaven? Just stick it in you sack and get out of here!"

I shuddered at the thought of carrying this particular action to its inevitable conclusion. Or was some power above testing me, I wondered, wanting to see which way I would go. There was no time, though, for metaphysical speculations. So I kneeled down at the bush, scratched the hell out of my hands and reunited mother and child. Alto and soprano, mother and child, now in perfect harmony, thanked me in bleat. Then I continued pushing myself through the ocean of woolly bodies, feeling proud of myself and full of love and compassion for all soft and furry little creatures.

A few steps more and I had reached a small opening devoid of sheep—live ones at least. There was a low fence, behind it a few crude tables and scaffolds. On the scaffolds, several butchered sheep were hanging; on the tables cut-up animals were piled, awaiting transportation to some distant army kitchen. But no trucks nor any of the butchers were in sight, and the only guard I had encountered was far away and hidden behind hundreds of sheep. Well, there I had it! God rewards those who do right and who are patient! The fence was not an obstacle; I quickly stuffed two meaty legs into my sack and hastily ducked away.

At home I was received like Santa Claus. Two families—a nanny, two mothers and nine children (the two husbands' fates unknown)— shared the house with us. None of us had seen meat for weeks. Meta, the nanny, had a lot in common with Emma: she was an excellent cook, and she swore a lot.

Gradually, in the course of the summer, we had traded in and spent nearly everything we had rescued from our original home. There was nothing left to take from the neighborhood houses. Russian soldiers, Polish Milizia, gangs of German teenagers, and I had cleaned up completely. There still were fish in the Oder, but due to tightened regulations, explosives were out of the question, so it was back to hook, line, sinker—and very few fish. The Poles had taken over, leaving nothing for Germans. A few weeks ago, I had taken the tires off my bike, thinking, "Who would want to confiscate a bike without tires?" Well, think again!

One day, a small group of milizia men entered our garden. They were carrying shovels, picks, metal rods and started poking around between the hedges, under trees, and on the lawn. Very strange indeed, but not all that strange, it soon dawned on me. They were hoping to find valuables the owners had buried. This activity certainly piqued my interest, and I followed their every move with fascination. The more I looked, the more one of the milizia men began to appear somehow familiar to me. A big hulk of a man—where had I seen that before? Like in a dream, a vision appeared to me: a wintry, dark evening, and then that hulk emerging. Antek! Yes, Emma's "saintly brother!" I ran outside and wanted to shout his name.

He turned around and recognized me instantly, but instead of hugging me, as I expected him to, he put one of his fingers over his lips and turned away.

After a while, having not come up with anything, the group departed, leaving me in a state of puzzled excitement. "Mama, one of these milizia guys was Antek. He would not talk to me. What's going on? How is this possible?"

"Well," she answered, "you know that he is from Upper Silesia. So he speaks both German and Polish, and as a result he probably doesn't quite know himself where he belongs. Whatever is best for him, that's what he'll be. Right now, the only way to be is definitely Polish. And of course, he doesn't want his buddies to know about his German ties."

What she said made sense to me. Later, in the evening, as I had expected and hoped, there was a knock at the door. It was Antek. I rushed to open, and this time there was a hug. The first thing he uttered was a question: "Do you know what happened to Emma?"

We reassured him that as far as we knew, she was safely with the Glaesers in that little village in the foothills of the Alps.

"Thank God," he sighed with relief, and then he asked us why we had remained here, how we were managing, and what our plans were. "Oh yes, before I forget, I brought a few things I thought you could use." He reached into the little sack he was carrying: bread, butter, a slab of bacon, a few chocolate bars. We were speechless.

My mother was the first one to regain her composure. "How can we ever thank you?"

"Hey," Antek grinned, "remember that Christmas dinner with the goose? Wasn't that great? Funniest thing I ever experienced. I thought I'd die. The memory of that evening is worth a lot to me."

"Did you really go to an orphanage to play Santa for the children that evening?" I asked.

"What do you think?" he replied with a wink.

Wow, what a great guy, I thought. Then the treasure hunting activities of the morning came back to mind.

"Have you ever found anything?" I wanted to know.

"No—you've got to know where to dig—at least you've got to have some sort of clue. Although, a friend of mine dug up a box with jewelry last week. But that was just a lucky shot."

"Hmm," was all I said, because pictures were appearing in my mind, early, very early morning pictures of a park, the park that surrounded the old mansion, the Hopf villa, where the Gestapo had stuck us. I don't remember what had gotten me out of bed that early, probably bathroom needs. Anyway, what immediately caught my interest was movement on the other side of a high, chain-link fence, which separated us from the property of an SS general. Then there was more movement. Two human shapes were engaged in something. Time to get my binoculars. This deserved closer attention. I adjusted the focus until I had a nice, clear, picture of two men who were about to perform some task involving shovels and a wheelbarrow.

They kept hovering around a large oak tree, pacing back and forth in front of it, apparently looking for something. Then they marked off a large square and measured the distance from there to the tree. Aha! Now the shovels and careful removal of the sod. They were working fast, efficiently, and methodically. It was getting a little lighter now, so I was able to get a good look at the men. They were wearing SS uniforms; one of them was an officer, the other a private. The officer was wearing a patch over his right eye. The private had a severe limp.

"Aha!" I had deducted, "two invalids. That must be the reason they are here digging, instead of fighting on some front."

The hole must have been about four feet deep when they stopped digging. The private, dragging one of his legs, disappeared with the wheelbarrow, returning a few minutes later with a crate which they lowered into the hole. This happened twice more. Finally they shoveled the dirt back into the hole; leftover dirt went into the wheelbarrow. With the sod back in place, I could hardly detect a trace of their activity. They were obviously well practiced in the art of burying. After a few weeks, you would not be able to detect anything. And that was probably the reason why I had not remembered this incident in all these months—until this very moment. Of course! Buried treasure! How could I have ignored this? An SS general, one whose powers were without limit, who could walk into any house, private or official, and appropriate whatever pleased him—he wanted these goods out of reach before the Russians got there.

Were those crates still in their hole? I wondered. Had these trusted men helped themselves to everything after the siege? Or had it all been blown to bits by bombs and artillery? I knew that this particular section of Breslau had been the scene of heavy street fighting in March.

This, I realized, was too big for me alone. I needed help with some muscle: official, legal, and armed. I could hardly wait for Antek to leave so I would be able to walk and talk with him. He had come by bike, a beautiful, three-speed bike with every imaginable gadget, I noticed with envy. As he pushed it, I walked next to him. He must have sensed something was on my mind, because he kept looking at me expectantly.

"You know," I began, "when you were talking about your digging and your lucky friends, you said you had to know where to dig, or at least to have some sort of clue. I think I might be able to find the spot where something is buried." And I told him of those early morning events.

"We can go over there and I'll show you." I was careful to stress the "I" and "we" factor, to make sure to be cut in later.

Antek stopped dead in his tracks and let out a long, low whistle. "Wow!" was all he said for quite a while. Clearly, he was mulling things over.

"Tell you what," he finally suggested. "Tomorrow I can't, but day after tomorrow I'll come and pick you up at—let's make it ten o'clock.

And let's meet at the corner down the street."

"Okay, fine with me. Do you have any idea where I used to live? It's at the other end of town. It will take us about two hours to get there."

"Not by car," he said with a wink. "And now go home and get rested up for all that digging and lifting and hauling you'll be doing. Boy, you are one crazy kid! Emma knew what she was talking about." He slapped me on the back and disappeared into the night.

To say that I was excited, nervous, full of anticipation and expectation, would be understating my condition considerably.

"Are you all right?" my mother worried. "You look like you might be running a temperature. Let me check." And she poked the thermometer into my armpit. I'd swear she valued this thermometer more than anything we had rescued from our home. Up just a little bit, it registered. "See? I knew you were sick the second I laid eyes on you."

"Mama, for God's sake, I'm not sick. Just a little tense and excited."

"Anything going on I should know about? You are not getting involved with Antek in any way, are you?"

I was so used to concealing things from her and of feeling automatically guilty, no matter what, that I had not realized that this time I was actually doing something that bore no danger—neither morally nor physically. What could be safer than working together with a member of the almighty Polish Milizia?

"Well, as a matter of fact, I promised him that I would help him."

"Help him—help him do what?"

"Help him dig."

"Dig? Aren't there enough of his milizia buddies around to help him?"

"Uh—yes there are, but they would not know where."

"But you would?"

"Yes, because I was right there when it happened, and I saw everything."

"Right where when what happened?"

I felt some irritation rising up in me. This was too much like an interrogation. Well, that's what I got for opening my mouth. "When we were still at home—I mean, at the Hopf villa."

"So what happened there? This all sounds a bit—uh—suspicious, you'll have to admit. Let me try to summarize up to as far as you have confided in me. About a year ago, give or take a few months, you watched something outside, perhaps in the Hopf park, which is now somehow causing Antek to ask you to help him dig. Am I right so far?"

"Yes, that's it exactly. I am so glad you understand, and that it is okay with you." I thought I could slip away quickly, but my mother was a little sharper than that.

"Not so fast, young man. Something is fishy here. I can smell it a mile away. Like you—trying to keep the "what" from me. So—what was it you saw?"

"Oh, not much. Couldn't see much at all. Just boxes—crates—I don't know."

"Now come on! You can do better than that. You are just trying to be difficult. This is getting to be like pulling worms out of someone's nose."

"Well, all right. There was that big hole behind one of the trees next door, and these two guys put these three boxes into it, and then they covered it up again and made it look like nothing had happened. And that is really all there is to it."

"Aha, I get it now. Antek's talk about hidden treasures suddenly reminded you of that episode, and you told him about it, and now he wants you to show him where to dig."

"Yup, that's it." What more was there to say?

I could see thoughts were going through my mother's head. She was moving her head slowly up and down and from right to left, now looking at me, then looking out of the window, then holding out her right arm with an open hand, moving it up and down, as if she was weighing something; the corners of her mouth were twitching. Suddenly she grinned. "Great, I am coming with you. Should be fun!"

V

Why my mother appeared to me like a knight in shinning armor, and what she meant by "our ticket to America"

THE SHOCK MADE ME close my eyes. When I opened them again, I beheld my mother standing there in a suit of shiny armor, a sword in her raised right hand, a crown on her head. It took several minutes before I fully recovered. But it was truly too overwhelming! My own mother, the woman who was so timid, who was afraid of her own shadow, who was so hung up on moral issues, who would not ride in a train because she was prohibited by law to do so, who did not dare to attend concerts or go to a movie theater for the same reason, who went crazy every time I was gone on one of my expeditions: that woman said with a smile on her face she was going with me and an armed milizia man on a treasure hunt, all the way on the other side of the town.

Then I understood her transformation: that woman had just cast off the bonds that had choked her spirits for fifteen years. And this here was my first encounter with a new person, bearing traits that were not familiar to me. Or were they? If this freshly hatched woman was adventurous and willing to take risks, then how did she differ from me? Was that how I got all those troublesome traits?

"Well, mother," I said, "I don't know what to make of this aberrant behavior. Have you really thought about this? Do you really want to be part of this—taking someone's possessions? And consider the danger! What if a Russian patrol comes along or one of these German teenage gangs? They sometimes have guns! And I thought you had come to your senses! And now this! Really! Don't tell me I have to take you to see your Pastor again."

"Now, where have I heard all this before?" my mother mused.

"Sounds awfully familiar, but don't worry, I'll behave. I am sure Antek won't mind. And those crates are probably long gone, anyway. If you knew about it, then there must be others who also knew about it. So what time are we going? Day after tomorrow, you said? Oh, shall I pack up a little picnic basket?"

I groaned, threw my arms up in the air and left. I could feel it: I was doomed; this whole undertaking was doomed.

Two days later, ten o'clock, the neighbors were treated to an unfamiliar spectacle: a mother and her son, obviously waiting to be picked up to go on a picnic. A few minutes later, a vehicle appeared, a former German Army truck, chauffeured by a man wearing the red and white armband of the Polish Milizia. The vehicle did not leave immediately. Some heated discussion seemed to be going on. The mother was seen getting in and out several times. Finally, they all departed together.

My mother was stunned at what she encountered on the way. You could see from one end of town to the other—no houses, just piles of rubble. Occasionally, we spotted small groups of shabbily dressed women and old men, clean-up gangs overseen by Polish Milizia.

"They'll need more than old people with shovels and wheelbarrows to clean up this mess," Antek commented. "Speaking of which, that's what I have in back of the truck: shovels and a wheelbarrow."

Groups of people became more frequent as we went on, gradually becoming a steady stream that emptied into a huge flat surface. It was a plateau, surrounded by mountains of brick, mortar and dirt that were adorned with occasional bathtubs, toilet bowls, and stove components sticking grotesquely out of the rubble and appearing to be completely out of place in this environment. Encountering bathtubs and toilet bowls in a Martian landscape couldn't have been more surreal.

Not that this area had always been a flat, empty surface. Blocks and blocks of apartment buildings had stood here not too long ago. Then the Nazi governor of Silesia, titled *Gauleiter,* had conceived of the grandiose plan to create a landing strip right here in the center of town. Thousands of women and children, including my mother, were drafted for this purpose, and block-by-block and street by street the transformation from living quarters to airstrip took place. It was completed the night before the surrender, so rumor had it, just in time for the governor to get into his little private plane and escape capture and certain death by execution or lynching. Ah yes, so much for the

Nazi boss of Silesia, Hanke, commonly referred to as "Hangman Hanke." If they had caught him, they would have hoisted him up on the nearest lamppost.

Now this area presented the perfect conditions for a major commercial setup, to which the presence of countless stands, booths, tables, cages with poultry and livestock, and truckloads with every type of merchandise bore witness: yes, the BLACK MARKET. My mother was amazed.

"Is this the place where you always go to take stuff to trade for food?" she asked; then adding reproachfully, "Why didn't you ever take me with you? This looks like so much fun!"

"Who is that woman?" I asked myself.

There were many detours along the way. Occasionally we met a trolley. They were running again in some parts of the city. Finally, our street, Gräbschnerstrasse, a long major artery from the center to the outskirts, appeared.

Our house emerged—more accurately, the pile of red bricks that used to be the Hopf villa. It had been a rather substantial structure, its brick foundation several feet thick. What went on there during the fighting must have been monstrous. Bomb and artillery explosions had turned the front yard into a moonscape. In what shape would the back yard—the park—be, I wondered, as I jumped from our truck and started out across the crater-riddled field.

"Stop," Antek yelled, "too dangerous! We must go around it. There may be duds in there and perhaps land mines. Follow me!"

He cautiously picked his way around the yard to the neighboring park where there was less evidence of fighting. The chain link fence was gone, unfortunately also the oak tree. "Well, where was it? I don't see any oak tree."

"No, it's not here anymore, but it must have been about over there. What kind of tree is the one lying over there?" I asked.

"Can't tell, it has no leaves. Go check the bark! You know what oak bark looks like, don't you?"

"Yea, then this must be it," I yelled, "and here is the stump where it was shot off."

It was really getting exciting. Mother was already emerging with the shovels, her face flushed, her eyes sparkling.

There were no shell craters near the tree, nor any evidence of recent digging—so, maybe, maybe! I paced around the tree stump trying to reconstruct the early morning activities.

I finally narrowed the area down to a section approximately ten by ten feet behind the stump. "Anywhere inside this square," I said and grabbed one of the shovels.

"Hold on," Antek said. "We'll save ourselves a lot of time and work if we use the metal probes. You know, if they had this dug up half a year ago, the ground must still be kind of loose. Let's start over here and work systematically right across to the other side. Push the rod straight down, about three feet, if possible, and then move one foot over and keep doing this."

Antek took one of the rods, while I tussled with my mother for the other one. I won and stepped next to Antek, waiting for his command.

"All right, push it in. Let's see what happens."

It was difficult to get it three feet down—nothing here. One foot over—nothing there. One foot more—nothing. Now we were almost in the middle of the square. One more foot. The rod went in as if we were playing in a sand box.

Antek whistled and grinned at me. At two feet down, the rod had hit solid resistance. One more foot over—same thing. One foot to the side—same thing.

"All right, let's start digging!" My mother was the first to sink her spade into the sod. After about ten minutes, we made contact with something that did not sound like rock or root—more on the hollow side. Ten minutes more and we had unearthed the outlines of three crates. Another ten minutes and we had all three crates completely exposed.

Antek jumped into the hole and tried to lift one of them. "Wow, that's some load in there!" This he repeated twice more within the next ten minutes. Now what? No way could we get the truck back here through this maze of craters. To navigate the wheelbarrow would be difficult enough. And then—it was still broad daylight, and there was some traffic in the street out in front.

"Best we wait until dark," Antek suggested. "Why take chances?"

My mother was delighted and all smiles, "Now aren't you glad that I packed us a picnic?"

I winced, and Antek gave me a curious look, like saying, is that woman for real? But there was no denying it, we were hungry by now and appreciated every bit of what she had prepared.

While my mother and Antek smoked his black-market Lucky Strikes, I left to inspect the rest of the park. It presented a sorry spectacle.

Hardly a shrub or tree had survived. Gone were my walnut trees, gone the hazelnut bushes, and the apricot trees at the far end of the park. How ironic: Mrs. Hopf had always gotten so upset each time a little branch was sliced off during one of my mock battles with a friend.

Darkness was slow in coming these summer days. More than once I glanced in Antek's direction. "Now? Should I get the wheelbarrow now?"

But every time Antek shook his head. "No, no, we can't take any chances. We don't want to lose this one."

I must have dozed off at one point, because I was really startled when someone shook my arm. It was my mother. "Okay, it's time. Antek has the wheelbarrow ready. So let's get one of the crates out and loaded up." She spoke and acted as if this were the kind of thing she had been doing for years.

I jumped into the hole and grabbed one end of a crate. Antek was at the other end, and together we heaved it up and out, and then into the wheelbarrow.

"Better let me handle this," advised Antek. He was referring to pushing our sturdy one-wheeler to the truck. "You go ahead of me and make sure we don't fall into something bottomless."

During the afternoon I had spent some time mapping out a safe route, but now, in the darkness, getting through was definitely a challenge. It took us about twenty minutes to reach the truck. We opened the canvas tarp and stowed the crate away.

"Best you stay here with the truck stand guard," Antek said. "If there is any sign of trouble, honk the horn and scream like hell. I'll try to get the next crate with your mother."

He vanished into the darkness. This seemed to be Antek's special trademark: appearing out of, and disappearing into—darkness.

I was relieved to hear the wheelbarrow's squeak after about half an hour. Then he was gone once more.

When he returned, my mother was with him. "Everything all right, Horst?"

"Sure, Mama, how about you?"

"She did a fantastic job," Antek said. "Couldn't have done it without her. Now, let's get the hell out of here."

Naturally, we were terrified all the way back. There were plenty of Russian military police vehicles now, patrolling the dark city. Not that they would have harmed us physically, but we surely would have lost our cargo. Having POLISH MILIZIA inscribed all over our truck in Polish, Russian, and German probably saved us, not to mention Antek's siren which he activated every time we spotted some Russians.

Toward the end of our trip, we had two Russian MP motorcycle escorts who thought we needed more siren support. Mother and I were alarmed by this, but Antek gave us his assurance wink.

Sure enough, when we came to a halt in front of our house and the sirens had stopped, he jumped out of the driver's seat, waving a bottle of vodka, and began jabbering at the two MPs in astonishingly fluent Russian. This went on for about ten minutes. Then the bottle was empty and the two vanished out of sight, racing their engines and sounding their sirens as they went. Antek gave us his low, breathy, relief whistle, which was quite different from his higher pitched, pleasant-surprise whistle.

Yes, the three crates! Each one measured about three by two by two feet of heavy pine boards wrapped in tarpaper and nailed shut. It would require a crowbar to remove the lids. The anticipation was almost unbearable—like just before cracking into the sealed burial chamber of a pharaoh, I imagined. We decided to wait a while because our arrival had probably awakened the entire neighborhood, which was nosily watching us now.

"Okay, let's take our haul into the basement," Antek finally said.

Electricity was still out, so we lit a couple of petroleum lamps. The wartime blackout shades were still in place. Antek went to work with a few tools from his truck, and then came the big moment—all three of them. Everything inside the crates was carefully wrapped in oilcloth.

I had read about treasures, about Pizarro and the Inca, about Schliemann digging up the Trojan treasure, and about that Egyptian pharaoh's treasure laden with gold and a deadly curse. This here now felt to me like all three of them rolled into one, except for the curse, so I hoped.

First, there emerged a box with all sorts of amber jewelry— necklaces, bracelets, various brooches and little figurines. Amber I knew from my visits to the Baltic. There were places on the Baltic in East Prussia where this prehistoric substance was actually mined, I had heard. On a lucky day, after a big storm, you could find small pieces of amber washed up on the shore; the largest I ever found was no larger than a fingernail.

Then there was jewelry; I mean the real kind—gold and silver and sparkling stones. Antek and my mother did a lot of whistling during this part of the show.

I had never heard my mother whistle before, but these pieces of jewelry brought it on. Having heard it from Antek, she must have thought that's the thing to do when confronted with unexpected, immense wealth—especially if it is your own wealth.

The crowning glory was a pearl necklace. "Genuine pearls," my mother assured us, after she had rubbed some of the pearls against her front teeth. "If it's real pearls," she explained, "they feel a bit chalky against your teeth, or something like that—or are they perhaps supposed to feel rather smooth?"

The surest way to find out if pearls are real, so I had heard, was to submerge them in vinegar. The real ones would dissolve. I offered to fetch some vinegar from the kitchen, but my mother declined, giving me a dirty look.

"Just trying to be helpful—," I huffed.

Next on the inspection list came a round box, very heavy, that was filled with old coins. All sorts of metals, centuries, and nationalities were represented. The large, gold coins felt unlike anything I had ever touched—so cool, smooth, and heavy. The silver coins tinkled when dropped on a wooden or stone surface. All of this was eminently suitable for the black market.

Oh, and then bundles of silver flatware appeared, also silver candlesticks and goblets. Stuff for the king's or the black marketeer's table, as the case may be.

The third crate was not as heavy as the other two. Groping around inside, I felt something like books, large books, just not as dense. What we had here, as it turned out, was a collection of eight stamp albums, all of them full or near full. A significant find, as Antek's whistle informed us.

There was more, carefully protected with a lot of padding—"Artwork," my mother remarked, always eager to strengthen my cultural awareness. While she gave us a little lecture on what to expect—oil paintings, watercolors, lithographs, etchings, woodcuts, rubbings, prints, and originals—Antek was pawing through the framed pieces. Suddenly he stopped, holding up one of them, studying it from all sides. He even looked at the backside. Then he set it on a shelf and stepped away from it.

All the time he kept on shaking his head in disbelief, in between chuckles. "Something is wrong here," he finally said. "Either the guy was drunk when he painted this, or I am now. Makes me dizzy just looking at it. Must be a woman, wouldn't you say? There is at least one boob—if that's what it is. The whole body seems to be constructed of squares and triangles, all in different shades of green. Oh yeah—there is also a face—must be a face because there are eyes. Wait a minute. Maybe there are two women here because there are two different eyes, the left one looking to the left, the other straight ahead. Different colors, too, and one of them has an ear attached to it—no, wait—that's a nose, I think. Actually, it looks more like a penis to me. On top of it all there hovers that little purple hat—way too small—sort of a figure eight, lying on its side. And yes, there is a mouth!—looks almost normal, but then the lower left of her face is missing. She is holding some musical instrument with three strings, and on the table there is a skeleton head of a bull—or goat—or rabbit with horns. Need I say more?"

"Is there a signature?" I had never heard my mother's voice quiver like that.

"Let's see—yes, there is something scribbled down here. Starts with a *P*, I think, and the last letter could be an *o*. That in the middle . . . could be an *n* or two *s*'s."

"May I, please!" My mother's voice was the scariest thing I had ever heard.

The frame measured about fifteen inches square. As for the painting itself, I had to agree with Antek. Although—there was something very intriguing about that picture. Made me want to look at it again and again, figure out what might have happened to the eyes.

"Have you ever heard of Picasso?" my mother asked.

I had heard the name; Antek had not.

"Well, my mother said, "this painting may be worth more than all the rest of this loot here put together."

"Ho, ho!" Antek challenged her. "If that's what you think, I am willing to make you a deal. This painting for the pearls."

"Deal!" my mother said.

"Mother!" I cried out. "What are you doing? This crazy little painting for those beautiful pearls? You can't be serious!"

But she was. They shook on it.

She turned to me and said emphatically: "This crazy little painting is our ticket to America. Until now, I knew we would not have a chance. But with this—," and she tapped on the frame of the Picasso, "we do, if we are lucky."

America! I had not thought much about it. Of course, I remembered what that old friend had said. I just had not given it another thought after his advice, because the realization of such a dream was too remote. And now it was closer? Apparently—at least my mother thought so. It was an intriguing thought. Perhaps she was right. I gave the picture a skeptical glance. Naw—as Antek had put it—ho, ho! But the idea had reached my brain and had established itself there. At night, I would lie in bed thinking of that place that had everything, where all could get whatever they wanted, if they were willing and able to work, where children could start as dishwashers, cabin boys and shoeshine boys, and would end up as millionaires after a few years. The land of unlimited opportunities—or was it unlimited possibilities? I always got this mixed up—not that it mattered much. I'd settle for either one.

From that day on, the word "America" came up more and more in our thoughts and conversation.

At the moment, we were facing a tricky problem: concealment of our treasure, while using it in order to obtain funds for our immediate survival. Okay, Antek might come in handy for that.

Yes! What about Antek? How to divide things up with him? Without him all this would not have happened—nor would it have without me. Perhaps there was enough for all of us. So far, Antek was like family to us, and I think he felt the same way about us.

The most troublesome question was how could this wealth be given some permanence, so we would be able to benefit from it, not just here and now, but also in the future? As in America, for example? We would have to make reliable contacts without attracting attention.

If we could just spirit everything to the West, to that little village in the foothills of the Alps . . . Sure, there were big-time operators who were shipping stuff all over the world constantly, but first of all, we did not know any, and secondly, from what we had heard, we really did not want to get to know these lads. Was this newfound wealth creating one of those situations about which they say, "Life will never be the same again"?

We all sat around our loot, not knowing what to do. I was still pawing through the crates, hoping to find something that would make *me* whistle, like some chocolates or a can of corned beef. But no luck. Antek comforted me, "Don't worry, with that stuff you'll be able to get anything you want. I mean it—anything!

"Well, until we can figure out something, let's hide everything the best we can," he continued. "Oh, and is it okay with you if I take a couple pieces of jewelry and a few of the coins now, to get us some zloty? At least then we can buy what we need."

Zloty was the name for the Polish currency replacing the Reichsmark.

After stowing our crates in the basement under a lot of old boards, boxes, and curtains, Antek did his disappearing act and was gone.

Journal entry, August 1945: I have never thought much of Providence, fate, or divine guidance, but this may make a believer out of me. How is such luck possible? It does not make up for all of our hardships and losses during the last ten years, but it is a step in the right direction. Is this a sign to strike out for America? I am sure Horsti would love to go, but for him everything is nothing more than an adventure right now.

VI

How I learned about mushrooms, and why Antek had to flee

THE NEXT COUPLE OF weeks were wonderful. Antek had not been kidding. With the sufficient amount of zloty, anything was available. Meta was in heaven. For years she had not been able to cook and bake as now, and I was treated to things I had been craving since the beginning of the war.

Two of my favorites, other than the familiar Christmas fare, were beef with potatoes and horseradish sauce, and the other was Streuselkuchen, the real thing, not the inferior imitations one encounters nowadays.

Streuselkuchen was a Silesian specialty that was famous all over Germany, but nowhere was it as good as in its place of origin—in Silesia. In fact, there exists a poem about it in Silesian dialect. But, strangest thing, whenever I implored Meta to bake one of these cakes, I met with resistance. No flat-out refusal, but all sorts of lame excuses came up: the butter was not fresh enough, the oven did not work right, there were worms in the flour, or it was too fattening. The real problem, or so it finally appeared to me, was that deep down inside of her, she carried a fierce loyalty toward her native East Prussia. To her, baking a Silesian Streuselkuchen was betraying her parents.

Other than that, Meta was a worthy replacement for Emma; in fact, I often called her Emma by mistake. There were so many similarities: Both of them were in their mid-fifties with gray hair fixed in a tight bun. Both were short with stocky figures, but quick and sure in their movements. Even their voices had a similar timbre, low with very clear diction. And whereas Emma's swearing had been colorful and mixed with Polish, Meta's was equally explicit but intermingled with Russian. Of course, their dialects were entirely different. Meta, as anyone would instantly recognize, came from one of the outer provinces of Germany, East Prussia, way up in the northeast corner of Germany, wedged between the Baltic and Russia. Wolves and moose thrived in this area of lakes and vast forests. Its natives, so rumor had it, still worshipped pagan gods.

Meta was a little suspicious of my culinary requests, but, except for the Streuselkuchen, perfectly willing to work on them. Besides, not only had I indicated that I wanted to participate, I also was the supplier of the ingredients.

Considering everyone in our house, including Antek, we had to prepare dinner for ten to twelve. So, soon after my talk with Meta, I set out for the market, carrying a bundle of zloty and a gold coin, just in case. The butcher greeted me like an old friend. I was sure we were among his best customers. I picked out a nice piece of bottom round, about five pounds. The only other item I needed was horseradish, which I finally discovered at one of the many vegetable stands. All the other ingredients, potatoes, onions, carrots, celery root (celeriac), milk and flour, would be at home, I figured.

When it was time to start cooking, two or three hours before eating time, I put two quarts of water into a kettle, added three to four medium-sized onions, quartered, five or six carrots, sliced, one cup of celeriac pieces, salt and pepper, put the lid on the kettle and brought everything to a boil. Only then did I add the meat. All this had to simmer for about two hours. Then we strained the broth and reduced it to about one quart to produce a strongly flavored beef broth. Next I made a smooth paste from two cups of milk and one cup of flour and stirred this into the boiling broth and let it thicken. The final step, of course, was adding the horseradish.

I prepared the fresh horseradish with a hand grater, which is a hellish job, due to the pungent emissions from this root. I had to make sure there would be enough to give the sauce a good amount of bite. A couple tablespoons of lemon juice finished if off nicely. A cup of whipping cream at the end ensured the best possible result.

We arranged the sliced meat on a platter; poured the sauce into a suitable dish, and served this with boiled, parsleyed potatoes. Everyone helped themselves to generous amounts of everything. Feel free to add a salad and a vegetable to this dinner.

All this we did and the end result was fantastic. Antek had tears in his eyes. Whether that was from too much horseradish or from nostalgia, we'll never know.

Toward the end of dinner, Meta suggested it was time to plan one of her East Prussian specialties. "You have probably heard of this," she began, "because it is really famous all over Germany. It's named after our largest city, Königsberg, the largest harbor on the Baltic, as you must know already."

"Oh, then you are talking about *Königsberger Klopse*. Yes, I have heard of it, but I have never tasted it." Actually, my mother had prepared it a few times before the war, but I did not want to spoil Meta's enthusiasm.

The next morning, Meta handed me a shopping list: one pound of lean beef, one pound of lean veal, one pound of lean pork, a small piece of bacon, six eggs, parsley, a tube of anchovy paste, one lemon, some shallots, half a liter of cream, a loaf of good white bread, a bottle of capers, soup bones for making stock.

Off to the black market I went again to make my purchases. There was a streetcar connection now, by the way.

All the storekeepers were super friendly and accommodating. They knew we were their best customers. It was so easy to get used to this: offer a brooch and get a pile of money in return. We had no idea if we were getting a good price for our valuables. It did not seem to matter. We had established a certain reputation by now and a definite group of customers, or were they suppliers? Or clients? Anyway, when we arrived, individually or as a group, all heads would go up; a kind of church-like silence would surround us.

Oh, what fools we were! Didn't we know about jealousy and greed? Didn't we notice how shifty little guys began to follow us around?

Instead of feeling threatened, we felt flattered when well-dressed and important-looking gentlemen would politely inquire if we were interested in some larger transactions. Well, actually, we were, but who would want to risk dealing with street vendors?

Back home, we went straight to work. All of the meat, including the bacon, went through the meat grinder. The shallots had to be minced and sautéed in butter. The rest was quite simple—just like preparing meat for making meatloaf. Except, in this case, we were making meatballs, about two inches in diameter. That was the *Klops* part of the dish. Klops means meatball. So, everything went into the meat mix: the sautéed shallots, six eggs, six tablespoons of chopped parsley, six slices of white bread softened in milk and then squeezed dry, two tablespoons of anchovy paste, one teaspoon of lemon zest, pepper, salt, a pinch each of nutmeg and of ground cloves. We formed the meatballs and simmered them from eight to ten minutes in about three quarts of stock until they rose to the surface.

Now, what really makes this dish unique and delicious is the sauce flavored with capers: capers, those highly aromatic, pickled flower buds from the caper bush of the Mediterranean.

We made the sauce by preparing a roux—that's a paste made of butter or oil and flour. We combined a stick of melted, bubbling butter with about three tablespoons of flour, cooked and whisked it into a smooth paste. Into this we poured enough of the Klops broth to make a moderately thick sauce, about six to seven cups. Finally we added about a cup of whipping cream, five tablespoons of capers including liquid, three tablespoons of lemon juice, and after the boiling had ceased, four egg yolks, beaten. As always, we served it with boiled potatoes. Actually, some pasta would do nicely.

Once again, the end product was a perfect blend of delight and nostalgia.

"What is this dish called nowadays," I attempted to joke, 'Kaliningrader Klopse'?" Kaliningrad—that was the new Russian name for Königsberg.

My innocent joke made Meta sad with homesickness for the land and city she had lost forever. It was not her style to dominate a conversation, but these Klopse must have brought on an irrepressible urge to talk about her homeland, more specifically, about its ethnic culinary specialties. These, except for the capers, had evolved from the land's natural resources: lakes, rivers and forest that had not been replaced by cities and industry. All sorts of smoked fish and the meat of deer, moose, wild boar and bear were prepared in every imaginable and unimaginable fashion. As she was describing an irresistibly delectable, sourish soup thickened with goose blood, her voice suddenly dropped to almost a whisper, and her eyes, half closed, gazed into the past. Was it a vision, she was having, a vision half obscured by towering trees and thick underbrush? The expression on her face resembled that of saints and martyrs on old paintings and sculptures: all transfiguration and ecstasy. What was that woman seeing?

Now, her eyes widened, her lips began to move, and she drew a deep breath. My mother looked disapprovingly at the empty wine glass and the empty bottle in front of Meta. But then there was a sound, a long sigh, followed by whispered words repeating over and over, "Mushrooms, mushrooms, mushrooms! There are mushrooms everywhere. Just look at them! Yellow and brown everywhere! All the woods are full of them. We have to go and collect them!"

"Meta, Meta, snap out of it! You've had too much to drink! There are no mushrooms anywhere!" my mother shouted and shook Meta's shoulder.

Meta's eyes focused again, and she looked at us with some embarrassment.

"Oh, I really thought I was in the woods back home, looking for mushrooms. That's what we did most of the time in the summer. Kids could make quite a bit of money, if they knew where to look. We took them into town on market days and sold them. It was such a—I guess I have to call it a thrill—when suddenly you saw that bright yellow of chanterelles shining through the leaves or pine boughs. Or the reddish-brown caps of the big boletuses. You know, the famous ones that cost a fortune, the *Steinpilz?* Well, in case you didn't know, in Italian they are called *porcini*, and the Latin name is *Boletus edulis*. I know things about mushrooms, because I've read some books on the subject," she added with an embarrassed smile.

Wow, imagine our Meta spouting off in Latin! I was fascinated.

Obviously, mushrooms to her were like fish to me. During that memorable summer—was that just last year?—on the Baltic, we had found and picked mushrooms a few times, never knowing if we would still be alive the next day. But Meta was clearly in a different league, and I decided to make the most of this opportunity. "So, if there are, or were, that many mushrooms in your woods back home—what were some of the things you did with them, other than selling them? And could you teach me how to tell the good ones from the bad ones?"

"I don't think there is enough time for all that right now, but I'll be glad to teach you, if you are interested. But just to give you an idea: we sautéed them, pickled them, marinated them, dried and canned them, made them into soups and salads; we even just put them into water to make a cold, refreshing drink out of them."

"Hey, I have an idea," I said. "There are woods around Breslau. Why don't we go there and see what we can find?"

Meta gave me one of those pitying oh-you-poor-child looks. "You call those woods? Nothing growing in there but garbage."

"Well, then I have another idea. There are really big, wild forests in the Silesian mountains. It's not all that far from Breslau. Took us about two hours by train when we went skiing there. Right, Mama?" That had been years ago, before the travel prohibition days.

Meta's interest seemed stimulated. She glanced expectantly from one to the other.

"I don't think any trains are going in that direction yet," said Antek, "but you know what? I could get some vehicle, a small truck or a jeep, and then a few of us could go. Sounds really interesting and fun."

"Great," I shouted, "and thank you, Antek! And Mama," as I turned to her, "you can pack one of your famous picnic baskets."

Two days later, Antek pulled up with a jeep-type vehicle. It got a bit crowded as six of us piled in, but we managed. A trip into the country, all the way to the mountains and not just by train but in a Polish Milizia vehicle! We felt sorry for the kids we had to leave behind.

For two hours we drove through barren fields and burned villages. Along the highway, endless columns of women and children were moving in a westerly direction. Another mass exodus, a major migration, was underway. The entire German population was being replaced by an incoming Polish population that had been replaced by an incoming Russian population. Must have made perfectly good sense to the politicians.

The farther we went the more silent and depressed we grew. Soon, we too would be on our way.

Bluish, misty ridges of mountains appearing in the distance revived our spirits. The majestic chain of peaks came closer and closer, dominated by the highest peak, their queen, the famous Schneekoppe,* object and subject of countless stories, tales, poems and songs.

Meta kept her eyes glued to the sides of the road, nodding approvingly. We were entering a densely forested area. Narrow paths, hiking trails, and fire lanes led off to either side. Suddenly she let out a yell, "Stop! Stop, back up a bit. Okay, right here. Try to pull over a bit."

She grabbed a bag and a knife, jumped out and got busy at the edge of the forest. One by one we followed and looked around.

Meta stood there like a general, pointing in different directions and ordering us to our posts. "You—over there to that big tree!

"You—follow me!

"And you two—look around across the road.

"This is what we are looking for," and she pointed to a spot between moss and pine needles where it gleamed like gold. Some mushrooms

*Snow cap

were the color of egg yolks—raw egg yolks—some a little paler, some approaching orange. Some were very small and very firm.

"The smaller the better! That's what the fancy restaurants use. But the bigger ones are good, too, and try to cut them off clean, without dirt and pine needles! We don't want to sit around and clean them for hours, do we?"

"Can't we just wash them off before we use them?" one of the girls asked.

Meta shook her head emphatically. Realizing, however, that she was perhaps a bit harsh and unreasonable in her expectations, she returned to her role as nanny and educator. "Well, you know what they call mushrooms in Bavaria and Austria? Of course you don't, so I'll tell you, and you can figure out why they have that name. They call them *Schwammerl. Schwamm* is German for sponge, so, Schwammerl means 'little sponge' in some dialects. If you run water over mushrooms— guess what happens?"

"They'll soak up the water like little sponges?"

"Right! And when you start to fry them or whatever, you'll end up with a soggy mess. So, when you are cleaning them at home, take a small brush, even a toothbrush, and clean them with that."

This was a dream come true! Like biology in school and cooking instructions at the same time. I loved it. Why didn't we have teachers like that in my school?

"Now, these yellow mushrooms are chanterelles, right?" I was pleased that I knew at least that much. "They are easy enough to spot and identify, but are there any bad ones that look similar?"

I could tell Meta was torn—should she get started on another little lecture or just go on with the picking? She sighed and grabbed one of the larger mushrooms and turned it upside down. "Okay, all of you! Come back and pay attention!

"Here, under the cap, do you see those tiny protruding ridges? Many different mushrooms have them, and they are called 'gills'. On a chanterelle, the gills are the same color as the rest of the mushroom— yellow—and they also go down the stem a little way. Can you see that? In other mushrooms, like the white ones you can buy, the gills are pinkish to dark and end where the stem starts. And here is another little trick I can share with you. Again, it has to do with the meaning of words. The German word for chanterelle is *Pfifferling*—P-f-i-f-f-e-r-l-i-n-g. Now, the German word for pepper is *P-f-e-f-f e-r.* See the connection and similarity? So, the meaning of Pfifferling is 'the peppery one.' And how does that knowledge help us, you may ask? Well, if you take a little corner of one of these and chew on it a few seconds, you'll get a peppery burning in your mouth. Here, give it a try!"

We all took a small piece, and sure enough, she had not been kidding. "That's a peppery one, all right!" was the general consensus.

"And don't worry," she concluded, "when they are cooked, the peppery taste goes away. Now go and fill your bags. If you spot any other kinds of mushrooms, let me know. Point them out to me, but don't touch."

Wow! that sounded downright scary. Would there be another mini-lecture? I could tell Meta was gathering up momentum for the next barrage. "No need to look scared, but I meant it! Every year people die of mushroom poisoning, did you know that? And why? Because they did not have anyone like me to teach them the basics and some common sense. So pay attention! Rule number one: focus on a couple of worthwhile types and know these very well.

"Rule number two: don't experiment. There are not many deadly kinds, but the ones that are, are vicious. You won't feel anything for hours and then it is usually too late. Even the smallest amount may be fatal. That's why you must not touch them.

"Rule number three: stay away from any all-white mushrooms. That means cap, gills, and stem. Most of these belong to the amanita family, which includes one of the most deadly of all mushrooms, the Destroying Angel.

"Rule number four: this applies to the family of the boletes, of which we have not found any yet. I'll show you the characteristics when we do. Anyway, if you find a bolete that has some red on the stem or underneath—stay away and don't touch. There is such a nice name for it in German: *Satanspilz*.* I don't think you have to be a linguist to figure out what that means. The good thing about this mushroom is that it won't kill you. But it will make you so sick that you might wish it would. Okay, but now, let's get busy and find some nice, young, firm, and wormless boletuses!" Meta definitely had the makings of a general.

Penetrating deeper into the forest, we came upon a small clearing, and there, beneath some birches, was a stunning sight: a whole colony of beautiful mushrooms. Thick, whitish stems beneath flawless, richly brown caps, sort of the color of an extreme suntan. It was almost

---

*Satan's Mushroom

like looking at families—there would be large adults surrounded by children of varying ages. Some of the adults were about six inches tall, and their caps measured about seven inches. The smallest of the girls actually sat on one of them. The little boletuses, the babies, were mere round balls sticking out of the ground, and their color was much lighter. All caps and no stems, it seemed. Meta was near tears with joy and nostalgia. "Just like home," she uttered over and over.

Cutting them off at the base, especially the little ones, felt almost like committing a crime. Murder and genocide came to mind. But Meta put our feelings, feelings made vulnerable by six years of war and concentration camp accounts, back into the proper perspective: the "buttons" are the absolute greatest eating. The huge ones, on the other hand, tend to get a bit slimy when cooked, but they are great for drying.

"Before taking one, feel the cap with you fingers. If it feels soft and spongy, it's too old and probably very wormy. And check each cut one carefully for any red markings. Sometimes the bad ones grow right alongside the good ones. Oh, and I almost forgot—there is one, looks exactly like the good ones, except that the sponge underneath is faintly pinkish. Not poisonous but incredibly bitter. Just one would spoil an entire meal. Guess what they are called—*Bitterpilz*. When in doubt, taste a small piece. You'll know immediately."

"I have a question," I said, intending to get as much out of this as possible. "You mentioned the word 'sponge' several times, and I don't see any gills under the caps. How come?"

"Ah yes, I forgot. Can't think of every little detail, you know, although, this is definitely not a little detail. All members of the boletuses have these little tubes underneath that look and behave a lot like a sponge. Remember Schwammerl? They may be grayish or beige, almost white, on the babies and a darker, almost greenish beige on the big ones. Again—watch out for anything that looks red."

"I think, I am colorblind," whined one of the younger girls, "what should I do?"

"Don't pick any mushrooms until you are sure that you are not colorblind. I'll tell you what you can do now, though. Look for mushrooms, and ask someone to check them for you. But don't touch! And I'll tell you a little secret while we're at it: girls are hardly ever colorblind."

This outing, with all its information, stayed with me forever and came in very handy many years later, after I had become known among the children of friends and colleagues as "the mushroom man."

One day during the mushroom-man era, we were visited by our newly acquired in-laws. It was August, and we thought it would be fun to have them camp out with us at the lake. Camping at a pristine Maine lake—what better way to make a lasting impression and lay the cornerstone for a harmonious relationship? There would be a campfire and a barbeque and beer and wine and song and pleasant conversation, after a refreshing swim in the lake.

Unfortunately, something came up, and I was forced to stay home. No big deal though, because there were plenty of people out there— eight adults, three of them medical doctors. So—why worry? as I turned my light off around midnight.

Little did I know that our in-laws had inherited a mushrooming interest from their European ancestors. But what good is the interest alone, without the know-how? Returning from a little hike in the woods, they proudly presented what they had collected on the way.

"Oh sure, these are good ones! My parents always collected them, and we fried and ate them. I think we have enough here for everyone. Got a large skillet around? And some onion and butter? Don't you worry! We'll fix them." Or did they say—"We'll fix you!"? I never did get a clarification on that, but my wife swears it was the latter.

Anyway, about 3 a.m. my phone rang. It was my wife. She normally does not call me at 3 a.m. I did not like the tone of her voice. It was shaky, sobby, with a lot of moisture being drawn up through her nostrils. I learned that, except for herself and her pregnant daughter-in-law, everyone out there was dying. "Oh yes, suffering terribly—cramps, vomiting, diarrhea—all at the same time. And all that with only a one-seater outhouse!"

What did I think could have caused this—the hamburger? the potato salad? the fruit salad? the cake?

"Now let's slow down for a minute. There are three MDs out there. What do they think?

"They don't think anymore. They are busy dying, remember? They don't have a clue."

"Okay. Let's see. Everybody ate everything? Did you and Betsy eat exactly the same things as all the others?"

"Well, yes—except, we did not try the mushrooms."

"The what?"

"The mushrooms."

Suddenly, there was a buzzing in my head, and I had not known, prior to this, that my forehead had an automatic hot-and-cold running perspiration option. It was working furiously.

"These mushrooms—they came from our woods? How so?"

"Skip and Louise found them and picked them. They said they are exactly the same as their parents used to bring home."

"Yeah, I'll bet! Exactly the same, except for one little difference," I snorted. "What did they look like?"

"They were those brown ones with the spongy stuff underneath."

"Are you sure they all were the brown ones?"

"Yes, absolutely!"

"Nothing white among them?"

"No. I am positive, because I helped with the cleaning."

"Well, that's a relief. No fatal poisoning then. They probably did not know about the poisonous boletes. They'll all be violently sick for a few hours, but no one is going to die." And I sent a blessing up to Meta, wherever she may have been.

Next morning, everyone but the two abstainers was sporting a novel hue—grey with just a hint of green.

Our in-laws soon drove off, lamenting the poor quality of hamburger in these parts. Oh well.

Everyone considered our Silesian mountains outing an outstanding success—about five pounds of chanterelles and considerably more boletuses.

"Hey, want to see what will happen if we take some of them to the black market? I have never seen any mushrooms there. Should be worth a lot."

"Nah, nah , nah, nah!" Meta ended our business ambitions.

"They shrink a lot when you cook them, and you'll love them so much that they'll be gone in no time. I want to dry some of the boletuses, too, so we'll have some for the winter."

"Meta," I said, "you don't really believe that we'll still be here in the winter, do you?"

There was puzzlement in her expression, puzzlement quickly changing to fear, then sadness. "Yeah," was all she said.

Gloom was descending upon us again. We looked at the westward migration along the roads, still in progress. Where would these people eat, where would they sleep, how were babies and children cared for on the march? Was that us, anytime soon now? Would our "treasure" benefit us in any way—and what about America? Too many questions, too depressing to let yourself get bogged down by them.

The musty, unique aroma of the mushrooms filled the cab, directing our thoughts toward more pleasant prospects: fried mushrooms with potatoes when we got home, and as Meta had announced, chanterelle omelets for breakfast and something with veal, cream, and Steinpilz for dinner.

Antek didn't want to miss out on any of this, but he had to get his vehicle back to the proper authorities. On parting, he assured us he would return for dinner the following evening.

Meta had not exaggerated. If the chanterelles tasted nearly as good as they smelled sautéing in some butter with a bit of chopped onion, they surely would not last very long. In my mind I was already planning the next mushrooming expedition.

I observed Meta as she worked. There couldn't possibly exist a more experienced mushroom cook than she, so I didn't want to miss a thing.

We cleaned the chanterelles with some brushes she had dug up somewhere, cut up the larger ones into thirds or quarters and left the little ones whole. Then we sautéed about two tablespoons of chopped onion in some butter and added the mushrooms, about one pound. We sprinkled some salt over them and turned the heat quite high.

Sometimes mushrooms contain quite a bit of moisture. If that is the case, let it boil down. If not, put a lid on the skillet and simmer them for about ten minutes. The moisture should be boiled down to the extent that the mushrooms begin to brown over a bit. At this point they are close to done and can be combined with a little cream sauce or sour cream or be eaten straight or, as in our case, be used as filling for an omelet. Just mixing them into a dish of spaghetti makes a delicious meal.

I think this was the first time I had seen Meta completely happy. She whistled and hummed little tunes and promised us even greater delights for dinner.

Later in the afternoon we cleaned about two pounds of the boletuses. They were so perfect that they required practically no work at all, except for the slicing. Since we were dealing with much larger mushrooms, we had to cut them into thin slices, about one eighth of an inch thick.

As we sliced them, I observed that Meta would take one piece now and then and pop it into her mouth. Noticing my curiosity, she encouraged me to try some raw. "Go ahead, try a good slice from a cap. The stems are a bit pulpy and not as flavorful."

I did as instructed, and indeed it was mild, nutty, and with a wonderful, new and unique kind of flavor, which I later always referred to as the "Steinpilz-flavor." (Sorry, this flavor vanishes in the drying process.)

"When they are sautéed that taste will be much more intense. You have to try a few pieces as they are cooking in the skillet. Take the ones that are starting to turn golden brown. And good luck trying to stop! There is nothing like it." Of course, she was right.

Toward suppertime, we sautéed them in the same manner as the chanterelles. When they appeared quite dry and tasted divine just plain, Meta added about two cups of cream and two tablespoons of sour cream and simmered everything together until it was a thick sauce. "Now stir in some chopped parsley, and we are ready to eat."

We had boiled some potatoes and string beans and had pan-fried some veal cutlets to complement the mushrooms. What a dinner that was!

As planned, Antek was with us, at least in body. He seemed strangely jumpy and preoccupied with something. We asked, but he just grimaced and shrugged his shoulders. Finally he came out with it, at least with some of it. "I need a bit more of the stuff from the basement, more than the usual for the zloty trade. I may have to get out of here."

This news came to us as an enormous shock. We had come to rely on his help and advice in so many ways—not to mention the friendship that united us.

I had never seen him depressed before. This was a new and very disturbing experience for me—and for my mother, too. "Anything we can do to help? Or would it help to talk about it?"

He just shook his head sadly. "Don't worry, I'll be okay. I'll see you in the morning."

Next morning, the roar of a heavy motorcycle disrupted the calm of our quiet neighborhood. It seemed to originate directly in front of our house. I opened the door, and there was Antek on a magnificent BMW. In back of him a couple bags and a suitcase were strapped. He was his old self again, almost; at least he was smiling and winked at me when he saw me.

When my mother joined us, he grew serious and shook his head with a worried expression. He sighed deeply. "Hate to leave you, but I've got to get away. We were too careless with our treasure. They are putting the pressure on me to tell them where I am getting it. They might use force to get it out of me. It's not safe for you anymore, either."

"Who is 'they'?" we asked.

"Well, some of my Polish buddies—former buddies. They are working together with a few Germans, former officers, I think. One has an eye patch, the other one walks with a cane."

"I have seen these guys," I gasped. "They were following me around. Oh, my God! Now I remember. The eye patch! That was the SS officer who'd buried the crates! I got away easily because the guy with the cane can't walk very fast."

"Well, there you have it," Antek said gravely. "Whatever you can do to get out of here, whatever it takes and costs, do it, and do it fast. I had hoped we might all be leaving together, but now—"

We were shocked and sick with fear and grief. Fear of the possible events in our immediate future, grief over parting with Antek who had become such a friend, companion and guardian.

"For God's sake," my mother cried, "where will you go, what will you do? Please take as much of the stuff as you want. Perhaps you can get some of it over the borders into the West. You have the Glaeser's address, don't you?" By now she had tears in her eyes, and I was blinking and swallowing hard.

"I think I'll be all right," Antek said. "I have some very good papers and documents, including a German passport that says that my home is in that village where Emma is. And yes, I'll take a few pieces from the crates, but I have to be very careful with that—they may be watching me all the time. Remember the pearl necklace? This," and he tapped on his motorcycle, "is what it has turned into. Should have gotten at least a Rolls Royce for it. Well, what can you do?"

"Can we get you something to eat or drink or something for the trip, a couple of sandwiches—anything at all?"

"No, thanks. I have all I need with me. Probably enough to last me all the way to the Alps. I've got to get going. Any delay may be dangerous for all of us. I'll just get a few things now, and I'll be gone."

He was back after a few minutes. We hugged and tried to be cheerful, "See you in the mountains—say hello to everyone."

He revved up his engine to a thunderous roar and disappeared in a cloud of dust. It was so terribly sad!

VII

How we fled from Breslau

JOURNAL ENTRY, AUGUST 1945: "What irony! But serves me right. Had to get overconfident, didn't I? How will we manage without our protector? Horsti is just too young and inexperienced, though one of the neighbors thought he was at least seventeen. Well, in looks perhaps. Now everyone is breathing down our necks. Those treasure crates sure backfired on us. Hardly dare to step out of the house anymore."

How was life to go on now? I had looked upon Antek as head of the family—as its protector and as a father substitute for me. We had trusted him and had expected him to lead us into the West. Now he was gone, and disaster could strike us at any moment. My mother's lighthearted cockiness had given way to her former pessimism and timidity. At every sound outside, she trembled and rushed to the window.

Antek's warning was not to be taken lightly. Obviously, we had to do something about it—the sooner the better. Was it still safe to go to the black market in order to get some money? What kind of money—zloty? Wouldn't do much for us in the West. Dollars! Dollars would be the answer. But how long would we be able to hold onto them, with the Polish Mafia lurking behind every tree and house?

Oh yes! They were out there. How closely were they watching us? Could we entrust our precious possessions to anyone other than ourselves? How about Meta? As far as we could tell, she did not know about our treasure in the basement. Perhaps it had occurred to her that there was something mysterious behind our ability to conjure up food and funds, but she had never shown any curiosity. But now, as Antek had cautioned us, how could she get out of the house without being watched and suspected? And wouldn't that be true for any one of us? In fact, from now on, nobody could come and go without running the risk of being—what?—followed, searched, beaten up, taken hostage?

"That's the third time now this car has passed by our house!" My mother was near hysteria.

"And did you count the times that blue bike has been around our block? What are we going to do? We can't just give up."

I agreed, yet was unable to come up with a plan. Our entire future was at stake. On the other hand—all those countless people on those nonstop treks—did they have gold and jewelry stashed away in their little hand wagons? Hardly! Oh yeah—and what about our American dream? How ironic: after surviving Nazi persecution and escaping deportation and concentration camps, we were dealt the final blow by our presumed liberators. Made me furious and really got me thinking. But this was a tough one. If only we were not being watched—or so well known among the marketeers!

All these factors added up to an almost hopeless situation—almost. Not totally. I had been in tight spots before and had gradually developed something like faith in divine intervention or enlightenment, because salvation had often appeared out of nowhere to save my hide. And now—I could almost taste it, it was so close—one of my "miracles" was about to happen. So I waited and waited, churning things over in my mind, until all at once something happened: an idea, a thought, a message had suddenly appeared and taken up residence in my head. I had a eureka experience of such magnitude that it literally tore me off my chair. The word "devil" had seeped into my consciousness and for no apparent reason. But I picked up on it and worked with it: Okay, I got that: devil. Could I please have another clue now? And indeed! Suddenly there IT was: I did not know if this was THE "it," or how we were supposed to benefit from it, but I suddenly found myself mumbling an old saying. No idea where I had heard or read it or how I knew about it, but there it was: "Driving out the devil with Beelzebub."

"Hey, Mama! What about the saying, 'Driving out the devil with Beelzebub'?"

"What about it?"

"Well, where does it come from and what exactly does it mean?"

"Gee, I don't really know. Possibly Luther or one of those religious thinkers, but more likely from the Old Testament. You know that

'Beelzebub' is just another name for 'devil', don't you? So, use the saying if you want to express the idea that you can get rid of one plague with the help of another. For instance, if we were to use the Russians to get rid . . . of . . . the . . . Poles . . . ?"

I think, at that moment she was having my eureka experience, judging by the expression on her face.

"Are you thinking what I am thinking?" she asked.

"You bet! But I was thinking it first."

For some time now I had neglected my Red Army scavenging and fishing buddies. Occasionally I had seen my friend Misha, by now a major, and we had waved at each other in recognition. So I knew he was still around. I also knew where he spent most of his time: at the Russian Kommandantura, the Russian Army headquarters, in charge of civil and military matters—infinitely more powerful than the Polish Milizia. What if I went to him and begged for help?

This was a plan, simple yet bold, perhaps a little risky—but compared to our present situation, downright child's play and definitely worth a try. At this point, what did we have to lose?

The risk here, once I had confided in him, was that he might simply come and confiscate everything. Might is right! But somehow I had faith in him. After all, hadn't we survived the big "boom" together? Shared experiences of such magnitude create bonds for life, I figured.

Without informing my mother of the details, I grabbed a couple of trinkets from our treasure chest, a delicate, highly polished, honey colored amber pendant on a gold chain, and a gold coin—I was careful to pick a Russian one from the 18th century—and a few stamps from the collection. I left, hoping I would not be stopped and frisked on the way.

The Kommandantura, a large, fancy villa, was draped in huge, red, hammer-and-sickle flags and decorated with larger-than-life pictures of Stalin, Lenin, and Molotov. Guards cradling balalaikas in their arms were everywhere. They were checking the IDs of all who wanted something. I was carrying mine, which stated in German, Polish, and Russian that I was a victim of Nazi persecution. Not once had it helped me in any way. Officials had always acted as if they had never heard of Jews. Only one German had looked at it more closely, then, staring at me, had said, "That's all right. They are humans too."

I paced back and forth in front of the Kommandantura, smiling at the guards, wondering how I could sneak into the building. Observing all the activities, I noticed that several of the guards spoke some German. One of them, a fellow not much older than I, had noticed me. We had made eye contact, and he had returned my smile. What was I waiting for? I took a few steps toward him, and he immediately leveled his balalaika at me. "*Stoi!*" he commanded, "What you want?" Gone was the smile. "Germany kaput, Hitler kaput. You go home now!"

"No, no, you don't understand. I want to see my good friend, Tovarishch Maior Ivanov. You know him? Is he here?"

The smile surfaced again. "Tovarishch Maior your friend? My friend too. He inside now making *robota,* work. You wait." He shouted something to an invisible interior guard, and then I waited for quite a while.

The Kommandantura was not a place of strictly enforced military discipline. A conspicuous presence of liquor bottles dominated the landscape. New jeeps arrived constantly, most of them transporting dolled-up young Fräuleins who disappeared into the villa. They seemed to know their way around, joking and kidding with the guards and an occasional officer. Finally, Tovarishch Maior appeared. He grinned and waved when he saw me. A beautiful young woman was very close behind him. "Hallo, Horst, my boy, how are you? Blow up any bridges lately or catch any good fish? I really miss our outings. Maybe I can get away one of these days. I know a few promising lakes in the country." He threw up both of his arms. "Boom! Remember?" And he roared with laughter.

His accent was still quite thick, but vocabulary and grammar were impressive. Was that beautiful woman perhaps the force behind his amazingly improved German?

There was something else, other than his progress in German, that caught my attention: the woman was carrying a thick German-English dictionary. Was he working up to some liaison officer's post in Berlin? And the young lady, as I could not help noticing, had little in common with the damsels that kept streaming into the house like fish on a spawning run. She was so beautiful—long blond hair and the most unbelievably huge, dark-brown eyes—that I just could not take my eyes off her. My friend the major smiled with amusement at my obvious reaction to her presence and introduced us, "Horst, this is my secretary, Anja. She is fluent in four languages and working hard to make some of this rub off on me. She grew up on one of the large estates outside of Breslau."

We shook hands, and I knew I would never forget the way she smiled at me.

"So, is there anything I can do for you now? Need any help?" He asked after he had given me enough time to reenter reality.

"Well, can we go to your office? Would be good if we could be alone."

In his office I gave him the items I had selected for him. He smiled and examined everything carefully. When he came to the amber necklace, his smile broadened. He now looked like an oversized boy Santa Claus who had the most wonderful toys for all the children on earth. He carefully took the gold chain and fastened it around Anja's neck. Again that smile, as she bowed her head ever so slightly.

I was afraid he might be so distracted by now that I would lose his attention. So, I risked a few discreet coughs, whereupon Anja gave him a little poke in the side. That brought him back.

Only now did I give him a brief account of our dilemma. He shook his head a few times; then he nodded approvingly, mumbling in Russian. Finally he fell silent, obviously trying to come up with a plan. "How much more of your stash is there?"

I felt he had taken the bait. I shrugged my shoulders. "I don't know for sure. Quite a bit. A lot of stamps, eight albums, I think, and coins, mostly silver and gold, but there are also some very old ones made of copper. My mother said they are more than a thousand years old. The jewelry is in a separate chest. They must have been in a hurry when they put it together because everything is just thrown in. Looks beautiful— like a pirate's chest from the movies. The amber is beautiful, too. I never knew that amber can come in huge chunks like this. And my mother said that there is enough silverware there for a royal wedding. I can't remember any of the names, but there are paintings from very famous painters. Twelve or fifteen."

"*Khorosho!* I'll have to have a look at it. I'll bring one of my friends. He knows about goods like that. In the meantime, it will help you if the milizia and the black market scum see that the Red Army is taking an interest in you. If you can wait a bit, we can drive over right now and see what's what. And don't you worry about the milizia and the black marketeers. I know how to deal with them—those scum! But just in case—I think I'll take Sasha along. He can stay with you and keep watch until we're ready."

Ready? Ready for what? I wondered. Ready to make a decision, or were there plans for something bigger?

"Okay, let me find my friend, the colonel, and prepare properly for our meeting. I am confident we'll be able to arrange something appropriate for you and your mother. And, oh, by the way, where do all these goods come from?"

I had worried he might ask that question, so I was rather brief.

"We had buried it out in the country and finally found someone to help us get it out." It was the best I could come up with, and he didn't seem all that interested anyway.

He was gone for about fifteen minutes, fifteen minutes of me being alone in one room with the most beautiful women in the world, as far as I was concerned. "Oh please, God, give me some ideas!" I prayed. But my brain had gone completely numb. Nothing would emerge, as if a giant vacuum cleaner had sucked out every thought. How embarrassing!

Sensing my predicament, Anja began to ask me all the customary getting-acquainted questions: age, parents, school, survival during the siege, future plans and hobbies. The numbness in my head vanished quickly. She was easily amused and laughed and laughed at my stories—in which I never failed to make her friend Misha the hero.

Misha returned with a tall man about the same age as himself, the colonel.

"Horst, this is Tovarishch Polkovnik* Petrovskii. He will come with us now. He is an expert on stamps and other valuables."

Both men were wearing dress uniforms. They were awe-inspiring. The medals gave their chests the appearance of armor plate. I recognized a couple of them: the prestigious Georgievskii Krest and the Geroi Sovetskovo. Misha commented on some of the others, "This one for the Battle of Stalingrad; this one for being wounded; that one for knocking out German tanks," and on and on.

I was seated in the front seat next to Sasha. He had his trusty balalaika with him and a small bag, probably his overnight gear. He also put a larger canvas bag into the car. It was about three feet long.

"What is this?" I inquired.

"Is balalaika," he answered.

"And what do you call this?" I pointed at his submachine gun.

"Is . . ." and he rattled off something incomprehensible.

Anja had overheard us and explained that the bag contained the real balalaika, the stringed instrument.

"I sing and play for you tonight, okay?" he announced proudly.

Memories of Baltic evenings appeared before me. That had been

*Colonel

only last summer, my brain told me, but life had piled up eternities
between then and now.

"You make music with instrument?" Sasha asked.

"No, but I sing. You can teach me some Russian songs, and I'll
teach you some German songs."

"Khorosho."

We were coming around the last corner now, just in time to scare
off a Polish Milizia truck. There were four men inside; the one next to
the driver wore an eye patch.

When we arrived at the house, my mother was scared half to death.
Nazis or Poles or Russians—it did not take much to transform her
once more into the hunted and persecuted persona of the past fifteen
years. Even so, there still was a little zip left in her, as I was later to
discover. But for now she simply said, "Oh, I am so relieved you are
here! I am sure they were about to break in. There were four men.
Antek's bloodhound with the eye patch was among them."

After introducing everyone, I informed my mother that I had
brought these two gentlemen officers on some business—and Sasha
for her protection. I had feared that she would go into shock, but she
remained uncharacteristically calm. Perhaps she had been able to put
two and two together during my absence: that her son had gone to
implore Beelzebub to deliver him from the onslaught of the devil.

Still, she seemed a little too cool and diplomatic to me. Had
her liberated personality made a comeback? Finally, I came to the
conclusion that she was trying to convey something to me—there were
little signaling attempts which I did not comprehend. I decided I'd
better be on my toes, in case there were some surprises lurking in the
basement.

Before we went downstairs, however, we had to pay homage to
ancient Russian traditions, rituals that preceded, accompanied, and
followed any business transaction. Only, this one probably surpassed
the norm. When Misha appeared with a bottle of vodka, some bread,
and a couple of tins of caviar, we could already hear Sasha entertaining
the girls with his balalaika. Again, my mother amazed me. Remaining
perfectly composed, as if she were conducting business with Russian
gentlemen every day, she withdrew for a few minutes and returned
with glasses and dainty hors-d'oeuvre plates.

The shot glasses were filled—even I had one—we all said *na
zdorovie,* and, just like swallowing an aspirin, down it went in one gulp,
as custom demanded.

For me, the caviar opened up a whole new dimension of culinary delight. First Anja, the emotional delight, and now caviar—and all this in one day!

We had another toast, and by the time I had reached the last step to the basement, I was in high spirits. Would there be any surprises waiting for me down there? I tried to focus on the importance of the moment.

Mother cleared away the camouflage over the crates, and when they lay open before me, I instantly knew what was wrong: some of the pieces of jewelry we had deemed more valuable were missing, the same was true for the coins and, most noticeable to me, the Picasso had disappeared. Was that the message my mother had tried to convey to me: don't give away any information because it might not be relevant by the time you get here?

Our business partners got busy taking inventory. They were thorough, taking notes and making lists. They now communicated strictly in Russian. Did their stony-faced expressions imply that they were impressed? Or suspicious? Were we worth the effort?

Finally, after about two hours, they were finished. Everything was packed away again and well hidden. That surprised me. I had imagined they would take all or some or most of it back with them.

Misha and Colonel Petrovskii sighed with relief, looked up at each other, at us, and at Anja who had observed everything with wonderment and delight.

No wonder, I thought, she will be the girlfriend of the richest major in the Red Army.

Misha now smiled at her and cleared his throat, "You are our friends, you came to me for help, and we will do our best—not only for your sake but for ours as well. You can't possibly begin to fathom what all this means to us."

He paused briefly, organizing his thoughts, so it seemed to me. "We have had plans for quite some time now, but no realistic way to carry them out. We think now we can—with your help. You have a very substantial fortune here. It's yours. We are not going to steal it from you. We'll buy it from you."

Amazing how sobering, literally, a serious speech can be. What did he mean: "buy it from us"? All kinds of possibilities reeled through my brain, but none made any sense. Never would I have come up with what was revealed to us during the next few seconds.

"You have probably noticed how serious we are about learning

German and English. That is because we want to be ready. Ready for what? Ready to cross over to the West. That's right! Defect, become traitors. Communism has no future; any idiot can see that. It's just a matter of time, and then it will collapse. Well, without us, thank you very much! All we needed to carry out our plan was money—or the equivalent thereof. We need the cooperation of certain people. It has to look legal, so—papers, passports, orders for the Russian, the American, and the German authorities. Without grease, the wheels can't turn. There is no one in this bureaucracy who can't be bribed, and this here is the perfect lubricant. Some of it, I'll tell you, is priceless. The stamp collection—wow! And of course, we also need some funds to get started over there. We might even make it to America, if all goes well."

Mama and I looked at each other. Could that be for real? And if it were, why would they mention it to us whom they hardly knew? What if we didn't keep our mouths shut? Didn't they know that it is standard procedure to execute deserters?

Misha had noticed our puzzled expressions. A slight smile appeared around his mouth. "I know what you are thinking: Why are they supplying us with information that could destroy them? Right? Well, we are aware of this possibility, but then we thought, in an undertaking of such magnitude, there has to be mutual trust. By telling you our plans, we are giving ourselves into your hands, as you gave yourselves into ours when you showed us your treasure. So, it's a simple equation: Without us you cannot get out of Breslau, which could mean for you loss of everything, including your lives. And without you and your wealth, we wouldn't stand much of a chance of getting out.

America! There it was again, beckoning to me, enticing me. Everyone wants to go there. Even the enemies of America!

"We are not going to force you," Misha continued, "But here is what we can and will do for you, if you are interested. You think it over and let us know. But don't wait too long. Things may change quickly here. Anyway, we—you two, Anja, and the two of us—would take one of our large limos and, everything legal and well documented, of course, drive out of Poland through the Soviet Zone and directly into the American Zone. We would drop you off wherever it might be convenient for you. Of course, we'll leave you enough to help you get started over there. In the meantime, Sasha will stay with you to protect you—and to guard the basement."

We were speechless for quite some time. This was truly an overwhelming revelation: Two high-ranking Soviet Army officers, financed by German-Jewish widow, defect to the West. What a headline that would make!

Nodding my head affirmatively, I awaited my mother's response. For me it was obvious. Sure, we would come out of this with next to nothing, but we had had a few very good weeks, and traveling all the way to the American Zone in a Mercedes, as well as having all the necessary papers handed to us, was unprecedented, as far as I knew.

"Of course," Misha continued, "if we all travel together in one car, there won't be much room for luggage. Besides, it would look suspicious if we carried too much. One suitcase per person and a handbag is about all we can take. We'll have papers made up that will state that your home is somewhere in the American Zone—otherwise the U.S. border guards won't let you in."

My mother wrote down all the relevant data, including an address in that village where the Glaesers were living now. So far, she had not spoken, but I could tell she was gearing up for it. "Tovarishch Maior and Tovarishch Polkovnik, we thank you for coming, for being honest, kind and fair, treating us like friends. It would indeed be easy for you to take advantage of a widow and her fatherless child, but that is not the way of Russian officers and gentlemen."

She raised her full glass, raised it to them and to me and tossed it down as before. Never had I heard her speak in flowery phrases like this before. Either, I concluded, it was the vodka, or she was imagining what my Glaeser uncle would say under similar circumstances. She continued: "No, to the contrary, in the true spirit of magnanimity and preservation of nobility even in victory, you are offering us the opportunity to escape a hopeless situation. Your glorious army has come and has removed the cruel yoke of Nazi oppression from us. Our gratitude will live on forever, and together our great nations will strive to build a better world for all of us. Together we will . . ." I could bear that nonsense no longer and gave her a sharp jab to the ribs. Her brows furrowed and she stopped, grasping perhaps that her speech was losing relevance and logic and that her verbal onslaught was beyond our friends' linguistic comprehension. They had nodded and smiled a lot during her speech, while refilling her glass repeatedly.

After a few minutes of silence, my mother must have realized that she had not really said anything definitive. She pulled herself together once more. "I think I can speak also for my son when I give my agreement to the terms you offered so graciously. I shall go now and pack."

But she didn't leave, rather remained seated at the little table where she picked at the last few morsels of bread and caviar. She was quite incapacitated.

Considering her condition, I quickly left to get Meta. Together, we put her to bed.

My Russian friends advised me that it would take about one week to get everything organized, and that they would come by every day to give us a progress report.

In the meantime, Sasha had made friends with all the kids and their mothers and was playing his instrument. It sounded a lot like a guitar. I had never thought much about it, but the Russian language, especially in songs, really appealed to me. It had something so mysterious, tender and sad, yet was forceful and wild.

"Khorosho!" he shouted when he spotted me. "Now you sing German song." He had no trouble accompanying me, and I sang many of the songs from the past summer. Soon the older girls joined in and held the melody so I could harmonize. Inge, the oldest of them, about fifteen, obviously was smitten with the visitor's voice and looks. She just stared at Sasha's blue eyes and blond hair, while his minor key Russian songs told of unending love and of death, forsaken maidens, endless forests and Mother Volga. At least, that was what I thought I heard in them.

My heart grew heavier and heavier as we sang so many old German songs. Too many memories were tied up in them. And now, the old familiar question—were we doing the right thing, leaving our homeland, our town, **our river**? Would it ever be the same again? But there was no point in getting sentimental, because we really had no choice.

This was the chance to escape the ordeal of joining the endless treks on the highways, which, incidentally, were not destined to terminate in the American but in the Russian Zone. And what we were planning— was that not a step in the right direction? How could we ever hope to get to America if we didn't even make it to the first stepping stone— the American Zone? Ah yes—America—and I comforted myself by singing the only American song I knew: "I've Been Working on the Railroad." We had learned it in English class.

Next morning, my mother did not remember a whole lot from

the previous evening. "They said that they would drive us to the American Zone if we give them our stuff? And what did we say? Are we going?"

"Yes, Mama, we—uh—you said we would be honored to travel with such noble and honorable gentlemen."

She winced. "I said nonsense like that? What did they do—get me drunk?"

"Well, you might say that. You had about six big shots of vodka and said a lot more than that."

"Oh my God! How embarrassing!"

"Don't worry Mama, you used mostly vocabulary they hadn't studied yet. But they did say it would take about a week to get everything organized."

That seemed to shock her. "A week—only a week? Leave everything?"

"Yeah," I sighed, "and there won't be much room for a lot of luggage."

That shocked her even more. She was near tears now. "But all our belongings are here. This is our home, our town, our river!"

First I pointed out to her that this remark hardly described our situation: what belongings? what home? what town? Well, except for the river part, perhaps. Then I attempted to direct her thoughts into different channels: "Think America—and, speaking of which, what happened to the Picasso and those few other items which didn't make it into the inventory?"

"Oh yes," she smiled slyly, "I was worried you might inquire. Anyway, I had a hunch that something like this might happen. You were not very explicit when you left, you know. So I picked a few things I liked—including the Picasso—and stashed them somewhere else. Our ticket to you-know-where. I'll have to really come up with a clever idea for hiding everything when we pack. I thought, for once in our life, there has to be something left for us. Something extra."

She definitely was learning. I was proud of her, for her thinking along the same lines as I had been for years. You just had to learn to be a little bit devious, if you wanted to survive. Reynard had taught me well. That's why I had done exactly the same as she: put aside just a few little inconspicuous pieces, easily hidden and easily turned into money or food. It wasn't even worth mentioning, so I didn't.

The next few days flew by. From the Russian point of view, everything was developing satisfactorily, so we were told. Whatever

we had to do to get ready did not take more than half an hour. The advantages of not owning anything.

I gave my kayak and most of my fishing gear to friends. Some choice items, however, I decided might come in handy, if we ever lived near water again.

My mother had taken the Picasso out of its frame, and I was watching her curiously as she loosened the lining of her suitcase enough to slip the painting in under it. She had been careful to save the original thread. Reusing it like a master surgeon, she deftly closed the incision without leaving the lightest trace.

The other pieces we just spread around. Why shouldn't we have been able to save a few pieces of nice jewelry from our former possessions?

Sasha was making astonishing progress in his German, while Inge was throwing around Russian sentence fragments and humming Russian songs. Her mother was not pleased.

By now, our Russian friends had been busy trading a fair amount of the treasure for dollars and cigarettes: cigarettes for dealing with Poles, Russians, and Germans, dollars for dealing with Americans.

"Okay, be ready tomorrow morning. We'll come, load up, and then we'll be on our way. Goodbye Red Army, goodbye Russia." That last part did not sound nearly as enthusiastic as the first.

"We'll have food and drink for all of us," Misha informed us. I knew from experience what he meant when he spoke of *drink*.

"Oh, so I can't prepare one of my famous picnic baskets?" My mother acted insulted. Apparently the history of our picnic outings had not yet reached my Russians' ears. They looked quizzically at each other, shrugging their shoulders. "Okay, but just a small one, please."

We said farewell to all the people who had become our friends. Meta, in particular, was grief stricken.

"*Ach, schade*, now we never got around to baking your Streuselkuchen," she lamented, "and good luck, Horst. Be more careful! You are a little bit on the wild, reckless side, you know. But this will keep you safe." She handed me a thin silver chain on which something shiny, pointed, and whitish was glistening. "It's from our woods. My father gave it to me. A wolf's tooth charm."

I was deeply touched and gave her a big hug. "Thank you for everything and for teaching me so much about food and especially about mushrooms. And we'll get to that Streuselkuchen yet, you can bet on that! As soon as you come over to the other side."

Sasha and Inge looked sad, but that was because Sasha would have to go back to the Kommandantura now.

Our suitcases barely fit; the picnic basket landed on my mother's lap, I next to Anja in the back seat. I had seen to that. Now the trip could go on forever, as far as I was concerned. I felt it: the tooth charm was working already!

Our friends seemed a little tense, understandably so. They spoke little and when they did, only in Russian, but we knew that they thought the trip would take about two days. A drop-off location had not been firmly established, but we had mentioned Munich a few times without encountering opposition.

So, as everybody else, we moved out of Breslau in a westerly direction, crossing the Oder bridge for the last time. I looked down into the swirling water. That's where I had seen the dead German soldier. Good luck, river, I thought, hope to see you again, someday!

Journal entry, September 1945: I have to tell myself over and over again: there was no way and no reason for us to stay. It was not a decision I made. It was made for me. I didn't even say goodbye to our little house. Couldn't bring myself to go near it. There was nothing left of it anyway, Horsti said. Better that way. Now we are at the mercy of these Russians. Hope they are honest and fair. Anja wouldn't be with them if they weren't, I keep telling myself. Still, leaving Oswitz and the family graves, Fidi's grave and all those places. At least I don't have to leave my memories behind.

We exited Poland at the city of Görlitz. There were a lot of detours everywhere and progress was slow. The areas we passed bore the evidence of fighting and bombing. It was depressing. Then it really got bad! I had always thought that Breslau was just about as level as *inhumanly* possible. What we saw now surpassed my wildest nightmares. Only when I read the sign with the town's name did I comprehend the incomprehensible: Dresden! We had heard about the devastation, the bombings, the refugees from Silesia, East Prussia, and Pomerania, caught and annihilated in the firestorm. But this left us stunned. My mother just sobbed and sobbed. Anja clutched my arm and started shaking. The two officers reached for the vodka and hurled fierce Russian curses at the ruins and the sky. It would not have surprised me had they changed their minds and turned around. Too late for that, though!

As evening approached, we drove through a fairly unharmed little town.

"Want to stop and find a place to sleep?" Misha asked. "One of us will stay in the car to guard it. We'll take turns. But you might as well get some sleep."

The colonel pulled up in front of a neat and cozy looking Gasthaus, got out and went to open the door. There he stood: tall, angry, and drunk after the Dresden experience, a high-ranking officer with medals covering his chest, pistol in his belt. The tiny, withered lady that emerged from a dimly lit hallway had obviously never seen a Russian soldier up close. She fell on her knees before him and started pleading in a high-pitched whine: "Bitte, bitte, nicht schiessen! nicht schiessen! bitte, bitte!"*

"Don't talk nonsense, Frau; we just want two rooms. Zwei Zimmer!"

"Ja, ja, natürlich, ja, bitte, kommen Sie!"

The kitchen was already closed, she regretted, but our friends just snorted an imperious laugh, "Njet, njet!" They fetched some bacon and eggs from the car and ordered her to prepare these together with boiled potatoes and salad or something green.

"Ja, ja, natürlich! Sie müssen paar Augenblicke warten, bitte!"

"And tomorrow morning—eggs and bread and coffee, verstanden? And here is some butter and coffee."

No German had access to genuine coffee these days—except for black marketeers, of course.

Next morning we left fairly early. There would be a few more hours of driving before we reached the border crossing into the American Zone. The closer we came to this point, the tenser and quieter we all grew. Again I thought they would change their minds and turn around. Again I was wrong. Signs in Russian and German appeared, stating that the Russian occupied zone would end in: five kilometers, three kilometers, one kilometer, then in 800 meters, 500 meters, 300 meters—100 meters. It was very slow driving now, because a few thousand German refugees, refugees whose homes had once been somewhere in that part of Germany which was now the American Zone, were having the same idea as we were. Near the barriers, barbed

*Please, please, don't shoot! don't shoot! please, please!

wire fences and guard towers, the traffic came to a halt. A little hand
wagon, pulled by two women, had lost a wheel.

The two officers looked at each other and discussed something. I
heard a lot of *da da, khorosho,* and *davai,* and suddenly they turned on their
siren. Now it looked as if we were on some important mission, and the
Russian guards directing traffic created a passage for us.

We had not asked our friends directly, but from Anja we had learned
that there was a four-power conference going on somewhere, at which
they were supposed to represent the Polish-German territories. That's
what the papers said, anyway. As for us, the three German citizens, we
were accompanying them as guides and interpreters on our way back
home to Bavaria. Good luck, I thought. Sounds pretty shaky.

It may have been the thousands of refugees waiting to be processed
or our impressive car with the Red Army flag and the siren or the
intimidating presence of these two highly decorated officers—we were
waved on through with a minimum of fuss at the Russian as well as at
the U.S. checkpoint. Personally, I believed that it was Anja's smile that
had this miraculously soothing, almost hypnotic, effect on the guards.

After the many swigs from the bottle along the way and at the
breakfast, lunch, and dinner table, our friends thought the time for a
formal toast had arrived. We had reached democracy, liberty, and the
pursuit of happiness. All this downright begged for a celebratory drink.
There were some small, metal tumblers in the car, packed exclusively
for this purpose, and I kept a sharp eye on my mother's intake. I
certainly did not need a repeat of that evening in the basement.

What I personally needed right now was some indication, in any
tangible form, that we were better off here than we had been at home.
But everything seemed exactly the same. House ruins, shabbily dressed
civilians queuing up in front of empty store windows, armed soldiers
in alien uniforms.

No caviar this time, just some slices of something salamiesque;
then came the phrase I had heard most frequently so far: Na zdorovie!
We all hugged and congratulated each other. "Good luck" and "let's
keep in touch" were repeated over and over. In this emotional turmoil,
I tried to sneak in an extra hug from Anja, but mother had kept her
eyes on me and yanked me back. "Horst!" she—it was almost a bark—
shrieked the way that always made me jump straight up in terror, as if
I had gotten too close to a snake poised to strike. She had developed
this very effective deterrent just recently and seemed to be very proud
of it. Reluctantly, I withdrew.

VIII

Bavarian interlude

W E HAD DECIDED THAT we would like to be dropped off just outside of Munich. There, in the small town of Planegg, lived my mother's cousin with three children. Well, last time we had heard, they were alive and lived there. Postal service into or out of Poland had not been established yet, so surprises were inevitable: for them, it would be our arrival, for us, if they and the house were gone.

Mother remembered the neighborhood from visits long ago, and there was very little war damage around this area. It was the most peaceful environment I had encountered in a long time. Shady, park-like gardens, immaculately weeded and landscaped flowerbeds, vegetables, and fruit trees still laden with apples, pears and plums, as I registered instinctively. No, these people had not been touched too harshly by the war. The huge beautiful houses were few and far between, and birds were fluttering and chirping around. The occupants of these dwellings, would they be tolerant of our arrival and our plight? Not by the looks of the drawn curtains and the closed garden gates and the high fences around their properties. As always, it would be up to me again to bring some balance to the scales of justice. "Okay, just around the next corner, first house on the left," my mother directed the driver.

A deafening ruckus suddenly enveloped us. There, on a large open lawn, about twelve children of varying ages and genders were engaged in a fierce soccer game. They paid absolutely no attention to us.

"Oh, my God," my mother said, "all the other cousins with their children must be here. Now what? We can't expect them to take us in, too? Well, we'll see."

A hush fell over the fighting teams when the two Russian officers appeared on the scene. I had envisioned that one of them would fire a couple of rounds into the air to achieve silence, but that proved to be unnecessary. Those kids didn't know what to do: huddle together, hide behind trees, or run screaming into the house to their mommies. I felt so superior to all of those lame softies! What did they know, what had they experienced compared to me, the battle-hardened veteran? A contemptuous grunt was all I could utter.

There we stood, facing each other: the five invaders from the East, still flying the Soviet star; and the home team, terrified and fearing for its turf.

In silence we stared at each other for a few minutes. Misha suggested timidly, "Should we offer some vodka? or cigarettes?"

Mother glared at him. "How about some chocolate, instead?"

"Yes, yes, excellent idea," and he whirled around to get a bag out of the car. The whirl must have looked a trifle too fast, somehow threatening to the children. Indoctrinated first by Nazi and now by American propaganda about Red Army atrocities, the children all huddled together. Some of the younger ones started to cry. They must have thought the massacre was about to begin.

I could not take it any longer. "You idiots," I shouted, "we are friends and relatives! Here, look! Chocolate for all of you!" And I pushed my way into the huddle, distributing the chocolate bars.

"Hey," one little wise guy griped, "hey, this is American chocolate! From K-rations. Tastes like crap." But he ate his anyway, as did the others.

Now, K-rations—that was a new one for me. And why did the Red Army have American K-rations? "Well," I figured, "they had American trucks, fuel, bombs, and planes, so why not chocolate?"

All the kids now came a few steps closer to examine something that was not "Made in U.S.A.": two genuine Russian officers. Especially the revolvers and the medals caught their interest.

One of the older girls, perhaps twelve or thirteen, cute, but definitely too young for me, hovered around my mother and looked her over from all sides.

"Excuse me, aren't you Tante Käte from Breslau?"

Finally! I thought. Took long enough. That girl and her mother had visited us just two years ago.

"Yes, I am. And you must be Monika. I am so happy to see you again. Is your entire family here?"

"No, just my mother and we three children. My father is a POW in France, and my brother is missing since Stalingrad. Shall I go inside and tell them you are here?"

"Yes, please! And tell them about our company, so they won't be frightened when they come out."

I dreaded the next few minutes or hours, during which visitors usually found out that all the adult males in the family were either dead or missing or, with luck, in a POW camp. Nowadays, no one ever knew where family members might be, except for those actually with you right then and there.

After a few minutes, the door opened, and four ladies came rushing out.

"Oh my God!" my mother muttered. "All my cousins with their children. Just as I suspected."

It was an overwhelming *Wiedersehen.**

"Oh, we have thought of you so often! How did you survive Breslau? We heard horrible stories. And Horst—we heard they drafted thirteen- and fourteen-year-olds in the end. How did you stay out? Or did they get you?"

"No! I was lucky, I guess." This scene was getting to me, so I was as brief as possible.

Actually, what had happened to me after my first stint as military messenger was that some time in April, when boys my age had become scarce, I accidentally ended up on the front line. A German captain flagged me down and drafted me right off the street. He needed a messenger because his former one had just been killed. "Here, kid, take this gun and put on this armband and the helmet. Report to me when you are ready. I'll be right here—I hope!" he grinned.

I snapped to attention, looked him straight in the eye and said, "I'd really love to, Herr Hauptmann, but I am not allowed in your army. I am half Jewish." Before he could recover from the shock, I was gone. *Scheisse*, there went my chance to earn a medal!

Our two officer friends were beginning to feel a bit awkward by now. What to do?

"Is there something among our possessions that has the power to cast a spell of well-being and tranquility over excited and tumultuous minds?" they may have asked themselves. This was a rhetorical question, of course, the answer was so obvious. Misha went to the car, returning with a huge, full bottle of vodka.

Without further ado, he opened it and passed it around. All the

*No direct translation, literally: see-again.

properly raised ladies, wives of bankers, of doctors and professors, were taken aback, but only for a few seconds. I could almost hear them think, "Act coy after six years of war and bombing and starvation? Don't be silly, and pass the bottle!" And indeed, it was passed—around and around and around.

Soon Misha was engaged in a fierce battle for ball possession; the colonel joined the other team. One by one, the ladies also took sides, including my mother and Anja. I kept close to Anja, hoping to bump into her in the heat of the game, or possibly to cause her to fall on me. "Welcome to the West, Horst!" my mother shouted as she hobbled past me.

One by one, the adults left the battleground. They had fought well and deserved to be strengthened. To a Russian mind and stomach, "strengthening," once more, can mean one thing only: vodka! And, well, yes, if absolutely necessary, some actual food may be added, but sparingly, lest the beneficial workings of the vodka be clouded or even neutralized. So, Misha made another trip to the car, returning with another bottle, along with a large loaf of bread, some cheese, and a ham. Knives, forks, and plates, even glasses appeared on the patio tables.

It was now about suppertime, and all the aunts and cousins anticipated long-missed food items. A bowl of potato salad, also cucumbers and tomatoes, were brought out of the house—probably what the ladies had prepared for this evening. For dessert, I became acquainted with *Rote Grütze*, a famous north German specialty. I loved it and asked my aunt from Hannover about preparation and ingredients.

Well, ingredients I could figure out all by myself: sour cherries, red currants, raspberries, all red berries, as far as I could tell. Hence the name.* So you boil them with some sugar in very little water and thicken this with some corn or potato starch. Chill and serve with vanilla sauce. How appropriate: red berries for the red officers. Ha, ha!

Tante Beatrice from Hanover paused and examined me more closely. "Ah yes, now I remember! You are the one who always wanted cookbooks for his birthday."

Several bottles of wine appeared, this time from the owner's basement. Only now we took the time to look at the house. It was truly magnificent. Built in the 1920s, it had three stories and a tower. As I was informed, it was in a style called *Jugendstil*.** Its size and the tower

*No direct translation: red pudding **Art nouveau

reminded me of the Hopf villa in Breslau, except that this house was half-timbered, whereas the Breslau house was all red bricks. Anja had a hard time composing herself. She had tears in her eyes. Over and over she shook her head. "This looks so much like our house in Keltingen. The same everything, the colors, the stained glass windows, the terrace, the tower—"

Tante Angelina was intrigued. "Really, that is most interesting. As far as I know, the architect did not build many in this style. Do you remember who yours was?"

"Well, let me think. As I recall, he was a professor at the University of Berlin. It was not a real German-sounding name. Something ending in i-u-s, I think."

Tante Angelina's jaw dropped by a couple of inches. "Was his name Margolius? Professor Margolius? Really short and wearing a monocle?"

"Yes, yes, now I remember. Oh my God, what a surprise! Well then, you must be Frau von Bergen."

"And you must be a von Woltershaag. The professor often mentioned a house he had built near Breslau. Is Keltingen near Breslau? Well, there you are! Oh, my God, what a coincidence! Tell me, are your parents there now? Did it survive the war?"

Anja shook her head. "The German Army had put a battle command post into the house, and it was completely destroyed in the fighting. Luckily, my mother and my sister left before this and went west. Well, I don't know about the *luckily*. They were heading toward Dresden. No idea what happened. My father—as an officer, he was involved in the July 20 events. Well, you know . . . I had to stay in Breslau, because I was drafted as an antiaircraft gunner's aid. Fortunately, I was rescued from the POW camp."

She gave a little smile in Misha's direction and blushed. I felt jealous.

Tante Angelina had regained her composure. She tapped on her glass. "Dear friends and relatives! I just want to take a minute to welcome our dear cousin Käte and her son Horst. We worried about them for months; we are so happy they are well and ready to begin a new life. We will do our best to help them as much as we are able. Of course, they will stay with us. Welcome also to their friends and our allies. It is an honor to give shelter to the victorious officers of the Red Army! Na zdorovie!"

All the adults raised their glasses and tossed down the clear liquid.

Now the colonel cleared his throat and stood up—not too steady on his feet anymore, or so it seemed to me.

"My dear, dear German friends, we are being treated like family. We are deeply touched and thank you for your friendship and hospitality. Tomorrow we have to drive on alone, leaving Käte and Horst in the care of their relatives! We shall miss them, and we wish them luck. May all of us have good luck. Na zdorovie!" And one more gulp went down to join the others.

I overheard one of my aunts whisper to my mother, "What the hell are these Ivans doing here, anyway? One of your conquests?"

"Shhhh," my mother hissed, "tell you later."

That night, I went to bed sharing a room with several of my cousins. We were all very tired and didn't talk much. But I couldn't help thinking of how we had left Silesia forever and of all the uncertainties lying ahead of us—and of Anja, her house, her family, her beautiful name: Anja von Woltershaag. Was she doing the right thing? Had that been just my imagination, or had she sounded a bit embarrassed at the table, talking about being rescued? Rescued, my foot!

Journal entry, September 1945: Made it! Was actually shaking, crossing the border. What if they had searched us? What a wonderful feeling to be among family again! So the treasure did

us some good after all—a lot of good. Poor Anja! How horrible! First her father, then her mother and sister. Misha seems nice enough. But a young woman with her background and a simple Russian? Wish Horsti wouldn't always have a crush on every young woman and girl he meets. Funny though. And to think that my cousins suspect me of having an affair with the colonel! Could do worse, I suppose.

Morning came and time to say farewell. The two officers had already turned over a fair share of the treasure to my mother. I had worried about that.

"Let's not mention any of this stuff to anyone," my mother said to me. "We were careless once, but we know better now. Actually, things evolved quite nicely for us, don't you think? We wouldn't even have made it out of the Russian Zone if we had been on our own. No! We were rather lucky in spite of everything."

We went outside where our friends were removing Red Army insignia from the car. The license plates looked strange with their Cyrillic lettering. I hoped they had it all figured out. One thing, though, I could not help mentioning: "Misha, why are you still wearing your uniforms?"

He smiled. "Well, we belong to the International Refugee Commission, remember? That meeting will be over in two days, and by then we will have made contact with our friends."

Frankly, I was worried about Anja's involvement, if anything went wrong. I wished she would stay here with us. At least she had the Planegg relatives' as well the Glaesers' address in Obergünzburg, in case of trouble.

One last hug, one last "good luck," and the car disappeared around the corner, leaving me with an entirely unfamiliar feeling: so empty and forlorn. My mother watched me, then came over and put her arm around my shoulder. She didn't say anything, but I knew she understood.

"Horst," she finally interrupted my brooding, "there is hardly anything to eat here for all these people. I think they need your help."

It was like a bugle blast calling me to battle. If there was anything capable of propelling me into action it was the cry of needy people for food. Twelve children and five adults, all near starvation except for mother and myself. What I could not figure out was that there were several teenagers among my cousins; one of the girls was even a year older—sixteen. What were they doing playing soccer and sitting around on their butts, instead of being out there in the surrounding forests, foraging for food, as I had been doing for the last five years? It was downright scandalous and disgraceful. Had I not seen trees bursting with ripe fruit? Didn't dense forests surround the town? And weren't there farms all over the place, just a few kilometers away? Farms with cattle, chicken, geese, potato and corn fields?

So I had a serious conversation with the two present cousins, Uli and Evi, who had grown up here. Of Tante Angelina's two older children, Ursi was working away from home and Peter had fallen in Russia.

After ten minutes of intense inspirational indoctrination, Uli, a boy my age, and Evi, one year older, were ready to follow me into unheard-of adventures and glorious expeditions. I told them of carp, lamb, mushrooms, and hand grenades, tales that made their mouths water and their eyes bulge.

Thus, the foundation was laid for my subsequent notoriety among friends and relatives, from Germany all the way to America. From now on I would be exposed to a large audience who would spread the news to countless cocked ears: watch out for that kid; don't have anything edible lying around; tell the neighbors to keep chickens, rabbits and ducks penned up; put barbed wire around your orchards!

Instead of being grateful for my efforts, which, for a while at least, resulted in some remarkable additions to the meager ration-card fare, these aunts would write to all their friends and relatives about my exploits. Perhaps they would praise me in these letters, but the result would be that wherever we showed up thereafter, warnings would spread like wildfire through the neighborhood: warn everyone, keep food supplies, dead or alive, locked up in the barn, post sentries! Poor Käte! As if I had ever taken anything from friends or relatives. Poor, poor Käte!

The thing was—coming into the American Zone was not exactly like entering the Promised Land, the Land of Milk and Honey. Oh yes, there were milk and honey and a lot of other things, too, but not for us. Once more we were disliked, resented. It was almost like a contest: Well, let's see—who is resenting us most now and for what reasons? First, there had been the Nazis, hating us for having Jewish blood flowing through our veins; then came the Poles, hating us for being German, and sometimes there was a double hatred—for being German and Jewish. Naturally, the Russians, generally speaking, disliked us for being the German invaders and destroyers—and it wasn't as if they loved the

Jews, by any means. But now, here in Bavaria, we experienced a new category within the string of possibilities: here we were the refugees, having arrived to stay forever and to deprive the natives of what was theirs and theirs alone. These refugees were Prussians, God forbid!— instantly recognizable by the way they spoke, namely East Prussian, Silesian, and High German, anything but Bavarian. And to make things worse, these intruders were mostly Protestants. So there we were, once more: on top of the most hated list!

Initially, I was not fully aware of how my survival efforts were setting the wheels in motion. Perhaps I had a hunch, but what was I supposed to do? Let them all starve? I was very focused on what needed to be done. I had a job to do! I was on a mission, come what may!

First, I organized a general-purpose foraging expedition. The target of this was the surrounding area, mostly forests, and possibly some orchards. I wanted to see what I had to work with. Every cousin ten years or older was instructed to get some kind of container, a bag or pail. Where there are woods, there must be mushrooms and berries, was my reasoning. I gave all a crash course on mushrooms: "Pick only the yellow ones, or if you find brown ones with sponge under the cap, make sure there is no red anywhere. And don't touch anything all white! When in doubt, ask me!"

When I entered the dense, fragrant forest, I inhaled deeply. This was what I needed to take my mind off the anxious moments throughout the escape, off Anja, and off Dresden.

I was not granted much time to reflect. The first questions were coming in:

"Is this a mushroom? But it is not yellow or brown. So what shall I do?"

"What about this one—the one with the red cap with the white spots on it? Can I eat it?" someone else asked.

"Horst, I just found a yellow one, and Fritz spat on it. Shall I keep it anyway?"

"Okay!" I yelled. "Everybody listen! Pick the mushrooms and bring them here, and I'll look them over and sort them out. And don't go far or you'll get lost!"

After an hour or so, quite a collection of mushrooms had piled up before me. I was pleased. A few old, slimy ones had to be thrown out, but the rest passed inspection: chanterelles and boletuses.

We changed location a couple of times, and then I thought that we had enough for some fine meals. Triumphantly we returned home. The mothers were impressed. "Well, all we need now is some meat. Chicken would be nice. Chicken with mushrooms and noodles. Hmmm!"

My ears went on red alert. Was that mother challenging me?

"Uli," I said, "you wouldn't know where I could find a burlap bag or some netting or something of that sort?"

He obviously had no idea for what purpose I made this request, otherwise he might have been shocked.

"Let me check in the basement. My father used to collect butterflies. I think some of his nets are in that one storeroom—'the bug and butterfly room', as we call it. I'll ask mother."

"Oh no, don't bother her. Let's just go and look for ourselves."

A butterfly net! What could be more perfect? Never had I worked with such tailor-made equipment. Still—a chicken is no butterfly.

I went to the kitchen where the mothers were cleaning mushrooms—with brushes, as I had instructed.

"I'm just starving," I said. "Could I have just a little piece of dry bread?"

In view of my earlier accomplishments this morning, I was granted this favor. Now I had what I needed: a net, some bread, and a shopping bag.

In Uli's eyes I could read the fervent desire to accompany me.

"What are you going to do Horst, catch fish? I know everything around here, you know? I could help you!"

True, true, true, but—could my conscience let me expose an inexperienced and innocent youth to the perils of an undertaking of such magnitude as I had in mind?

He looked at me imploringly. His brown eyes moistened. That was more than I could endure.

"Okay, Uli! But stay close behind me, don't make any noise, and don't ask any questions."

One item I had almost forgotten: my pocketknife. It was a gift from my uncle, my father's brother—oak handle with a large blade, which I kept razor sharp. That part of our quest, the one involving the use of a knife, weighed heavily on my mind. I had watched Meta a few times and knew exactly what to do, but the thought of performing this act myself made me shudder.

"Now Uli, in order to save time—do you know of any farms nearby where the chickens are running free?"

"Chickens? I thought we were going to catch fish somewhere.

Chickens? Wow! Let me think! Yeah, okay! There is a farm about half an hour from here. Woods all over and I have seen chickens running around in there. No fence—or anything." He was obviously taken with the audacity of the plan.

As he had assured me, we soon entered a patch of forest. There we gathered a few mushrooms as proof of our harmless intentions. When I spotted a flock of chickens, my heart started pounding so violently that I could hardly hear. They were a peaceful bunch, scratching, picking, and looking around. We sat on the ground. The rooster came a little closer to inspect us, as was his job. I threw him a piece of bread. He examined it, tried it and looked expectantly for more. When I cast a few more morsels in his direction, he started to make clucking sounds to invite his harem to partake of the feast.

Uli stared at me, terror in his eyes. His lips were trembling, trying to form words. I could tell just by looking at them what they were trying to say: "Don't, don't, don't! Please don't do it!"

Oddly, they were expressing exactly my sentiments. I just couldn't do it. Fish—no problem! But furry or feathery warm creatures? Sorry, count me out!

Angrily, I crumbled up the rest of the bread and threw it at the birds. They flapped their wings, fought over it, and fully enjoyed the extra ration.

Somehow, I had suspected it might end like this. So I had something in reserve: plan B. I quickly briefed Uli; then we boldly approached the entrance of the farmhouse and knocked. After a few minutes we heard sounds, the door opened and we were face to face with a large and fearsome looking woman and her growling watchdog, a German shepherd. Why does this woman need a watchdog? I wondered. What a redundancy!

She looked us over carefully, probably suspecting we were some of those refugee kids who kept coming around begging for anything edible. I was wearing my lederhosen, so at least I looked ethnically correct. She nodded approvingly and grunted sentences of which I could not understand one word. It sounded as if someone was falling down a flight of wooden stairs. Uli uttered similar sounds in response. Was this the legendary Bavarian dialect I had heard about? Their discourse didn't sound altogether hostile.

While they were talking, I was clutching a pair of small amber earrings in my right hand. Now I stepped forward and held them out for her so see.

When she said "Oh!" it was actually recognizable to me. She inched a bit closer. This was apparently not an everyday occurrence for her. How refreshing! Not just the boring old begging, but someone who offered something in return.

"Oh, very pretty! Amber?" She switched into High German. Was it the way I combed my hair that had tipped her off?

"Yes. They are my grandmother's. Her engagement gift from my grandfather. But now we have to feed all her little grandchildren. So . . ." I tried to make my voice sound like falling logs. Uli turned beet red and coughed violently.

"How many are there?" She now sounded friendly and interested, speaking very slowly and clearly.

"Eight," I said. "My father is still missing. So I have to . . . well, you know."

"And so is my husband. But come on in and have some *Brotzeit*," as Bavarians call any snack-time meal, usually a bowl of milk into which you break slices of rye bread.

"So these earrings—how do I know they're real amber?"

"Well, real amber burns. But that would not be a very practical test, would it?"

She chuckled. I continued, "Real amber floats on water. But with all that silver? What do you think?"

Now she actually laughed and slapped me on the back so hard that I nearly fell off the bench.

Uli looked worried. What would I come up with next? Little did he know that I was not making any of this up, for once.

"Okay," I said, "if you rub real amber against wool, it will become magnetized and you can pick up small bits of paper with it. Here—let's try it. Is this tablecloth wool? Okay if I tear off a few little pieces from this newspaper?"

"Sure! Whatever you need."

She now looked and acted like a child watching a magician in the circus. Probably the most fun she had had in years, I guessed.

I rubbed the amber over the wool surface and then held it above the paper scraps, and sure enough, the paper shot up and clung to the amber. She shrieked with delight. "You boys are really something!"

I braced myself for another slap on the back. Even her dog, Siegfried, came closer, sniffed us over and forced himself to a halfhearted attempt at wagging.

She disappeared into an adjoining room. Returning, she was carrying more bread, liverwurst, and a baking sheet with plum cake. "Come on! Boys your age need to eat a lot, so they can grow big and strong."

Who were we to argue with that?

Plum cake—that was something new. A Bavarian/Austrian specialty, though known in other parts of Germany as well, I was informed. It was baked on a flat cookie sheet, and the bottom was a yeast dough, just like the one for Streuselkuchen. Very interesting!

She left once more, this time returning with a dish full of whipped cream. "Well, you can't eat plum cake without whipped cream, can you?"

We shook our heads emphatically.

It was quickly established that she and Uli were practically neighbors and that her family's name was Moosbacher, a typically Bavarian name. On an envelope on the table I also noticed her first name: Lindhilda! When she found out that I had lived through the siege of Breslau, she sighed deeply, shook her head and heaped another dollop of whipped cream on my cake. "Must have been horrible. Your poor mother!"

This time she gently patted my arm. I began to like this woman. Her presence made me feel safe and optimistic. There was strength and kindness in her face and certainly immense physical strength in her body: someone you wanted to—and could—count on.

I was amazed how good her High German was when she tried. More amazing, however, was the fact that I had not understood one word before. All those dialects that I had encountered so far! There was the dialect of the lowland areas in northern Germany, called "Low German" for that reason; then there was Emma's Upper Silesian; Meta's East Prussian; the dialect of the mountain people of Silesia; and now Bavarian. The differences between Low German and Bavarian were probably as pronounced as those between Dutch and German. When spoken, they were virtually two different languages. Good thing High German, the official German, was taught in schools and spoken over the radio and on stage.

I would have liked to actually learn some Bavarian from her, but she had the earrings on her mind, and yes, we had, after all, come to conduct business that would put food on our table.

Now that we had become friends with Frau Moosbacher, the transaction was no longer strictly business, which was a little unsettling. Was each side expecting preferential treatment now? "You are our friend, so we'll give you a good deal" or, "You are our friend, so we expect a good deal"? I did not know what to say.

Similar thoughts must have been running through Frau Moosbacher's mind, because she didn't say anything, either. Finally, she took the initiative.

"No idea what these earrings may be worth in terms of butter and eggs. How old do you think they are? They are beautiful, I think, and I can use them. So they are worth something to me. On the other hand, without a husband things are often so difficult, and I have to think ahead. Why don't you tell me what you are really short on, and I'll see what I can do about it. Well, of course, I already know what you are short on: food. So, right now, I'll give you some butter, eggs, cheese, and some smoked pork, and when you need more staples, you can come back and visit, okay? Or is there anything in particular right now?"

I thought of the chicken assignment, but didn't dare to bring it up. Seemed a bit greedy. But I did mention fresh meat.

"Ja," she said, nodding thoughtfully, "ja, I might have just the thing for you. Yesterday we slaughtered some of our rabbits, so I can give you a couple of them. How does that sound? Oh, and you know what? I just had a great idea! Next week we'll slaughter one of the pigs. Why don't you and your cousin come and help? There is always lots to do: cutting meat, making sausages, stirring blood for blood sausage, mixing up the headcheese ingredients, grinding up liver for liverwurst, and things like that. Wouldn't that be fun?"

I looked at Uli, who had turned white as a sheet. "Yes!" I said enthusiastically. "I love to do stuff like that. But I might come alone. I think Uli has to go somewhere next week."

"Fine. Come by in a couple of days, and I'll let you know the date. And don't worry! The pig will be already dead when you arrive. Now I'll get your things together."

"Better not mention the earrings at home," I cautioned Uli. "We'll just say she paid us for helping her with the apple and plum harvest. My mother doesn't know I have my own cache of treasure loot. Far better to trade some of it than to kill a chicken with my bare hands. It's just awful! They fight and peck and scratch, and then they poop all over you. No thanks!"

All this was a bit much for poor Uli. His earlier enthusiasm had vanished. The tales of guts, blood and gore had exhausted him physically and mentally. He could hardly carry the rucksack with fruit, butter, bacon and eggs, which Frau Moosbacher had strapped to his back.

"Did you understand all that talk about blood sausage, liver, and head cheese?" he groaned. "I think I am going to be a vegetarian. But first—I am going to be sick."

For me, our outing had quite the opposite effect. What a woman, that Lindhilda Moosbacher! Lindhilda! That name alone! Like something straight out of a Germanic epic: For example, the *Nibelungenlied,* which we had studied. Or how about out of one of those Icelandic sagas, in which some Gunhilde, Hildegunde, or Gudrun would serve her unfaithful lover wine in a goblet made out of his son's gilded skull? But our Lindhilda, behind this fierce, heroic exterior, had a soft, sensitive core, I felt. And to think of what new culinary adventures lay in wait for me, challenging my imagination: to be invited to penetrate the veil of secrecy around liverwurst, smoked pork sausage, *Bratwurst,* and *Landjäger.* Then, after all the work was done, when hams and sausages were hanging in the smoke chamber, and everything else was canned and preserved, there would be the customary, legendary slaughter feast, where large amounts of meats were heaped onto huge platters, together with sauerkraut and dumplings. That's when the infamous blood sausages and the grey-colored ones composed of mysterious innards, including some of the liver, were served—sausages that had been known to make strong men weep with delight and weaker ones throw up. I was going to try it all, no matter how revolting!

IX

*How I helped Lindhilda with the pig slaughter and turned
into a Bavarian*

A LREADY ON THE GRAVEL path to the house, I could smell
it: enthusiastically we inhaled the sautéing onion-and-mushroom
aroma that swirled through the air. A healthy pink hue began to spread
over Uli's ashen face.

"Well, any meat to go with the mushrooms?" some hungry voice
called out.

I felt a little ashamed that we had only two rabbits for so many
mouths, but there were enough other victuals to create a near prewar
meal.

Everyone, with the exception of my mother, was absolutely
amazed at our success. She, of course, was used to it and could not
quite understand what all the fuss was about.

Uli and I didn't say much, just kept referring to this fairy godmother-
like lady, the owner of that farm, Frau Lindhilda Moosbacher.

"Yes," I lied. "We helped her with her plums and apples, and then
she invited us in and gave us *Pflaumenkuchen* with whipped cream. Next
week we are supposed to help her with making sausages and other
porky delicacies. They are going to slaughter the biggest pig you have
ever seen. Uli said he can't wait to dig into some weird blood-and-
innards sausages."

"Really? He did?" His mother shook her head in disbelief as Uli
dashed out of the room, pressing one hand over his mouth.

That was on Friday. Monday morning I hiked out to the Moosbacher
farm. Frau Moosbacher was happy so see me.

"Ah, Horst! Grüss Gott!" The standard, good-for-all-times-of-day
Bavarian greeting. Not *Guten Morgen* or *Guten Tag* or *Guten Abend* but

always *Grüss Gott,* which, I was told, meant something like, "God's greeting to you." I responded in kind. That's about as far as I had progressed in learning Bavarian.

"Listen, Horst, one of my helpers can't make it. Wednesday is the day, you know. The slaughterer is coming at seven in the morning, so if you could come around eight, that would really be helpful and most appreciated. Oh, and wear something old—or I can give you something from my boys. Things might get kind of messy, you know. No, wait! I'll find something for you right now. Then you can get dressed at home."

Carrying a bundle with some old pants and an old shirt, along with a few eggs and a hunk of butter, I went home.

Tuesday arrived and with it my anxiety mounted. I had read about actors or musicians having stage fright and concluded that my feelings were akin to that. If I were able to perform as expected of me, then, I thought, I would be just like one of these superman-like Bavarians and not a wretched refugee mooching off them. I decided to be tough.

The children were acting strangely around me. What had they been told? They were whispering behind my back, observing me shyly and apprehensively, as if they expected me to be sacrificed any minute now to some Bavarian god on an Alpine mountaintop. I noticed Uli talking to them in low tones and guessed the rest. All day long he kept inventing increasingly gross "delicacies" which I would encounter tomorrow. Almost every dish contained chopped testicles, penis parts and eyeballs.

Getting back at him was not difficult. "Ah yes, Uli, before I forget, Frau Moosbacher has already promised that she will have me take a package of *Blutwurst* home for you. I'll heat them up and slip them under your covers while you sleep. So, if you wake up and feel something warm and mushy all over: don't worry, just start eating!"

Wednesday morning I got an early start. Fall was approaching; it was cool, windy, and overcast. In the distance I could see a chain of mountains: the Alps. Some of the higher peaks had patches of white. Suddenly I stopped. An unearthly sound had invaded my consciousness. It was a high-pitched squealing sound, resembling car tires under stress. But there were no roads and no cars here. The closer I came to the farm, the louder the sound grew. And then I comprehended—what was the matter with me? Hadn't I ever been told of squealing pigs?

That's funny, I thought. The pig was supposed to be dead when I arrived. Well, obviously not this pig!

Frau Moosbacher appeared. She was wearing men's clothing and over her head a babushka which was barely adequate to contain her thick, reddish hair. Actually, she was quite beautiful in a fierce way, face flushed, eyes blazing. She would look very impressive on a Wagnerian stage, I thought, perhaps as one of the Rhine Maidens or even as Brünhilde herself, the banished Valkyrie. I did not have the opportunity to convey these flattering notions to her.

"Horst, things are a little bit different from the way I had planned. The slaughterer was an hour late, and his assistant is sick. You'll have to fill in for him. I know you can do it," and her arm came crashing down on my back.

I felt too flattered to be scared or injured. I nodded and smiled confidently.

"Here is the gentleman you'll be assisting, Herr Hinterhuber. And these three gentlemen are his other helpers. And then I'll have a couple of women coming in to help with the cutting and stuffing."

Herr Hinterhuber looked me over, shook my hand and gurgled something in Bavarian, of which I did not catch one single word.

I'll be a great help if I don't understand his instructions, I thought.

But lo and behold! Frau Moosbacher whispered something in his ear, and he switched to High German. "First, you have to steady the head. Right! Nothing to it! It's just like wrestling. Headlock, you know? Get your arm around that porker's head and lean on it, so I can stun it. Then we have to get it up on the table. See that big bucket there? That's for catching the blood. You have to get it right under the point where I slit the throat. What? No, when the blood starts pouring, you can let go of the head. Now—and this is very important—actually, everything is very important. As the blood spurts out and into the bucket—don't spill a drop—you have to get your arm into it and keep stirring it around. And you have to keep opening and closing your fist, so you can break up any clots that may form. Fresh, warm blood coagulates very quickly, and once that happens, it's not much good for anything. When one of your arms gets tired, switch to the other one, okay?"

"Yup, okay, I think. And for how long?—"

"Well, can't really predict, but it has to cool down to about room temperature. I'll keep checking. It's in my blood, when."

Amazing, I thought, if he were an Indian, they'd call him He to Whom Blood Speaks.

I had not known that slaughterers have little gadgets that shoot little bullets. The squealing ceased abruptly and a torrent of hot blood poured over my arm, rising steadily in the bucket until it was halfway up to my shoulder. And all the while my hand worked the blood as my arm kept rotating.

How much blood in a pig? Let's just say that it was a very large bucket.

By now, Uli would have vomited at least five times, I thought. I felt fine, but that warm, sticky liquid did have an odd odor: sickeningly sweet and unlike anything I had ever experienced. I would have to be awfully hungry to be able to swallow sausages made from that red slime. Suddenly, Uli's aversion didn't seem so absurd anymore.

Finally, after I had alternated my arms several times, Herr Hinterhuber indicated that his blood had just spoken to him, informing him that the pig's life juices had been adequately stirred and cooled. All likelihood of curdling and coagulating had been prevented, and we could now prepare for the actual offensive, the final drive toward the Promised Land: BLUTWURST.

Spices were selected and lined up: salt, white and black pepper, cloves, marjoram, ginger, and ground dried pimentos appeared next to the huge kettle where, to my complete bewilderment, the blood was being heated.

Mountains of the pig's skin and fat belly meat were first cut up and then put through a coarse meat grinder, before they were dumped into the steaming brew. The master himself added the spices, following an ancient, proven procedure—taste and add. After each addition, he would spoon up some of the dark, gruel-like mixture, put it into his mouth, and then he chewed and shifted it around inside to get a full report from his taste buds as to the adequacy of the spicing process. He followed the same procedure for each of the spices, one at a time. Now and then, when not satisfied, he had to repeat the spice check two or three times. That added up to a lot of Blutwurst-gruel. Watching this, my intention to never eat Blutwurst turned into a vow. By the time he was finished, he must have consumed about three cups of this mush—savoring every swallow.

I must say, five hours of actively participating in these activities had exhausted me emotionally and physically. My clothes were stiff with dried blood; my arms up to the shoulders were encrusted with layers of dry blood. Frau Moosbacher took pity on me. "Well, Horst, that was quite a battle, I must confess. You have fought well and deserve a rest. You'll find hot water and clean clothes in the laundry room. You must be hungry, too. I noticed you didn't have any of the blood mix as all the others did. Well, they love it because they are used to it. So, what would you like?"

"Just some milk and dry bread," I said weakly.

Even though I had asked to be assigned to a different post, I still was curious as to the ultimate result of my labors. Some of the mixture was stuffed into natural casings, then processed for 60 minutes at 85 degrees Celsius. The rest was canned. This took 120 minutes. Most of the sausages were designated for tonight's feast.

I don't think there was any part of the pig that was not turned into a choice delicacy for the delight of the unsqueamish. Well, except perhaps for the parts Uli had mentioned, but at this point, who cared or could tell?

Now there were new smells emanating from the kitchen, familiar ones, conjuring up images of Christmases past and other family feasts: sauerkraut! My optimism, rooted in inexperience and hope, whispered reassuringly, "Sauerkraut is sauerkraut."

"Well, we shall see!" a cautious voice answered. In the meantime, the mere smell revived me.

I entered the room, where Lindhilda, amidst dense vapors, appeared to be floating from pots to kettles. She was periodically obscured by massive billows of steam which enveloped her whenever she lifted one of the lids. On the floor I noticed a huge earthen crock. No mystery what that might be! Oh yes, I had been around when cabbage was shredded and layered into one of those brown, glazed vessels: one layer finely shredded cabbage, one layer coarse salt!

And then I had had to tamp it down with a wooden mallet until the cabbage gave up and released its natural juices that collected as a frothy brine on top. Mercilessly, layer upon layer had been added, until my arms ached and blisters had formed on my palms. As a finishing touch, a large flat stone had been placed on top, so that not one sliver of cabbage would dare rise above the brine.

The odors of the fermenting cabbage, rising into the air and spreading throughout the house, were not pleasant—something between cheese and manure. But that would stop after a while, and a kraut tasting would be conducted. Raw sauerkraut, ready for human consumption, should be almost white, crunchy, and quite acidic. The sharp cabbage flavor should be at a minimum. If the new sauerkraut measures up to these requirements, it is ready to be eaten, raw or cooked. It keeps quite well in a cool place, but cautious housewives prefer to preserve it in jars.

With Frau Moosbacher's permission, I dug a handful of kraut out of the crock and started to eat. Yes! Just as if Emma and I had made it. Lowering my head over the crock, I drew in a deep breath of pungent, raw, kraut-scented air.

"Now, don't fall in, Horst! Don't worry; you'll have your chance a little bit later."

Smells of boiling and frying meats, combined with essence of sauerkraut, instantly had me under their mouthwatering spell. Even the Blutwurst didn't smell too nasty when fried to the crusty stage. Other types of sausages were also boiled or fried, together with some actual meat.

"What about the dumplings? Can I help? Dumplings was always my job back home." I was really curious to find out what went into Bavarian dumplings.

"Sure! Moisten your hands and start rolling. We'll need about one hundred. The water is already boiling."

Probing around in the dough, I was shocked. What had gotten into these people? Not one potato in the entire batch. "What is this? Doesn't look or feel or smell like anything we ever made into dumplings."

"Well, Horst, you are in Bavaria now. So, naturally, we eat Bavarian dumplings. Bavarian bread dumplings, made from stale bread, sautéed onions, eggs, milk, and a lot of fresh parsley. Try some raw! Tastes damn good the way it is, doesn't it?"

So I rolled and I rolled and I rolled, and by the time all the meats and the kraut were ready, so were the dumplings.

Then came another devastating blow for me: the sauerkraut! What lack of imagination! Who would want to eat it like that, with nothing added to it—no bacon, no raw onion, nothing worth mentioning! Just the boiled kraut with a bit of caraway in it—a simply revolting combination, by the way. I was barely able to conceal my disappointment. The dumplings were good, though. But again: no gravy! Dumplings without gravy? You really had to be awfully hungry for that! Good thing I was—by then.

Watching the natives' blissful abandon to chewing, I wracked my brain for an answer. What was their secret? How did those barbarians manage to devour these immense portions of food? I soon was onto them. They put little samplings of everything from their plates into their mouths, layering them in, as it were, and then they mushed it up. Yes, this might be the answer: create a new dish inside your mouth. "It's the only way to endure this meal," I concluded, after some further careful observation, analysis, and personal experimentation.

Wrong again! This was only half of the story. The other half had to do with the huge one-liter mugs in front of each chair. Until now, I had seen these steins only as decorative collectors' items on shelves and buffet tops. Who would want that much of anything all at once? I had wondered. Now I had the answer—Bavarians! They needed it. It was essential for their survival. How else could they get the mush that was clogging up their mouths down into their stomachs? You had to have something to produce a torrent that would sweep away everything in its path. Images of broken dikes, tidal waves, and collapsing hydroelectric dams came to mind. No piddling little wine or water glass would do here!

It wasn't as if I had not encountered alcohol before. I had tried wine at holiday dinners in Breslau, and I certainly had experienced and witnessed the effects of vodka. Now I raised the stein for my first taste of beer. Disappointing! Bitter—and those annoying little bubbles that made me burp after each swallow! But there were songs, songs probably composed by brewers to boost beer consumption, in which after each verse everyone would jump up—later, up onto the table—to shout: "Eins, zwei, drei: g'suffa!"

I had no trouble with the eins, zwei, drei, but *g'suffa* didn't remind me of anything within the German language. So I did what everyone else was doing: I shouted "G'suffa!" and drank up. And that, not surprisingly, was exactly what g'suffa meant, as Uli explained to me later.

Anyway, the lesson learned here was that beer drinking, singing, and high spirits mix well, whereby my personal well-being increased proportionately with the quantity imbibed. The once annoying bubbles were now conceived as a pleasantly tingly sensation in my throat and mouth; the burps, originating deep down in my stomach, burst forth with primeval force, creating a wonderfully liberating sensation. Best of all, after the third song, everything on the table tasted just marvelous. Gone were my misgivings about Blutwurst. Now, rejecting it would have been an insult to the pig, the owner, and to the master sausage maker who, at this very moment, was standing on the table shouting, "Eins, zwei, drei, g'suffa!"

Frau Moosbacher had kept a watchful eye on me. Bavarians are virtually immune to the effects of beer. It is regarded not as an alcoholic beverage, but as nutritionally important food, essential in measured quantity for your child's healthy development. I, on the other hand, a Prussian, had not benefited from such childcare practices. Therefore, it did not seem prudent to her if I went beyond two steins.

Personally, I had already reached the point where I did not care what happened to me, but my hostess gently pulled me back by the collar as I was about to receive my third refill. "Horst, I promised your mother I would take care of you. I know what too much beer can do to someone who is not used to it. If you drink too much on top of all that fatty food, you'll become awfully sick. Believe me! It's a horrible feeling! So, just stay and sing and have fun, but no more eating or drinking!"

She had spoken very softly and with a gentle smile, but for an instant I had caught a glimpse of that fierce, steely look in her eyes that had intimidated me the first time. No way could I disregard her orders!

"Oh, and Horst, I talked to your mother about this. It's okay if you spend the night here. I have made up a bed for you in the boys' room. So, anytime you feel like it, just go on up."

Feeling very full, a little dizzy, grateful, and like a real Bavarian, I soon followed that invitation, mumbling, "G'suffa, g'suffa, g'suffa," as I climbed the stairs.

X

How we left Munich

BACK HOME IN PLANEGG, we were anxiously awaiting replies to the many letters my mother had written, replies that would determine our next step. From the start it had been clear that we could not expect to stay there permanently.

First of all we expected a reply from the Glaesers. They were our closest relatives who had been part of our lives as far back as I could remember. That little village in the foothills of the Alps sounded rather intriguing to me. Obergünzburg! I had found it on an old map. Not far from Kempten and from there just an hour's train ride to Oberstdorf, a famous ski resort, below the Nebelhorn. A cable car, one of the first in the Alps, took skiers to the top. That aspect alone could have persuaded me to move there. Skiing was another one of my passions, along with skating, fishing, cooking, mushrooming, singing, and kayaking.

Several letters had been sent to America: Chicago, Albany, New York City, wherever these fugitives from the 1930s had found a new home. What would we learn from them? Was there any hope for us? Every day, when I came home from some excursion, my first question would be, "Any mail?"

And every day my mother would lecture me on the virtue of patience. "It takes time, Horsti, lots of time! Think of the distances! Who knows if the mail delivery is working reliably again!"

"Okay, okay, okay!"

But one day there was a letter from Obergünzburg. I recognized my Onkel Pippi's handwriting. Wouldn't you expect my mother's own sister to write? Very ominous!

And indeed! It was devastating news we received. My aunt had not survived the hardships of the long trip from Breslau. Constant bomb-

Otto, the eldest of the sons

ing, strafing, torn-up rails, over-crowded trains, and days and days without real sleep or food had proven to be too much for her poor health.

We were both in shock. My mother continued with the letter but after a few seconds suddenly stopped and gasped, "Oh my God, oh no! Not Otto! Otto, too! Oh, my God!"

She was unable to go on reading.

Otto, the eldest of the sons, had been the one who had discovered Obergünzburg and who had orchestrated the family exodus. It had been after the surrender that he suddenly came down with some unidentifiable illness. He was taken to the Kempten hospital where he died, leaving behind his wife, child, and mother- and grandmother-in-law. All of them lived in Obergünzburg now. As a matter of fact, everybody even remotely connected to the Glaesers had migrated to Obergünzburg.

"Any word about Emma and Antek?" I broke the silence.

"Yes, here! Read for yourself!"

It was a note to me from Antek. He had made it out of Poland in good shape. His BMW was a lot faster than the Polish bicycles without tires. He was working with refugees, learning English, and experimenting with making jewelry. "Hope to see you soon! Got some great ideas! Emma sends her greetings. She is saving up butter for a Streuselkuchen for your return."

Well, at least that part of the letter was good news.

More and more letters kept arriving. My father's brother in the north invited us to live with them. Their only son, Paul, was still missing. He had last been seen during the battle of Berlin. As one of his returning comrades had reported, they had run out of food and ammunition.

His family spent years hoping for his return. There never was any trace of him—then or later.

Paul, no trace

Gradually, letters in unfamiliar envelopes with exotic stamps arrived: America!

"What do they say, what do they say?" I always shouted. "Are they inviting us? Are they going to help us? How long do they think it's going to take?"

Usually mother just sighed under my onslaught. "You've got to be more patient! Right now, almost no one is getting out. It's going to take a lot of time. Before the war, it was much easier. Now there are millions who want to emigrate. Everyone has to be carefully checked. They don't want to end up with a bunch of ex-Nazis over there. There are top Nazis with fake IDs and lots of money, running around free. But all the relatives are optimistic that they'll get us out in time. The most important and difficult thing is that they find someone who is willing and able to supply us with affidavits. That means someone—actually we need two sponsors—who would swear that we will not become a burden to the government and that they will take care of us if we are unable to do so ourselves. And all of our friends and relatives over there are recent immigrants themselves, unable to meet the government's minimum income requirement for sponsors.

"But Mama—what about—you know—our ticket to America?"

"Yes, I know. If we are clever and careful enough—who knows. So far, I don't have even the slightest idea where to begin. Once we are in Obergünzburg, we can look into the possibilities."

Every time there was some mail for us, I would check all the envelopes with hope in my heart. "Is there nothing else? Are you sure?"

"Well, we have heard from just about everyone now. What on earth are you expecting—a personal invitation from the president of the U.S.?"

I would just shrug my shoulders and wander off, with obvious signs of discouragement and melancholy.

"Oh, now wait a minute—don't tell me you are waiting for a letter from Anja! Is that it?"

I just grimaced and nodded.

"Well Horst, this may not make you feel any better, but it's something to think about. There are going to be many times when you will feel this awful pain, but one always gets over it. Think how I felt when your father died, and I was only thirty-four! There are so many things happening in your life now. You don't have time to feel sad, and you'll meet many wonderful girls to fall in love with—girls your age, not someone six years older. There is probably some sweet girl in America right now, just waiting to meet you. And, I might as well tell you: girls do seem to like you. Can't imagine why!"

I risked a little smile and did feel better.

Then, two days later, contrary to all expectations and my mother's pessimistic predictions, there was a short letter from Anja in the mail: they were renting a small apartment in Munich; our Russian officer friends were making contacts; she would like to study languages at the university; she had not found any of her family, and she missed us. No return address. Hmm!

I would have loved to write an endless letter to her—and say what? No! Mother was right!

We felt that we had stayed long enough in Planegg. I had trained the children to be fairly competent foragers who could work independently now. Only Uli was unhappy—because I hadn't taken him fishing yet.

"All right! Let's see what we can pull out of one of your Bavarian lakes! First, we have to get some worms and two long poles. Those hazelnut shoots over there should work. I'll get everything ready."

It was mid-September by now and suddenly quite hot once more. So the idea of going to a lake appealed to me. My last good swim had been in the Oder. In fact I had crossed the river then, a feat highly regarded in my circle of friends. Suddenly the idea of swimming in another body of water seemed like a betrayal. But what was I betraying? A river? How silly did that sound? I decided not to reveal my feelings to anyone, not even to my mother.

We mounted a couple of old bikes. Uli led the way to a totally hidden and never frequented—as he assured me—jewel of a lake. For the final kilometer, there was nothing but a narrow, overgrown footpath. I could easily believe that not many passed through here, because on both sides of the trail there was dense growth of stinging nettles.

Uli had not exaggerated. The path finally ended at a little sandy cove, and there was the lake—clear, sparkling water surrounded by cattails. A little rowboat was there, with oars, attached by rope to a small tree. A scene from a picture postcard.

"Of course! It's all right to use the boat, Uli! We are just borrowing it. Let's row over there where it seems to be a bit deeper. I think we can just drift with the wind."

I instructed Uli in baiting the hook with a worm, a task which made him squirm more than the worm. Then we watched the bobbers. Nothing! What was wrong with this lake? Had word gotten out that I was Prussian? For Uli's sake, I wished we would catch just one fish.

"Well, why don't we go for a swim and then try again later. A little lunch wouldn't hurt, either." Our mothers had packed us some sandwiches.

Rowing slowly back to our cove, I peered into the crystal clear water for any signs of aquatic life. My heart rate increased by several beats when I discovered something on the bottom: a line or a wire, it seemed. A nightline, like I used to put out? This I had to investigate.

The water was about four feet deep. I dove under and grabbed whatever it was. It turned out to be a fairly heavy wire that was tightly stretched along the bottom of the lake. I could raise it a couple of feet, but was unable to pull it in either direction. It had to have some fishing purpose! What to do? Well, definitely not give up! Of course, I could not possibly dive along the entire length of the wire, which might reach all the way to the other side of the lake. And who knows how deep it might get? Then I had an idea. There were, after all, two of us.

"Uli, I'll stay here. You row back to shore and find a sturdy stick, about three feet long. Bring it here! I have a plan."

Uli and I would swim side by side, carrying the stick between us, the wire running over the center of the stick. Swimming forward, we could raise the wire as we went along. There was enough give to allow for this maneuver. Before we started out, I strapped my knife around my waist. Uli turned out to be a competent swimmer, and we made good progress.

I had been right. After about twenty feet, we came to the first hook; a nylon leader was attached to the wire. No fish! Another twenty feet and another empty hook. Then our luck changed. Since the wire was probably running along the bottom of the lake, I had anticipated eels, and so it was. A beauty of an eel! Getting it back on land was a problem, though. I cut the leader, wrapped it around my hand and swam ashore, towing my captive behind me. Uli remained where we had paused, holding up the wire and waiting for my return.

We continued as before, but it became increasingly difficult to hold up the wire in the deeper water. We took one more eel and then let go of the stick. I had never seen eels that large and was quite elated. So was Uli. Not exactly what he had envisioned, but the results were satisfying.

In view of the nature of our activities, we decided it might be prudent to disappear quickly and quietly. At home we had a hard time convincing the younger children that it was not snake we were having for supper. Luckily, there was dill growing in the garden. So mother prepared her famous dill sauce, which, with boiled potatoes, created a delicious meal with the poached eel.

For weeks, for months—it seemed like years—come to think of it, my mother had kept lamenting the absence of continued schooling in my life. Through no fault of my own, I had not seen the inside of any school for over a year. That situation had to change, the sooner the better.

In spring of 1944, when it had become prudent to ship entire schools—student body and faculty—to some countryside location in order to escape bombings and invading armies, my blood was deemed not pure enough to qualify for survival rights. So there I was left, pushed into a little private—I cannot bring myself to call it a school—which I hated. We had to sing strange, unfamiliar songs and accompany them with a sequence of, to me, totally alien and somehow embarrassing body movements. I blushed at the thought that one of my friends might catch me in one of these poses. My attitude changed when I was seated next to Gisela. Usually German schools were strictly segregated according to gender, but this place was the exception. We never spoke a word, but her mere presence had an Anja-like calming effect on me, giving me complete contentment. And I must say, on her these awkward, effeminate poses looked rather appealing. I saw her one more time after the siege of Breslau, but by then I had that crush on Mechthild.

Altogether, from the spring of 1944 on—virtually zero schooling. I had kept up my reading though, always carefully screening the bookcases wherever we were living. Among my interests were books dealing with hunting, fishing, cooking, expeditions to exotic and dangerous places, and stories dealing with America. Authors such as Mark Twain, James Fennimore Cooper, Jack London, and especially Edgar Rice Burroughs and his Tarzan adventures were thoroughly familiar to me—in translation, of course.

Getting me back into academics was foremost on my mother's

agenda now: get that fellow back into a school to cure him of those nasty foraging and black-market habits. I was not remotely eager to be once more subjected to the regimentation of education, nor did the prospect of being stuck in a class with a bunch of "children" appeal to me. But I realized that there would be no escape, and deep down I felt somewhat embarrassed at how far behind I was. Uli was two grades ahead of me, and his English surpassed mine by far.

"Don't worry," my mother comforted me. "There will be others exactly like you. And just think, no more Nazi teachers to harass you. You will be able to do and to say whatever you like. I just know it will be a whole new and pleasant experience for you, and you'll be so far ahead of everyone else—in terms of experiences. Think of what you know and can do compared to them."

"Well, yeah, perhaps. I hope you are right."

The time for our departure was set. The Glaesers had written that they were expecting us. Initially we would be staying with them in an old inn that had been converted to accommodate refugees.

As so often before, it was time to say goodbye. Only some seven months ago we were still living in the Hopf villa. Since then, our lives had been an endless procession of partings: from houses, apartments, possessions, cities, rivers and lakes, smells and sounds, countries, friends and relatives. All this was and would be with us forever—and travel with us wherever we went, because everything and everyone had, in some way, been memorable. Now the list was expanding once more: my aunts and cousins, their magnificent home, the orchards and farms, the Valkyrie-like Frau Lindhilda Moosbacher, yes, and also the poor pig, whose sudden and violent departure had contributed so significantly to my transformation into a Bavarian. Uli and I had become fast friends, vowing to keep in touch and visit each other. Frau Moosbacher nearly suffocated me in her final embrace.

XI

How we fared during the train ride, how refugees and Black troops had transformed Obergünzburg, how I learned to jitterbug and fly-fish, befriended a Black captain, and met Brigitte

THE TRAIN RIDE FROM Munich to Obergünzburg was nothing we were looking forward to. No luxurious ride in a Mercedes was awaiting us this time.

Normally it was a three-hour trip, but these days passenger trains were often sidetracked for hours. The U.S. Army had priority, causing huge delays.

There were still millions of German civilians moving in every direction, like ants after someone has leveled their hill. If you were not quick and aggressive, you might see train after train leave without you.

Taking the local commuter train into Munich was not too bad. Two of my aunts and Uli accompanied and guided us. The main station had been completely destroyed by repeated bombings. Now hundreds of people, mostly women and children, were crowding the makeshift platforms between the tracks. They were sitting patiently on their bundles and suitcases. Red Cross ladies occasionally came through to distribute some bread and water. The lucky ones received K-rations.

Rumor had it that our train was to start empty from Munich. So we might have a chance! Our relatives were still with us because we needed them to carry out our plan: when the train arrived, they would hoist us up from the platform, through a window, into one of the compartments, and our luggage after us. Closed windows would not be a problem. In all of Germany, there existed probably not one train compartment with windows. They had all been shot out by strafers or blown out by bombs.

Two hours after the scheduled time, a train was approaching. Was it ours? As if a storm were whipping up a stagnant pond, there suddenly was movement everywhere. The masses were preparing for the assault on the train. Mothers fixed bayonets, summoned children, moved belongings to more advantageous locations, and counted heads and bags one more time. How had they ever gotten that far? Not much of a chance for them here.

Hissing and wheezing, the train came to a stop, and the rush for the doors was on. I leaped toward the nearest window, jumped, pulled myself up and rolled into the compartment. It was a new world record! Then my mother's head appeared, her arms were straining to raise herself, there was shouting, even laughter outside, as she was pushed, heaved higher and higher, until she managed to swing one of her legs over the window ledge. The rest was easy. Our two suitcases and the small bundles followed, and we were safely inside, proud occupants of two window seats. The entire operation had not taken more than thirty seconds.

More and more people piled into the compartment. Pressure from all sides built up so fiercely that it would have been impossible to fall over. What if anyone had to go to the bathroom? Indeed a terrifying thought! I had given my seat to a mother with twin babies and tried to dismiss toilet nightmares.

When the train finally began to move, we waved. "Goodbye, thanks for everything . . . maybe Christmas."

On the platform there still were hundreds of swearing or crying or resigned travelers.

My last train ride had been the return from my Baltic summer—just a little more than a year ago. I kept thinking about that journey as we went bumping along. Back then I had been filled with the excitement of all my summer activities. Now, even though my recent adventures made any previous ones pale by comparison, I felt nothing but apprehension. Perhaps someday, when and if I had a real home again, I would be able to find pleasure, pride and amusement in remembering the feats and exploits of the last six months. I felt that it would be a long time yet before this happened.

A hideous odor rescued me from sliding deeper and deeper into gloom. God forbid! The twins! The diapers!! And there was nothing that could be done. I seriously looked around for the emergency brake.

Mother, sensing my desperate intention, gave me that stern "don't you dare" look.

An elderly lady now struggled wildly to reach the window. As her husband held onto her, she leaned way out and vomited. Screams of outrage and disgust from the adjacent compartment and some from further on down the train reached our ears. What were those nasty, sickening, smelly, greenish, wet particles that kept coming in through the windows?

Whenever in later life I encountered the word "chain reaction," it would conjure up before me a long train with hundreds of desperate people hanging out of windows, all doing the same thing: vomiting.

I too was among the stricken. Beads of sweat were forming on my forehead, saliva was collecting in my mouth at an alarming rate, and my stomach was convulsively heaving. As I vainly attempted to pry and tunnel my way toward the window, I and all my fellow travelers received overwhelmingly convincing proof of the existence of a good and merciful God. It was a classic example of a miraculous salvation, the perfect *deus ex machina,* provided by divine intervention, so it appeared to me. But to my disappointment, this intervention was not heavenly, but manmade, probably in Detroit, Michigan.

A highway crossed our tracks—on it, a convoy of U.S. Army trucks. The train had to stop. All but a few vehicles had successfully passed, and then it happened: there was a small explosion from one of the trucks. A bang, followed by black smoke, and that truck would not budge from its position smack in the middle of the intersection. The convoy ground to a halt, we were safe—and not one second too soon.

In one desperate effort I overcame the last obstacle between me and the window: an enormous lady, eyes bulging in terror and pain as I lunged forward, scaling her as a leopard would an elephant, finally reaching her shoulders with my knees so that I could just let myself drop to the ground outside.

Oh, to be outside! Oh, to breathe fresh air! Oh, to lower my head between my knees, and oh, the relief of saying farewell to my last Planegg breakfast!

Passengers from other compartments started to emerge. Only now I noticed that a number of lads my age had been riding on top of the wagons. Wow, did that ever look like fun!

"Don't even think it!" My mother squelched my hopes.

By now, most of the passengers were milling around alongside the train. They all seemed to have the same goal in mind: find a bush or a tree! But alas, no such comfort was in sight. So, inhibitions were cast aside, and everyone did nature's bidding, ignoring friends, neighbors and strangers. What an opportunity for the GIs to complement their WWII photo albums with more action shots.

Quite a bit of fraternizing went on, too. Cigarettes, chocolate bars, canned ham, and that strange, spongy, cotton-like bread emerged from trucks and pockets and were passed around. After a while some of the younger ladies from the train actually went back to their compartments, fetched their baggage, loaded it into trucks, and climbed in after it. More breathing space for the rest of us.

By following the progress of the trip on a map we knew that we were approaching our destination: Günzach. From there it would be a twenty-minute bus ride to Obergünzburg. What I saw outside now appealed to me. It was quite hilly. Large pastures in between dense pine forests were alive with light brown cattle. Little wooden racks piled with fresh hay were standing like puppets among the cows. Whenever the train slowed down or stopped, I could smell that good old, reassuring, comforting country smell, fresh hay and cow manure. This I could get used to, I felt.

At this point, a few words about the region known throughout Germany as Allgäu may be of interest. It is not a political unit in Germany. Some parts of it are located within Bavaria, others within Baden-Württemberg, but it belongs to neither. It's just there, a region in southern Germany. The name, historically dating back to the fifth

Obergünzburg im Allgäu

and sixth centuries, was used when referring to "that region where the mountains are," or something like that. The name occurring in documents is Alb Gau: "Alb" as in Alps and "Gau" simply meaning region or landscape. It abounds in natural beauty. Hills and lakes attract vacationers. The elevation is reputed to be ideal for promoting healing and well-being. Famous pure-air health spas invite the ailing from all over Germany and beyond. A little further to the south, the Alps form a natural boundary that separates Germany from Austria.

But more than for all these attractions, the region owes its renown to milk products. Chocolate-bar labels proudly announce: "Made from the milk of happy Allgäu cows." Butter and various cheeses also owe their fame to the mammary secretions of these happy critters.

Aside from resorts and recreational centers, the Allgäu is—or rather had been—primarily inhabited by cows, but due to the sudden influx of people like us, the despised "foreigners," the population had multiplied. Still, towns were small, the infrequent farmhouses were separated by forests and pastures, and most of the Allgäuers performed some cattle-related job. If it had been Otto's objective to find a remote cow town, Obergünzburg fit this description.

During the last few kilometers of the trip, nervous excitement built up inside me. By now the train was a couple of hours late, so would there be anyone at the station to greet us? What about the bus? Would it run that late?

We were the only passengers getting off at Günzach, apparently not a center of commerce and culture. In fact, except for the station house, no other structures were visible. But the smell was present: light on the hay, heavy on the manure.

"Mama, are you sure we got off at the right station? This is the deadest place I have ever seen!"

"Yes! Positive! Remember, Otto wanted a place were everyone could sort of disappear. Ach, poor Otto! Couldn't have found a better place!"

What a disappointment! No bus, no relatives to greet us, and a low sun that was about to disappear behind a hill. Somewhere in the distance—cowbells. Downright peaceful!

But now—oh no! There was a rumbling of thunder in the distance. But how was that possible? There were no clouds in the sky! Yet, the sound came closer and closer, culminating in a deafening roar. A trail of thick dust was speeding toward us. Whirling wheels and flashes of shiny metal began to emerge. A motorcycle! Could it be? I began to shout and dance. Yes! I'd know that hulk of a man on the motorcycle anywhere! "Antek! Antek!" I shouted and raced over to where he had stopped. I just jumped up on him and clung there like a bur. Only now I fully realized how much I had missed him.

"Horst! God, it's good to see you again!"

Mother was less demonstrative with her feelings, "What a relief to see you, Antek! I feel a lot better about our future now."

An hour later we arrived in Obergünzburg. Humbly by horse-drawn cart—the only wheels Antek had been able to arrange for us—as it behooves poor refugees.

The turmoil of the lost war had cruelly torn this peaceful community of dairy farmers out of its daily routine. No longer did the old Nazi slogan, "One nation, one will, one Führer," carry any weight. Hitler would have been very disappointed! Fellow citizens of this once single-willed nation now were intruders with wives and children—as yet without possessions or food—who had come to inflict hardships on the natives: one had to share housing, victuals, firewood, and provide school facilities.

The population of Obergünzburg had nearly doubled in recent months. It was noted with some suspicion that many of these newcomers bore the same last name: Glaeser! There were all my cousins and their mates and children on my mother's side, and then an entire additional tribe stemming from the Glaeser side, people I did not know at all.

But all this was nothing in comparison to the upheaval brought on by the presence of U.S. soldiers—an all-black infantry unit! There was very little the Catholic priest was able to do to assuage the fears of the natives. Clearly, these soldiers were the instruments of the devil. Nazi propaganda had instilled an irrational fear of them in the population. On the eastern front it had been the Mongolian troops that had struck panic into the hearts of the population; here it was the black troops.

But this fear did not affect everyone the same way. Despite most parents' diligent efforts to keep their daughters under lock and key, these shameless creatures found ways to escape surveillance. The lure of the exotic—not to mention chocolate, cigarettes, silk and even nylon stockings, liquor, and wild, new, never-before-heard music—proved to be far more persuasive than anything parents or priests could do. And so it happened that every evening the young ladies would cleanse themselves of the livestock odor, dab on a little cologne, and head into town where loud jitterbug music would blast forth from one of the inns. The Goldene Engel* was the place where they would—"oh, just for a little refreshment"—disappear.

The non-fraternization order had recently been rescinded; PXs with liquor stores had been established in nearby Kempten and Augsburg; jeeps filled with cases of gin, rum, whiskey, and vodka were unloaded in front of the inn several times each week; the innkeeper's son was given a crash course in basic cocktail mixing, and it didn't take long for the ladies to acquire a certain fluency in spouting little sentences that carried words like, "gin and tonic," "daiquiri," "margarita," "Tom Collins," "martini," and "pink lady."

In the evening, in little groups, the GIs emerged from their billets, all dressed up in their class As and carrying little packages which contained items they hoped would win them the favor of some local beauty.

The ladies loved the unusual liquid concoctions; the GIs on the other hand fell in love with the local brews which, just like the ladies, surpassed anything they had ever experienced or so some claimed.

The horse cart which Antek had managed to mobilize for our rescue deposited us in front of the Goldene Engel. It was a warm evening, the door was wide open, and I could see male and female shapes moving in rhythmic ecstasy. The beat of the music had invaded every body, forcing every muscle and sinew to follow it. Couples were whirling, twisting, flying through the air. Girls were tossed up high, flipped over shoulders, bounced off knees. There were some rough landings, accompanied by little screams and followed by painful withdrawals from the dance floor. Feet that were accustomed to stomping through soggy manure were attempting dainty maneuvers; hands trained to extract milk from udders were clapping to the music or clutching their partners. Occasionally, rings of cheering spectators would gather around some particularly outstanding couple.

The crowd was going wild with the "Boogie Woogie Bugle Boy of Company B." In Planegg I had heard it a few times over the American Forces Network station, and now my own feet were beginning to twitch, making the same little dance steps as everybody here. Suddenly I felt a tug on my shirt. A little hand came and pulled me into the turmoil. It was a girl about my age, probably someone's younger sister. She wore long pigtails that went horizontal when she whirled.

*Golden Angel

"Tomorrow," she whispered, and "Brigitte,"* as Antek came to whisk me away.

Already halfway out the door, I turned around. She still stood there.

Pointing at my chest I shouted through the music: "Horst!"

My mother was more pleased than annoyed, I think.

"Well, Horst, that didn't take very long, did it? Told you! Remember?"

I sure did.

In the meantime, Antek had put all of our belongings into a small handcart which we pulled to our final destination, the Gasthaus zum Schwan,** on the other side of the market square. All the relatives lived there now. The Glaesers and their kin had taken over the entire place. The owner, a Nazi official, was in prison, and his family had moved away in disgrace.

A warm, emotional welcome took place. There, in the center of the dining room, stood the huge, round family table, the chairs arranged around it, the buffet, even the carpet, exactly as I remembered from our last Christmas dinner in Breslau. All this made me feel at home, up to a point.

It was a joyous reunion; we were all glad to be together, but the losses weighed heavily on our spirits. We knew we would never be able to recover from them. My aunt's and Otto's death cast a pall on the occasion, and all the familiar furniture, though comforting, seemed to say, "We want to go home now! Enough of this!"

And that was the problem: there was no more home. Or was it merely a "not yet"?

Emma encircled me over and over, examining me from all sides. "My God, you have grown so tall—you have turned into a man! That will take time to get used to. Are you still into food and cooking? Not much going on here in that respect. They just don't know how to cook in these parts. But we are managing—will be, as long as the GIs are here, at least."

The others had eaten already, so Emma brought in some food for us. Very disappointing. Must have been U.S. Army rations, but toward the end she disappeared and, smiling at me, returned with a sheet of Streuselkuchen. "I just had to come up with something special for your return."

*Pronounced with a hard g as in "get": Brih-GIT-te.   **Swan Inn

My uncle now addressed us. "Don't be surprised or alarmed if some guests drop in later on. Yes, we have become good friends with some of the officers and men in town. Well, you have probably noticed the black soldiers already? Wonderful, fascinating fellows. They visit almost every evening. We talk and learn English; of course, quite a bit of alcohol is consumed, but that's all right. During the day I paint little watercolors for them: houses, farms, the church, cattle, landscapes, even portraits. They are crazy about things like that and pay me in cigarettes and even in dollars. I hope they'll stay here for a long time."

There was a knock at the door. Every head turned expectantly in that direction. I had a feeling that something incredible was about to take place, a feeling akin to starting a new chapter in one of my adventure books, taking me to Africa or the world of Tom Sawyer and Huckleberry Finn. One of my earlier heroes came to mind: the greatest, most famous black man of all—Jesse Owens, the hero of the 1936 Olympics, the man with the "inferior blood" who had broken so many world records and whose hand Hitler would not shake, just because it was the hand of a black man. That fact alone created a feeling of solidarity between the likes of Jesse Owens and me. Jesse's people, just like mine, had been and were being persecuted because of their race.

My eyes were fixed upon the door. Would they be tall and athletically built like Jesse? Of course, I realized that not every black man could be a huge super-athlete. But perhaps one of these guests would? Please? Just for me?

The door opened, and I could hardly believe my eyes. I instinctively jumped up from my chair and started gaping—a giant—at least ten centimeters taller than Jesse. I almost clicked my heels. Well, he was a captain, after all. He smiled with the whitest teeth I had ever seen and, spotting me as a newcomer, stepped forward, welcoming me with open arms, thereby raising me to his level.

Two of his friends were with him, a lieutenant and a sergeant. They too, were tall, nice-looking men. I couldn't get over how friendly and cheerful they were, laughing and joking all the time, passing out cigarettes and chocolates and setting a battery of bottles on the table: scotch, gin, rum, and cognac, and some stuff I had never heard of before. What was tequila?

Later, the giant came over to me. "Hi-ya buddy! You must be the kid who gave all that trouble to the Ruskies and Polskies in the East.

I am Captain Moses Underwood, but you call me Mo, understood? And what's your name? Horst? Say that again? How do you spell that? That's a terrible thing to do to a nice kid like you. Say, you got a middle name? Christian? That I can relate to. All right if I call you Chris? Now I can call out to you. With that other name, I'd always be scared to call out to you. How old are you, anyway? Almost sixteen? Really? Well you look older than that. But that's old enough to smoke and drink where I come from. No? That's okay. Then how about some chocolate, or? Oh, I know! All the German kids go nuts over this—how about some chewing gum?" And he handed me a whole box.

In Planegg I had studied some of Uli's English textbooks. This and listening to the AFN (American Forces Network) Munich and Stuttgart station all day long had improved my language proficiency greatly. But Mo here was a definite challenge. It would take an awful lot of practice—listening and speaking—before I would be able to carry on a conversation.

"Well, Horst," my mother said, "looks like you've made a new friend. That makes two in one evening. Not bad!"

"Two? What do you mean, 'two'? O yeah, I almost forgot: Brigitte."

"What? You have her name already? But you didn't have time to say anything! So, where is she from? How old is she? Is she a refugee? Who are her parents?"

"Yeah, yeah, yeah. Why don't you come along tomorrow and interview her, mother?"

"Oh my God! So you have a date with her? Wait till I tell Anja!"

We had not joked around like this in quite some time.

"Chris, Chris!" someone shouted.

It took me a few seconds to realize that it was I who was being addressed.

"Chris, I have an idea. What about if I pick you up with the jeep tomorrow morning. Do you like to fish?"

Do I like to fish? Was this man toying with me? My second reaction was, oh my God, here we go again! A captain who wants to take me fishing! Almost got me killed last time that happened.

Mo looked at me, waiting for an answer.

"Fishing? Oh yes! I love fishing. What do you use to catch fish? Hand grenades, bazookas, or just dynamite?"

Poor Mo! I could tell he was shocked. Suddenly the conversation and the laughter in the room had subsided; all eyes, grave and concerned eyes, were focusing on me. I could tell what they were thinking: "Poor Käte!"

Fortunately, Mo did not comprehend the seriousness of the moment. He smiled again and continued, "No, no! This is not the Russian front, you know. I have some very fine rods and reels, and I can teach you how to use them, if you like."

Wow! Rods and reels! That had been a dream for a long time. Not even my "fishing uncle" from Berlin had equipment like that!

"So, do you want me to dig up some worms?"

"Oh no, trout don't care much for worms. They go for different kinds of flies."

"So, do you want me to catch some flies? Do they have to be kept alive?"

"No, no, no! I'll take care of everything. We'll be using artificial flies, dry flies mostly, that will float on top of the water. You'll see! That's a beautiful trout stream here in the valley. Full of fish. So—agreed! I'll pick you up around ten."

I don't know how long the others kept on talking, smoking and drinking, but mother and I were dead tired from that horrible trip on the Vomit Special.

Emma had taken care of everything and showed us to our room. Wow! What a day it had been! And tomorrow: fishing for trout with a fly rod—and a black captain. Nobody would believe me if I told them about this stroke of luck. Suddenly, a warm feeling entered into my body, culminating in a brief shudder. I closed my eyes and thought: Brigitte.

That night I dreamed that I was on a train. I was all alone and filled with anxiety because I had to be home by a certain time, and the train was barely moving. Again and again it had to stop, because there were hundreds of cows all around us. They wouldn't move out of the way, closing in on the train from all sides until they were pushing against it, making it rock from side to side. They had bells tied around their necks which rang and rang and rang, louder and louder. Now they rammed their horns against the train, attempting to push it over, and all the time their mooing was piercing my ears. "Shut up, shut up!" I shouted. "Get away from me!"

Something shook me, over and over. I awoke. My mother had grabbed me by the shoulders. "It's all right, Horsti. Just a dream! It's all right."

But it wasn't—because I still heard the bells and the mooing. Day was breaking. I climbed out of bed and went to the window which faced the marketplace. And there was my dream: hundreds of cows, mooing and ringing their bells, marching by our window. Boys my age, shouting and swinging sticks, were driving them toward some distant destination. Exhausted and haunted, I dropped back into bed. Luckily, I was able to fall asleep again.

At the breakfast table, I talked about my reality-induced dream. "Oh yes, you'll get used to this. Happens every morning," someone said. "In the evening, guess what, the whole migration happens in reverse. It's a matter of finding good pastures. Careful where you step, though, when you are walking out there!"

Antek had already left for some job in Kempten. So there would be just Mo and I.

We drove a few kilometers until we came to a swift, meandering mountain stream, the Günz. Mo assembled the rods and explained the mechanics of fly-fishing to me. It didn't sound too difficult, but then trying it was a different story. It was very tricky to land your fly where you wanted it.

Mo selected a wide-open stretch of water where accuracy didn't matter too much. "Now just watch me a few times before you try it."

He pulled out a lot of line before he set his fly onto a patch of calm water. He instantly had a strike.

"Whoa—we came to the right place at the right time with the right fly! It's a biggy! Better get the net, Chris!"

This was exciting! These fish were fighters, unlike lethargic carp! And they were so beautiful with their multicolored, sleek bodies. Good name, rainbow trout!

My turn came. It was not pretty. All my previous fishing experiences were worthless here. The fly landed everywhere except where I wanted it to, mostly behind us in the field. Finally! I hit right where Mo had made his first catch. And again, there was an instant strike! Reeling the fish in proved to be much simpler than casting. But every time I got it close enough to net, it shot away again. Mo ended the fight by stepping into the water and netting it.

After two hours of this my arms were beginning to ache. No idea how many trout we had so far, but it must have been quite a few. "Uh—Mo—how many do you think we need? What do you want to do with them?"

"Well, I thought it would be nice if we had enough for everybody at the house. Let's have a look."

We counted twenty-three, not one under ten inches. We had released countless little ones. What a river! I learned later that this portion of the river had been reserved for visiting party dignitaries. Even Reichsmarschall Göring had fished there once.

"I think this should do," Mo said. "Might be a good idea to clean them right here. Then you wouldn't have that mess at home."

I was shocked. "No, no! We can't clean them yet. These are trout! You have to be very careful not to injure the skin. Otherwise they won't turn blue."

It was very difficult, considering my meager language skills, to explain *Forelle Blau* to Mo. He was more than skeptical.

"You mean, you don't fillet them, dip them in cornmeal and fry them in butter?"

We kept on outgrossing each other by describing the various possibilities for preparing fish. For Mo it was all fried; for me, mostly poached. At last, I won out by announcing that Emma would take care of everything, provided she had some butter, cream, and horseradish. Even after I had found "horseradish" in my little pocket dictionary, it didn't mean anything to Mo. His skepticism grew.

"Perhaps I should bring some hot dogs, too," he mumbled in resignation.

Hot—what?—dogs? I understood "hot" and "dogs." But together? A terrible thought crossed my mind: I had not seen any dogs in the streets of Obergünzburg. Had they all been—heated? As in heat and eat? Perhaps Emma would know. Pig's blood I had managed to endure, but under no circumstances would I ever surrender if it came to dogs.

I was so upset that I hardly opened my mouth all the way back. Mo sensed that something was wrong. A furrow appeared between his brows, his eyes shaded over, an expression of melancholy covered his face. What could have gone wrong? Silently, we pulled up in front of the Schwan. I jumped out of the jeep and ran inside to warn my cousin. He was ten years older than I. He was the one who had recently married Gaby during my Baltic visit. And now they had a dog, a cute fox terrier—presently, the only living dog in Obergünzburg, as far as I could tell. "Werner, Werner, where are you? You have to put Mecky on the leash or hide him!"

I told Werner what I had learned, and he just laughed and laughed. Then he explained.

"Well, damn it! Why do they call them 'hot dogs'? Doesn't make any sense!"

"Well, yes, on the other hand, why do we Germans call pickled herring 'Rollmops'"?

Laughing, I ran outside to snap Mo out of his gloom. "Come on, let's go into the kitchen and show Emma what we caught."

Emma was overwhelmed, but there was more apprehension than joy in her voice. "Twenty-three trout? And who is going to do all the work? Do you think they are self-cleaning?"

"But Emma, these are trout! You told me yourself they are not supposed to be scaled. Aren't we going to make them blue?"

"Blue doesn't mean you don't have to clean out the guts. I hope you'll take over here. The head stays on and don't scrape away any of the slippery stuff. Well, you know what to do. So, grab a sharp knife and get busy. I have to see about the rest of the meal. Could have given me some warning, you know!"

"Right! I'm sorry. I had no idea it would be that easy. Just like pulling fish out of a carp pond. Oh—and Mo should be coming by with the rest of what we need: butter, cream, and horseradish. Can you think of anything else? How about sauerkraut?"

"Sauerkraut? With trout? Are you crazy? The flavor of trout is much too delicate for sauerkraut. No—but a green salad would be nice. Mo should be able to come up with some greens. They have everything in that mess kitchen."

Having a restaurant kitchen at our disposal was of enormous advantage. We even had a gas stove. No shortage of helping hands, either. It was fun to get to know the new in-laws this way.

Gaby's brother Sebastian, Bastel to all who knew him well, had just gotten married to Ursula, called Utte. While we worked, she told me how they had managed to always stay just one step ahead of the Gestapo's last-ditch effort to do away with as many of us "mongrels" as possible.

Then Gaby spoke: She and Werner were both half-Jewish. Thus there were no Nazi objections to their marriage. Bastel, however, was not permitted to marry the blond, blue-eyed Utte. The Nazis had a special term for such unions—Rassenschande (racial pollution). Had he been caught with her, KZ would have been his final destination. But they had been fortunate, and two days after Germany's surrender, they were married in the Obergünzburg church. The party that followed the ceremony was such that it overshadowed all political events. Having arrived just one day before this event, the black GIs were thrilled to be invited to a genuine German wedding. Little did they know that it was partially their beverages and edibles that made them so irresistible. But since then, a genuine bond of friendship had developed.

I found it to be a bit distracting to work with these two young ladies. They were so attractive, laughing, joking, and teasing me about my date with Brigitte. I wished my mother had kept her mouth shut!

"So, how old is she? About twelve? And still wearing pigtails, we've heard! Why didn't you ask us? We would love to go to the dance with you. Perhaps we'll go anyway. I think we should keep an eye on you. Can't trust those native girls! Even if they are only twelve. They say being around cows all day makes them kind of crazy. And just think of the manure smell. Better take some cologne along for her. Well, we'll check her out for you and let you know if it's safe."

They were merciless, but I enjoyed the attention I was receiving.

Mo arrived in good time, delivering butter, cream, and horseradish.

As if we had planned and worked on this for days, everything was ready to be served as planned. Artfully arranged on huge platters and decorated with lemon wedges and parsley, our trout provided all with an unaccustomed visual delight. Never had I nor any of the diners seen a lovelier hue of blue. Sauciers with melted butter, Meissen bowls and platters with parsleyed potatoes and salad completed the picture. But were there no breads, no flaky, buttery rolls for our captain? He sorely missed them, and we had trouble explaining to him that breads are not part of a German dinner.

So, after all the adventures, triumphs, defeats, victories, even deaths and births, now, surrounded by the familiar furnishings, new and old faces, anticipating sensational and long-missed culinary joys, we took our seats, as if nothing had happened. Almost every space at the table was occupied. I counted eighteen, including the guest of honor, Captain Underwood. We all realized that without him this gathering would not be happening, at least not as planned and prepared. Not only had he been instrumental in providing the main attraction for the feast, he had, as a soldier and officer of the U.S. Army, been our liberator, rescuing us from harassment, persecution, and probable death. The fact that he had arrived for this dinner carrying a case of Moselle wine and two huge cans of pineapple only added to our love and admiration for him and the United States.

Of course, I knew exactly what would happen first. No sooner had all of us settled into our chairs, than there was the familiar tapping of silver on glass. My uncle arose, nodding, as his glance swept over the expectant company.

The blond, blue-eyed Utte

As always, his words, though sometimes a bit overbearing, were well chosen. It was not a joyous, triumphant message we received. He briefly welcomed all, especially my mother and me, then quickly and uncharacteristically came to the conclusion: "We mourn our losses but also thank God that he has guided and protected those present, so that they may sit here together, enjoying good food and each other's company, finally free of fears. May they all be successful in using this freedom to rebuild their lives. Amen!"

Quietly, subdued by the solemnity of the moment, we passed the bowls and platters from person to person. After a few bites and several swallows of wine, conversations returned to normal. My mother observed with concern that I was not up to my usual appreciation of fine dining. Hastily I dissected my trout, carefully removing the entire skeleton in one expertly executed motion. A few pieces of potato drizzled with butter and a dollop of horseradish cream completed my plate. There was no denying it: best fish I had ever eaten!

But matters of greater importance were on my mind, seriously interfering with my appetite. Time for the evening festivities at the Goldene Engel was approaching. Would she be there? And when she had said "tomorrow," did that actually mean that she wanted me to be there? My palms were sweaty. This heart-pounding anxiety was a new experience for me.

"Okay, Mama, all right if I go now?"

Leaving the room, I turned once more to wave to everyone. Onkel Pippi had a surprised look on his face. Antek, giving me his blessings, winked at me.

Gingerly tiptoeing across the cow-dung-peppered marketplace, I headed for the Goldene Engel. There was a steady stream of small groups of young ladies and GIs heading in the same direction. Already, the amplified pounding of the drums dominated all other sounds, including the evening bell of the Catholic church. Excitedly, I hummed along with the melody that had invaded all hearts, minds and bodies within the reach of the U.S. Army radio network—"In the Mood." Uli had played an old recording of it from morning till night, driving all the adults crazy. Glenn Miller—another one of my idols—along with Jesse Owens, Hawkeye, Huck Finn and Tom Sawyer.

I peeked into the dance hall: a few dancing couples, but no pigtails anywhere. It was still relatively early, I consoled myself. No acrobatics or cheering sections, so far. I stationed myself just inside the door: in front of me the dance floor, the small tables at either side, the bar in the background. From here I could also keep my eye on the street.

A full moon appeared behind the church steeple. Nine loud bell strikes rang through the night, strangely offsetting the rhythmic pattern of "Chattanooga Shoeshine Boy." I was beginning to feel very disappointed and depressed. If she didn't come, how would I ever be able to find her again?

Activities inside the Goldene Engel were intensifying. The air was filled with laughter, screeching, smoke, airborne human shapes, and loud, loud music. It reminded me of those barroom scenes in the Western movies with which the military government hoped to win the German people over to democracy and the American way of life. No sooner had I made this observation than a loud crash occurred. One of the soldiers had landed on a table, reducing it to kindling. This, however, was not a miscalculated jitterbug maneuver or a clumsy landing, but an act of hostility and the beginning of a regular Western-style brawl, evolving as if choreographed by a master director of action movies. When a beer mug, one of those liter-size monsters, missed my head by just inches, I decided to wait outside for the cessation of hostilities. And there, underneath a lamppost, just like Lili Marleen in that famous soldiers' song, was a young, dainty girl, but she was not waiting for her soldier, nor was she passively standing there; she was struggling desperately to avoid being dragged into the ballroom by a GI. Brigitte—and wouldn't it just be my luck—was squirming, kicking, and swinging her fists whenever she was not hanging onto the lamppost.

Recognizing me, she let out a scream, "Horst! Help, quick!"

When the soldier saw me, he instantly let go and vanished into the night.

If I had expected Brigitte to cry or shake, wanting to go home to mother, I was mistaken. "Thank you, Horst! That was just in time! One second more and I would have killed him—pow!" And she executed a sweeping, powerful blow through the air, followed by a kick higher than my head. Then she calmly smoothed her hair and straightened out her blouse and skirt. "I think we can go inside now. Really feel like dancing after this!" she said.

"What the hell was that?" I asked.

"Was what?"

"Well, that kick! I saw something similar in a movie once. Is that some sort of Japanese fighting? Like Judo?"

"Yeah, you are close. It's called karate. My father was really good at it. He worked in Korea for a few years. You should see what my brother can do! You wouldn't want to mess with him."

I was totally dumbfounded. This young and beautiful creature, so lithe and svelte, with her pigtails—how did all this fit together with her combative nature? I could not take my eyes off her. Her hands and feet were so small and delicate! And ach! Her nose! Never had I seen a more appealing nose: small and straight until you came to the ever-so-slightly turned-up end. She smiled at me, took my hand, just as yesterday, and pulled me onto the dance floor.

She knew all the moves, teaching them to me as we went.

Where did she learn to dance like this? it flashed through my mind.

As if she had read my mind, she said, "My brother and I have been watching and practicing. I hope, you'll meet him."

"How old is he?"

"Seventeen."

"And how old are you?" I asked.

"Almost sixteen. How about you?"

"Same."

For some reason that seemed to please her.

"Oh, I thought you might be older. I don't like older boys."

She knew the names of most of the songs they were playing: "Don't Sit Under the Apple Tree," "String of Pearls," "Hey—Daddy," "Give Me Five Minutes More," and the all-time favorite, "Hey! Ba-Ba-Re-Bop."

Now a hush fell over this excited, sweating, panting collection of humanity. Couples came to a stop, moved closer together and just stood there motionless as if turned into pillars of salt. Had our reckless abandon to wild and frivolous music so provoked the wrath of God that He had found it befitting to send down His punishment? But the earth did not shake; no fire and brimstone fell upon us. Instead, the lights were dimmed way down low, and then the music resumed, soothing the overheated, frenzied creatures: slow, low, utterly lovely music and a woman's voice, so honey dripping, sweet and mellow, that my whole body tingled. Actually, what caused my body to react in this unusual but hugely delightful manner was not just that woman's voice but primarily Brigitte, who was snuggling up to me, putting her cheek on mine, her arm cradling my neck.

"'Sentimental Journey'," she whispered, "just follow my lead."

But there was not much to follow. We, as every other couple, just stood there, gently rocking back and forth with the rhythm. Made me think of another one of my favorite tunes: "Cheek to Cheek."

So I was not the first one to notice the close association between "dancing cheek to cheek" and "heaven"! Now, finally, the words made sense. I had to admit, whoever had written that song knew what he was talking about. As the music played on, I had but one wish, "Please, don't ever let this song end!" But I needed no heavenly powers to grant me this wish, for quite some time, anyway. It may have looked funny, but from then on we did not let go of each other, no matter what song they played, no matter what the other couples around us were doing.

I was familiar with "Good Night Ladies"; I knew what it meant, but I could not let go.

"Horst," she whispered, "Horst, they are going to lock the doors. We have to go! I have school tomorrow, but I'll be back. You can meet me at the bus stop at 1:45. Come, and walk me home now. It's not far."

"Not far? But I need *far*. Can't you make it far? Ten kilometers would be just fine with me."

"Yes! With me too! But just think how lucky we are that we can see each other every day now, if we want to. Isn't that a happy prospect?"

I put my arm around her and we started to walk. Naturally, she led the way: once around the church, twice around the church, three times around the church. We did not say much. We talked, yes, but our words had nothing to do with reality. We just pretended that they were important so we would have a reason to keep walking.

Back at the Schwan, my mother was nervously waiting up for me.

She started firing questions at me but suddenly stopped. "Well, I am glad you are back. Perhaps you'll be able to tell me about it tomorrow."

What a sensitive, sensible woman!

It took me a long time to get to sleep that night. My thoughts kept revolving around Brigitte. Over and over I relived every moment of our evening together. The outcome was the same every time. This was the most powerful feeling I had ever experienced. It was so strong it made my eyes moist. I had read about human sexuality and had had the usual juvenile discussions about it with friends. But they and the books had been wrong: there was not the slightest bit of erotic longing for her. Holding her—yes! But beyond that—nothing. I looked at my watch—thirteen hours to go!

Over breakfast, my mother looked at me quizzically. "Well, did you have a wonderful evening with Brigitte? Will I get to meet her?"

I nodded, but was not ready yet to talk about the evening. "Later, Mama. And what did you and the others decide in the meantime? Are we going to stay? I would really like that, but I think I should start going back to school again now. What do you think?"

"Well, that's a shocking development. Of course, Brigitte has nothing to do with this! I think I like her already. Does she travel by train to Kempten or Kaufbeuren to attend the Gymnasium there?"

"I am meeting her at 1:45 at the bus station. I'll find out then."

"Hm-hm."

XII

Maternal interrogations, transition from bombs to the big band sound

SEVERAL SCHOOLCHILDREN EMERGED FROM the bus. They must have been mostly refugees from Germany's eastern provinces, because I was able to understand what they were saying. Brigitte was one of the last ones getting off. This was the first time I saw her in broad daylight. Her hair, light brown, almost blond; her eyes, blue-grey with a few specks of green. I was unable to take my eyes off her because she looked so familiar. Had I met her before?

And then a name from long ago came back to me: *Das schöne Marlenchen*, the beautiful Marlene. I suddenly felt as I had when I was a little boy, and Oma, for the umpteenth time, read to me from my favorite book, and I could look at the pictures of Marlenchen. There were several color pictures of her, and that's why I could not take my eyes off Brigitte; to me she looked exactly like the beautiful Marlene.

As on the previous evening, I was surprised at how, with all her daintiness, she carried herself with such strength and agility. She was happy to see me, but a little bashful in the presence of other students. "Let's get out of here!" she said.

"Out of here" meant walking about two blocks. We did and found ourselves surrounded by cows.

She took my hand; we looked at each other and started laughing. Nothing mattered anymore—neither that I had just stepped into a cow pie, nor that an enormous bull was watching us suspiciously. We would have liked a place to sit, but that was not so simple. Finally, between some boulders, we found a log. Fall was in the air, the sun was still warm, but the wind made us shiver. We put our arms around each other and huddled together.

"Tomorrow I'll bring a blanket," I said.

We did not sit very long because it was getting chillier by the minute.

"Wouldn't be surprised if we get some flurries. No big mountains around here, but I'll bet we could find some nice hills for skiing. Do you like to ski?" I asked.

She shrugged her shoulders. "Don't know. Never tried it, but it sure looks like fun, gliding silently through thick, fluffy snow. Why? Do you have skis?"

"No, not yet. But that's one of the items on my list. Skis, and a bicycle."

She shook her head skeptically. "To get things like that you either have to be a farmer with a lot of extra butter and eggs, or you have to have something good for the black market, cigarettes, dollars, or jewelry."

I didn't say anything, but I still had a few nice pieces from our treasure hidden away.

We strolled back to the marketplace, undecided what to do next.

"Feel like coming over to my place to meet everybody?" We said it in almost perfect unison and thought this was hilarious.

"My mother has already said she likes you and hopes to be introduced soon," I continued.

"Okay then, let's go to your place, because my mother doesn't know anything about you, though she asked a lot of questions. On the other hand, if she doesn't meet you, she might not let me go out again tonight. If we hurry, we can do both places. Let's go!"

That sounded just as determined as last evening when she had said, "One second more and I would have killed him—pow!"

Three minutes later we were in our kitchen. My mother was there, and Emma. I had never been in a situation like that and felt a bit awkward. Not so Brigitte! With the sweetest smile on her face, she walked up to my mother, extended her hand and said, "Guten Tag," not Grüss Gott, "I am Brigitte Hilgendorf."

My mother shook her hand, smiled back at her and said, "And I am Horst's mother. So you probably know my name."

"Uh—gee—Mama, actually, she doesn't. We haven't really had enough time for details like that. So—uh—Brigitte, this is my mother, Frau Küter," whereupon they shook hands once more.

I should have warned Brigitte about this, because here came the questions which, in my opinion, could be quite tedious. But Brigitte handled everything beautifully, and perhaps it was even useful to know a few of the basic facts about her family. For example, where they were from: Danzig; her father's occupation: architect; was he living with them? No, he had fallen on the Western front near the end of the war—a major; and her mother: a violinist, trying to establish herself locally as a teacher.

"Oh Horst, did you hear this? Her mother is a musician! Did you tell Brigitte that your father played the viola in the symphony orchestra?"

"Mother! I told you that we haven't had time for stuff like that."

Brigitte seemed to enjoy herself more and more, especially after Emma had brought in the remaining Streuselkuchen. "Do you like to cook and experiment with recipes like Horst?" she asked. "I am sure he must have told you about the goose and the carp!"

"Well, no," Brigitte replied. "Actually, we have not had time for stuff like that."

Emma and my mother exchanged meaningful looks.

"Do you have any brothers and sisters?" mother asked.

"Oh yes, one brother, Erhard, seventeen, and two younger sisters. We take the train to Kempten every day to go to school."

"Well, with your mother being a musician, do you and your siblings play instruments?"

Aha! Now we had arrived in the territory that was closest to mother's heart. Not, as mentioned earlier, that mother was in any way endowed with musical talent, she simply loved music and, as the widow of a musician, felt morally and emotionally obligated to promote her husband's profession. Brigitte's anxiously awaited answer would forever determine mother's attitude toward her and her family. I held my breath.

"Oh yes! We all do! Erhard is really good on the piano. He can play anything! I play the cello, Margrit the viola, and Annemarie the flute. We often play together and give little concerts. You must come and listen. Next Sunday evening we'll be playing in church."

I must say, Brigitte had an uncanny instinct for what really mattered to my mother. If she played the cello as well as she played my mother, she had to be a master on her instrument. She went on and on about their studies, their concerts, and the competitions they had won. Suddenly she stopped and turned to me.

"What about you, Horst? Your father was a musician, so it must be in your blood, too. Do you play anything?"

Uh-oh! Apparently, this was something that mattered to her. I groped for an acceptable answer, but mother, sensing my predicament, came to my aid.

"Yes, he studied the violin for a few years, but then with the war, and his teacher gone, we gave it up."

She did not mention that this teacher, a colleague of my father, had to wear the yellow star and that he, as so many of our friends and relatives, had ended up in Theresienstadt. It had been my mother's experience that the less said in regard to the Jewish connection, the better. "But Horst has a wonderful voice and loves to sing."

"Really! That's great! Voice and cello sound beautiful together. We'll have to try that. Oh, it's going to be so much fun!" She skipped over to me, hugged me, and threw her arms around my neck.

I blushed as my mother quickly bent down to fix something on her shoe.

"Okay," Brigitte said, "it must be getting late. We better go now."

"Will you be back later on tonight?" my mother asked me, not entirely without a trace of sarcasm in her voice.

"Oh sure," Brigitte answered happily. We are just going over for introductions. Then we'll be back."

"You will?" my mother asked. "I mean, do you mean the two of you?"

That question seemed to surprise Brigitte. "Why yes! We want to go to the dance again. They are having a jitterbug contest tonight. We are going to win!"

That was news to me. But for the moment, the thought that the "I" of me had turned into a "we" was utterly intoxicating.

"Well then, perhaps I can invite you to have a bite to eat with us before you go to the dance?"

"Oh, thank you! That would be lovely."

"Lovely"—where had she learned to say exactly what my mother would say under similar circumstances? I could see it now. My uncle would have a ball with this young lady—or she with him!

My mother seemed favorably impressed, and Antek, who had just dropped in, gave me an encouraging and approving wink.

I immediately liked Erhard. He was tall, slender, with wavy hair, and cool serious blue eyes. He was practicing the piano when we entered but got up to greet us. "Great!" he said when he found out where I came from. "We have a little soccer team here—all refugees. We play the local boys and usually kill them. You look real fast, somehow. Do you play?"

"Sure do! I played a lot in school. We had a very good team in our class."

"Okay, I'll let you know when the next practice is. And I can get you some gear to wear. The Amis* help us a lot with equipment."

One by one, I met the entire family. Frau Hilgendorf was a bit intimidating. Her dark hair was pulled back tightly, which gave her face a rather stern appearance, but she had kind eyes and a warm smile, as she interrogated me in very much the same fashion as my mother had Brigitte.

"And Horst and I are going to have a duet together," Brigitte broke into the dialogue. "He is going to sing, and I'll do the accompaniment. This is so exciting! I can't wait to give it a try." And she scooted over and embraced me, just the way she had done in our kitchen. I guess that left no question in her mother's mind as to my role in her daughter's life.

Frau Hilgendorf cleared her throat discreetly and subjected me to an intensified continuation of the interrogation. I did my best to be as vague as possible when points of political consequence were raised.

Brigitte did not like this lengthy talk. She had more important things on her mind, like the jitterbug contest tonight. "Erhard," she said, "you have to help us! There is that contest at the Goldene Engel, and we want to win."

"Well, what do you want me to do? How can I help you?"

"You always have such great ideas. Why don't you play one of those jitterbug tunes? We'll dance and try to come up with a routine; you check it and tell us how to do it better."

"Okay, so, what do you want me to play? Any idea what they'll pick?"

"Well, not really, except that they have been playing "Hey! Ba-Ba-Re-Bop" more than anything else. I'll bet that's the one."

"Okay—here we go."

I was so stunned at his performance that I forgot all about dancing and just listened. He got more rhythm into that tune than the band on the record. I applauded when he stopped. "Wow, that was absolutely super! I wish you could play for us at the dance."

Actually, why can't he? I reflected. After all, what good is it to have the commanding officer of this town as a friend, if I can't ask him for favors?

Then we got to work. Dancing with Brigitte was so wonderful! She

*Germans routinely used this term when referring to Americans.

had so much rhythm and athletic ability and grace. Tossing her around was simple because she was light as a feather, yet her legs were like steel springs. It did not take Erhard long to come up with some really innovative ideas. He knew what his sister was capable of doing, so he had her do some flips and handsprings, which simply amazed me. "Where did you learn to move like that?" I asked.

"Oh, I took gymnastics for a couple of years back home—helps with the karate."

"I don't know! That's almost unfair competition."

"Oh, come on! They won the real war! We can win this one!"

I hoped Mo would visit us early in the Schwan, so I could make my suggestion to him. Suddenly I was in a hurry to return. "Oh, I just remembered. There is something I have to do at home. I better get going."

No doubt: the devil had made me say this. There was no room for happiness like ours in his manual. He required the presence of distrust and strife in the hearts of mankind, so he could win them over for his evil intentions.

I instantly regretted my words. Brigitte stopped her dancing around, looking reproachfully at me with her big eyes, that were slowly filling with tears. *"I?"* she uttered, seemingly without comprehension. *"I?"*

Oh, what a creature! Were all women like that? It dawned on me that there was nothing more fragile and complicated than a woman's heart. On the one hand, Brigitte was tough as nails; on the other— what did I know?

"I am so sorry, Brigitte. But all this is so new to me. I have never been a *we* before."

"Really?" she asked, visibly relieved. The thought of her being a first in my life seemed to comfort her.

Frau Hilgendorf had witnessed this interlude with considerable alarm.

"Just a couple more minutes, please!" Brigitte said. "I have to change a bit for tonight. You know—if I do flips and things."

Aha! This was the chance I had been waiting for! This might help her to understand. *"I?"* I said, *"I* have to change? What happened to *we?"*

She blushed and chuckled.

Her mother glanced at me with disapproval. "I'll help you, Brigitte," she said quickly.

That left me alone with Erhard and the two younger sisters, who were sort of sniffing me over like the new puppy in their litter.

"Hey, why don't you get your instruments and we'll try to play that song together," Erhard suggested to his sisters.

To my surprise, they were eager to display their musical prowess to me. They fiddled and fluted around Erhard's melody, as if they had been rehearsing for weeks. Occasionally another one would take the lead and the others would harmonize.

"Hey," Annemarie said to me, "you can sing, Brigitte told us. Do you know the words to this song?"

"I'm not sure, but what the heck! I can always fake it." I hummed along for a few bars and then began to fit in the words, first very softly, but gradually working up to full volume, trying to imitate the American accent the way I remembered it from the recording. By the time Brigitte and her mother reappeared, we were in full swing.

Oh my God! I thought. How will she take this? Am I doing an *I* where I should have waited for the *we* to happen?

Fortunately she was too impressed to spend time trying to analyze our quartet. So I quickly took the initiative and called to her. "Hurry up and give us a hand with your cello; we've been waiting for you!"

She quickly did, and it was amazing to hear how we all blended in together. Even Frau Hilgendorf managed a big smile and modestly tapped her foot to the beat.

But now it was really getting late.

"Okay," I said, "we have to go, but we'll surely get together again. I'm so glad we did this."

Everyone was awaiting us at the Schwan. Mother, Emma, and Antek must have been busy giving their versions of the saga of Brigitte and Horst. Entering the dining room was like running the gauntlet. There were people present I had never seen before. Brigitte smiled right and left, like a princess striding to her coronation. At the end of the line, there stood my uncle, tall, white haired, beaming in delight, arms opened wide, intent to receive us—probably only her—into his embrace. I had alerted Brigitte to his somewhat unusual personality and to his flowery language. "Oh my blessed little princess, how delighted we all are to make your acquaintance. I am sure everyone here knows who you are, but it would be pointless, indeed cruel, to try to tell you the names of all these lovely people. So, if you will allow me, I'll escort you to your place. Please, grant me the honor and let me be your dining partner tonight. Horst on your right, I on your left."

He paused briefly, glancing from side to side. Was he gathering ammunition for another barrage? An expression of joy suddenly appeared upon his face. Had he found a way to turn this elaborate greeting of an individual into a more general address? He must have come up with something extraordinary because now there was a triumphant smile on his lips. And boy, was I right!

"Our table may not be laden with exquisite culinary delights, but"— and his voice gathered strength—"I challenge any group of diners anywhere to equal, never mind surpass, the perfection of feminine beauty that is assembled here tonight: my two daughters-in-law, our new dear in-law Utte, my very own daughter Sophie, and my wife's sister Käte, and now, still a child, but ready to burst into full bloom, this little princess, Brigitte. Please, be seated, all of you. And, as our beloved poet Heinrich Heine expressed in his immortal poem: 'I pray that God may keep you, so pure and fair and sweet'."

I had to hand it to the old romantic—a little overbearing the whole thing, but closing his address with the Heine poem was pure genius. My mother kicked me under the table, a reminder that we had heard the poem many times back home, set to music by—was it Schubert or Schumann?

Actually, the poem "Du bist wie eine Blume"* was set to music by both composers, but I could not remember which one I had liked better.

It was indeed a modest meal, disappointing after my uncle's elaborate speech. Just some cold chicken, courtesy of Uncle Sam, a bit of green salad, and the customary sliced dark bread with a little cheese and butter.

In view of the coming events, neither Brigitte nor I ate very much. Furthermore, I was nervously awaiting Mo's arrival. When he finally entered, I jumped up and, before he could settle down with a drink, ushered him into a corner. Then I beckoned to Brigitte to come over to meet him.

"Oh, I have noticed you," he said. "You sometimes come to watch the dancing. And now you are Chris's friend! He is so lucky! I am jealous!"

*You Are Like a Flower

"Chris? Who is Chris? This is Horst." Brigitte sounded indignant.

"Yeah, yeah, I know. But I have a hard time with the word—that name. So I call him Chris. Please, forgive me."

He turned to me. "So, what's up, buddy? Can I help you? Coming over to the dance later? There is that contest tonight, did you know that?"

"Yes, we know," Brigitte replied. "We are going to win!"

Her English was as amazing as her high kicks, and the determination in her voice startled Mo. "Well, I hope you do! More power to you."

"That's what I wanted to talk to you about," I said. "Brigitte's brother is a truly outstanding pianist. You should hear him sometime. He can play all those songs. Could you give him permission to play at the dance?"

"How do you mean? Play all the time, instead of records?"

"Oh no! I don't mean that. Just a couple of times. In between numbers, you know? Or could he possibly play for the contest? I've heard him play 'Hey! Ba-Ba-Re-Bop'. He could really make the place rock."

"I don't think it would be fair to have him play for the contest. But in between numbers? I think it's a great idea to bring in some local talent. If he is anything like Brigitte, I can't wait to meet him."

"Are you going to be there?" I asked. "Are you one of the judges?"

"Yes, I'll be there, but no, I won't be a judge. Officers can't be judges. Enlisted men and some locals will be the judges, six altogether. Well, I better get over there. It's getting late."

Brigitte had disappeared for a moment, and now she was back. What a transformation! She had undone her pigtails, leaving her hair loosely held together by a silvery barrette. Mo looked at her, shaking his head and said, "Now, this is what I'd call unfair competition! I think you have just won the contest."

She smiled at him and nodded as if to say, "Told you so."

My uncle, joining us now, placed a light kiss on her forehead. "Good luck, my little princess!"

Gaby said, "I think we should all go over there and cheer and take along some rotten potatoes we could throw, in case they don't win."

There were already many couples on the dance floor when we arrived. You could tell that they all had worked out little routines. Several of them looked rather good. There was one slender and very athletic private who really knew what he was doing. Fortunately for us, his partner, though attractive, just couldn't get her feet off the ground, at least not both of them at the same time. I almost felt sorry for her. I could see it in her eyes; at this moment she would have given anything to be back home, surrounded by the warm safety of her bovine friends. Her face was already bright red, little rivulets of perspiration had dug out channels and canyons through the make-up on her cheeks, the white blouse of her *Dirndl* clung lifelessly to her back and bosom. It was a hopeless situation. She knew it, her partner knew it. Later on I tried to find her again among the dancers, but she and her friend had vanished. I hoped she had found her way back to the reassuring company of her cows, which expected nothing of her but warm fingers and a gentle touch.

Brigitte and I danced conservatively. We did not want to reveal what we had in store for later. Erhard was there, waiting for Mo to arrive and introduce him. His sisters had also come, to watch and listen.

We were beginning to feel a bit nervous, wishing something would happen. When would Erhard be given the chance to play—if at all? And the contest? Everyone would be exhausted if this dragged on much longer. I had not seen Mo at all. Was there a problem? Finally he appeared, signaling me to come to him. He asked, "Is your friend here, and can he play right now?"

He beckoned a few of his men to push the piano into the foreground. Erhard was following closely, ready to go.

"Ladies and gentlemen," Mo began, "just today I was informed that there is a special talent in our midst, a master, though very young, on the piano. What a wonderful change from nothing but recordings! Feel free to dance or just listen. Please, welcome—" And he leaned over and whispered, "What's his name?—Erhard Hilgendorf!"

The wrinkled brows and critical comments lasted only for a few seconds; then there were smiles, nodding heads, and tapping feet. "In the Mood" ended with shouts, clapping and whistling. Erhard kept right on playing, producing a seamless string of melodies, one popular song after another, now and then weaving in the latest German hits. Many of the couples were dancing again, applauding when he finally paused for a break.

Mo was more than pleased. "Young man, that was absolutely outstanding! I hope we can do this again. In the meantime, here—," and he handed him two cartons of Lucky Strike, not to be smoked by Erhard and his buddies, for sure, but to be traded for anything of value.

Erhard beamed. This was worth about ten pounds of butter on the black marked or two pairs of shoes or fifteen pounds of sugar—or 200 marks, for which one could not get anything useful.

"And now, ladies and gentlemen! What you all have been waiting for, rehearsing for, losing sleep over: the U.S. Army all-Germany, uhh, I mean, all-American-Zone-jitterbug contest!"

Huge applause.

"We will be playing a number of familiar tunes. Our judges—three Americans and three Germans—will circulate around the dance floor. They will eliminate couples by tapping them on the shoulder. The four remaining couples will continue to dance to the melody of 'Hey! Ba-Ba-Re-Bop' for ten minutes. After that the judges will cast their votes. May the best team win!"

Dancers lined up for their numbers. There must have been fifty couples. Someone pinned the number twenty-three onto our backs. Looking appraisingly at all these competitors I concluded that our chances had to be better than average—just from the physical appearances alone: there were those huge, lean GIs and their not-so-lean, short-and-cuddly partners. True, I had seen them fly through the air, but unfortunately, landing was part of the deal. And there, but for very few exceptions, lay the problem: they screeched, stumbled, fell, lost the rhythm, and totally frustrated their partners.

Brigitte seemed cool and calm, but her hand clasping mine was hot and moist. In her mind she was probably running through her varied routines, from sliding in split position between my legs, to doing a backward flip with minimal help from me, to several handsprings and cartwheels. An ambitious routine! Her nerves had to be as taut as the strings of her cello. Repeatedly she bent over to check the oak floor, whose smoothness and polish were so crucial to a successful slide.

The music started. We enjoyed the rhythm, dancing very close for a few beats, then separating in the typical jitterbug fashion, back and forth, in and out, whirling simultaneously in opposite directions and coming together again without missing a beat. Nothing fancy yet, but I think the judges looked upon us with favor. Gradually, certain couples discreetly withdrew from the dance floor.

I signaled to Brigitte. "Let's do that split and slide."

She nodded, danced a few paces further away from me than usual, then with lightning speed she approached me, went into the split position and slid, carried by her momentum, through my spread legs, catapulted back into an upright position, whirling around and returning to me as if nothing had happened. We beamed at each other while the bystanders' clapping and whistling swept over us.

"God, let's do this again!" I outshouted the ruckus.

Perhaps the maneuver itself was nothing too remarkable, but what really made the difference was the perfect timing—the slide and instant return to her feet without missing a single beat, holding that smile all the while.

It did not take long until we were one of the four finalists. And here was our song, "Hey! Ba-Ba-Re-Bop"! The song we had rehearsed to! We did the entire routine the way Erhard had choreographed it for us: slides, handsprings, cartwheels, and as the climax, a somersault high up, complete with perfect landing, and again, without missing a beat.

The music stopped and we retreated to the corner where our support team had congregated—all of Brigitte's siblings, my mother, Gaby, Utte, Bastel, and Antek. Antek winked at us. "If you didn't win this one, I'm going back to Poland," he said.

Fortunately, it didn't come to that. Mo finally showed up to make the announcement, giving a little speech praising the spirit of reconciliation between the nations, expressing hope for future joint activities, and looking forward to the day when Germany would be a democratic country, a trusted ally of the United States.

All who understood his message, and that included very few of the Fräuleins, applauded halfheartedly, as if to imply, can we please get on with it now?

Brigitte kept squeezing my hand, probably wondering why I was so calm. From what I had seen, there was no doubt in my mind who would be the winner. More intriguing was the question, what would be a worthy first prize? Would it be something valuable, useful, or merely a token item of no significance? Perhaps the all-purpose, universally appreciated gift of the day, the month, the year: a couple of cartons of cigarettes? I hoped it would be something more imaginative, but who knows, some officer may have made the decision: cigarettes for all winners. Simple, practical, cheap.

Mo paused, went over to the table where the judges were still deliberating.

Soon he returned with a piece of paper. "Ladies and gentlemen! We thank the judges for performing their difficult task so well. All four couples danced well and are worthy of being finalists. And my congratulations to all the couples who came to compete. In my book they are all winners—winners in our efforts to rebuild after all the destruction. For the first time, perhaps, Americans and Germans united to achieve a common goal in truly democratic fashion."

I began to wonder if my uncle had assisted him with this speech. They had been up drinking and talking for a long time the night before.

"But, sad as it may be, this was, after all, a contest, and as you all know, there can be only one first place so—"

There was a third, and a second and a first runner-up couple. Our number was not mentioned among them.

I began to feel a little guilty, because having Brigitte perform with all her training and ability was a bit unfair. Mo's voice snapped me out my morose thoughts. "Now then—and it was such a difficult decision—let us applaud couple number twenty-three, whose last somersault will be remembered for a long time. As for the prize—I think you'll be surprised—but just yesterday they shipped us a few of these wonderful items, which you'll see in a minute, and what better place to use them than here?"

He motioned to two GIs who quickly left, leaving us excited and puzzled as to what he might be talking about. A few minutes later the two soldiers returned, pushing in two apparently brand-new bikes, sturdy, heavy-duty vehicles with headlights and baggage carriers. Schwinn it said on them. I had seen ads with that name.

Bikes! I could hardly believe it. Ever since that Polish Milizia man in Breslau had abused our local cobblestones with the steel rims of my bike, I had longed for the day when I would once more be able to enjoy the mobility of my own set of wheels.

As Mo came over to shake our hands and to congratulate us I said, "Thank you, Mo. How did you know? This is what I have been wanting for a long time. Thank you, thank you so much! We will think of you when we explore the countryside together."

Brigitte gave him her sweetest smile and a peck on the cheek. He took a little step backwards in surprise, and an expression of mild shock appeared on his face. Just a fraction of a second it lingered there; then he regained his composure and concluded, "Thank you Brigitte and thank you Chris, for bringing Erhard, for dancing, and for winning. This has been a great evening. I am so happy that everything went the way it did. Enjoy your bikes!"

We biked around the marketplace a few times; then we placed both bikes in a secure room in the Schwan. Biking was fun but in no way matched the pleasure of walking with our arms wrapped around each other.

That night was the first time we kissed.

"Now we belong to each other forever," she whispered.

In the Schwan everyone was still up, waiting to celebrate us. They were disappointed that I came alone.

"And where is Brigitte? Oh yes, I almost forgot, she is only twelve," Utte teased. "So she had to get home to her mother. No! Seriously though! You hold onto that girl!"

As I lay awake later, I reviewed the events of the evening in my mind. Everything had gone so well, but behind it all, like a shadow, hovered Mo's face with that expression of shock. Strange, but it was the only way I could picture him now, as if there existed no other Mo. The longer I puzzled over this, the more convinced I became that Brigitte had probably been the first white woman who had ever touched him, touched him affectionately and in a totally natural way. I could not come up with any other explanation. What was really going on behind all that talk about American freedom and equality, I wondered.

XIII

How I encountered local cuisine, how and why I fought with my mother, and how the priest enforced God's will

FOR THE MOMENT IT was a wonderful, almost idyllic, existence for the occupants of the Schwan. We were all together, without being too cramped; food supply was adequate; socializing with the GIs, as well as exposure to comic books, newspapers and magazines, were stimulating and educational.

Brigitte and I explored the surrounding countryside, riding our bikes along dirt roads that wound their way up and down through forests and fields, past isolated farms and little lakes. It was a beautiful autumn's end. Occasional patches of beech trees, birches, and oaks lit up the darkness of the pines. Though there were some night frosts, early afternoons were often warm and sunny.

We all knew it could not go on like this forever, and gradually, family by family, the Schwan crew shrank in size. First, Utte and Bastel had found an apartment, then Werner and Gaby, followed by Gaby's parents, and then by Carla, Otto's widow, with her son, mother, and grandmother.

When Sophie's husband suddenly appeared after having escaped from a POW camp in France, he and Sophie decided to move to his hometown, Baden Baden, in the French Zone. They took Emma along. That left my mother and me; my uncle was soon lucky enough to find a little apartment in a little house owned and occupied by an amusing landlady, Frau Steck.

Situated on the outskirts of Obergünzburg, the ivy-covered, half-timbered old farmhouse was the kind that photographers and artists would seek out for commercial or personal reasons. It did not take our GIs very long to decide that if they wanted any memento from

Germany at all, then it would have to be a picture of that house. So, Onkel Pippi, who was a good artist, produced watercolor after watercolor for them. He smiled sweetly, acting like an embarrassed child, when his customers insisted on leaving cigarettes or liquor, even dollars, with him.

Over the years I have often wondered how many homes there are in the United States today with a small picture of that farmhouse hanging on one of the walls: "Oh that? I don't really know where that is. My father brought it back from Germany after World War II."

Frau Steck, a single, middle-aged woman, lived there all alone, happy to rent a couple of rooms to a famous artist. This woman was a curious creature. She had a rather deep voice, and her favorite topic of conversation was the merit and nature of all sorts of shaving paraphernalia. Already by three o'clock in the afternoon, blue shadows on her cheeks and chin proclaimed impatiently that it was time for a second shave.

While my uncle lived in her house, he became witness to a passionate courtship between his landlady and a male nurse. Common interest laid the foundation for their relationship—both of them used the same brand of razorblades and shaving cream. As a matter of fact, they had met in a drugstore while queuing up for these objects.

The wedding date was set, and my uncle presented them with a nice oil painting of the house, as well as a year's supply of American shaving cream.

One thing flawed their happiness. In order to be at work on time, Joseph had to get up at six every morning. Why then was the

Carla

alarm always ringing at four? Not just occasionally, but every morning? Finally, my uncle could not bear it any longer. "My dearest lady, how awful that you have to get up at four every morning. Is there some sort of sickness that requires special round-the-clock attention?"

She blushed, which gave her cheeks an eerie shade of purple, and stammered, "Oh my, you see, we are still on our honeymoon, and early morning is the only time when no one will bother us."

Though a bit scary, she was a very sweet lady who occasionally prepared some regional specialty for us. Among these was a dish I grew particularly fond of. I had heard the word before and often wondered what it would taste like. The name itself did not give me any clue: *Spätzle*, the diminutive form of the word *Spatz* (sparrow). So, "little sparrows"—not exactly something to make my mouth water.

I had asked my mother and Emma, who had shrugged their shoulders: "Nothing to get excited about, just little noodley things." Thus, when Frau Steck one day proudly invited me to have some Spätzle with her, I did not jump with joy.

As I entered her house two days later, my nostrils immediately assured me that I would not be disappointed. An unbelievably sweet aroma combining sautéed onion, butter and cheese filled the air, making my stomach growl with anticipation. This I had to investigate! Perhaps it deserved to be incorporated into my repertoire of memorable dishes! Following my unfailing instincts in such matters, I found my way into the kitchen.

Frau Steck was a little startled to see an unexpected visitor in her domain but offered me her polite Grüss Gott, which I returned. Then there was silence. These Allgäuers are not known for their loquaciousness.

"This is so enticing, I just could not resist coming into the kitchen. Is it the Spätzle that produce this wonderful fragrance?" I asked.

This question seemed to bother her. A furrow appeared on her forehead, and she shook her head in bewilderment.

Was it my pronunciation or the choice of vocabulary? I wondered. After a few seconds I tried once more: "Good smell here! What is it, the Spätzle?"

Now she smiled and nodded vehemently: "No, no!"

This was turning out to be more difficult than I had anticipated. I had always been under the impression that a nod meant yes. "May I look, see the Spätzle? I am very interested in cooking, and I would like to learn from you how to make this."

"Ah, yes, of course," she nodded and smiled. "Look into that pot over there. That's where they are."

I lifted the lid and peered into the pot. Whitish, noodley looking things filled it. No smell at all. "Very interesting, but what smells so good?"

"Ah," she nodded and smiled. "Look into this skillet here!"

Yes, of course! A lot of onion sautéed in butter, as my nose told me. Next to it stood a bowl of shredded cheese—local Swiss, I guessed, about half a pound. Now I had all the parts together. I nodded and smiled.

"Very good, very interesting. What do you do with all that? Mix it together?"

Again she nodded, but she said, "No, no!" The nodding had to be her way of indicating to me that she had comprehended the question. But this time there was a follow-up. She must have decided to take on the role of guide or educator for this poor, homeless foreigner. There was no stopping or interrupting her now. She was even making an attempt at speaking High German.

She got out an ancient-looking book, handwritten in the old German script. "From my grandmother," she explained. Then she deciphered with difficulty: "Combine 250 grams of flour with two eggs and a pinch of salt; then slowly add 1/8 of a liter of warm water and beat this mixture until it is very smooth; pass this through a *Spätzlemaschine,* letting the drops fall into boiling salted water. When these rise to the top, take them out and submerge them in cold water." So much for the handwritten recipe.*

Then I learned how to turn this rather bland product into a memorable experience. She instructed me to layer, into a casserole, one inch of Spätzle on the bottom, then onion, then about half an inch of grated cheese, and so on until we had repeated the sequence three or four times. The top layer we covered with breadcrumbs, then sprinkled it with grated cheese, and finished by covering everything with little flakes of butter.

This we baked at moderate heat until the top was golden brown— at which point we took it out and devoured it.

As I found out, there also exists a variation on this dish, called

---

*For the benefit of all who love to experiment with new things, I would like to add that Spätzle-machines, very simple and inexpensive manual gadgets, basically a can with large holes, can be purchased in cookery stores, complete with recipe.

Krautspätzle: combine the Spätzle with precooked sauerkraut, sautéed onion, bacon or cubed ham, and fry it all in a skillet—a dish for hearty eaters. Spätzle also go well with gravy-rich meats: venison, beef, and pork roasts, even sauerbraten.

Returning to our Schwan after such an outing—now all alone in that large house—had turned into a depressing event. Something had to be done, because heating this place would be impossible. We discussed various options with relatives who supplied us with well-meant but not very satisfactory advice. One of the options was to move to Kempten where my mother could work in my cousin Hannes's pottery, art studio and store, while I could attend the Gymnasium there. Naturally, I was opposed to any plan that would separate me from Brigitte. True, she would be taking the train to school in Kempten every day, but in those days there was no coeducation, and after classes she would be taking the train home again—without me. A horrible, unacceptable prospect for either of us. So the battle was on—the first serious one.

Whenever mother was at odds with me over some major issue, she would address me as "son," whereupon I would call her "mother." That happened a lot these days. Words like "selfish," "one-track mind," "hooked," even "possessed" and "traitor" entered her arguments, while I countered with adjectives such as "mean," "self-centered," "unsympathetic," and "jealous." I don't remember how I had meant that last one, but at the moment there was a satisfying ring to it, especially since it really seemed to upset her.

Of course, she had the perfect bombshell saved up for this very occasion. I knew exactly what was coming and winced in anticipation, just as when you drop something huge and heavy on your bare toe, and there is that fraction of a second between the impact and the registration by your nerve endings of this event: you clench your fists, grit your teeth, and hold your breath, but all this does not help one bit, and it hurts like hell anyway. "Well, my dear son," she said, "I guess I should write to our relatives, then—that they need to apply for just one affidavit. That should make matters a lot simpler. Things should move right along now. I might even make it for Christmas."

Anyone in his right mind would have been subdued by this, but I had one more stupid thing to say.

"Okay, fine! Then everyone will be happy! I am sure I could move in with any of the Glaesers or even with Antek. And merry Christmas to all the relatives over there—or is it going to be Chanukah, now, or whatever they say!"

Boy, was I mean. For a second I thought she was going to hit me. She should have. I certainly deserved it, or so I thought later on. Instead, she just glared at me for what seemed like several minutes. "Sounds like you have been planning this for some time," she finally said. "Don't wait too long, if you want to change your mind."

The truth was that from the very beginning I had been fully aware of the fact that the time would come when I would have to choose between Brigitte and America. It was a dilemma for which I could find no solution. I pondered and pondered. Nothing! No sudden eureka experience this time. I could tell myself a thousand times—as mother had—that I was far too young, as was Brigitte, for a binding relationship; that Germany was no place for us; that Werner and Bastel were also anxious to leave Germany as soon as possible, and that I had made a pact with my mother to accompany her to the new world. That contrived-age concern bothered me a bit: How old were Romeo and Juliet, anyway? Well, look where it got them! Though their problems were hardly comparable to ours.

As often is the case, there exist old German sayings, proverbs, which are versatile enough to lend themselves as comforters and consultants to all kinds of situations. In this case it was *Kommt Zeit, kommt Rat,* roughly translated: give it enough time and a solution will turn up. So, I found comfort in the fact that nothing was going to happen anytime soon. The letters from our relatives were not encouraging. Sponsors were impossible to find, and so far hardly anyone had been granted an immigration visa. It would take one to two years, they guessed, before U.S. immigration restrictions would be lifted. A short time ago, this information would have utterly depressed me; now it made me rejoice.

I managed to appease my mother by pointing out to her that everything was so vague and distant that no final decision was necessary at this point. Besides, shouldn't we try to implement some action from our side of the ocean? "Remember the Picasso?" I asked. "Shouldn't we try to find out what that would do for us? Hannes is an artist and has connections. Perhaps he can come up with some ideas. And the most important thing right now is that I get to go to school. Let's take the train to Kempten and talk to the school officials. And let's also go to the Bürgermeister's office here to find out if there is some apartment available for us."

I figured if I bombarded my mother with a multitude of issues, she would be so befuddled that she would not be able to focus on any single one and thus not object to our staying here. She did not put up any argument. In retrospect, it is more than probable that she was onto my scheme but as eager as I to be on speaking terms again. So we did travel to Kempten that very week, and we did find a satisfactory apartment not far from the Schwan. But then, nothing in Obergünzburg was very far from the Schwan.

Journal entry, October 1945: Everyone is so full of "good" advice, but I need action, not just words. What I really could use now would be a strong father figure. That boy is determined to sacrifice his—our—future for that child. Sure, she is sweet, gifted, and beautiful—but at their age? That was a horrible confrontation with Horst the other day. And yet, I can so identify with him after all that has happened—first finding out about our Jewishness, then Oma's death, followed by the destruction of our town, and leaving it—this girl must be like an anchor to him, something that brings stability and security into his life. If only I knew—is it really necessary to leave Germany behind? For Horst, leaving Germany is leaving Brigitte, and Brigitte has become synonymous with Germany for him. Perhaps I should have a serious talk with her mother— Pippi is continuing to make advances toward me. My sister's husband?! Mo is awfully nice to me, too. That's all I need—from the life of a Jewess in Nazi Germany to the life of a white woman with a black man in America. I just pray that Horst, after all his wild experiences, will adjust to school discipline. And here's another thing: if it were not for Brigitte, I don't think I alone would have gotten him to go back to school. Should I talk to any of his teachers? Have to get some help with the Picasso. Soon!

As my mother had predicted, I was neither the oldest student in my class nor was I the only refugee. There even was one boy from across the street in Breslau. We had not known each other back then, but now found great comfort in each other's presence. The other nonnative boys were from all over the eastern territories. There were eight of us, comprising about one third of the class. All of us were about one year older than the normal class average, and we were bigger, stronger, and wiser than the home team. They were already well into the school year, so I was painfully aware of being behind in everything except English, German, music, and gym.

Supposedly, all the teachers who had been Nazi Party members were prohibited from teaching. Depending on the outcome of the investigation know as *Entnazifizierung* (de-Nazification), they were either kept out indefinitely or reinstated.

Somehow, that one teacher, Doktor Zorn, must have slipped through the cracks. He was our physics and mathematics teacher and of the type I had come to hate in Breslau. He was in his fifties and spoke local dialect exclusively, which enabled him to express the typical native's irrational dislike for us Prussians. After he had interrogated me in class, he ended by suggesting that I "avail myself of the customary language of the region as quickly as possible." I was dumbfounded but instantly remembered what my mother had said to me in Planegg: "And you won't have to take crap from Nazi teachers anymore!"

I was standing at that moment, as was customary when being addressed by a teacher. I smiled at him and said, "Oh, I am sorry. I thought we were here to learn German."

My seven fellow foreigners cheered me on. After that I was the hero of the day and their trusted friend for the school year.

Quite the opposite of Zorn was Doktor Schweitzer, our teacher for German and history. He had been a medic during the war, and he loved us foreigners, for he too came from one of the eastern provinces. He quickly discovered that there were three of us who were good and eager writers, and he promoted a regular spirit of competition for excellence among us. He made us read our compositions to the class, which was then invited to comment and evaluate—a very effective method to motivate us. After a few weeks of this, he called us to his office. He had an idea, a suggestion, a plan. "Why don't you get together with a few more students from other classes and come out with a, well—let's say monthly for now—school paper. I'll be glad to be your faculty advisor. You know, school issues, sports, some humor, fiction, perhaps art and music—whatever comes to mind. But be sure to invite a few of your indigenous schoolmates to participate. We need something to bring the two factions together. Working together on a project like this might just do the trick. I can recommend Schlegel, Lohmann, and Marder. Really sharp and articulate! And of course your friend Horst Faas, with his new camera, can be your photographer.

Writing for a newspaper! I was instantly *Feuer und Flamme* (fire and flame), as the saying goes. Some of my adventures, I thought,

were worthy of retelling, and if the Allgäuers could be made to see
us not only as impoverished, homeless and hungry refugees, but as
fellow humans, then everybody would profit. In my mind I was already
planning the whole thing. I wanted them to understand us in general,
me in particular: What it was like, as a boy, to be shot at with a machine
gun; to loot abandoned houses together with a bunch of drunk Russian
soldiers; to paddle a drunk Russian captain around, who, for the sake
of getting a few fish, was holding enough explosives in his hand to
blow up an entire bridge; and what it was like to leave your town, your
home, your lakes, and your river—your past, forever.

Perhaps I could create a series of episodes that would appear in
consecutive issues and write them in such a manner that readers would
anxiously await every new chapter. The more I thought about it, the
more exited I grew.

Riding the train back to Günzach, I talked about this with Erhard
and Brigitte. Erhard, in his usual serious manner, cautioned me to
choose my words very carefully. "You know, parents, teachers, and
officials will also read this. So you have to make sure that you don't say
anything critical or even hostile about anyone."

"Well, perhaps you could join us as an editor," I replied. "Also, I
thought that you would be the ideal person to write articles on recent
trends in music. You know more about this than all the others. Would
you consider it?"

Erhard smiled and nodded. "I'll be happy to contribute."

These were wonderful weeks. Being with Brigitte was on top of the
list. We were together almost every day. I was best friends with Erhard
and good friends with the rest of the family. Brigitte and I still biked,
weather permitting. Often we studied together, or she played to my
singing, as she had planned. We tackled many German folk songs and
a few Russian ones, dating back to the days of Sasha's balalaika music.
Then there were pieces from Brigitte's mother, songs with wonderful
melodies and texts, dating back to the 16th and 17th centuries. We even
attempted a few Schubert songs, but those proved to be too much for
me. Frau Hilgendorf tried to be encouraging, "You know, with your
natural gift—a few voice lessons could make all the difference."

Some of the old songs were arranged in four parts. Brigitte's
sisters were happy to take two of these with their instruments, Brigitte
one with her cello, and my voice would be the fourth. Whenever all
the parts blended together in perfect harmony, Brigitte would be so

overwhelmed that she would put down her cello and rush over to hug me. Her siblings got used to this after a while, but could not resist the urge to roll their eyes in disgust. And then there were the times when only Brigitte and I would work on something, and she would simply go wild with her accompaniment, playing counter melodies and harmonies of such intricacy that I had a hard time holding onto the melody. On such occasions, her mother would appear and just gaze at her daughter in awe. "Daughter, where did you learn to play like this? Is this an angel or a devil in your soul?"

"I think, it's an angel and the devil fighting for my soul," she answered, exhausted. Such a performance left Brigitte always completely drained and in need of a walk. She would then cling to me so tightly that I was almost carrying her. Those were my happiest times.

Of course Erhard added his talent, too. But he was more into modern melodies and chords, playing all of the latest American hits, with the rest of us filling in the best we could. It was he who suggested, "Man, if we had some drums, we could really be great."

I mentioned this to Mo.

"Well, let me see what I can do. One of my sergeants, Smitty, used to play in a band. I think he was the drummer. Let me check that out."

A couple of days later he was back, informing me, "Okay, we are all set. Smitty is your man. When do you want him?"

"How about tonight, about seven, in the Schwan?"

"Sure thing! See you then."

We had already rehearsed for an hour when Smitty arrived. His full name was Archimedes Smith. He was very short, chewed gum, and was more than surprised at our ages, which ranged from eleven to seventeen.

"What's this, the wunderkinder band?" he asked with a smirk. "Let's hear what you've got."

We played "Chattanooga Shoeshine Boy," and his expression went from smirk to broad smile. "Hey, man, that was real smooth. You kids! And I thought you were going to play chamber music, considering the choice of instruments. Now let's play that again."

He set up his drums and deposited his gum under one of the tables.

Erhard had been correct. What had been good before now sounded like a professional performance. Curious townspeople poked their heads through the door and enjoyed the free concert. Some began to dance, not as wildly as the Goldene Engel crowd, rather more subdued and in keeping with the low-key temperament of the band.

At one point Erhard just had to play his favorite. "Okay, 'Capri-Fischer'!" he whispered—a song that had nothing to do with the events of the present, but told of men, boats, nets, sun and moon, and of Bella Marie, waiting in the morning for the return of her lover.

I smiled at Brigitte as I sang; she smiled back and began to perform rather provocatively on her cello, never turning her eyes from me. It was the most exciting, seductive "conversation" I had ever experienced. Incidentally, both of us felt we were emotionally and biologically mature enough to find out what some of these adult games were all about.

Not long thereafter, Mo appeared one evening, looking rather somber and depressed. He was the bearer of sad news: our U.S. Army friends were soon to leave our little town and the hospitable maidens of the surrounding dairy farms, who, suddenly forsaken, would miss the weekend dancing—now, just when all that jitterbug whirling and flipping had begun to make sense.

And what about the few unfortunate ones who had to make it clear to their boyfriends that excessive acrobatics on the dance floor might not be in the best interest of the tender new life that was beginning to stir beneath their hearts? What would be their lot in this fanatically Catholic region? The priest had done his best, had admonished the commanding officer and the more apprehensive than proud fathers- and mothers- to-be. He had heaped fire and brimstone upon the heads of the sinners, but had also uplifted them again, pointing out that, after all this death and bloodshed, God in His boundless mercy had chosen them to repopulate the world with His creatures.

Witnesses to this occasion, both Americans and Germans, later agreed that the Holy Spirit himself must have spoken from the mouth of the priest, giving him not only the power to move the hearts of the sinners, but also the English vocabulary so necessary to the successful conclusion of the matter. Yes, indeed, there were tears and solemn promises, followed by application forms in triplicate, consultations with army chaplains and terror-stricken parents. Somehow, shortcuts were found, so that within a couple of weeks, on a wintry Sunday, nine couples received the Holy Sacrament of Marriage in the Catholic Church, after which the Hilgendorfs gave a memorable performance of the Bach-Gounod *Ave Maria.*

For us personally, the departure of Mo and his men meant the loss of good friends and of endless supplies, ranging from butter to toilet paper. Mo walked around, shaking his head, saying "Jesus Christ" over and over. He promised he would visit on weekends and bring truckloads of army surplus for us. His company had been reassigned to an installation near Nürnberg.

On the evening before his departure, his jeep stopped once more in front of our house. "Chris, would you come out and give me a hand, please?"

I went outside with him. It was darn cold—light snow was falling. He opened the car door and started to unload. "Here, Chris. You wouldn't want to be without this next summer, would you?"

It was a fly rod and a small tackle box.

Having heard it so many times from him and his men, I thought I couldn't find a better way to express my delight: "Jesus Christ, Mo!" I said. There was more in the car—the drum set Smitty had used, and then came another huge surprise.

"I had planned to make this my Christmas present to you and Brigitte. A little early now, as it turns out, but look! Everything is turning white. The snow is sticking. So, here you go. I know you wanted some. It's from the 10th Mountain Division, so it's got to be damn good quality." And out came two pairs of skis, boots and poles.

"Jesus Christ, Mo! This is too much! This will be so great! Thank you so much! When you come in the winter, I'll teach you how to ski, if you like. Now you must come in for a minute, because I, we, have something for you, too!"

Mo responded with an "Oh," and I could not tell if it was followed by a question mark or an exclamation mark.

We had thought about this for some time. What to give to this man who had everything? After some discussion, we all agreed: it had to be something personal, something that would bring back to him these, as he put it, "best times of my life."

So we had made a little album for him. Werner was an avid photographer with his own darkroom. He had accumulated piles of pictures of everyone and everything: people, animals, houses, trees, mountains, clouds, festive gatherings, marriages (all nine of them), dancing couples, soldiers with their girlfriends, fly rods bending under the strain of a trophy trout, Brigitte somersaulting through the air, me singing, our little band and, of course, Mo from every angle, on and off duty. It was the summary of his life here, of his happy six months in Obergünzburg. We had assembled everything into a photo album, labeled each picture, and Brigitte had decorated it beautifully with watercolors. Mo was totally overwhelmed. For quite a while he could not say anything. Finally, he hugged all of us, murmuring, "God bless you, my friends." Then he was gone.

Once more, that awful empty feeling had entered my chest. Now Mo had joined the procession of vanishing friends. Being with Brigitte was an enormous comfort, and I knew, as long as I had her—I didn't want to, could not, think any further than that.

XIV

How Doktor Zorn could not give up his Nazi habits, and how we fixed him

IF IT HAD NOT been for Doktor Zorn, school would have been something to look forward to every day. What a relief not to see teachers with their NSDAP pins and not to have to dodge older students wearing their HJ *(Hitlerjugend)* uniforms; not to be herded out into the schoolyard every morning to salute the swastika flag and to sing, "Deutschland, Deutschland, über alles" and that other one, its companion piece, "Die Fahne hoch," the entire time standing at attention, right arm rigidly extended, but your hand under no circumstances raised higher than eye level!* And every day the apprehension lest one of my teachers, most of whom knew about my shame, would make some remark in class, thereby branding me as an outcast.

Doktor Zorn would have fit right in with some of my old teachers. Rumor had it that his continued employment as teacher was the result of close ties to some influential member of the board of de-Nazification. I was just waiting for the day that he, by force of habit, would come to class with that hateful pin in his lapel. But no luck. He just kept harassing all of us foreigners, in particular me. I soon had my suspicions why.

Our pleasant little apartment was the upstairs of a villa that belonged to Doktor Bucher, a former, less fortunately connected colleague of Doktor Zorn. I had seen Zorn visiting the Buchers, and on this and other occasions everything about us and the entire clan

*Hitlerjugend: Hitler Youth; Deutschland, Deutschland, über alles: Germany, Germany, above all; Die Fahne hoch: Hold high the flag

must have been discussed: our friendship with the black soldiers, a few mysterious and suspicious privileges we seemed to enjoy, frequent letters from America with telltale names like Freund, Rosenthal, and Frankfurter on the envelopes. Could there be any doubt, then? Beware! Don't let that Aryan name, that kid's blond hair fool you! Just look at the mother—curly black hair! That's approximately how it must have gone. So the old bloodhound's killer instinct had been reawakened and the hunt was on, I being the prey.

His objective must have been to vanquish me academically. Physics and mathematics were major subjects. Anyone failing two major courses had to repeat the entire year, and if this happened in two consecutive years, then you were out, expelled, finished, kaput.

Zorn was relentless in his attempts to trick me in oral work. But I had an equally tricky ally: Erhard was not only excellent in these subjects but had had Zorn in the past. So he knew what to expect, and he drilled me accordingly. This way, I not only managed to totally frustrate Zorn, I also became quite competent in the subjects in question.

When the time came for the dreaded one-hour written math exam, I had no problems with any of the questions. I was done well ahead of time, but I did not turn in my paper. I had better things to do.

I hoped Erhard would go into psychology someday because he could read people's minds like a book. At least he didn't have any trouble predicting what Zorn, the old slimeball, was going to do. "No matter what you write on this exam, Doc Zorn is going to flunk you. Believe me, he'll work your paper over with a red pen until you yourself won't believe you deserve to pass."

"If you are right—and I don't doubt it a bit—then how am I going to pass? Sounds downright hopeless to me."

I should have had more faith in Erhard. He wouldn't have said all this if he hadn't already mapped out a battle plan for me. "So here is what you have to do! I think I know well enough what's going to be on the exam. We'll work on the problems together so you can finish the test really fast. Don't turn in your test booklet, though. Write down the questions and how you answered them and hide those pages. Then turn in your test booklet.

"Now, when Zorn returns the tests, you'll have ten minutes to look things over, and then the booklets will be collected again. That is customary. If, as I predict, he flunks you, then I'll take the pages with your copied test and answers to Direktor Krause. He is a math teacher and knows me quite well from the students' workgroup. I'll tell him what has been going on, and he'll check your exam, and God help Doktor Zorn if he does what I predict."

It was a simple, logical, beautifully devious plan, and that was why I did not turn in my exam until the bell rang.

Three days later Zorn appeared with the exam booklets in his hand. He returned them, arranged according to grades, best exam first, mine last. "I am sorry, Horst, but I am afraid your intellectual gifts are not quite adequate for the challenges of higher mathematics."

Zorn had not been stingy with red ink, marking up my pages so they looked like a chart of the circulatory system. There was more red than black: question marks, exclamation marks, entire pages crossed out, "No," "False," and "Incomprehensible!" written all over the place, and in such a fashion that you could never figure out what it related to. At the end there was a note: "This exam is a demonstration of a complete absence of any degree of comprehension. At times I was under the impression that the student was hallucinating. My recommendation is that the student withdraw immediately from this course, if not from this institution. F."

The grade did not come as a surprise, and the sheer malice of this man was of Auschwitzian dimension.

"Horst," I heard Doktor Zorn's voice, "would you mind reading my comment at the end aloud? I think the class will find it educational."

As I read aloud his little message, I felt the blood draining from my face and the urge to vomit rising from my stomach. Without saying a further word, I rose from my seat and walked out of the classroom, leaving the test on my desk. Three of my closest foreigner-friends and even one of the local students, Kurt, followed me.

Kurt Marder was the son of the local newspaper's editor. He was dependable, very good in all subjects, outstanding in German, competing with us for the best compositions. We had invited him to join our newspaper, an offer he gladly accepted.

Normally controlled and thoughtful, he was now beside himself with rage. "That miserable *Nazisau** has some nerve shooting off his big mouth. I am not supposed to talk about this, but he used to come to class in his shit-colored SA uniform and his gold Nazi pin, and he made sure that none of the inferior Jewish blood was infecting the minds of his students. One by one he tracked them down, even

*Nazi sow

the half and quarter mixes, and caused them to flunk out of school. They say that one boy committed suicide on account of him. That was early in the war. But then, after the war, all this was hushed up because he had friends in high places. So he even got his teaching job back. Well, I think his time here is up. Let me do a little research and then—

"I mean, why did we start our little school paper if not to take a stand on scandals like this? And it would not surprise me at all if my father published a few well-chosen facts about this gentleman's past. Oh, and one more thing, Horst," Kurt said, looking embarrassed and uncomfortable. "I don't know if you are aware of the fact that there are rumors going around about you, but if we are to follow up on this, I think that it would help our cause if we knew. Of course, you don't have to answer if you don't feel comfortable about it. Just keep in mind that we are all your friends."

Considering the circumstances, there was no question in my mind as to what Kurt was driving at. I thought of my mother's stern warning: "Never tell a soul about your Jewish blood." But by now I had grown utterly tired of this cat-and-mouse game. So, when the question came, I nodded and said, "Half."

There was absolutely no reaction to this revelation.

"Okay," Kurt said, "we'll proceed as planned, then. In the meantime, let's see what we can do to make the good doctor's life a little miserable."

Naturally, we were curious as to what he had in mind, but he just grinned. "You'll see soon enough."

Three days later, entering the classroom for our first-period math class with Doktor Zorn, an unusual scene awaited me: half the class was crowding around the blackboard. There was whispering and giggling. All heads turned toward me, then silence; a path to the blackboard opened up. What I saw amused and frightened me at the same time. There, white on black, was a picture, a caricature, created by a master, summarizing all the elements of that final confrontation scene in the room: unmistakably Zorn, oversized, dwarfing everything around him, the desks, the students with frightened faces, cowering in their benches, Zorn himself standing there spread-eagled, SA uniform, high leather boots, an enormous Nazi pin on his chest. All this frightening enough, but nothing compared to the expression on his face, grinning in fiendish pleasure. With one hand he cracked a whip, while holding back a snarling German police dog with the other. In front of Zorn and half his size, a frightened student wearing my lederhosen and reading a sentence from a booklet: "I am inferior scum, not worthy of being part of this institution."

Manfred, my friend from across the street in Breslau, clasped my shoulders, otherwise I would have walked out again. "No, no! That's exactly what he would like you to do. If this is to work, you have to stay."

Breathless tension descended upon the room when Doktor Zorn appeared a few minutes later. Calm before the storm, before the unleashing of boundless fury? What were the possibilities? Shouting and screaming, ordering a student to wipe the blackboard clean, sending a student out to summon the principal, collapsing from a heart attack and suffering an ignoble death in front of everybody? Someone should have written out a list and taken bets. Funny thing, though. There wouldn't have been any winners. No! The old Nazi did the only thing he could: he studied the cartoon a few minutes, grimaced a bit, and shrugged his shoulders. "Typical students' prank," he said in a tone of voice as if announcing, "And tomorrow will be another day."

He paced back and forth a few times, smiled as he continued to address the class. "A bit exaggerated, of course, but that is, after all, what a good caricature is all about, isn't it? If I had to grade this work, I would not hesitate to give it an A. But let's end it with this. We have better things to do."

He grabbed the sponge, performed the first cleansing sweep across the drawing. The class had expected a huge spectacle, an investigation taking up the entire period, now—nothing! How disappointing. Give that round to the man with the golden Nazi pin!

Kurt Marder must have envisioned a different course of events. Or had he? From what followed I would say that he had anticipated every move the "good" doctor made. "Excuse me, Herr Doktor Zorn," his calm voice could be heard saying, "this won't take very long, but I think the class and I need clarification on a few things."

"Sure, Marder, as long as it contributes to this class." Zorn's voice sounded a bit shaky now. He knew he could not refuse Kurt's request. If he did, it was as if he had something to conceal; on the other hand, if he let himself in for a discussion with Kurt—who knows where that would lead?

"Oh, it does!" Kurt assured him. "Herr Doktor Zorn, there are records revealing that between the years 1935 and 1942 there were eighteen students who had to leave this school because they had reportedly failed mathematics and physics. Do you know anything about this?"

"Well, you know, I was not the only teacher of these subjects. There are always some who have trouble with this. Unfortunately, most of my records did not survive the war, otherwise I would be happy to review them."

"Herr Doktor Zorn! Survive the war? There never was any bombing or shelling or looting in this town! Fortunately, the school kept and still possesses most of the material from these years, including the test booklets for math and physics. Do you remember names like Schapiro, Landau, Levi, Schatz, Goldstein, Silbermann, Rosenberg, Rosenthal, and Herz?"

Kurt's voice volume had intensified; there was a staccato effect to the speech pattern; each syllable rang out like a gunshot. Standing there with the sponge still in his hand, Zorn suddenly seemed shrunken in size; the color of his face was ashen. This round was definitely not going to him. Merciless punches were driving him around the ring. Where was the bell, so he could sit in his corner to think a few minutes and recover? But his opponent kept up the relentless attack. "Herr Doktor Zorn! Our Direktor, Herr Doktor Krause and several other qualified teachers have reviewed the tests of the students whose names I mentioned. Those students were all members of your classes. The results of this investigation indicate that you had a method of marking up papers which was deliberately so confusing that students were unable to protest the failing grades they received. It was a fiendish scheme, the success of which was guaranteed by the simple fact that the victims thereof were of Semitic blood. Opening one's mouth in protest would have meant deportation. And by the way, according to Doktor Krause, Horst's grade on that last exam has been changed and recorded as an A minus."

Zorn was breathing heavily now; beads of sweat appeared on his forehead. He was losing the match. All he had left now was some wind in his lungs for screaming. "I'll put an end to this infamy! There will be expulsions; I can promise you that! The Board of Education will receive a full report and so will the Minister of Education."

The possibility of this course of action seemed to revive the fighting spirit of Doktor Zorn. He staggered back into the ring where the knockout punch was awaiting him.

"Herr Doktor Zorn! This is really important, so please allow me! It should not take very long. Does the name Konrad Goldschmidt mean anything to you?

"It doesn't? Well, it should, because he was your student in 1942. Yes, his test booklet is also in Doktor Krause's office right now. He was the top student in his class. Straight As in every subject, except for math and physics. Isn't that strange? He consistently failed every test in these subjects. He had a tutor and his mother came to your office to discuss the matter. All in vain. You told her that Konrad was simply of inferior stock and unfit for the Gymnasium. And this is my question: do you still think that people of Semitic blood, like Einstein for instance, are inferior to Aryans? You better have something to say about this because soon you will be interviewed about it by one of the reporters. After all, it's only fair that you should receive the opportunity to express your opinion, because Mrs. Goldschmidt's interview will be in the paper tomorrow. Ah, yes—before I forget it: I have here a short newspaper article; your name is mentioned. I thought I should read it to the class because it's rather educational. Okay, the date is Monday, October 3rd, 1942. 'After a two-day search, the body of Konrad Goldschmidt was recovered by local fishermen. Goldschmidt, a gifted student and musician, was a student at the Maximilian Gymnasium. His mother stated that her son had been severely depressed in recent weeks. Doktor Zorn, his faculty advisor, had no comments other than that Goldschmidt was unable to cope with the intellectual demands of his studies and really didn't fit in'."

A bell rang. Was it the bell announcing the end of the match, or the end of the class period or the end of the Doktor Zorn era?

Doktor Zorn was never seen again. Later we heard that he had moved—no one knew where.

There was not too much in the papers about Doktor Zorn's departure and the background details leading up to this event, just enough to allow for all sorts of speculation. Who were those kids who had made it their business to hunt down war criminals? To some we were villainous troublemakers, to others champions of justice.

Our own little school paper reviewed the case, listing the names of the eighteen expelled students and honoring the memory of Konrad Goldschmidt. The caricature on the blackboard which had triggered the investigation was described in detail, but we never found out who the artist had been. I suspected that it was someone on the staff of the local paper. Kurt must have known, but he did not tell.

The four classmates who had walked out on Doktor Zorn with me became my best friends. Fellow students and teachers alike respected us, and the few remaining Zorn sympathizers did not dare open their mouths.

Of course, it was clear to me that now everyone in school and in town knew about my background. There was no hostility, quite the opposite, but I often noticed how people were staring at me with interest, if not fascination. The effects of fifteen years of intensive brainwashing just could not be obliterated without leaving a trace. My friends must have been aware of this because they often acted as if they were my bodyguards.

Predictably, my mother was horrified. "Ach, Horst, didn't you think of what I told you hundreds of times since you were five years old: don't let anyone know about us! It may seem safe right now, but believe me, some little incident involving a Jew, and the anti-Semitism will flare up, as it has been the case for centuries. I hope I'm wrong, but I know I am not. Well, too late now. We really have to get out of Germany if we ever want to feel safe again. It's the only way."

"Mama! Don't get all timid and scared again. Hitler is dead, the Nazis are gone; in a few years, no one will remember what anti-Semitism was."

"Oh, what a child you still are! But tell me, how are things with Brigitte and the Hilgendorfs?"

A good question! One I had worried about, not a whole lot, but still . . . They might find it strange, even dishonest or cowardly that I had never confided in them.

Erhard behaved exactly as I had expected him to. He looked warmly at me, shook my hand and said, "That was a wonderful thing you did in school. I wish I could have done something to help."

"But you did! Without your idea with the test, we couldn't have done anything."

"True, but it would have felt so great to know that I was really getting involved with something so important."

Brigitte, in keeping with her more impulsive, playful personality, reacted differently. Riding back home on the train, I noticed how she kept looking me over now and then, raising her eyebrows occasionally, while a little mischievous smile appeared on her lips. At home, she managed to get me away from the others. She put her arms around me and gave me a long kiss. "So that's what it feels like to kiss a Jewish boy!" she said with that same smile. "Now I'll never go back to Aryans again!"

Frau Hilgendorf acted as if nothing at all had happened. I wondered if the topic ever came up when I was not around. I asked Brigitte about this, but she just shrugged her shoulders. Then she added, "My mother said that my father would have been very upset. No explanation, nothing."

Journal entry, November 1945: I am still in shock. All this worrying and fussing in vain. Now everyone knows. But it would have happened anyway with Bucher constantly snooping around. Do the Germans still have that obsession with "who is Jewish?" Apparently. I hope they won't take it out on Horst. What about Brigitte now? And what about that mother of hers? Now, there is one enigma! She is kind to Horst, but somewhere there must be a dark secret. The Nazis surely did a thorough job inseminating Germany's population with anti-Semitism.

If I had been a little smarter and a little bit less in love, I would have been suspicious of the fact that Frau Hilgendorf never made an attempt to befriend my mother. Once, she even declined politely when my mother had invited her to meet the family. And shouldn't my mother have cautioned me: "Listen, Horst, these are not good signals I am getting from Frau Hilgendorf." Or perhaps she had said this, and it just hadn't registered, because too many other things were occupying my mind, matters that had to do with our day-to-day survival. This was the winter of 1945-46 rattling its saber, threatening to annihilate those who had escaped the preceding five and a half years of slaughter.

XV

How we ended up with a seventy-pound wheel of Emmentaler, how we prepared for Christmas, and how Brigitte learned to ski

IT WAS THE BEGINNING of December: cold, wintry, snowy. Our supply of firewood was shrinking at an alarming rate. Never in all the years of the war had there been less food. The area farmers showed little compassion, and trying to barter with them was pointless because by now they had everything they needed. My first question everyday upon returning from school was, "Any package from America?"

Rarely, perhaps in three- or four-week intervals, there would be a smile on my mother's face as she led me to the table, pointing at that package which contained all the riches of America—a brick of strangely orangey yellow cheese, corned beef, chocolate, something wonderful called Spam, powdered eggs and milk, Crisco, a huge salami, a few bars of soap, and a carton of cigarettes, everything cushioned in a bed of wondrously soft and spongy paper. Only much later did we find out what that was: paper towels! But to us it was a long-missed luxury—toilet paper! So soothing to the touch that you felt caressed by angels when making contact with it. Chocolate, soap, and cigarettes we gladly shared with others, but these crumpled scraps of heaven we guarded with our lives.

As everyone was becoming more irritable and skinnier by the day, memories of excursions that had yielded rich bounty began to haunt me. Was it not my duty, my obligation, to revive the spirits of relatives and other loved ones? Just as the warmth of spring days ends the dormancy of wintry nature, so did witnessing the suffering around me end the dormancy of my survival instinct.

One early morning, as the delivery truck from the nearby dairy factory rumbled by our house, I felt the spark of reinvigoration. This truck had for some time now been the object of my reflections on the relationship between dishonesty and starvation. Was it not logical that in times of famine every accumulation of food would be viewed not only with desire but also with suspicion, lest there be dealings in progress that were depriving the masses of nourishment while enriching a favored few? There were in fact rumors flourishing to that effect. Could it be that the ample yield of regional milk was, as it were, flowing into the wrong pockets? I called upon my hero, Robin Hood, for inspiration. Ideas and plans which always ended in fairytale-like visions of piles of butter and cheese raced through my mind. "This can be done," I told myself over and over. "But how?"

The vehicle in question was a small, simple truck, merely covered with canvas. No obstacle for a determined entrepreneur, but neutralizing the driver was the real challenge. And I would need help, once I had figured out what to do. Surely Erhard would be more than happy to put something substantial on his family's table.

So the driver was the major obstacle. I pondered and pondered, and ever so gently something took shape deep within my mind. It added a new dimension to my plan: Antek! I had not seen much of him lately, but from time to time he visited. He was working in Kempten, transforming German armament stockpiles into household items. Americans were in charge of these storage facilities, and he had made friends with several GIs. The next time he showed up, I took him aside.

"Antek, we need food badly. This is getting ridiculous. No, no! Don't worry, I don't want you to get us any. But I have an idea that might help all of us. Do you think you can get a hold of an American uniform? One that would fit you?"

"Are you plotting to get me killed? You want me to impersonate a U.S. soldier? Can you imagine what would happen to me if I got caught? But you know me, always ready for one of your crazy ideas. Sounds like fun. Is this going to be some spying operation? But I believe you mentioned food just now?"

"Right!" And then I told him about the dairy truck, its presumed content, its route and timetable, and what I envisioned as his part in the operation.

Antek was impressed.

"Wow, Horst, I must confess, you've still got it. A little bit more sophisticated than throwing grenades into a pond. But I think this can be done. I'll let you know when I have everything together."

"Great! Oh, and Antek—wear a revolver holster, empty of course, an MP helmet, and an MP badge?"

"Yes, sir!" and saluting instead of winking, he vanished into the darkness of the December evening.

With Erhard I had a little more trouble. He was so incredibly conservative. I think his grandfather had been a minister, one of those unsmiling preachers who struggled diligently and earnestly for the salvation of illiterate men and women living deep in the primeval forests near the Russian border. Acquiring goods for personal gain by devious means was not anything Erhard had ever aspired to. I talked and talked, feeding him romanticized versions of some of my earlier exploits, trying to convince him that really all we were about to do was to bring the scales of justice back into balance. To reinforce my point, I gave him an impassioned account of the feats of Robin Hood and his men, the noble outlaws. Finally, I detected a gleam in his eye.

"And you think this will work? What if . . . ?"

His arguments were not pointless, but there is hardly anything worth doing in life that does not bear the weight of possible danger, I mused.

"What do you think would have happened to Robin Hood and the poor, oppressed peasants if he had been unwilling to stick his neck out?"

"I'll go, if you won't," Brigitte snapped.

"Not a bad idea," I said, "but not instead of Erhard, but in addition to. The more we are, the more we can carry away on our bikes."

"Great!" She jumped up and hugged me the way she always did when overcome by emotion.

"Oh, all right then," Erhard grumbled. "I wouldn't do this ordinarily, but I have a responsibility toward my family. I sure hope you know what you are doing."

"Well, don't worry. Remember, Antek will be with us. He wouldn't touch this if he didn't think it was safe."

Several days went by. Our impatience grew proportionally with our yearning for some nourishment. Actually, these waiting days proved to be rather valuable. I studied and recorded judiciously the arrival and street-to-street progress of our truck, picking a spot which appeared to be the most suitable station for Antek—a well-concealed side street in proximity to a streetlight.

Relief came one afternoon when I heard the familiar BMW-roar of Antek's motorcycle outside my window. He appeared carrying a package and giving me numerous winks and thumbs up. My mother was still at work, and that was good. She wouldn't have been pleased to see me revert to my old ways. Why couldn't she ever understand that my seemingly shady undertakings were an absolute necessity for our survival? Where would we be if it had not been for me? Penniless, starving and freezing in Breslau.

"Sorry it took so long," Antek said. "I actually had to bribe one of the MPs to do me the favor."

"Really? What did you give him?"

"I didn't give him anything, but I fixed him up with that Polish girl he said he could not live without. Hope she doesn't disappoint him. Anyway, we should make our move tonight. There is snow predicted for tomorrow, lots of snow possibly. That could make things difficult— footprints and bike tracks in the snow, you know, or great delays. So we'd better move tonight, that is, early in the morning. What time did you say again, five o'clock?"

I nodded, and we left for an on-the-scene orientation. On the way we picked up Brigitte and Erhard. Erhard was apprehensive, Brigitte scared. She clutched my hand, nearly squeezing the life out of it. "Sorry," she whispered when I winced. "I guess I am not used to undertakings like this. It's just like that movie we saw last week. Remember how those guys got caught and shot? I actually felt sorry for them."

"Don't worry, no guns around here."

We came to the spot I had chosen: a side street with some shrubs which would conceal us from possible main-street traffic and pedestrians. "Okay, that's where the three of us will be with our bikes. Antek, you should post yourself over there where it's still quite dark. Try to halt the truck there; then make the driver walk with you to the streetlight, so you can have a better look at him and his papers. Ask him all sorts of questions, offer him a cigarette, do whatever is necessary to give us enough time to remove a few items from the truck. You can also park in the side street. After about seven minutes give the driver permission to proceed—in your best American accented German. I have the key to the workshop in the Schwan. That's where we'll take everything. I will let you in there now, so you can get some sleep and change into the uniform. We'll come by at a quarter past five to pick you up."

"Sounds like child's play, Horst. Can't imagine how anything could go wrong . . . I think—no, you've covered every possibility."

As the little delivery truck contentedly rattled down its customary route at the usual time, the young driver suddenly slammed on the brakes. There, in the middle of the street, not too far from a streetlight, this hulk of a figure suddenly emerged as if rising out of the pavement. One of those damned MPs, the driver thought. Those guys are going nuts these days. Must be after someone or something. Hope that guy speaks some German, at least.

I watched from the shadows as the hulk stepped up to the driver's window. Good old Antek would have fooled anyone. No doubt about his new persona: MP badge and helmet, mean face, pistol holster on his belt. "Aussteigen, aber maken snell!" he said in that typical GI-flavored German. "Papiere, bitte!"

He carefully looked at and studied everything, finally ordering, "Kommen zu Laterne! Brauke Licht." As was true for most GIs, our MP mispronounced that "ch" in "*Licht*," the word for "light," making it sound like "licked."

In the light, Antek studied the papers some more, suddenly offering the driver a cigarette.

"Alles okay?" the driver asked.

The MP hesitated a few seconds, then looking at his watch, handed the papers back. "Alles okay! Weiterfahren!" And he performed some official looking hand-and-arm motions.

It struck me how similar to some scenes in gangster movies this had been: the boyish, frightened driver, the equally frightened character playing the part of the soldier, and the gang, concealed by shrubs, waiting to perform its task. And did we ever perform! By the time Antek had joined us, our bags and basket were filled and securely fastened to our bikes. Just one item had remained in the middle of the highway. In the dim light it looked like a spare tire. Antek shook his head. "What the hell is that? Is that from the truck?"

"Sorry," I replied, "it's sort of an accident. It suddenly started rolling. It's a whole Emmentaler. About seventy pounds. If you bring your vehicle we can strap it on."

Triumphantly we returned to the Schwan. The entire operation, including travel time, had not taken more than thirty minutes. We pushed our bikes right into one of the unheated storage rooms, eager to inspect what we had grabbed in the dark. Shouts of joy and gasps of surprise filled the room. All that butter! Look! A box of eggs! And all those cheeses: Gruyère, Brie, Camembert, Gouda, Tilsiter, Port Salut, and some I had never heard of. Erhard grabbed one of the smaller pieces, ripped the wrapping away and bit off big chunks. Then he passed it on. "This is certainly not for the local stores. I have never seen or tasted cheese like that. It's like eating butter!

Well, you can bet on it that this place does not only work for the good of the community." Antek had arrived, rolling in the Emmentaler. "They must be doing a lot of illegal trading with their local products. Look at that! Do you think *that* is made from local milk?" He held up a liverwurst and a salami. "And here! Cigarettes and a bottle of brandy!"

Erhard was outraged. "Those robbers! Those bastards! Someone ought to come and do something about this!"

"Erhard," I said, "you just did. You have in this very hour become a champion of justice, the savior of the poor. After this, you will be famous like Robin Hood."

"Yeah," he said with a grin. "Finally I have done something important. Thanks for talking me into it."

Uncharacteristically, not a word had come from Brigitte. She was sitting on a box, a blissful smile was on her face. On her lap there was an open box of Swiss chocolates, and the floor around her was littered with many little golden wrappers. "Oh, would any of you like one, too? They are divine!"

Long pause.

"Oh no! They are all gone."

As predicted, snow started to pile up during the day. It was very still, and the grey sky seemed to be filled with a simply inexhaustible supply of large, white, fluffy flakes. It was so beautiful! As always when watching falling snow, I could not tear myself away from the window, fearing my disappearance might end the magic. All traffic had long since ceased to exist; silence had transcended everything. A few bundled-up pedestrians were wading along the sidewalks; children were getting their sleds ready, heading for the nearest slope. I was itching to get out on our skis and to teach Brigitte a few simple maneuvers. But we had things to do. Erhard had designed and fashioned a number of decorative little cards which read, "Merry Christmas from the Allgäuer Robin Hood and his Merry Helpers!" These cards accompanied all the little packages that were waiting to be distributed to the numerous households within our family. This was not an entirely selfless gesture: if they had the necessary ingredients, all these people would be forced to produce some scrumptious Christmas treats. So—cheese, butter, eggs and sugar for all!

Everyone was truly grateful, although demonstrative expressions of feelings, as well as an overt display of these recently acquired riches, had to be kept to a minimum. One must never stir up the envy or curiosity of one's neighbors. It did not go unnoticed, however, that there was an awful lot of cheese cookery going on. Odors of cooking, frying, baking, melting Emmentaler were present in every puff of air that blew through the wintry streets. "CARE packages and Christmas supplies from friends and relatives in America," was our precautionary defense against possible accusations.

Of course, I was familiar with some of the better-known dishes like cheese soufflé and cheese fondue. But here, in the land of cheese, the list went on: you could make a salad from cubed cheese, oil and vinegar, and mix it with some chopped onion, celeriac, and apple; you could take a slab of cheese, about half an inch thick, bread it like a schnitzel and fry it in oil or butter; and finally there was the most famous of all regional dishes—as I had found out and learned to appreciate and prepare—*Spätzle,* in this case *Käsespätzle, Käse* being the German word for cheese.

Also, Frau Neuhofer, formerly Frau Steck, my uncle's happy, early-rising landlady, received a Christmas package from Robin Hood. There had been a small box with toilet articles in our loot, and when I spied those few packs of razor blades, I knew exactly what to do with them. Before this, she had complained bitterly, "Joseph and I have to share the same blade over and over. That's why there are so many nicks and scabs on our faces."

I asked my uncle if the alarm still went off every morning at four.

"I think so," he answered. "I have gotten so used to it by now that I hardly ever hear it."

What a happy couple!

When I met Frau Neuhofer the next time, it was obvious that she had something important on her mind. First, she begged me to give her an address, so she would be able to thank Mr. Robin Hood for the precious Christmas gift. Then she beckoned me to follow her to a corner, as if we were coconspirators planning the overthrow of the government. "Want to learn something new?" she asked, appraising me with a cunning gleam in her eye. "Christmas cookies!" she whispered. "Very special in this part of Germany. They are called *Springerle—Anis Springerle*. Have you ever heard of this before?"

When I shook my head she continued her whispering. "Well, all right then. Come tomorrow afternoon, and we'll do it together. I'll teach you."

She nodded and smiled.

"Would it be all right to bring Brigitte?"

My heart sank when she put on her frown. But then she smiled again and nodded vigorously.

Now—was that the yes or the no nod? I wondered.

The following afternoon Brigitte and I appeared at the Steckhaus at about three o'clock. Greeting us cordially, Frau Neuhofer ushered us into her kitchen, the setting for decades—if not centuries—of food preparation: baking, brewing, cheese making, pickling, and roasting had permeated everything in this room, giving it a very characteristic scent. But today, there was something unusual in the air that made me lift my head and sniff: very unique, very pleasant, very mysterious. I could not identify it.

"Can you tell what this smell is?" I asked Brigitte.

She acted bored. "That is anise. You know, those little seeds they use for flavoring and also for medicinal purposes and for that famous liquor, anisette?"

There were huge gaps in my culinary education, I concluded. "Must ask mother about this," I made a mental note to myself.

Scanning the kitchen table, I noticed the famous family cookbook, next to it a rolling pin, richly decorated with rows of all sorts of carved images: birds, flowers, stars, castles, rabbits, snakes, dogs, squirrels,

angels, nutcrackers, Tyrolean hats, musical instruments, a mountain goat, a bear, a dancer, a Christmas tree. All of these were carved expertly and artistically into little rectangles measuring about one-by-two inches.

She held up the rolling pin: "Just look at the movement in this rabbit and at all those turrets on the castle.

"Let's start by making the dough, which is very simple: just two eggs, flour, and sugar. Here, you can read it for yourself. It's simple, but it takes a little time and a lot of muscle, because you have to keep kneading until it is very smooth. So for the dough, proceed as follows," she read and elaborated. "Beat two eggs until they are thick and lemon colored. Gradually work in one and a quarter cups of sugar and a dash of salt until the mixture is thick and smooth. Beat in three cups of flour. If you don't have a heavy-duty beater, knead the dough with floured hands until it is very smooth, about ten minutes. Shape it into a ball and place it on a floured, smooth surface. If it feels sticky, add a little flour. Then comes the more interesting part: the imprinting of the images into the dough."

We proceeded as instructed, finally watching her get ready for the last step: she first wiped her hands on her apron then dipped them in flour, creating a white cloud by clapping them together. "You'll need a regular rolling pin to roll out the dough until it is about a quarter inch thick.

"Next, sprinkle the wooden images in the pin with flour; then, with a pastry brush, remove all excess flour. But no matter what you do, there will always be some little corners where the dough will stick to the wood, unless you sprinkle a little bit of flour onto the flattened-out dough and wipe it, so that only the thinnest film of flour remains—and you won't read this in any cookbook, at least I never have. But this is really the only method that has worked consistently for me.

"Now, bearing down with nearly all your strength, roll the springerle pin slowly over the dough, hoping that all the figures will come out sharp and clear." It was now difficult to follow her words because they were so muffled by her panting and grunting.

Finally, she took a knife, cut the pictures apart and placed them on the baking sheet which we had prepared by spreading a tablespoon of butter on the sheet and sprinkling it generously with anise seeds.

"That's very good, Brigitte. And you can place them very close together. It's all right if they touch each other. No, not you and Horst! You know what I mean. Now gently press on the cookies to make sure the anise will adhere to the bottoms. Whose bottoms? You are terrible, Horst! The bottoms of the cookies, of course. Allow them to dry for twenty-four hours, then bake for twenty to thirty minutes at a very low temperature—oh, I would say 135 to 150 degrees Celsius*—until they are firm but not brown. I'll take care of this tomorrow. They will become rock hard as they cool and will keep for years. But if you store them in a closed jar together with a few peelings of apples or oranges, they will become soft and delicious. If you want to use them as Christmas decorations, poke holes into them before baking."

We doubled the recipe so there would be enough to go around.

Christmas was fast approaching, and the matter of the traditional Christmas Day feast began to weigh heavily upon me. Most family members seemed to be resigned to dine on Spätzle or other cheesy dishes. Not so I! Too much tradition stood behind Christmas. For me, of course, tradition meant carp and goose.

"Oh, Mo, Mo! Where are you in this my hour of desperate need? Hadn't you promised to visit us with truckloads of food?" To me, his promise had carried an almost religious significance—like the promise of the Savior's birth. But no guiding star emerged, not even a postcard.

I consulted my mother: "Should we risk sending him an SOS?"

"Better wait a few more days. It's still a bit early," she suggested.

We were already on school vacation, earlier than ever due to the shortage of coal. A generous blanket of snow covered the area. Horse- or ox-drawn sleds with little bells traveled through town and countryside. The thought of silently sliding through the snowy forest on skis became irresistible.

I could tell Brigitte was a little apprehensive to entrust her limbs to those narrow boards, but my enthusiasm, optimism, and confidence in her athletic ability weakened her resistance. Already, weeks ago I had adjusted the bindings to the boots; now I applied a little wax to the bottoms of the skis. This was the first time I was examining—never mind owning—skis with steel edges and these new cable-and-spring bindings. I was anxious to test their advantages over my old leather-strap bindings.

"All right," Brigitte groaned, "if I must! But nothing steep!"

*275 to 300 F

"Don't worry! There isn't even anything steep around here."

"Oh yeah? What about that hill on the way to the Steckhaus?"

"That? A ball wouldn't roll down from it if you gave it a push!" I laughed. "Anyway, today I just want you to learn to walk on skis, sliding a little with each step and using your poles as you go."

I showed Brigitte how to hold her poles and how to get into her bindings, which I adjusted for walking. Then I put on my skis and we were off—at least I was.

Perhaps I did get carried away a bit with all that fresh snow and those new skis. I sort of went crazy, sprinting forth without turning my head until—suddenly, loud wailing reached my ears.

"Oh?" I stopped dead, jumped straight up, turning 180 degrees. There she was, helplessly flailing around, unable to rise. Each time she thought she could muscle herself up, the skis would slide out from under her, and she was down again. This was serious! Not so much for the potential of physical harm, but handled poorly, skiing could easily become an unbearable frustration. I frantically tried to recall my ski instructor's way of dealing with near-hysterical students.

That had been about seven years ago in a little resort in the Silesian mountains, right next to the Czech border. Skiing was slowly evolving into a popular pastime back then; equipment and technique were still at a Stone Age level, but there was something mysterious, almost mystical, about every aspect of the sport. The smell in the equipment room, a mixture of leather, damp wool, and ski wax made of pine pitch, could put me in a nostalgic trance.

Ski instructors were revered like gods. Beyond their ability to perform the most amazing maneuvers on those treacherous boards, somersaults included, they all had several things in common, attributes which were considered prerequisites for becoming an instructor: a perpetual suntan, a good singing voice, complete with the ability to yodel, competence on guitar and accordion, and never appearing drunk, no matter what. Ladies expected instructors to be outstanding dancers until three in the morning, yet to be on the slopes again by nine. Of foremost importance, however, was their ability to build and restore a pupil's faith in the sport and in him/herself: "Sure you can make it down here! Just keep your knees bent and don't sit back!"

"Sure you can get up! I'll show you how it's done." And they would plop down next to the frustrated student.

"First, do not throw yourself, ski poles and all, into the abyss!

"Then, roll onto your back so you can lift your legs above you, and untangle your skis. Bring your skis down next to you, making sure they don't point downhill—or uphill, for that matter—and sit up as straight as you can; put one pole into the snow, basket a little beyond your knee; now put one hand on the basket of that pole, the other over the top of the pole. Rock forward a bit and push and pull with your arms. *Eins, zwei, drei*—push! Now that wasn't so hard, was it?"

And that was exactly how I got Brigitte up, her body as well as her confidence and spirits. Of course, what worked for her didn't always work for customers over two hundred pounds.

"Wow, that was easy! You are a terrific teacher, Horsti. Maybe there is a future here for you."

She tried to shuffle forward for the traditional hug but had to abort. "I'll postpone it for now. Or can you quickly teach me how to do this on skis?"

"Sure! Just stand still and don't fall over."

I pushed off gently and slid forward until I bumped into her.

"Oh, I am beginning to like skiing. But I think I need to practice this for a while."

We did, taking turns. I think I had actually discovered a new exercise for developing balance and stability. Then I decided it was time for teaching her the fine art of walking, involving the weight shift from one sliding ski to the other as we increased our speed. We put more and more force into each stride, and soon we were moving fairly fast. When I performed a few skating steps in front of her, she was stunned.

"Hold it! This I've got to learn! How do you do it?"

"Do you know how to skate?"

"Sure!"

"Well, this is called 'skating.' Same principle. Stay on your inside edges and push out as you do when you skate. Watch me, and try to imitate me."

I took off, taking long, slow, sliding strides, pushing off with both poles simultaneously, and judging by the squeals of delight behind me, I gathered that Brigitte had caught on. She was beside herself with pride and joy. "This is so incredible! But I think what I need right now is a refresher course in that first exercise you taught me."

We accomplished a lot that afternoon. Brigitte's training and athletic ability made everything so easy. No awkward moments, no incorrect weight shifts. She instantly comprehended "inside edges," "outside edges," "downhill ski," "weighting the downhill ski," and all those maneuvers like sidestepping, herringbone, kick turn, and snowplow, which were essential in those days when skiing still entailed coping with ungroomed terrain, and mountaintops—save for a few exceptions—were reached one step at a time.

Thus, by the time the setting sun cast a delicate pink hue over all that snow, we had accomplished much more than I had planned—straight runs down a gentle decline, snowplow stops and turns, fast-forward walking, and skating.

There were no clouds, and temperatures plummeted rapidly.

"Let's get out of here," I urged. "We are wet and sweaty, and we are really going to freeze if we don't hurry."

"Jawohl, Herr Skilehrer!* Catch me if you can!" And she took off on the level trail so fast that I had a hard time keeping up.

*Ski instructor

XVI

How we got our Christmas roast, and how we had our very own Christmas miracle

SUNNY, CLEAR WEATHER PERSISTED, so we skied every day, farther and farther into the forest, until there were no more roads, just narrow trails which rangers and forest workers had laid out. Animal tracks abounded, deer, fox, and hare mostly.

Occasionally, there would be a shot tearing through the silence. A shot? How could that be? The possession of firearms was strictly forbidden. Obviously some bold poachers were out there, looking for their Christmas dinner. But who would have the nerve to keep guns around? Like a magnet, some force pulled me in the direction of the shots. If there were shots, there had to be poachers; if there were poachers, there had to be meat; if there was meat, there was a potential Christmas dinner waiting for us. I was like a wolf on a trail of warm blood.

Deeper than ever before, we penetrated the forest. It was still early, so I was not concerned about nightfall. Brigitte was a bit worried, I sensed, but she kept up with me. A path from the right met ours. On it there were ski tracks from two skiers in single file, as I could see by the number of pole marks to the right and left of the tracks. And something else! Marks from the runners of a sled were plainly visible. Index finger on my lips, I signaled Brigitte to be absolutely quiet. After a few minutes we heard voices in the distance—talk, occasionally interrupted by laughter.

"Quick, let's get to that big tree. We can hide there and pray they won't notice that we left the trail." We released the bindings and slipped behind the tree. A ridge of trees cast its shadow around us, creating twilight and giving us some protection.

The voices came closer and closer. Soon we could see two men, each leaning forward into some sort of harness, pushing with their poles, straining to pull a heavy load on the sled. A few minutes later and we knew what the cargo was: a large buck, so large that parts of it dragged in the snow. We also knew who one of the sharpshooters was. When I recognized him I grabbed Brigitte's arm so hard that she let out a little groan. It was Doktor Bucher, our landlord, ex-teacher at the Maximilian Gymnasium, fired from his job because of his past as a prominent Nazi. Now we could also understand their conversation.

"That buck didn't know what hit him. It was perfect. Biggest one we've gotten this year."

"Yeah! But we have to be careful. I think people are getting suspicious. That good smell coming from our kitchens all the time, you know. After today, we'd better lie low for a while. Anyway, let's hide it where we always do, and tomorrow morning at three I'll pick you up, and we'll drag it to your garage."

They had reached the intersection with our tracks but were working so hard that they did not notice anything. What a relief!

"Okay, let's go home," Brigitte said. "I'm getting cold."

I looked at her in amazement. "Go home? Are you kidding? That was our Christmas dinner sliding by here just now. We have to follow them and find out where their hiding place is. That old bastard Bucher! You should see the way he looks at us in the house."

"Oh, wow!" Brigitte whispered. "We are going to snatch that buck away from them? You are bad, but I love it—and you—and venison. So, let's go!"

We followed at a safe distance. We could see them ahead of us most of the time, trees permitting, but suddenly they had vanished. That had to be it. Then we saw and heard them again. They were moving much faster now. We waited until they had completely disappeared, then we looked for the spot that had swallowed them up. Following their tracks, it was not difficult to find. They had been very careless, making no effort to obscure their moves.

What they had created was a very primitive hiding place, just a snow cave covered with canvas, snow-covered pine bows camouflaging the entire structure. Yet, from the trail nothing was visible.

"Not too bad—," I commented, "for amateurs. So now we know exactly where it is, right?"

"Right!"

"Will we be able to find it in the dark?"

"Blindfolded!"

"Okay, let's get home. We have work to do. I think we'll need help."

"I think you are right! That was one big buck!"

Back in town, I first went to Werner's place. I knew he had skis and a big sled for firewood. He also liked dinner parties with good food.

"I have a date with a big buck tonight," I greeted Werner and Gaby. "He said he wants to be at our Christmas dinner. I told him we'll pick him up at twelve. I promised we'd give him a sleigh ride into town."

Werner was no stranger to foraging strategies, but he was no match for me. He was amazed at what I told him, but could not find any flaws in the plan. Besides, we had not—nor were we about to—do anything illegal.

"Sounds outrageous, yet simple and logical," he said. "That old bastard Bucher! Always acting so superior. I am glad it's him and not some poor schmuck. The only difficulty I foresee will be the transformation of the buck into table meat. Have you considered that? Skinning, cutting, aging, and marinating? Where is all this supposed to happen? Of course, there is still the Schwan. We could use the storage room and the kitchen, and we'll need the large dining room, anyway, if we are all going to eat together."

I could tell he had caught fire and was licking his lips in anticipation. As for the predicted difficulties, I had thought of all this and was confident I would be able to handle everything with a little help. I knew Bastel had assembled quite an arsenal of cutting tools. So that was my next stop.

"Search no more, worry no more! Your Christmas dinner is on its way," I announced as I entered the kitchen where he and Utte were eating supper: boiled potatoes with a cheese sauce. What else would anyone be eating these days?

Though not intentionally, I often managed to drop in on them during suppertime. And this time too, I was not disappointed. "Here, have some," Utte said. "It's all your fault, you know, that we have to eat this crap seven days a week. But what can you do! Without it, we wouldn't be eating anything. So what did you do this time, rob a train? And can we please have some of it?"

"No, not a train, just that Nazi swine Bucher," and I gave them all the relevant information.

"Can you come and help tonight, Bastel, when we make the pickup at twelve?"

"You can count on me," he said enthusiastically. "Let me get my skis ready and two of my heavy ropes. I'll help with the butchering, too. I have some experience and also some good saws and several very sharp knives."

There was one major person who had yet to be informed—my mother. Contrary to my expectations, she did not explode. Instead, a delighted, triumphant smile appeared on her face. "Good! I am glad you are doing this to the Nazi cretin, Bucher. He deserves it. Can't you turn him in for possession of firearms?"

"I could, but his rifle is out there in that hiding place, and we would lose the buck if I did."

At midnight we all met in front of the Schwan. There were four of us. Brigitte had insisted on coming along, and I was glad because by now I needed her presence for my general well-being.

It was cold; the snow reflected the starlight just enough so we could make out the old ski tracks. We were wrapped up in German Army parkas that had never made it to Stalingrad, white parkas with hoods. A wonderful sense of adventure overcame me—the skis, the ropes, the sled—like setting out for an Arctic expedition. The only thing missing to make the scene complete was a team of howling sled dogs.

Brigitte led the way. Hadn't she used the word "blindfolded"? She followed the trail with the ski tracks until we came to the thicket where I had broken off a couple of branches to mark the spot. Yes! There they were! We gathered around in a circle.

Werner unstrapped his backpack, opened it and fished around in it. "The most important thing in an undertaking such as this is to fortify your mind and body," he lectured.

He came up with a little flask, uncorked it and passed it around. It was Obstler, that clear, sharp fruit distillate that went down your gullet like lava. I think it was the first time Brigitte experienced something that potent. Almost immediately she started to giggle and bump into me on her skis. One more swig and she would have started to sing.

"All right, let's get that critter," Bastel said and was gathering up momentum to entertain us with one of his humorous sayings, when the forest around us suddenly lit up, and we stood there like actors on a stage, caught in the convergence of several floodlights.

"Hände hoch! You are surrounded! Do not move! This is a special unit of U.S. Intelligence."

The voice spoke excellent German with just a trace of an accent.

Two men approached us, pistol in hand, and started to frisk us for weapons. Brigitte just stood there with a grin on her face and started to giggle when she felt those hands sliding up and down her body. "Horst, he is tickling me," she squealed. It was so embarrassing!

Fortunately, Werner and Bastel had their IDs along, which stated that they were victims of Nazi persecution. That eased the tension considerably.

"And what is the purpose of this—uh—expedition?" asked the German speaker, a lieutenant.

"We were just picking up a buck, you know, our Christmas dinner?" Bastel tried to joke.

"And how did you get possession of that buck?"

"We found it."

"You found it? What? Did it suddenly fall over dead when you were coming? You do know that it is a criminal act for a German to carry a firearm, don't you?"

"Yes sir! But it was not our rifle, nor did we do the shooting."

"Can you prove this?"

"Excuse me! May I please say something?" I joined the interrogation. "The rifle is in that cave there. I looked it over. The owner's name is on the barrel, hardly noticeable. It belongs to Doktor Ignatius Bucher, and I saw him carrying it."

"Go—check the barrel," the lieutenant ordered one of his men.

He turned to me again. "Bucher, you said? And you recognized him?"

I nodded.

"How do you know him?"

"We live in his house."

"Is that a joke?"

"No sir! He is our landlord."

"Do you know what Bucher does for a living?"

"Nothing. He hunts a lot, I guess, because it always smells so good from his kitchen. He was a teacher but has been dismissed because of his Nazi past."

The lieutenant had nodded repeatedly.

"Yes, we know all about Herrn Doktor Bucher. We have had an eye on him for some time, and I think, now, with your help, we have something that may put him away. And your name is? And that Fräulein's? Addresses, please? Very good! We'll be in touch—very soon."

Now he was talking to his men.

"What are we going to do with that buck?" one of them asked.

"I don't know. I don't think we have any use for it."

"Excuse me," I ventured forth once more, "I think we might find a use for it."

"I am sure you will," the lieutenant grinned and saluted briefly. "See you soon."

And they were gone on their skis, carrying with them two rifles and our blessings.

"I think—this definitely calls for another round," Werner said. "And then let's load up and get going."

Our spirits soared! We had survived a close call, we had accomplished our mission, we had bagged another Nazi, and we had our Christmas dinner and then some. We were so exuberant, we actually started to sing. The song we came up with after a heated argument was "Erika," the song about a little beauty blooming on the heather, besieged by thousands of bees. It had been the German Army's favorite marching song, most effective when sung by at least five hundred men marching through Poland, or France, or Africa, or Norway, or Holland, or Russia, though by that time there was not much singing anymore. Sing to a flower? In December?—but at this point, who cared? Apparently, there was one creature that did care: at some distant farm a lonely dog let out a piteous howl every time all of us roared the famous refrain that ended with "AIHHH-ri-ka!" Thus we arrived at the Schwan, by now ski-stepping in cadence, singing loudly and not quite sober anymore.

My mother, Gaby, and Utte were waiting for us. They had unlocked the doors and had brought up the inside temperature to above freezing, so we wouldn't have to deal with a solidly frozen buck in the morning.

"Have you guys lost your minds?" my mother scolded. "Do you want the entire neighborhood to know that you are poachers and thieves?"

"Don't worry, Mama! It's all legitimate. It's a Christmas present from an American lieutenant."

For the next couple of days we were sawing and cutting from morning till dark. Oh yes! We had detailed directions for the processing of a deer. An old hunting manual told all, from skinning to roasting, but the transition from print to praxis never quite works as one expects or hopes. So we ended up with huge heaps of scraps and meaty bones, except for the thick muscle portions, of course, which had been designated for Christmas dinner. Fortunately, there was no shortage of grateful recipients who, just as had happened with the Emmentaler, now received meat parcels. Finally, the era of cheese cookery came to an end. The natives lifted their heads, opened their nostrils, sniffed the air, and welcomed the aromas of venison concoctions. No good meat or organs wasted here! In fact, aside from the hoofs, skin, and antlers, I don't think there was any part of the animal that didn't end up in someone's digestive tract. There were fried liver, sweet-and-sour kidneys, lung hash, stuffed heart, and any number of soups, stews and goulashes. Bastel's father, who was a bit squeamish when it came to food, asked his son suspiciously, "And what did you do with the asshole?"

My mother, calling upon her earlier experiences at the family estate with its annual hunts, took charge of preparing the large roasts. There was just enough time left for the aging and marinating. An animal of this size and age, male moreover, needed to marinate about five days, and then, before going into the oven, it should be larded, otherwise the dense muscles would end up rather dry. Larding, I found out, meant inserting strips of pork fat into meat. There were larding needles in the Schwan kitchen, but finding pork fat proved difficult. Finally, my uncle was able to make a deal with the landlady, a deal involving a new kind of aftershave lotion and some brandy. As my uncle put it, "I hope they'll know which one to drink and which one to rub on their faces—not that it would make a whole lot of difference!"

Two kinds of marinade were concocted: one was composed of wine, juniper berries, bay leaves, sliced onion, and peppercorns; the other, which my mother favored, substituted buttermilk for the wine.

As the leg and loin roast portions were awaiting their day, we, the night raiders, and by special invitation, Gaby, Utte, and my mother, prepared to reward ourselves for our efforts. We had set aside the tenderloins—juicy and ready to fall apart on your tongue when cooked—for a little celebration. We heated up the Schwan kitchen, sliced the meat into thin steaks and pan-fried them in butter. Into the pan drippings we stirred cream, a little sherry, and as it began to thicken, a jar of lingonberries. As we ate and drank, we all raised our glasses: "To Bucher, the old bastard, and may he get what he deserves! Too bad, he can't be around to witness the happiness his generosity and marksmanship have generated!"

Yes, it was tragic! He was prevented from enjoying himself with us, because he was in a little cell, awaiting a trial in which the charges of poaching and possession of firearms were mere trifles compared to other allegations.

Ever since Germany's surrender, a Nazi terrorist organization which existed throughout Germany had carried out attacks against U.S. forces in our area. The group was well armed, trained, and informed. The name: Wehrwolf—comprised of young men who couldn't accept that the Aryan race was not a bunch of invincible supermen. Its members were mostly former Hitler Youth leaders.

Several U.S. Army vehicles had been ambushed; U.S. soldiers had been killed or wounded. A special unit of army intelligence, working together with German intelligence, came to investigate. A few suspects turned up, but their activities yielded nothing to justify an arrest. One name had cropped up more than others—Bucher. The agent assigned to him could not report anything unusual, other than that the suspect liked to ski with one of his friends. When a small ski unit looked for some clues in the woods, they came across ski tracks: Brigitte's and mine. Following them, they were led to Bucher's hideaway with the dead buck and the rifles. If they staked it out, so they must have figured, at least they would apprehend some poachers with illegal firearms. Naturally, they were delighted that in the process of doing so they had stumbled across Bucher. He was arrested; I had to identify him as the person I had seen with the buck and the weapon that had killed it. Now a thorough investigation of Bucher's contacts and activities took place. Some witnesses came forth, and their testimony led to more arrests. Several older students, as well as two of our teachers, disappeared. Bucher, a World War I officer, finally confessed that he was the commander of the local Wehrwolf unit.

Even though there had been nothing that I had planned or instigated in connection with Bucher, I was regarded by many as the troublemaker who was responsible for yet another defeat of the Germanic fighting spirit. I realized that it would take a long time before the motto etched into the blade of every Nazi dagger—Our Honor Is Loyalty—would be forgotten.

Perhaps, so I thought, the Bucher episode would contribute a little to obliterate the memory of the Nazi era, and deep down within me I perceived a feeling of satisfaction that, though unwittingly and unintentionally, I had been an instrument of justice.

It did not take my mother very long to tumble me from my lofty perch. "Ach Horst, Horst! Why can't you understand and accept our position in this country. You think you have done something noble, but whenever one of us causes the spotlight to turn in our direction, we, the older generation, tremble with fear. It's inborn—instinct and conditioning developed during millennia of persecution."

The time before Christmas raced by, gaining in speed, so it seemed, as the 24th approached. God knows, there was little to get excited about, yet a festive mood had descended upon all of us. Small batches of cookies were baked; little presents were assembled and carefully wrapped and labeled. An air of joyous secrecy surrounded it all. With the forester's permission, we had selected, cut, and re-erected in the dining room, a stately fir tree. Around it we assembled the famous old crèche from Breslau. Papa Glaeser was tuning his lute, humming the familiar carols and threatening to perform his music, as usual. Brigitte secretively confided in me that she and her sisters were preparing a little Christmas concert for us. I had seen to it that she and her family would be invited to our celebration. As always, her mother had politely declined but had thanked us for inviting her children.

As we discussed this, my mother shook her head. "I wish I could put my finger on it. Is there ever any indication of her political or racial orientation? Do you think our Jewish blood could have anything to do with her attitude?"

I shrugged my shoulders. "All I can tell you is that Erhard would sooner die than have anything to do with Nazis. And so would Brigitte."

Then, on Christmas Eve, without a guiding star, without angels, without a heavenly host or mangers with shepherds and sheep, oxen and asses, our Christmas miracle occurred. It was not the Three Kings that arrived, merely one of them, and not on a camel's back either, but in a U.S. Army jeep—Mo! The old son of a gun! Without heralds or even a phone call, and what he had in his jeep was not myrrh, gold and frankincense, but hams, turkeys, fruit, wine, and cigarettes, and believe it or not, two large carp and a bag of poppy seeds. He must have paid close attention whenever we had talked about Christmases past.

A feverish activity ensued. All that food! If we intended to use any of it this evening, another miracle was needed. Everyone available sprang into action. Naturally, Brigitte was with me.

"Would you please go and ask your brother to come to our aid? If he wants a chance to finally get involved with something important, this is it!"

So we all worked together. The old Schwan kitchen had never seen busier and happier days.

Actually, there was now too much fresh meat for our immediate needs. One ham and one of the turkeys disappeared instantly into the oven; the other pieces we took to one of the balconies. The temperature was well below freezing, and remembering the acquisition of the '43 Christmas goose, I decided to use the second floor balcony for safekeeping.

Originally we had planned to serve a venison roast with Spätzle and red cabbage; now the menu had changed into a veritable meat orgy. From time to time Mo showed up to cheer us on. It was obvious he was concerned about our ability to handle a thirty-pound turkey the proper American way. He had brought a large bag of cut-up bread with some strange spices in it, referring to it as "stuffing." Instructions for preparation were included.

"No, no! You cannot have roast turkey without that stuffing. It would be a sacrilege!" he shouted.

So, back out of the oven the turkey came to be stuffed.

Gradually, the number of helpers in the kitchen began to shrink. Some had to participate with the preparations in the dining room, which included decorating the tree; others, such as Brigitte and Erhard, had to go home to change, and Brigitte wanted one last rehearsal with her sisters. That left a core of four in the kitchen: Utte, Gaby, my mother, and me, more than enough to complete everything.

Just one problem remained unsolved, a huge one: what Christmas gift would adequately express our feeling of gratitude and friendship to Mo?

Papa Glaeser had the answer. "I have just completed a wonderful little watercolor of that charming baroque wayside chapel buried under two feet of snow with a setting sun and a pinkish light on everything. It's perfect!"

Our guests started to arrive, some looking forward to culinary delights, others in somber moods, homesick, yet grateful for this haven. They lingered in the entrance hall, conversing in hushed tones. Then there was the familiar sound of the little silver bell, and the double doors to the dining room swung open. It was a beautiful tree: tall, straight, perfect. And all the familiar ornaments had survived the long journey from Breslau; on top hovered the angel with the silver gown and long golden hair, spreading wings protectively over the tree and the manger scene below. Glass balls in many shapes and colors reflected light from wax candles.

"Horst!" someone called, "why don't you go to the tree and light all the sparklers. But be careful."

Papa Glaeser sat solemnly next to the tree, the huge family Bible on his lap, his lute leaning against the wall. He read the Christmas story, then he reached for his instrument, strummed a few chords, and all of us followed him in the first song, "O Tannenbaum." Gone were the days of off-key singing. Gaby, Bastel, and their parents, not to mention the Hilgendorfs, were superb musicians.

Most of the guests were surprised when the three girls, led by Brigitte, appeared with their instruments. This was turning out to be quite the gala event, a feast for ears, eyes, and palate. Brigitte in particular was a visual pleasure for the audience. Propelled out of his complacency, my uncle jumped up when he saw her in her full black velvet skirt, her dark green satin blouse with mutton sleeves and a high neck with ruffled edge. He rushed over, begging her to let him carry her instrument. She smiled and graciously tolerated a peck on the cheek. For the first time ever, as far as I knew, she had put on lipstick and was wearing high heels.

The musicians set up next to the tree and started to play some of the traditional carols, some less familiar ones, and two short pieces which must have been Bach or Händel. Everyone was moved by the performance, though the younger guests had their eyes glued to the kitchen door, whence the more tangible delights were expected to emerge. But the time was not ripe.

A discreet throat clearing interrupted the expectant silence. Mo had risen and was approaching the musicians. He shook their hands, then he turned to us all, thanking everyone for letting him join. "Dear friends, I am deeply touched by the beautiful singing and playing. You have wonderful music, and listening to it I feel a little sad, because I miss my Christmas music which, I think, is also beautiful. With your permission, I would like to give you a sampling of our American Christmas music."

I had no idea what to expect and was surprised when he began to sing. What a rich, mellow baritone!

"Must ask him where he studied voice," my mother whispered to me. "What a talent!"

Though I knew quite a few English and American carols from singing in the school choir, none of his were familiar, and I found them to be far more beautiful than the ones I knew. He started with one called, "In the Bleak Midwinter." After the first few measures, Brigitte started to play some experimental accompaniment which quickly reached the virtuosity she sometimes achieved when playing with me. Then came "Bells of Norwich," followed by "Lulay, Thou Little Tiny Child." By the time he ended with "What Child Is This?" all the instruments were playing along. I thought this had turned out to be the best Christmas present we could have given him.

XVII

How we were reminded that anti-Semitism is not dead, and how we dealt with the coal shortage

AFTER ALL THIS PLAYING and singing, I could not imagine that Papa Glaeser would deliver one of his well meant, though often overdone, speeches. Besides, what more was there to say that had not been said already? And, mercifully, this was precisely what he did say: that we all were still hoping and praying and thankful for the same things we were thankful about at the last gathering.

The last sound waves of his amen were still hovering over us when something horrible, ugly, and life threatening happened. It shattered our hopes and made us relive our worst experiences during the war. An enormous crash occurred, glass broke, splintered, fragments were flying through the air, humans were screaming and diving for shelter under the table—an almost instinctive reaction acquired during six years of war. A large rock had crashed through a window, a rock with an attached note. It had landed next to the crèche, smashing a couple of shepherds. Mo had leaped toward the door, revolver in hand, but it was too late, as the disappearing roar of two motorcycles indicated.

Antek approached the rock and examined it carefully. Silently he handed my uncle the note, who studied it several times, shaking his head over and over. Finally he looked up. "Humans are curious creatures, carrying within the potential for good and evil. The Nazis made good use of this duality. They systematically suppressed the good, thus creating a society in which evil outweighed goodness. What we have just witnessed is the living proof of the decline of humanity in Germany. This here—," and he raised his hand with the note, "is so vile it defies our imagination and makes us ashamed to share the name 'human' with creatures such as the authors of it. I refuse to dignify this infamy by reading it to you or to permit it to disrupt our Christian celebration. If you really are interested, you can read it after dinner in the entrance hall. In the meantime: "Guten Appetit!"

I looked at Brigitte and Erhard. Obviously, they had never experienced anything similar before. Judging by their expressions, they understood that they had just witnessed an outburst of hatred. Were they capable of making the association between this hatred and the presence of a largely Jewish gathering? I thought so. Brigitte was trembling and pale, looking at me with frightened eyes. Erhard's face was angry red, and he was breathing rapidly. The two younger girls were wailing, begging to be taken home.

Good thing Mo had brought an assortment of bottles, among them some high potency beverages, because this was what it took to recover from the shock. Human nature, in addition to being saintly or vile, also has the capacity for being resilient. This, as I witnessed, is true particularly when the violated spirit is soothed by delectable food and strong spirits.

If the attack had been designed to prevent our enjoyment of good food and drink, it had been a dismal failure. Our appetites gained momentum with the appearance of each additional course: crabmeat-asparagus salad, cold curried consommé, carp, roast turkey, followed by Virginia ham, and finally, only for hard-core gluttons, the poppy-seed dumplings. It was a most unusual assortment of food, bestowed upon humans by unusual circumstances.

Watching all this chewing and swallowing around me, I could not shake the suspicion that some of the diners were driven to extraordinary gourmandise by a subconscious fear that this might be their last good meal—the hangman's meal before the execution? I guessed the note on that rock weighed heavier on everyone's mind than outward behavior would otherwise indicate.

Of course, like everyone else, I read the note which was pinned to one of the walls in the hallway. It was nothing more than a repeat of the party hate mongering of the past twelve years, guaranteeing that Germany would soon be rid of all of us parasitic subhumans: "We shall carry on the holy war set in motion by our beloved Führer and his disciples. Don't deceive yourselves! Your last hour will come—much sooner than you think!"

No amount of liquor could outweigh this message. My mother gave me a meaningful glance. I knew what it meant and avoided her eyes.

The prevailing mood for the rest of the evening was subdued, to say the least. The unwrapping of presents, accompanied by mumbled thank-yous and silent embraces dominated the gathering.

The entire evening, Brigitte did not budge from my side, reaching for my hand all the time and putting her arms around me whenever possible. "You need me to protect you," she said, and her tearful glance gave way to her fierce karate expression. "I am not going home anymore," she said over and over. "How can I, after what happened?"

She was now wearing my present: a delicate gold necklace with a large blue, oval stone. It was one of the last pieces from my Breslau collection.

"I have something for you, too," she whispered. "It's out in the hall."

She returned, smiling proudly, and handed me a small package. She had knitted a ski hat for me, Scandinavian style, which she had designed herself. It was very attractive, but somehow my enthusiastic comments failed to satisfy her. She kept looking and looking at me, shaking her head repeatedly. Finally I could not stand it any longer. "What? What am I missing? It's absolutely beautiful. What more can I say?"

Now she was near tears, sniffling delicately into her mother's hanky. "Oh, you did not really look carefully. Here . . . see this curved section?"

"Yes?"

"And here, another curved piece?"

"Yes. You are right. It is a curved section. So many colors in it. Stunning."

"Oh, you are hopeless. Use your imagination! Put the two sections together and what do you get?"

Oh, what a Dummkopf I was! How could I have missed this? A heart?—Her heart! "Oh Brigitte, I am such an idiot. I am so sorry. What can I do to make up for this?"

"Well, at least let me see how you look in it. Put it on."

"Yes! But not here. It's too hot here. Let's go to the storeroom and try it on there."

Journal entry, Christmas 1945: So that is the new, free, democratic Germany? What a morbid joke! That's one Christmas I'll never forget! The killer government is gone, but they forgot to get rid of the killers, too. Perhaps this will help Horst to make up his mind and to be more careful in the future. How naïve of us to think that we would be safe now. I hope Mo can do something to help.

As happens so often with incidents of this nature, there immediately arose a deluge of rumors surrounding it: that a Wehrwolf unit was on its way to "clean up" the town; that similar outbursts of anti-Semitism were occurring all over Germany; that Jewish homes and businesses were being looted and destroyed, just as had happened during the infamous *Kristallnacht* in the 1930s; that Jewish women were being molested, men beaten up.

Mo tried to assuage our fears and promised to help. He had phoned in a full report to his headquarters, requesting that an MP unit for our protection be set up in Obergünzburg. This actually happened—ten men under the command of a lieutenant.

Did we file a complaint with German authorities? After cautious analysis of the situation and considering the apparent attitude of the indigenous population, we decided it would be in our best interest not to say anything to anyone. Once more my mother's credo was observed: "Don't ever tell anyone that you are Jewish!" Of course, by then everyone knew anyway.

A few days after the incident, Brigitte, Erhard, and I were pulling a sled to the forest for some firewood. We soon noticed that a group of five sturdy lads, about fifteen to eighteen years old, was following and closing in on us. We tried to disappear into a side street but no luck. They caught up and surrounded us, ordering us to stop. The oldest, at least eighteen years old, acted like some official. "Where are you going? Do you have a wood permit? Well, then we'll have to get your names and confiscate the sled. We can't allow any wood thieves around here."

One of the younger ones had been looking Brigitte over from all sides. With a malicious grin he addressed her. "You must be that dirty slut, that Jew whore they are all talking about."

I could tell that Erhard had taken all he could. His face had that angry, dark red color, and his sister's eyes had narrowed. She had dropped the sled rope, taken off her gloves and had assumed a threatening stance.

"Listen," Erhard said firmly, "we are freezing and looking for wood like everyone else. We don't want any trouble. So let us through."

The leader of the group stepped closer. "You don't want any trouble? Did you hear that, boys? They don't want any trouble! So what are you going to do about it if we feel like giving you trouble, lots of trouble? You and that slut and that Jew bastard."

He was now just inches away from Erhard and gave him a push. What happened next lasted about ten seconds. Erhard and Brigitte seemed to be flying through the air, kicking and striking with incredible speed and making blood-curdling sounds with each punch. Then there was wailing and groaning. Three of the five attackers were on the ground, twisting in agony. There was blood in the snow now, and one of the boys was crawling around, crying, "My teeth, help me find my teeth!" But his comrades had vanished. We helped him up on his feet. He stared at us with a mixture of fear, hatred, and defiance.

We notified the MP unit who came to investigate. Later we learned that we had flattened one of the Wehrwolf assault squads. Fortunately none of the boys was from Obergünzburg. After that they left us alone.

"Can you teach me to fight like this?" I asked Erhard. "Looks like a must for me, if I want to stay alive here."

"Sure I could, but it takes a long time to become effective."

"Why do you want to learn?" Brigitte interrupted. "You don't need to know. You've got me."

Nineteen forty-six began with an unusually severe cold snap, inflicting suffering on man and beast. Hardest hit, of course, were the refugees. Every stick of wood was jealously guarded. Groups of people would hike out to the nearby train tracks to gather up pieces of coal that had fallen off freight trains. There was a little hill called Jägerkuppe where the trains slowed down considerably, so much so that we were able to jump aboard and assist the coal in falling off. This act of self-preservation became a sort of sport among my friends and me. I even invited my school friends from Kempten for so-called coal rides. At one point we would jump on, unload all we could, and jump off again when we spotted that white towel on the tree that marked the spot where the train started accelerating down the other side of the hill. Sleds with crates were used to transport the precious cargo home.

"Where do you get this coal?" Antek asked with great interest while on a surprise visit. "Grade A black gold and worth a fortune," he mumbled, as his fingertips fondled the smooth, shiny surfaces. He knew coal because he had grown up in the Upper Silesian coal mining country.

"This operation I've got to see," he said after I had described everything. I could not begin to guess what it might be, but I had the distinct feeling that something big was brewing in his head.

Next day at the proper time we walked to the Jägerkuppe. If there was anything in this world you could count on, it was the punctuality of German trains, provided there was no troop transport, no bombing, and no torn-up tracks. Exactly at 2:37 we heard hooting in the distance. Five minutes later the engine had started to pull the flatbed wagons up the hill, slowing down with every meter. Antek timed, counted, took notes. As the last car passed us we jumped on. But we did not unload any coal. Antek just looked, examined, made entries in his little notebook. At the towel we jumped off.

I'll never forget that expression on Antek's face: glee, exuberance, and the certainty that he was going to introduce me to a plan that was bigger than anything we had ever undertaken.

"You know what we are going to do?" he asked. "I saw it in a movie once. There was that train, and in the last wagon they carried a shipment of gold for Fort Knox, you know, where they store all the gold. Well, the outlaws jumped on the train, balanced their way along on top of the wagons until they came to the last one. And then, you know what, they just uncoupled it and let it roll to a stop. Well, yes, there was a lot of shooting, and they did not really get the gold, but the idea was there. Simply brilliant! And that's what we are going to do. You bring the labor force; I'll arrange for a couple of trucks. When the wagon rolls back down the hill, it should just about make it to the railroad crossing, where we'll be waiting. Well? What do you think?"

I had to admit, it was a brilliant plan. "And what's going to happen with the two truckloads of coal?"

"That's simple. One truck for all the participants, contents to be delivered to each door; the other one I'll drive to Munich to the black market, and we two will divide up whatever I get."

"What about that abandoned wagon sitting all alone on the track in the middle of nowhere? Couldn't it cause a horrible accident if a passenger train crashes into it?"

"Hm, yes! Hadn't thought of that! The next train isn't due for two hours. So we can call the nearest station and tell them, 'Hey, in case you are interested, there is an empty railroad car sitting all alone on the track near Günzach.' That ought to do the trick."

The date was set for the following Wednesday. That gave me a week to organize a work crew. Without being too specific, I told my friends to arrive at the Günzach station on the 12:30 train. "Wear old clothes and bring shovels and buckets and an old towel for clean-up. This operation will keep you warm for the rest of the winter."

There were twelve of us as we marched down the icy, isolated country road toward the railroad crossing. Two large trucks were already in place. Antek and the other driver grinned at us as we arrived. Antek bestowed his usual greeting ceremony upon me: a wink and thumbs up. "Shouldn't take more than twenty to thirty minutes to unload. I want two guys on the coal car, the rest form a chain to pass the full buckets to the trucks. It's going to be hard work. Coal is heavy."

Most of my friends were a little nervous and apprehensive. Clearly, they had never done anything illegal in their lives. But then again, how illegal or criminal was what we were about to do? As Antek had lectured me, most of that trainload was going to the black market anyway, making millionaires of some racketeers. At least we were helping a lot of people survive by our action.

"Think Robin Hood," I reminded Brigitte and Erhard. Then I informed the others briefly about the exploits of my hero and how we had formed our own little group to promote the redistribution of wealth—the Allgäuer Robin Hood.

I must have chosen the right words, because I could see fear on faces giving way to interest, even enthusiasm. After all, none of these boys except Erhard was much over fifteen. All of a sudden, our little shady undertaking had become a noble, romantic, daring feat.

Antek had followed my account with keen interest. He kept nodding his head, saying over and over, "Yes sir! Yup! You bet!" while my fellow students looked at him with expressions of ever-growing admiration radiating from their faces. I had seen these starry eyes before—not too long ago. "Führer befiel, wir folgen dir." (Führer, command, we'll follow you.) Antek, too, took note. He intensified his vocal volume by a few notches, put on a fierce face, and continued his—now full-fledged—speech, as if addressing thousands, "Yes sir! We'll show them! We have rights too! And if they think they can starve and freeze us to death—we are not entirely helpless, right boys?"

What has got into Antek? I wondered with alarm. Has he gone crazy with power? Did he see himself as the hero of tales and ballads or as something bigger? What did it take to create a monster?

Antek fell silent. He now stood there, giving me a sheepish look for a few seconds. When he opened his mouth once more, his voice sounded different—cool, dispassionate, and carrying a fatherly undertone, "Listen boys, we are not a bunch of medieval peasants rebelling against a tyrant. We are peaceful German citizens in desperate need of warmth. There is a difference. We'll do this job, and then it's back to school. Don't you agree?"

I looked around. Some of the boys blinked, bewildered, as if awaking from a trance; I did too—with relief.

Antek looked at his watch. "Getting close. Everyone ready?"

There he stood, smiling confidently holding up a gigantic wrench. "Just in case," he said, noticing our questioning glances. "The coupling link may be stuck and require loosening."

At 2:37 the hooting of the train broke our tension; five minutes later Antek hoisted himself up and onto the last car. Another five minutes and Antek reappeared, slowly rolling down the track away from the train and doing a little dance on top of the pile of coal. We had laid a small log across the tracks so that the car would stop exactly where we wanted it. The two strongest boys jumped up and started filling the buckets, handing them to Antek who passed them on. It really went fast. Any fire brigade would have been pleased to accept our services. In twelve minutes we had filled the first truck; another fifteen minutes and the second one was also ready to roll. There still was quite a bit of coal left in the car, so we just dumped it in a pile on the ground. Imagine the delight of the lucky coal hunters who would stumble upon this treasure!

Work completed, we all looked at each other and burst into laughter. Everyone was blackened from the coal dust. With the aid of snow and the towels, we managed to make ourselves presentable enough to rejoin the civilized world.

Antek had a list of all participants' addresses and promised to leave nice piles of coal in front of cellar windows.

"When are you going to Munich?" I asked.

"Day after tomorrow. Want to come?"

"Sure, but—" I felt a severe pain in my arm. Brigitte had pinched me hard. "But, what I wanted to ask, can Brigitte come?"

There was some hesitation, brow wrinkling, head waving, and then a resigned, "Yeah, yeah, sure."

"Great! Why don't you pick us up at the station in Kempten? That way we won't attract any attention at home. We'll be coming in on the 8:20. By the way, will we be back in the evening?"

"I expect to be. I have to be at work Saturday morning, you know."

Erhard's face expressed skepticism as we later discussed this matter. His little sister going off to Munich did not strike him as a splendid idea.

Even I felt a little uncomfortable. "What about your mother, in case we don't get back on time?"

"Oh, she never worries about us. Never said a word all those times I left real early or came home real late. She knows I can take care of myself, and she trusts me."

"Well, okay then," Erhard agreed. "Still, I wish I could join you, but we are having a major exam that day."

My mother wasn't ecstatic about the trip either. "I don't know," she mumbled over and over. "I don't know what it is, but I have an uneasy feeling about this trip. At least you can always go to your aunt in Planegg if there is trouble. And let me also give you Anja's address."

Brigitte watched quizzically as my face turned beet red. Later she asked me sweetly, "And who is Anja? Not that it matters."

"Oh, she is the fiancée of the Russian officer who helped us get out of Breslau."

Even though I thought that I had spoken totally nonchalantly, my tone of voice must have set off some sort of female alarm mechanism in her brain. "And were you good friends?"

"Who? Misha and I? I guess so. We used to go fishing together—and looting through abandoned houses."

"No. I meant you and Anja."

"Oh no! She was my friend's fiancée and six years older than I." This was getting to be a little uncomfortable. "You know, maybe we can drop in on them. I'd love to have them meet you."

"Oh, they live together? Are they married?"

"I'm not sure, but I think so." Sweat was forming on my forehead by now.

"Yes, that would be nice," she said, giving me a long thoughtful look through narrowed eyes.

XVIII

What happened in Munich, and why we visited Misha

MUNICH HAD NOT CHANGED much since September, except now the destruction was mercifully hidden under a thick, white layer of frosting. Jagged edges had disappeared under dollops of snow, piles of rubble and bricks looked like hills for sledding. People were scavenging through the landscape, pulling and digging free anything that looked like it might burn. If these hunters had known what we were hauling, they would have stoned us without giving it a second thought.

We zigzagged through the city until we saw, high up on a pillar and looking at the city across the Isar River, the Friedensengel (Angel of Peace). Under her spread wings, receiving a blessing, as it were, the black market flourished. To me it appeared even more chaotic than the Breslau market. There it had been mostly victuals that were being bartered; here, anything from real estate to cars to art to trainloads of cigarettes was attainable for the right price. We began to feel kind of silly: one truckload of coal, what was that? But there were smalltime businessmen as well. As soon as we had taken the tarp off our load, merchants began to swarm around us. It did not take long before Antek had made a deal with a smiling Rumanian who could scarcely count to three in German but who knew a little Polish and a little Russian. I don't know who cheated whom, but both Antek and the Rumanian seemed more than happy with the outcome of the transaction. The truck was quickly unloaded, and we were ready to spend some of the dollars we had earned.

We strolled through the alleys with their multitude of booths and actual stores. Brigitte had a little shopping list from her siblings. I had nothing particular in mind, but one storefront caught my eye.

ART AND JEWELRY BOUGHT AND SOLD!
PLEASE COME IN AND CHAT IF YOU LIKE!

That sounded friendly and inviting. It could not hurt to make some possibly useful contacts, so I naïvely figured.

I turned to Antek. "Mind if we go in there and look around for a few minutes?"

"Ah yes! You have that interest in artwork. Do you still have that bizarre wonder-woman at home? The one with the cube boob and the figure-eight hat?"

"What?" Brigitte blurted out, "You own a Picasso?"

"Shhh! Not so loud! You want us to get killed? I'll tell you later."

Am I going to tell her everything? I wondered. Alarming her with our ticket to America?

We entered the store, and both Antek and I stared in horror at the man behind the counter. The man, too, was scarcely able to control himself. His right hand kept twitching and jerking in the direction where once a pistol holster must have been. But those good old days were gone! Now he just stared and shouted, "Hans, Hans! Schnell! Komm' schnell!"

Nothing happened for a few seconds. Then we heard repeated thumps, each one followed by a dragging sound. Even before the door opened, I knew whom I would encounter—the man with the artificial leg, the shadowing companion of the one who was at this very moment adjusting his eye patch, which had shifted in the excitement.

"Brigitte, run! Follow us!" I yelled as we rushed out.

We had a hard time finding our truck. For a few moments we thought we had lost our pursuers, but one young fellow wearing a Tyrolean hat kept appearing behind us, stopping to write down our license plate number as we climbed into the cab.

"Damn," Antek mumbled, "now they know where to look for us. From Breslau all the way to Kempten and now this! Damn! And how could we be so stupid and lead them directly to our truck?"

"That's easy," I said. "We panicked. Now what? Should we try to find Misha? He helped us once. Perhaps he can come up with something."

Antek grimaced and shrugged his shoulders. "Yeah, what the heck. Can't hurt to try. But we have to hurry if we want to get back home tonight. And you don't want to draw those criminals to your relatives in Planegg! So let's give Misha a try. Got an address?"

"Yes, here. Let's see. Okay, Luisenstrasse 56."

"I think I know how to get there. Back across the Isar and then it's somewhere not very far. Let's get going."

Of course, Brigitte had no idea what was going on and kept shaking her head. "Why are you running away from those guys? Did you do something to them in Breslau? Does it have to do with the Picasso?"

"Yes! They think we have it, and they want to take it from us."

"And do you? And do they own it in any way?"

"Yes, we do, and no, they don't. Those two were after us in Breslau already. They are probably members of an underground SS organization who will do anything to get something that valuable." Shortly thereafter we arrived at our destination—Luisenstrasse 56."

The door opened a few seconds after we rang the bell, and there stood Anja. As four and a half months ago, I found her to be indescribably beautiful. She made a sound expressing surprised delight and stepped forward to hug me. What I would have given for this back then! Now I quickly took half a step backwards, extending my right hand. Shaking hands with all of us, she very formally asked us to come in.

His portion of our Breslau treasure must have done very well for Misha, because it was a beautifully furnished living room we entered: oriental carpets, tasteful curtains, massive dark furniture, a grand piano, and paintings, some of which looked familiar. In the middle—Misha. A little heavier than before, wearing a mustache, which gave his boyish face more dignity, and grinning broadly as he came forward to hug me. "Horst, you old fish-killer, so great to see you again! I still dream about our kayak adventure. Remember? Boom!" He roared the way he always had and stretched both arms into the air.

In mid-roar he suddenly stopped because he had discovered Brigitte. "Horst! I am sorry, but I can't allow this! She is far too beautiful for you!" He used his raised arms to give Brigitte a big hug.

All the while Antek had remained in the background, smiling awkwardly.

"Did you ever meet Antek back then?" I asked.

They all shook hands and I never got an answer to my question.

"Horst, my old friend with the criminally pretty girlfriend, I have the distinct feeling that you are in deep trouble again, and you want Onkel Misha to help you. Am I right?"

"Yes, unfortunately you are right and guess what? It's the same people who were threatening us in Breslau. We just ran into them. They pursued us, and now they know how to find us, because they got the license plate information from our truck. Did you know in Breslau who any of them were? Is it a gang, an international organization? Or just a group of individuals? Did you have any idea back then?"

"We did not make any arrests in Breslau, but I think there were two groups after you. One was a bunch of black marketeers; the other was very slippery. Never got a good look at any of them. When they realized the Soviet Army was getting involved, they became invisible. Obviously, you recognized them immediately today, as they you. Can you describe them to me? Anything special about them?"

"Well, that's easy. One wears a patch over his right eye; his comrade has an artificial leg. What's the matter? Do you know them?"

Misha was whistling through his teeth and pacing excitedly back and forth.

"We certainly do."

"Who is *we?* You and Anja, or?—"

"Can't tell you, Horst. Let's just say that I am part of an organization that is tracking down war criminals. Anyway, these two are former SS officers: Kaminska and Gruber. They sort of run the black market. Totally ruthless, evil killers. I'd give anything if we could arrest and try them before a military tribunal."

"If you know what they have done and where to find them, why don't you put them under arrest? Looks straightforward to me."

"Yes, you'd think so. We tried once. Big mistake! These guys are devilishly clever, you know. They are fluent in Russian and English and they know everything about every country's armaments—extremely valuable qualifications these days! So valuable that the CIC* snatched them up as agents. That was it! Can't touch them now. But someday we'll get a break."

It began to dawn on me that Misha's defection to the West had not worked out the way he had envisioned—or had the entire defection story been a masquerade from the beginning? Well, no matter how you looked at it, they had gotten us out of Breslau in style, and we had to be grateful for that.

"I am puzzled," Misha continued. "Why are they still after you? Back then you had all those valuables, so it made sense. But now? There can't be a whole lot left, unless they know something I don't. I don't want to snoop around in your business, but it would help me to know everything. Does that make sense?"

*U.S. Counter Intelligence Corps

"Yes, of course!"

"Wait!" Misha added. "Before we go on, we'd better park the truck somewhere else. They know where I live, and they know that you know me, and they must not suspect that we are together now. Perhaps Antek could drive it to some other street?"

"All right! As you were about to tell me—," Misha picked up the thread after Antek had left.

"Well, among the paintings, most of which you got, there was one Picasso. My mother knew what a treasure we had stumbled upon and hid it somewhere away from the rest. It was to be, as she always called it, 'our ticket to America'."

Brigitte was so enthralled by all this adventure that she failed to grasp the implications of the last revelation.

"Okay," Misha nodded, "I can comprehend all this, but how does Kaminska know that you have that painting?"

"That's precisely what I couldn't figure out until it came to me why that man with the eye patch looked so familiar. When they buried the three crates in General Strasser's grounds at five in the morning, it was still quite dark, but I remember distinctly that the officer in charge of the operation wore an eye patch. That officer must have known exactly what was packed away in each of the crates. After the war, sometime after we had dug up and taken the crates, he must have come to do the same. How upsetting for him to find nothing but empty holes! Then, not long thereafter, various items from the crates began to show up on the black market. All he had to do now was to observe who was selling them and where this person lived. Very simple, isn't it? But the Picasso never surfaced. So this person or persons had to be still holding onto it. Kaminska surmised that I, Antek, and my mother had kept the painting. But suddenly we had vanished. Until today."

Antek returned. He looked worried, shaking his head repeatedly. A thin layer of snow stuck to his coat. "It's too late to start for home now," he grumbled. "Besides, it's beginning to snow."

"Wonderful," Anja suggested, "then you must all stay with us. We often have guests, so don't worry. Brigitte, let's go to the kitchen and fix something to eat. You must all be starving."

They disappeared. In the distance I heard the reassuring clatter of dishes, interrupted by occasional laughter.

In the meantime we continued our discussion. Misha thought it would be prudent if he had a car with a couple of his men follow us tomorrow. "We can assume they will leave you alone if they want you to lead them to the Picasso. But then again—what guarantee do we have that they won't try to kidnap you and torture you to get it. You can never be sure of what those people might do. Sometimes they think the faster they strike the better."

All of this began to look more and more mysterious to me. What sort of operation was Misha running here? He had vehicles and men under his command, clearly working under the auspices of the Soviet Army but in cooperation with the CIC. "And what are we going to do once we get home? Now they know we live somewhere in or near Kempten. How hard can it be for guys like that to track us down?"

"Exactly what I am thinking," agreed Misha, "but I have not come up with any answers. If they were not with the CIC, it would be a simple matter. As it is, I have very strict orders regarding them. However—," and he paused.

"How badly do you want those two, Kaminska and Gruber?" I asked.

Misha just scratched behind his right ear.

Perhaps it was the years of being constantly threatened with extinction and having to come up with simple yet clever ways of protecting myself that had developed in my brain the ability to find creative solutions to problems. As so often before, I found myself thinking feverishly of all kinds of schemes, all of which had very definite shortcomings. Finally, again, as so often before, there was something that appeared like a breakthrough to me, an idea that withstood critical analysis. Misha and Antek observed with alarmed fascination as my face turned redder and redder.

"Are you all right, Horst?" Antek asked. "You look like you are going to have a stroke—or a baby. Can we do something for you?"

I shook my head, but I appreciated the birth-giving analogy, because I, so I felt, was about to deliver a healthy idea.

"Misha," I asked, "do you know what a sting operation is?"

He shook his head but seemed to sense that I was onto something.

"It's setting up an all-fake situation in order to catch someone—in other words, an elaborate trap."

By now I had Misha's undivided attention. "Yes, so what are you saying?"

"I am saying that this trap will both save us and also give you the men you've been after for months."

"Okay?"

"Well, we have to subtly leak some information to the Kaminska gang that the Picasso will, at a certain time, be at a certain place, and when they show up to . . . kill and steal, you and your men will be waiting for them. Then you load them into your vehicle and cross over into the Russian Zone. I'm sure you'll know how to get them out. No one will ever know that you were involved. They simply will have vanished in pursuit of their own black-market dealings. What do you think?"

Misha had risen from his seat during my discourse. Now he bowed and applauded discreetly in my direction. "I knew it was for a higher purpose when we didn't blow ourselves up that day on the Oder. This calls for you know what! Let's invite the ladies for the celebration. I'll have to discuss this with my officers, but I don't see any reason why this should not work. It will be a great victory for us to deliver those two to justice. Anja, Brigitte!" he called out. "Time for a little toast!"

Brigitte and vodka? I worried. This is bound to be embarrassing.

"We'll be right there with supper," Anja answered.

We proceeded into the dining room where platters with meats, cheeses, and salads awaited us.

"Na zdorovie," Misha said, and we all raised our glasses. "Na zdorovie, and especially to Horst who is a genius, as I have always known. That's why I didn't shoot him when he caught the biggest fish away from me." And once more he roared with laughter.

Brigitte looked a bit lost, but not for long; the vodka worked its magic.

Misha was amused and delighted. "You remind me of my sister Lara. Same giggle. But it takes more than one shot of vodka to get her going. Here, Brigitta! One more! Want to dance?"

"But there is no music."

"Uck, music! Who needs music?" And he started to hum one of those dismally melancholic Volga songs, not exactly music suitable for dancing. In fact, in Brigitte it triggered the opposite of a giggle on the vodka-induced emotional scale.

"Oh, I am sorry," Misha mumbled when he saw Brigitte's eyes filling with tears.

Later, when I told the story of the very brief Wehrwolf battle, he looked at Brigitte with renewed interest. "I could use someone like you," he said.

"Really?" she asked enthusiastically, and then sweetly, "Anything or anyone you would like me to break?"

"No thanks. Not right now," he said with a worried look.

"That's too bad," she said sadly. "I really feel like fighting. Pow!" was her last word. Then she was sound asleep on the couch. I covered her with a blanket.

"I think she is the perfect girlfriend for you," Anja said.

"Yes. Isn't she great?"

Misha had to make a couple of phone calls about tomorrow; then we all went to sleep.

We awoke to the aroma of coffee and bacon. What a way to live: hot radiators, hot water in the pipes, wonderful food in the icebox. And they owed it all to me!

Antek was worried because there were two inches of snow on the ground. "We'd better get going. This may take a while."

Anja had packed up some food for the trip. She and Brigitte hugged. "I hope you will come and visit again and stay a bit longer."

"You will soon hear from me," Misha said. "One of my men will contact you. Remember, those guys are clever and ruthless. So don't take any chances."

We walked several blocks to the truck and left. All the way home we never noticed a trace of either our pursuers or our protectors.

XIX

How we used a Picasso as bait, how Onkel Pippi became an armed guard, and what we caught in the trap

BRIGITTE WAS SOMEWHAT CONCERNED about the reception awaiting her at home. The best way to diffuse possible tension with her mother, I advised, was to provide evidence that the time away had not been wasted: a couple of pounds of butter, a Black Forest ham, a pork loin, sugar, eggs, two chickens, and a few chocolate bars. Coal, of course, had already been delivered. That should appease even the most enraged spirits, we thought.

Erhard was shocked when we informed him of our adventures. "Oh why didn't I insist on going along? I knew there would be some kind of trouble."

"Here, Erhard! Look what I got you," Brigitte patted his arm. "Exactly what you wanted: mittens, fur lined and waterproof. And what do you think you would have been able to prevent or change if you had been along? Not a thing."

"Thanks! Of course you are right, but still, I always think that I am responsible for you—and what about those three guys now? What if they find us and kidnap and torture us?"

"Oh, they'll find us all right," I said. "We want them to find us. They must. That's part of the trap we are preparing for them. They'll be caught in it, and we'll be rid of them—for good. Perhaps you can help us think. What would you do if you had to find out where a teenage boy lives around here?"

"Do I know what the boy looks like?"

"Yes."

"Then I would patrol the schools which that boy may be attending. He would have to show up somewhere."

"Yes! That's the only way. So we have to be on the lookout for unusual-looking characters hanging around our school. I doubt whether Kaminska or Gruber will be doing this, but there was that third fellow who was running after us. Can't say much about him: medium height, slender, good runner, about thirty years old. And he was wearing one of those Bavarian hats.

"So let's assume they will locate us eventually. What do you think will be their next step? We have to develop a keen sense of brutality and shiftiness, mixed with cunning and ruthlessness, if we want to be able to think and act the way they do. So, if you had all those attributes, how would you proceed?"

Erhard was mulling over the possibilities. "We don't want them to break in and turn your house upside down. The way to prevent this, in my opinion, is to give them hope that there is an easy way."

"Yes! The piece of cheese for the trap. You know, my cousin Hannes, the artist, might have some ideas. I think I'll consult him."

When I mentioned the Picasso to Hannes, he thought I was kidding or that I had lost my mind. "A Picasso? And you have that lying around your apartment somewhere? Don't you realize that there exist people who would kill you for that?"

"Funny you mention that possibility, because that's precisely our concern." I gave him the background as well as some of the most recent developments.

"You know," he said, "I have dealt with Herrn Kaminska. He has a couple of my paintings in his very nice store. And I thought he was friendly and fair!"

That was quite a revelation, perhaps opening up some real possibilities. At the moment I had no idea what those might be, but it seemed like a beginning to me.

"One thing for sure, Kaminska must not find out that you and I are related and working together," I told Hannes.

So Hannes knew Kaminska professionally, perhaps even liked him, or had liked him. What could I make out of this? I had a feeling that the answer was just around the corner, but the eureka experience of days gone by was not happening—yet. Perhaps, if we kept talking, my mental block would vanish. "Hannes, do you know a lot about Picasso?"

"Well, as much as any art student. I studied his paintings and read about him."

"Do you have books on him and prints and reproductions of his works?"

"Yes. I have some books, and I have some reproductions."

Hm! Could this line of thinking lead somewhere? Let Kaminska know that there is a Picasso expert in town? "Hannes, in your store, could you put a little Picasso display in the window?" At that moment my brain shouted "Eureka!"

"Hannes!" I grabbed his arm in excitement. "Do you think you yourself could make a quick copy of our painting and display it? The rat will recognize it when he sees it and ask you about it. It's like smelling the cheese at the entrance of the trap."

"The trap? What are you talking about now?"

"Still the same thing. Everything is leading up to catching these guys in a trap."

"And how dangerous is this going to be for me? Am I part of the bait?"

"Well, in a way, yes. But don't worry. We'll be working together with Russian Intelligence. They have been trying to get Kaminska and his team for a long time. Must have been some horrible war crimes they committed. So what do you think?"

"Russians, eh? I like that. Great fellows! My Russian is rather good,

 did you know that? I spent some time in Russia during the war, working with prisoners to set up some factories. We did everything we could to slow down the German war machine. Manufactured detonators for grenades and bombs. Most of them would not go off after we got through with them. Almost got shot for it. Anyway, you can count on me. Tomorrow I'll come to your house to make a copy

"Am I part of the bait?" Hannes (left) and Author of your Picasso."

So that's where Hannes had spent some of the war years! He would never talk about it, but we assumed that he had experienced horrible things.

"Some brainstorm you had," Erhard said when he, Brigitte and I were heading home on the train again. "I just hope they will think as logically as you."

"How could they not? I can see it all now. Envision something like this: Kaminska walks down the street, stops in front of an art display. After all, this is part of what he does for a living. He looks around, suddenly seeing something familiar—the Picasso he had buried in Breslau. Excitedly he enters the store, recognizes Hannes as one of his customers.

"You here? Small world! That is such a beautiful painting out there. I just love it. How did you get to copy it? Oh, a friend owns it? Had it for years? Well, do you think I could see it sometime? Check it to make sure it is not a fake? You know, I might have a buyer for it. American millionaire. I am sure there would be a healthy commission in it for you, and not just money.

"Well, I'll inquire for you. The whole thing must be very confidential, of course. You understand. A widow can't be too careful these days. Why don't you check with me tomorrow on this? So nice to see you again. Have a pleasant evening."

Brigitte and Erhard had nodded repeatedly during my act. So it had made sense to them? I hoped.

As arranged, Hannes arrived the following day at our apartment.

It had been difficult to convince my mother of the importance of his visit. "Mother, you don't want three killers to come in here and turn everything upside down, do you? It would take them about one minute to get our secret out of you. Would you keep silent if someone put a pistol to my head?"

This convinced her of the urgency of this visit. "Oh, Hannes! Come on in! Here is the painting. Put it into the light over by the window and work fast. We don't want anyone to catch you here."

Hannes appeared awed in the presence of the master's work. He touched it almost tenderly with his fingertips; then he went to work. It did not take very long before he had what he needed.

"The rest I can fill in at home," he said, "and it will go into the display tomorrow."

He grinned at me, "Good trapping!"

By now I had conscripted some help from the ranks of my train robbery buddies. Without going into details, I asked them to be on the lookout for some very easy-to-identify men—one with an eye patch, one with a wooden leg, and a strongman with a Tyrolean hat.

First, a Tyrolean hat was sighted near our school. He had followed me to the railroad station. The following day Kaminska and Gruber were in town. High time to communicate with Misha and his team.

In the meantime, Misha's men, who had escorted us from Munich to Kempten, were shadowing everyone's moves. Indeed, Kaminska had noticed the Picasso display and had talked to Hannes. Both of them had acted as if they were very pleased to meet each other again, exchanging raves about Picasso.

So far, so good! The lure of the bait had permeated everything. It hung heavily in the air, drawing its unsuspecting victims closer and closer to their doom.

One major problem had remained unresolved so far: What was to be the location of the final act, the place where Misha and his men would be waiting, and where Hannes would escort his client to meet his captor, and where bullets might fly.

Well, there was the house in which we had our apartment. Frau Bucher, once her husband was out of the way, had turned out to be a very warm and friendly woman with whom my mother often had tea. I would even go so far as to surmise that she was grateful that the old buzzard was gone. So that was one possibility. She would surely play along. But Misha, just having arrived with four of his men, rejected this option. "Too many houses too close together. What if there is some shooting? We don't want the police involved. No! It has to be somewhere out of town."

What came to mind immediately was the Steckhaus, ideally located far away from the nearest neighbor. The owners would be away at work, anyway, but Papa Glaeser, superbly proper in such matters, asked his landlady if she would mind if he invited some business acquaintances, art lovers, for a business meeting at her house. Predictably, she was delighted to be accommodating. "And should I bake some cookies or cake for the gentlemen?"

"My dearest lady, you are too gracious," my uncle cooed. "No no!

I don't think this will be necessary. The gentlemen will not be staying very long."

Hannes had informed Kaminska at an earlier meeting that the Picasso was out of town, entrusted to an extremely competent guard—filling this role was the last remaining problem. It did not take us very long to arrive at what at the time seemed the ideal choice for the part of the guardian. Who could be more convincing than Hannes's father, my Onkel Pippi, an elderly, distinguished and scholarly looking gentleman with a vocabulary and a gift for flowery speeches capable of keeping any audience spellbound—if not numbed—for hours? Question was, would he be willing to expose himself to possible harm? What a question!

"Ever since my heart murmur prevented me from serving my country in World War I, have I felt unfulfilled, as if I have not lived to my full potential. I have always longed to prove myself in a dangerous situation and a noble one at that—not only liberating my dear sister-in-law and her son from mortal danger, but aiding our brave Russian friends in capturing long-sought enemies, fiends so vile they don't deserve to share the company of decent human beings."

Misha had listened with increasing fascination. "So was this a yes?" he asked.

"I guess so," I whispered. But we better get out of here now. We don't want them to find us together."

Kaminska had been to Hannes's art shop twice more, we found out. He had confided to my cousin that he indeed had an interested buyer who had entrusted the entire transaction to him, giving him carte blanche in the matter. "And when and where would I be able to see the painting?" he had asked again. "Do the owners keep it in their apartment?"

"Oh no! Like I told you, it's in the country. There is a guard to take care of it and to protect it. Wonderful older fellow. Used to work for Göring. Can shoot the center out of the ace of spades at ten meters— with a Luger."

"Well then, could we make an appointment with the gentleman? When might it be convenient for me and my partner to call on him?— in your company, of course."

"If you don't mind coming by here again tomorrow morning, I'll have the answer for you then."

That night we all met in a remote village where Misha and his men were staying in a Gasthaus. Two large Mercedes limousines were parked in front when we arrived. One of them looked awfully familiar. I wondered if the wad of chewing gum was still stuck under the floor mat where I had deposited it.

"Okay, we are on!" Hannes announced. "All we have to do is say when."

"Well, we are ready to go anytime," Misha said. "The sooner the better. If we hesitate something may go wrong. So, tomorrow at 14:00 hours? How does that sound? That's when you will arrive with our customers. We'll be waiting inside the house."

He turned to my uncle. "Are you sure you want to do this?"

"My dear man! I have been waiting for an opportunity like this all my life. You know, back in good old Breslau—"

"Oh, one more thing," Misha was quick to cut off my uncle, trying to prevent another torrent of words, "before I forget it." And he pulled out his not-so-little flask and passed it around.

"Na zdorovie!"

"Na zdorovie!"

That evening I sat together with Brigitte and Erhard. We went over everything, making sure no detail had been overlooked. Actually, there wasn't much that could go wrong, unless they had somehow grown suspicious. But there were no indications pointing to that.

"I don't see why you have to be there," Brigitte said. "I'm really worried."

"No need to be. I just want to be there for the pure pleasure of witnessing when they nail those bastards. If I could do what you can do, I would delight in breaking a few of their bones at the occasion."

"Hey! Just say the word, and I'll be there, doing your bidding." She was smiling again.

The following morning, about ten o'clock, one of the Russians dropped us off at the Steckhaus. Then he drove back to put the Mercedes out of sight. The barn of the Schwan was the ideal place for this.

There I was now, with Misha and three of his men, all of them armed, of course, four hours of waiting ahead of us. In addition, there was my uncle, who by now appeared to be having second thoughts about the operation in general and his role in it in particular. Nervously he kept pacing the parlor, mumbling to himself, as if rehearsing a speech. Misha tried to calm his nerves.

"There really is no need to worry. When they come in, we'll pounce on them and have them handcuffed in no time. I have known my men since Stalingrad. This is nothing! But perhaps a little swig will help?" He pulled the inevitable bottle of vodka out of his briefcase and handed it to my uncle.

"Thank you, my good man, thank you! Wonderful stuff, that vodka. I feel better already."

As I watched him I could tell that his brain was working feverishly, sending through his body messages that activated his legs and feet, forcing them to continue their rounds through the room.

"Perhaps, if I might bother you again?" he addressed Misha. "That little swallow I took had a remarkably calming effect on me. May I?"

He took the bottle from the table and, lifting it for several seconds above his head, gulped down a hefty bit. The Russians were amused; Misha raised his eyebrows. This was one problem he had not foreseen. He looked at his watch, then at the bottle: two hours and two thirds of the bottle to go. At this rate, the bottle as well as my uncle would be gone by the time our guests were due.

"Horst," Misha whispered, "does your uncle have a problem? A drinking problem? We've got to stop him. I don't want to take the bottle away. That would upset him and increase his insecurity. What we don't need now is drunk or angry people. Go and talk to him!"

Indeed, my uncle had started his pacing again, closing in on the bottle in ever tighter circles. I noticed a certain unsteadiness in his steps. If I had been a little less respectful, I would have called it staggering. "Onkel Pippi—," and I put a lot of worry and alarm into my voice, "Misha says this is black-market vodka. Sometimes it's mixed with wood alcohol. Last week there were six people who got blind from it. Better not have any more."

"Blind, eh? Well, I have a long way to go, then, because right now I am seeing everything double. Maybe this will fix it," and he reached for the bottle.

I leaped forward and ripped it from his hand. In desperation I called out, "No, no, I can't let you do this! I promised my mother to watch out for you."

He cocked his head in a queer way, like a dog observing the progress of a big bug ascending a wall. "Oh! My dear Käte! Oh, she worried about me? Yes! A wonderful woman. We must not do anything to disappoint her." He collapsed in a chair, wiping tears from his eyes.

We had forty minutes now to make him operational again.

"Horst, can you make some strong coffee—really fast?"

Not too long ago we had presented Frau Neuhofer with a small jar of Nescafé from one of our CARE packages, and I quickly heated some water in the kitchen.

"Here, Papa Glaeser, drink this! Come on, some more! Come on, come on! And now we'll walk." Never before had I heard Misha's voice sound so cold and commanding. Two of the Russians grabbed my uncle, one right, one left, and marched him around the room. Finally they halted in front of Misha when he yelled, "Detail halt! Ten-hut!" It looked as if they had rehearsed this scene many times before.

My uncle, who never in his life had worn a uniform, stared fearfully at Misha, but he stood there as if he had just completed basic training: heels together, palms pressed against the seams of this trousers, chest out, chin up, staring straight ahead with terror in his eyes.

Prussians! I thought. Snapping to attention, obeying orders—it's inborn. My uncle is the proof of this theory. I was sure an Austrian would not have been able to perform like that.

But Misha was not finished. Somewhere along the way he must have taken a course on dealing with drunks. This was the Russian Army, after all.

"Private Glaeser," he shouted, "do you know what day this is?"

"Yes sir! Thursday, sir!"

"Do you know what is happening at 14:00 hours?"

"Yes, sir! Two gentlemen are coming to examine a painting."

"Do you know what your mission is in regard to these gentlemen?"

"Yes sir! I am supposed to act as if I am the guard of that painting."

"And?"

"And to get out of the way as fast as possible."

"Yes! And don't you forget it! Dismissed!"

My uncle acted perfectly sober again. He executed a perfect about-face, but seemed a bit confused as to what had happened to him during the last few minutes.

It was almost 14:00 hours now. Two of the Russians and I disappeared into an adjacent room from where I could peek through a crack in the door. Misha and one of his men, pistols drawn, positioned themselves near the entrance behind a curtain, leaving my uncle in charge. Then: motor sounds, a car stopping, doors slamming, my uncle's voice—calm, charming and jovial—asking his guests to please come in and to have a seat while he would prepare some tea. Then there was the shuffle of feet, a chair falling, some swearing in German; finally Misha's ice-cold voice: "Hände hoch, meine Herren! Well, gentlemen, I have been waiting a long time for this moment. A welcoming committee is already expecting you on the other side. And to think that a boy of fifteen was capable of tricking you! Hey, Horst, come on in and meet some old friends."

When I entered the room, Kaminska and his assistants were already handcuffed. They looked at me with hatred. Kaminska said, "Du Schweinhund! You'll be sorry for this. And you," as he hissed at Misha, "aren't you forgetting that I work for the CIC? You'll never get away with this."

"Oh, don't worry about me," Misha replied. "They'll never find out what happened to you. This is not Munich, you know, but as we say, 'when greed takes over, the brain goes numb'. Never thought you'd be stupid enough to leave that town."

He checked his watch. "We'd better get going now. It's a few hours to Innsbruck. Easier to get across the border in the mountains, you know. From there we'll be flying you to Vienna and from there," he shrugged his shoulders, "perhaps Berlin, perhaps Moscow. In the meantime, goodbye to all. I'll be in touch. The Red Army thanks all of you. Oh, and here, this is for you," and he handed my uncle the half-empty vodka bottle.

"Thank you very much, kind sir, but you see—I never touch that stuff. I am proud I could be of service." And he clicked his heels as they shook hands. Now where did he get that? Instinct, I guessed.

Once more fate had been kind to us, or was it our ability to foresee danger and to harness every available assistance to our advantage that had saved us? Just as centuries of rigorous militarism had instilled in the Prussian mind a rigid soldierly bearing, so had centuries—or was is millennia?—of pogroms and other forms of persecution developed in us an inborn wariness and the ability to avoid disaster. So what had gone wrong with the internal warning system within the millions who had perished during the past fifteen years? Actually, I rationalized to myself, most of all we had been damn lucky once more. We were safe and the Picasso was still in its hiding place. The fact that everyone in the family knew about it now did not bother us much.

But what was I to make of Frau Hilgendorf and my mother's cautioning words regarding her apparent dislike for us? Not for me in particular but for us, the "racially tainted"? Skiing filled my days, along with music, schoolwork, some cooking, sometimes together with Erhard and the girls, and Frau Hilgendorf was always pleasantly involved. So I just could not imagine that her standoffishness was anything other than—well, what—a personal dislike? But who could dislike my mother?

How we got to visit Switzerland, how the Swiss were treated to unusual food, and how they learned American slang and song

WINTER WAS AT ITS best now; that is, at least for those who loved skiing and the outdoors. We had discovered a few steeper pitches, never good for anything more than two or three turns, but that was enough to prepare us for long and steep alpine descents—so we hoped. Almost every day, from the top of our little hill we eyed longingly the white peaks in the distance. Finally, we could stand it no longer. So we decided to skip school and take the train to Oberstdorf, gateway to one of the highest ski mountains in the German Alps. On top of the Nebelhorn (2,224 meters) there was a hotel, as well as a number of short ski lifts opening up a variety of ski trails, the shortest of which was probably fifty times as long as our little practice hill. What an exciting thought, to ski on and on, linking turn to turn, surrounded by an endless sea of white peaks below and a deep blue sky above!

When we arrived in Oberstdorf, we immediately realized the significance of the word *Nebel*, fog, in that mountain's name. Half way up a dense grayness enveloped our gondola in a cotton shroud. It even sent shreds and threads into our little capsule. Gone were the mountain peaks, gone trees and snowy slopes. This persisted until we were about 200 meters from the top. Suddenly it grew lighter; we could see swaths of fog swirling around us, then a blinding light reflecting off snow and fog—the sun! We had risen above the fog! Below us a thickly woven, impenetrable carpet of grey, above us that blue sky we had dreamed of, and under it, endless slopes of white. Brigitte could not help herself. In front of all these people she hugged me.

We grabbed our sunglasses, deposited the knapsacks with our

lunches and extra socks and gloves in some corner of the gondola terminal, and headed for the nearest lift, a T-bar. I had never been on a lift before, nor had many of our fellow skiers, judging by the number of casualties littering the snow next to the T-bar. It was amusing to see one couple after another fall off. Analyzing the causes for their failure, I soon realized what it was in most cases: people were trying to sit down on the wooden bar, rather than letting it push them forward and up the hill.

"Okay, Brigitte, hold your poles in the hand away from the T-bar, and don't sit down!"

Even that was fun. Gliding smoothly uphill, rather than sidestepping endlessly up, up, up, sweating and panting.

With the aid of some instruction manuals, we had gotten quite proficient at making Christy turns—stem Christies, to be exact—and linking four or five or ten together was an unforgettable experience. This was in the days before elaborate grooming machinery, and just a little off to the sides we could ski into untracked powder! After the first few turns I knew that I was hooked forever, as was Brigitte, on that unearthly, blissful sensation of gliding almost effortlessly in perfect silence through unblemished whiteness: virgin snow.

By early afternoon the fog had dissipated to the extent that we could see the village down in the valley. The question now was, should we take the gondola when the time came, or should we ski down? There were warning signs that gave us some concern: steep slopes ahead! For experienced skiers only! So, what were we? That of course was merely a rhetorical question. We knew very well what and where we were: a long way from being experienced. But what we were lacking in experience we made up for in guts.

"Think we should?" Brigitte asked when we were already well on our way. "What if we suddenly can't handle it?"

"Well, there is always the snowplow option, or you can sideslip or even sidestep down if it gets too steep."

But then came a section that was neither terribly steep nor overly long—just very, very narrow; steep cliffs on the right, abyss on the left, and since everyone skiing down had no other option, the snow was worn and packed down to a slick, icy, rock-hard surface. I stood there and, for the first time since having been bombed and machinegunned, experienced real fear. Too steep and icy for snowplowing, too narrow for sideslipping.

How did experienced skiers handle this section? They just schussed through it! Then I remembered something I had witnessed in my Silesian mountains. Our instructor had given a panic-stricken lady in his class the following advice: "Take your poles and, holding the handles up, put them between your legs, points onto the icy crust; then sit on them as you start sliding. The more weight you put on them, the slower you will move. Try it!"

She did—and proceeded in slow motion down a fairly steep, slick trail.

I'll never do anything as disgraceful as that! I had vowed to myself—unless absolutely necessary, I should have added. Obviously, this here was one of those absolute necessities. I quickly demonstrated the maneuver to Brigitte, and then I tried it. As if sitting on a little sled with chains, I inched my way down "suicide chute." Brigitte followed closely.

The rest was easy. Nice wide-open slopes, but the powder down here had worn off. It was a strangely sobering, depressing feeling that seized us in the valley with its dirty snow banks. Noise, traffic, and the thought of riding back and going to school again overwhelmed us.

From that day on we were possessed, addicted, forever checking the weather and the papers for travel opportunities. Like a climber who is driven to conquer peak after peak or the seafarer who sets out to solo around the world in his little craft, be it sailboat or even a kayak, we were lured into the mountains in quest of untracked powder.

Wherever there was a ski lift, that's where we were heading, by bus or train. One day we received a call from Mo, asking if we would like to meet him in Garmisch where a large U.S. Army recreation area was located. Who had not heard of Garmisch, the site of the 1936 Winter Olympics? Clearly an opportunity we could not let slip through our fingers.

This excursion would require several days, because we would first have to go to Munich and from there in a different direction on to Garmisch. But it would be worth it to ski on Germany's highest peak, the Zugspitze. And Mo? I vaguely remembered having promised to teach him how to ski. He must have realized that it would be a horrible sacrifice for me to confine myself to the bunny slope with him, so he declared cheerfully that he had already signed up for lessons and that he would see us in the evening.

The top of the Zugspitze, as far as skiing went, was disappointing: not much skiable terrain on the incredibly cold and windy plateau. So we descended one level down and skied the Olympic Kreuzeck ski

Germany's highest peak

area. No powder snow there, though. Too many skiers had packed down every last flake.

I don't know if this ski area was for GIs only, but the entire day we did not hear one word of German. It was definitely intimidating, and I imagined that arriving in America would have the same effect on me. It was a scary sensation, and I mentioned it to Brigitte. She nodded thoughtfully, but then smiled confidently. "I don't think it would be so bad if we were together."

"Right," I agreed, but dark thoughts stayed with me the rest of the day.

We took the train back to Günzach, richly laden with Mo's food contributions.

The outlook for the rest of the winter was bleak. Schools had closed down for lack of coal. If it had not been for Mo and occasional shipments from compassionate relatives in the States, we would have had nothing but potatoes, turnips, and bread which, as rumor had it, consisted mostly of sawdust. Sure, there were food stamps that rationed out minute amounts of everything from meat to sugar, just enough to remind you that these items really existed. But as the saying suggested, there was "not enough to live on but too much for dying."

Despite our addiction to powdery, downhill descents, Brigitte and I still loved to explore the forests as cross-country skiers. Once, not even all that far from town, we found a small, dead doe. She must have fallen prey to dogs or foxes. There was a gaping wound at her throat, and the fur was still wet from blood.

No reason not to supplement our diet with some meat, I figured. We always carried knapsacks on our outings, and I had my razor-sharp knife. So, all we needed to do was to carve out a few good chunks of meat and carry them home. I was surprised at the reception I received. How many times in the past had I been greeted as the food guru? And now this disappointing treatment? There were skeptical, downright horrified reactions to my dinner invitations.

"Are you nuts!"

"Are you trying to poison us all?"

"You can't eat carrion!"

I was devastated but unwilling to surrender.

"Well, let's try a little experiment," I said.

Frau Bucher kept a few chickens that were scratching for food under the snow, the guinea pigs for my experiment. I cut a piece of venison into small cubes and discretely offered it to the rooster who immediately summoned his harem to partake. Eagerly they devoured the meat. And then we waited and watched: no indications of discomfort anywhere. In fact, several times the rooster gave us proof of renewed vigor and well-being by favoring certain hens with his amorous attention. Next morning I counted the flock: all present and accounted for. What further proof would it take to convince the still squeamish?

I never discovered the answer to this question, because the believers were in the majority and demanded action, leaving behind a few disappointed, hungry relatives who were left with nothing but the memories of our Christmas venison dinner. So you couldn't really blame them for periodically dropping in on us after our feast. But if they had harbored hopes of seeing us in agony, retching and vomiting, they were disappointed.

Not long thereafter a letter arrived from my cousin Uli. It was addressed to me. In it he passed on to me the invitation to travel to a country that had not been part of the war, where food abounded, where no ordinary Germans were allowed to tread and where mountains, snow and skiing were part of every citizen's inalienable rights: Switzerland. One of our many cousins, instead of choosing England or America in the thirties, had managed to be admitted to this haven of neutrality. Apparently the Swiss had recently agreed to accept a few qualified German children as guests, giving them the opportunity to escape the cold and starvation at home. "Qualified" meant the absence of Nazi ties. So who could be more qualified than Uli or I? The letter Uli had received was not just a "come and visit some time" letter. It was an invitation by our cousin Peter to come and join him and his friends, male and female, on a two-week skiing holiday in a remote little village, Stierva, above Tiefenkastel, high up in the Alps. He had suggested that perhaps cousin Horst, Tante Käte's son, would like to join the group. Uli urged me to write to Peter directly, indicating my interest.

I immediately set out to compose a letter in which I expressed my gratitude, my friendship with Uli, my eagerness to meet yet another set of cousins, and most of all, my love of skiing. I wrote and wrote, and as I progressed my words began to flow slower and slower until I just had to put my pen down. I knew I could not continue because I knew that I would not go without Brigitte. Could I possibly ask if it were all right to bring a friend, a girlfriend at that?

"It can't hurt to ask," my mother suggested. "I am sure our cousins would not have any objections, but they are not the only ones involved. Write a polite letter, and don't just mention 'a friend' or 'my girlfriend', but present Brigitte as an individual who would be a valuable asset in any setting. Oh, and mention her music! Our Swiss cousins are all crazy about music."

I followed my mother's advice, and as I wrote I felt a huge weight lifting off my chest. Eight days later I received a thick envelope from Switzerland. It contained a cordial invitation to Brigitte and application forms for our visitor's permits.

Getting ready did not require much time because we did not own much. It was not any more difficult than getting ready for our trip to Garmisch or moving from apartment to apartment in Breslau. There was just one item we did not possess and without which we would be utterly helpless, they assured us: skins. Once made from sealskins, now synthetically manufactured, these long, furry strips could be strapped onto the bottom of your skis, enabling you to walk up fairly steep inclines. Yes! There would be no lifts where we were going, and yes!— we would be using these skins not only to reach the mountaintops around us but also our quarters—a large old farmhouse—from the railroad station, two hours uphill by skis. "So don't bring more than you can carry uphill in your rucksack."

It was not like going off to uncharted lands in the Arctic Circle, but we in our state of ignorant excitement identified with Amundsen preparing for his expedition into isolation amidst ice and snow, with just a few basic belongings and relying primarily on one's own powers and one's trusty skis. What an incredible adventure lay before us! Even Brigitte's mother was affected by the—to us novices—exotic nature of the trip. She asked to see letters and forms and took notes of names, addresses and telephone numbers. She even conversed with my mother. If we thought that this was the beginning of a more civil relationship, we were sadly mistaken. Once more my mother cautioned

Stierva, high up in the Alps

me to be prepared for shocking surprises. Once more I shrugged it off because I had more important things on my mind—like finding skins.

"Perhaps in Munich," a sales clerk in a sporting goods store suggested.

"How about an ad in the paper?" one of my friends advised. "You know, with so many men gone, there must be a lot of unused equipment like that around."

Finally, in a dingy side street of Kempten, we came upon a second-hand store: toys, used clothing, cookware, furniture, musical instruments, artwork, weapons from wars past, tools, books, and sporting goods, everything surrounded by decades of mustiness. Amidst all this, a white-bearded man was perching on a pile of carpets. Like an owl, he stared at us with watchful eyes, blinking every few seconds. Asked about ski equipment, he pointed to a corner in the rear of the store. "Check back there. It's a bit messy, but there is quite a collection accumulating. Women bring in more stuff all the time. No use keeping it at home if their men have no legs or are not coming back."

His voice was unlike anything we had ever heard: a toneless gurgle, like something coming in fractured, from a very distant radio transmitter. Raising his head he pointed to an ugly scar across his throat. "Grenade fragment—France—1940," he uttered. "Just ignore it. What are you kids looking for? Want to try some skiing? Great weather for it right now. Used to do it a lot myself . . . until they got me in the knee in Africa in 1942."

"Actually," I said, "we are looking for skins—you know, for walking up mountains?"

He blinked at us, alarm in his look. "Oh kids, be cautious! The white death is out there, every year swallowing up careless skiers, even entire villages. Be sure you know what you are doing. Lost a brother that way when we climbed the Wildspitze in 1938."

Avalanches! If my mother heard about that possibility there would be trouble. "Well, I think we will be all right. Several experienced Swiss boys are going to be with us. They know when and where it is not safe."

"Yeah! That's what we thought, too. And then suddenly—whoosh! That white wall came after us. I was able to duck behind some cliffs, but our guide and two other skiers were swept under. By the time the dogs found them they were gone. Terrible tragedy!"

"Still want to go?" I asked Brigitte.

"What? And leave you alone with all those Swiss maidens? Not a chance!"

We rummaged through the winter sports piles and actually came up with two pairs of skins which had the correct length and all the straps and buckles in good working order. "Whew! What is that horrible smell? How do we get rid of that?"

"Soak them overnight in a vinegar solution, or boil them with some lye. But not too strong or they'll dissolve!" reached us in fractured syllables.

"Great advice! Thank you!"

"Hey," he gurgled after us as we were leaving, "let me know how it went. Love those mountains!"

Just the challenge of reaching my Swiss cousin would have been enough of an adventure in itself. It was one of those "can't get there from here" situations. We had checked the map, had talked to experienced older travelers, and finally to someone at the Kempten Bahnhof. We had collected the following information: there were three major obstacles between Kempten and Zürich, where my relatives lived—mountain ranges without tunnels, Lake Constance, and, blocking the most direct route, the Austrian border, which prevented us from entering Switzerland by way of Bregenz on the most eastern corner of the lake. That left us with no other choice but to take several short train and bus rides to a town on the northern shore of the lake, Lindau or Meersburg, whence a ferry would take us across to Konstanz. Konstanz, our informant whispered, as if this were classified information, had two railroad stations, a German and a Swiss one. Somehow, one little corner of Konstanz belonged to Switzerland, and from that Swiss Bahnhof one could reach Zürich in a little over an hour.

Considering all this, we left very early in the morning. A little bit later in the year it would have been a fantastic springtime trip through rolling countryside dotted with blooming orchards, past old churches, and an occasional castle ruin on a hilltop. "Must do this someday in the summer," I said. "Or in the fall, when the apples, peaches and plums, and the grapes in the vineyards along the shore of the lake are ripe—or when they try the new wine. Some of these vineyards are really famous, they say."

Onkel Heinrich and his son Peter, accompanied by Uli, were awaiting us at the station. It was a strange experience reentering a world where everything worked and where you would not be surrounded by piles of rubble the minute you stepped out into a street. People looked well dressed and well fed and most importantly: everyone we saw was in possession of all his body parts.

When we entered the large townhouse apartment, it was immediately obvious that we were in the home of art lovers. Wherever you happened to look, there would be a painting or sculpture, a fancy plate or tile. Most of these stemmed from ancestors on both sides of my uncle's parents, and there was a little story attached to every one of them. Some of the paintings depicted scenes from my mother's childhood: riverboats on the Oder, the gardens and estates where she had grown up, portraits, and some of the family-owned townhouses in Breslau.

Brigitte was astonished and a little intimidated. As always in situations bearing unknown quantities for her, she remained within clutching distance of me. "All that belonged to your family? Were they nobility or something?"

"No, just intelligent and hard working. Both of my mother's

grandfathers had their doctorates, one of them even had two, and my grandmother's sister was the first PhD at the University of Breslau. In physics or chemistry, I think. Had to defend her thesis orally in Latin, if you can imagine that. And just think, if Hitler and the war had not happened, I could be back there, owning everything—or part of it, anyway."

"Yeah, but what would all this be worth without me?" she asked with a reproachful expression on her face while reaching for my arm.

"True," I agreed. "So, thank you, Mr. Hitler, for accomplishing all this for us."

I don't think my clumsy response had quite the desired effect, but at this moment Onkel Heinrich saved me by calling us for dinner. I had detected a very familiar smell in the air, and his words confirmed my worst fears.

"No better way to introduce a country than by one of its national specialties. You've probably never heard of it—cheese fondue. Not my favorite, but heck, we are in Switzerland, after all. Might as well help to get rid of the number-one national product—Swiss cheese. Best part of it is the holes, I always say. The nice thing about fondue is, we can all sit around this pot and get to know each other."

Swiss cheese fondue! Hadn't he heard the saga of the seventy-pound cheese wheel that had rolled into our lives, nourishing but also instilling in us an aversion to the product? Good thing we were starving from the long trip. And it wasn't as if the fondue was the only dish for the evening. There was a first course. This time indeed something new and exciting—artichokes, as I was informed. Large, green shapes, resembling pinecones, in a way. Neither Brigitte nor I had ever seen one before, and I was very curious, if not apprehensive as to their suitability for the human palate. I imagined it would be like eating spiked, green leaves. Tante Charlotte explained that these strange shapes were related to thistles and that they were cultivated in warm areas such as Italy and Greece. Great, I thought, thistles! What am I, a donkey?

"There are many ways of preparing them," explained Onkel Heinrich, "but we prefer to eat them the way a farmer in Italy showed us, when he invited us to his home one evening. Boil them until you can easily pierce them with a knife. Once the artichoke is on your plate, remove one leaf at a time with your fingers, dip the thick end into olive oil, and scrape the fleshy part off with your front teeth. A little salt and lemon juice may be added to the oil. When the leaves are gone, remove the fuzzy stuff, slice up what's left, and dip the pieces into the oil. You'll be surprised how good this is!"

We watched for a few minutes and caught on quickly. Ever since, artichokes have been a favorite of mine. As for the fondue, amazing what a difference adding the jigger of kirsch made. Also, the bread we used here was bringing back memories of Sunday mornings in Breslau, when my mother would give in and bring a breakfast tray to my bed: crusty, light and fluffy hard rolls, regionally called *Semmeln,* with butter, liverwurst, and a soft-boiled egg. God, what a memory!

So I dipped sparingly into the fondue and devoured large quantities of bread instead, trying to obliterate the memory of that sour-bitter bread-mush we had to endure in Obergünzburg.

For dessert another Swiss specialty was awaiting us.

"We have heard you are a great cook and food expert. I wonder if you can tell what this is?" Tante Charlotte put a bowl on the table—next to it an implement that looked like a super-sized hypodermic, that is, a metal tube, one end sealed with a perforated metal plate, the holes about two millimeters in diameter; the other end had the pusher. Into the tube she spooned a light brown paste from the bowl, put the pusher into the tube and started pushing—and pushing—and pushing. I could guess what she hoped for, but it just didn't happen. Nothing came through the holes.

"Here," she sighed. "You know what to do." She handed the syringe to Peter.

There were six crystal bowls on the table which Peter gradually filled with swirls of long, light-brown worms. By the time he had finished, he was breathing hard; beads of perspiration had appeared on his forehead.

"Thank you, I think I can manage the rest," she said.

Large swirls of whipped cream from a pastry bag completed the dessert. Just gazing at it cranked up the saliva production in my mouth. I knew it would be an unprecedented delight, because from the first moment on I had it all figured out—chestnuts, my favorites! As for the syringe, I had to confess that I had read about this Swiss/ Italian dessert implement in some international cookbook. It is called *Vermicelles-Presse* (worm press), but I added that I had never seen one in action, and that I would definitely try to purchase one because what it produced was so unique.

Onkel Heinrich was more interested in Brigitte's musical talents than in desserts and engaged her in a conversation which went way beyond my level of knowledge. After he had brought his examination to a satisfactory conclusion, he let us in on his scheme.

"I have that old instrument which has not been played in decades. When I heard you were such a wonderful cellist, I had it checked and reconditioned. So, after dinner, if you are not too tired, I would love it if you played. You know," and now he addressed me, "our great-grandfather was a collector of fine, old instruments. That's how my family ended up with this cello. I believe your father played one of his violas."

Now he turned to Brigitte once more. "I am not very good, but I do play the violin a little bit. Would it be all right to try some duets?"

By now he was so excited that he was unable to restrain himself any longer. He jumped from his seat like an eighteen-year-old. Brigitte followed. His wife watched him with concern. "He never has a chance to play with anyone, you know. I hope this is not too stimulating for him," and she pointed to her heart.

When the tuning process had ended, we moved to the adjoining room.

Brigitte was ecstatic and hugged me as I entered. "Oh Horst, what an instrument! Just listen to this! And I thought my cello was great."

She played an unfamiliar passage, but to me, lacking the super-refined ear of the true musician, it sounded as wonderful as it always did when she played.

Onkel Heinrich listened enraptured. "I can't play with you," he groaned, "you are far too good for me."

So she soloed for a while, playing some Bach which I recognized and some others which I didn't. Then came the moment my uncle had been waiting for; she stopped playing and insisted he pick up his violin. "Your turn now! It's much more fun to play together. Just pick something you like, and I'll come in and accompany."

He played nicely, a little stiffly and nervously at first, but improved quickly, adjusting to the nuances of her improvisations. After a few pieces his wife demanded that he take a break. But by now Brigitte could not let go of the cello. It was as if it had taken possession of her.

"Horst," she said sweetly but in a tone of voice you would not dare to ignore or refuse, "why don't we do some of your songs together?"

Groaning on the inside, I walked over to her. We did several of our folk songs, and now I could hear the difference between this cello and her own, and I could understand why she would want to keep on playing.

"You two truly sound wonderful together. As if you have been rehearsing for weeks," Onkel Heinrich commented.

"Well, actually, we have. It's been about five months by now. We love to make music together." Brigitte smiled at me.

During all this Uli had not said anything. He must have looked forward to kidding around with me again, and now I had spoiled his fun by showing up with a girlfriend, and I, the great pig killer and fish robber, had turned out to be a singer. How low could one stoop!

"Hey, Uli, have you told them the story of the eel and the Blutwurst orgy yet?" I tried to cheer him up.

"Yes, please tell us some of your adventures," Tante Charlotte said. "You could fill volumes, I'm sure. We just got the big news all the time, never the day-to-day experiences."

So, Uli and I proceeded to entertain these poor, deprived Swiss with some of our exploits, all tastefully exaggerated and hammed up, but I think they sensed that there had been a good deal of desperation and angry defiance at the root of our actions.

Quite late into the evening cousin Peter reminded us all that tomorrow would be a long and hard day. I had noticed that his accent

A few years later, author (left) and Uli

was different from that of his parents. Whereas they were speaking real High German, Peter's German, although I could understand every word, was moving along in a melodious almost sing-songy fashion.

Yes," he informed us, "that's what it sounds like when a Swiss speaks High German. Wait until you hear my friends' Swiss dialect tomorrow. You won't get one word, I'll bet. But don't worry. I told them they have to converse with you in High German."

I gave Uli a look, but he just shrugged his shoulders.

"No, Uli, Bavarian is not going to be of much help to you. Even within Switzerland, it can happen that people from one valley are unable to communicate with the people from the next. Mountains are language barriers. That's why there are so many dialects."

It had been a long day, followed by a harmonious, stimulating evening: such wonderful people, the art, the music, the food, the anticipation of tomorrow's climb to our destination, but best of all, the knowledge that Brigitte was just one thin wall away from me. It took a long time to fall asleep that night, and Peter's alarm clock at six cut me like a knife.

There was hot chocolate, bread, butter, and an unbelievably delicious homemade apricot jam on the large kitchen table; then we were off to the station. At the next streetcar stop, Peter's girlfriend, Stephanie, joined us. She was not introduced as "my girlfriend," but by the way the two interacted, it was obvious that such mention was superfluous. The others were already assembled on the platform, waiting for the train. It was a lively bunch, singing and joking around. One of the boys even had a guitar.

"Is he going to carry that up the mountain?" Brigitte asked.

"Oh no! They'll bring it up by postal truck. That's how we'll get all our supplies, too," Peter informed us.

I turned to Brigitte, "See? You could have brought your cello."

One of the girls, Annelies, had overheard my last remark. "No need for that. Our landlord has one. How long have you been playing, Brigitte?"

Before she could answer, Peter burst forth, "God, you should have heard her last night! My father said she is ready for Carnegie Hall."

"Carnegie Hall? What's Carnegie Hall?" I exposed my criminal ineptitude.

"Horst, you've never heard of Carnegie Hall?" a chorus of voices assaulted me.

I could have mentioned the fact that I had been rather busy and preoccupied by our survival requirements, but that might have triggered some awkwardness. So, after my enlightenment, I just put on a big grin and said, "Oh! THAT Carnegie Hall! Why didn't you say so?"

Peter's warning concerning the language had not been an exaggeration. As he had said—not one word! I would not have wanted to even guess at what any uttered word might mean. Even the first names were totally alien to me, names such as Urs, Beat,* or Oliver. One of the girl's names was Yvonne. No German had ever carried such names. As far as I knew, they were not listed in that little Nazi publication of authorized first names.

We changed trains once, got off at Tiefenkastel, a small town so deep in a valley, or surrounded by such high mountains on all sides, that during the winter months the sun was never seen. It was kind of depressing, and everyone was anxious to rise above this realm of gloom. We strapped on our skins, something we had rehearsed at home, and took our places in a single-file column. Everyone was chatting excitedly, but the heavy packs and the constant climb soon put an end to any exuberance.

Was this still skiing? Sure, there were skis on our feet and we were moving through snow, but not in the accustomed exhilarating fashion we had come to love. This was work! Hard, boring drudgery! A couple of times I managed to walk next to Brigitte for a moment. "This is what we will be doing every day for two weeks?"

"Let's give it a chance," she replied. "Can't be all bad if the whole damn country is doing it."

We arrived at our village, Stierva, just as the sun was disappearing behind a chain of mountains in the west, turning all the peaks east of us pink. Everyone stood still and watched as the color slowly faded. It was the first time we had ever experienced the famous *Alpenglühen,* and that alone was worth a two-day trip and the long climb. Brigitte inched over silently and put her arm around me.

"This was an unusually beautiful one," Peter informed us. "I don't think I have ever seen colors that vivid—except on those picture post-cards. Well, let's go inside and get started. We have to build fires, unpack, cook, and make up the beds. We are completely on our own here.

"All the ski equipment stays in the shed. Might as well leave the skins on. We'll be climbing in the morning. Come on in now, I'll show you around."

---

*Pronounced with two syllables: BAY-aht.

What caught my attention more than anything else was the cleanliness. Everything was swept, dusted, and polished to the spotless stage. When we entered the kitchen, two of the boys were just putting matches to huge chunks of split wood in an enormous fire hole which extended about twelve feet into the adjacent dining room, where it heated up one of these "live on top" ceramic stoves. Long rods were used from the kitchen to push the fire deep into the next room. To ignite the wood they had carved curls into the sides of the logs. When lit, there was instantaneous fire. I have never seen this technique before or after, but it made perfect sense, and I practice it to this day.

"Come on, I'll show you the most important part of the house," Peter said with a grin. Up a flight of narrow stairs there were two side-by-side doors. Behind each one there was a twin-seat two-holer with tightly fitting lids. I lifted one and peered down: a scary dark shaft with no end in sight! Never have I been able to receive a satisfactory explanation as to why the privy existed on this penthouse level.

Someone must have gotten up awfully early that first morning, because the stove tiles felt warm; hot chocolate was on the table, as well as bread, butter and jam. So far, we had been treated like guests, but we tried to pitch in whenever possible. Little did I realize at this point that I was the designated cook. I became aware of it when Peter asked me if I would mind preparing the evening meals and could I please assemble a shopping list.

Wow! What a challenge and what a responsibility! My failure might terminate centuries of Swiss neutrality.

"Of course, there'll be several of us to help and to clean up," he elaborated, "but since you have all that experience and reputation, we are eager to taste something different for a change. So just tell us what you need, and the truck will deliver it. Unfortunately, cost is a factor."

So here I was, in the land of plenty, given the chance to do what I knew best, and my mind went absolutely blank. Had Peter said, taste something different? How was I supposed to know what was ordinary to them? What is this kitchen capable of producing? I wondered. There was that huge wood-fired cook stove. If you wanted to adjust the heat you had to remove or insert some metal rings in the cooking surface so the pots or skillets could be exposed to more or less direct heat. No subtle controls here! No cookbooks either! When I mentioned beef, Peter shook his head gravely. "Better stick with pork. Beef is too expensive for us."

"What about fish?"

"Fish? You don't get to see much fish around here, but on a Thursday we could possibly have some delivered."

"Brigitte!" I wailed in desperation, "They want something novel. What the heck can I make that's cheap, exotic, filling, delicious, not too labor intensive, and does not require sophisticated equipment?"

"I don't think that has been invented yet," she replied, "but if you can come up with some good ideas for these requirements, it might make you a millionaire. In the meantime, how about a shortcut version of Königsberger Klopse?"

"Okay, that's a good start, if we can get capers. Keep on going."

"Well, remember that bean stuff we had at the army mess hall in Garmisch? It was interesting, looked simple and was certainly unlike anything I had ever eaten before. We asked Mo what that strange spice was. Remember?"

"Yes! You are a genius! I just can't come up with anything. So we'll need ground meat, onions, canned tomatoes, several cans of beans and—was it chili powder? Can't quite imagine that they'll find it around here."

"If we put the order in early enough, perhaps they can have it shipped up from somewhere. Let's at least try. Oh, and remember that Chinese food Mo kept raving about?"

"Yup, great! Ginger, pork, different kinds of fresh vegetables, and rice. And that brown salty sauce? What did he call it? Soy sauce? This is going to be international week. If I had known about my part in it, I would have gotten a frozen turkey from Mo. So we have Mexican, Chinese, East Prussian, so far. What else did Mo keep raving about? Oh yeah! Italian spaghetti and meatballs. Simple enough: ground pork, eggs, onion, garlic, spaghetti, and tomato sauce. Perhaps some white crusty bread to make garlic bread. Bet they'd love that."

"Can't wait to eat all those things," Peter said. "We can make out the list tonight after we get back. I think we have enough food here for a couple of days, so there is no hurry. In the morning we always make enough hot chocolate, so we can take a few bottles on our tours, along with bread and cheese and oranges. Everyone carries something. So let's get going!"

I must confess that as novices we were a little apprehensive, setting out to conquer some unknown mountaintop. But everyone assured us that this was going to be a very easy tour, a warm-up exercise, in preparation for more demanding excursions. Besides, Yvonne was a real beginner, and no one was going to push anyone beyond their ability.

We marched off in single file, up untracked snow that was as light as down feathers. The sun was out, the sky of the darkest blue I had ever seen. Further up there were white peaks, one of which was our destination. Gradually the tedium of the slow step-by-step ascent gave way to a feeling of contentment. Everything was in harmony: man with man and man with nature. No wonder the Swiss had been neutral for centuries. They were content! And who would be crazy enough to invade this fortress of peaks and narrow passes?

After two hours we stopped for lunch and a rest at one of those little alpine shelters where shepherd boys and girls would lead an idyllic life during the summer, milking, making cheese, tending cows, and making hay. It was a sturdy little hut, looking to me like something straight out of *Heidi*. The doors were not locked, but we had no reason to enter. It was not customary, if not illegal, to lock mountain huts, lest some hikers or shepherds had to find emergency shelter in a sudden storm.

But there were stacks of boards to sit on or to prop our skis up against, so we could recline on them. The February sun was quite hot up here, and suntan lotion was passed around. We ate chunks of bread with Swiss cheese and drank cold chocolate. Never had I tasted such a delicious meal. Oranges were peeled and every last little shred of waste was carefully collected into a bag and carried with us for the rest of the day. Suddenly skiing uphill was not such a dumb idea anymore.

"Think we could do

In single file on seal skins

something like this every

year?" Brigitte asked.

"Oh sure, why not?" I answered naïvely, without thinking beyond our momentary bliss.

After three more hours, we had reached a fairly high up plateau. There were higher peaks around us, but they appeared quite inaccessible. It was colder up here; the sun was low already, and an icy wind was blowing. Still, the view all around was so spectacular that we took our time unstrapping our skins and adjusting the bindings for downhill.

I could tell that all of the Swiss were dying to see us fall all over the place, disappearing in bottomless powder. They were whispering— why they bothered, I don't know, since we could not understand them anyway. Some were chuckling, looking at us not altogether kindly. This was, after all, their mountain, their snow, and their sport. How could they have known that in just a few more years they would do anything short of moving mountains to get us foreigners to come and spend money for the thrill of sliding down their ski trails?

I did not foresee any problems for the descent; the snow was perfect, the slopes wide, and the grade moderate. During the climb we had often had to traverse up the steeper climbs; now we would take these slopes straight. We were standing in a random sort of line. Two of the boys pushed off and curved their way elegantly down to a flat area. There they waited. Annelies and Sylvia went next—not so elegant this time. Snowplow all the way, two wipeouts.

"Okay," Peter called to us, "you two are next, or you can wait until later and really take your time."

Made me kind of angry and I called back, "I think—we'll be all right. But just in case—tell my mother I love her. You can have all my money! Goodbye!"

We pushed off vigorously and sailed through that powder as we had done so many times before, linking turn to turn, Christies all the way, until we stopped, kicking up a cloud of snow onto the first four skiers.

Up on top behind us, we heard hooting and applause. Then the rest came, all together, some more graceful than others, whooping and yodeling as they went.

As I stood in the ice-cold kitchen later, inspecting what I would have to work with, I remembered the essence of one of Emma's cooking lectures: anyone can read and follow a recipe. But the real cook will be able to create a decent meal, not out of the ingredients he would

Something straight out of Heidi

like to have but out of what is available. Keeping this in mind, I surveyed the situation: spaghetti, eggs, some ham, two heads of cabbage, plus some of the basics such as salt, oil, onion, and vinegar were there. Milk was being presently picked up at the barn next door, whence wonderful, warm, animal odors issued forth, reminding me of childhood explorations around my grandmother's barns.

While some very skeptical Swiss helped with the fire, I put on a large pot to cook spaghetti. Brigitte was chopping up onions and about two pounds of ham. There were some truly gigantic skillets hanging from one of the beams, just the right size for a party of fifteen. Did I see a gleam in Uli's eyes? Now I was again the old Horst he remembered.

"Okay mon général," he asked, "what can I do for you that does not involve Blutwurst?"

"See those two heads of cabbage over there? Get a sharp knife, quarter them and cut out their cores. Then take a large bowl and shred them. We are going to have some cabbage salad. And I think that's a shredder hanging over there. Tell me when you are done."

The water was boiling; the onions with the ham were sautéing, spreading their aroma throughout the house.

"Annelies, if you are not doing anything, get a medium-sized bowl and the eggs. Crack twenty into the bowl and whip them up with a bit of milk." I showed her how to break two eggs at once, one in each hand, a trick Mo had taught me. They all looked at me as if I were a circus performer.

I checked the spaghetti by picking one strand up and throwing it against the wall. Now they all thought I had snapped under the pressure.

"That's how you can tell if they're done. If the spaghetti sticks to the wall, they are done." Mine slowly slid down, so I gave it a couple of minutes more.

"Okay, someone get a strainer and pour the water off. Yes, of course into the sink."

"Ready with the cabbage, Uli? Then get the oil and the vinegar. For that much cabbage, let's try one cup of oil and half a cup of vinegar, two tablespoons of sugar, one of salt, and about one cup of finely diced onion. Let Brigitte do that. She is good at it."

This was fun. I had never commanded a crew of workers before.

"Ready with the spaghetti? Then dump it into the ham-and-onion skillet and crisp everything up a bit. But be careful not to let it get burned!"

When I gave the signal to add the eggs to the skillet, a murmur of disbelief, disapproval and protest arose.

"Eggs into spaghetti? That's crazy!"

"How so?"

"Well, no one has ever heard of adding eggs to spaghetti. It's disgusting!"

"Have you ever tried it?"

"Of course not. It wouldn't occur to anyone to try cooking it."

"Well, you see, then you don't really know, do you? This, I'll have you know, is an old Texas specialty," I lied. Texas always worked. Whenever you mentioned it, a hush of awe would descend upon all present creatures.

"My friend Mo, a captain from Texas, showed it to me. It's called *Texas omelet.*"

If to a German the word "Texas" was synonymous with "superlative" in some mysterious, manly, adventurous way, then why would it not have the same effect on my Swiss friends? And indeed! Who, after all, would want to defy John Wayne and a time-honored Texas tradition? So the platters went around the table, and the diners couldn't get over how delicious everything was.

"And that cabbage salad," Urs inquired teasingly, "is that also a Texas specialty from your friend Mo?"

"Yup, you bet! That's what they call *Texas slaw*, except over there they also add some mayonnaise and hot pepper sauce."

From that day on, everyone except Brigitte, who knew the truth, called me Tex. "Hiyah, Tex!" they greeted me next morning. They must have heard it that way in one of the many Westerns that were playing undubbed all over Germany and Switzerland.

The events of that evening triggered a veritable Western craze. "Howdy, pardner," became the standard greeting for all occasions, even among the ladies. It was amazing what their little bit of school English enabled them to say. I introduced them to new and wondrous agrammatical structures and to vocabulary that had not yet made it into their dictionaries—nor ever would—things I had learned from Mo and his buddies.

"Don't think that you will find any of this in your English grammars," I advised them. "And don't let your English teachers hear them."

Things like, *ain't gonna, he don't, you ain't seen nuttin' yet,* soon rolled off their tongues as oil does off a hot skillet.

These kids, trained to rattle off the conjugation of any verb in any tense, mood, or voice, just couldn't get over the simplicity of this system. "So how do you conjugate this?" they wondered.

"Very simple," I replied. "I ain't, you ain't, he, she, it ain't, we ain't, you ain't, they ain't. But don't try this on a test."

No, their English teachers would never be the same again, though one addition, I was confident, would find favor in everyone's ears: "How much wood would a woodchuck chuck . . ." It sounded hilarious whenever the entire group would rattle off the whole thing in unison, especially with all the *w*'s sounding like *v*'s and all the *d*'s like *t*'s.

I had noticed with satisfaction that Uli and Annelies delighted in hurling uncouth American idioms at each other, a sure sign, I decided, that a bond of mutual fondness was beginning to develop between them. But the glue that held all that cowboy mystique together, reinforcing and nurturing it, was music. Brigitte had been able to get a hold of the village cello, Sylvia was playing a violin, and Urs his guitar. They worked hard together and the results were respectable. Soon, "Don't Fence Me In" had become our theme song. We sang it whenever and wherever possible or even impossible: on the climb, during lunch breaks, while cooking, and especially when we would all sit together after dinner.

Knowing that this would be a musically interested group, I had brought one of Mo's gifts, a songbook, *American Folk and Western Songs.* This came in very handy. Brigitte would play a few of the songs to decide which ones we would like to learn, then she would play the chosen ones until we could handle them on our own. The one that ran close in popularity to "Don't Fence Me In" and "Deep in the Heart of Texas" was "The Cowboy's Lament." We instantly grew fond of the word *lament.* There was an air of nobility about it. Not just anybody, we felt, was capable of *lamenting,* only kings and queens and, apparently, cowboys. It became our favorite English word. We used and misused it in all its various grammatical forms: as verb, adjective, noun, adverb, participle, and imperative. The privy walls were used to record the visitors' inspired outbursts: "This is a lamentable place," "Lament no more!" Others followed and added their heartfelt thoughts: "Hear my lamentations, oh Lord!" "Have I not reason to lament? No more paper!" One, poetically gifted, wrote:

What's the use of lamentation?
This, no doubt, is constipation.
Lord, oh hear this stuck lamentor,
Grant what he came here to pray for.

Fortunately for me, evening meals rarely gave occasion for lamentations. There were a few tense moments brought on by the unusual taste of the chili, though, not to mention its peppery heat.

"And this is really what cowboys eat every day when they are on a cattle drive?"

"Well, that's what Mo told me, and he ought to know. He was a trail boss before the war."

XXI

How we almost died on a mountain

WE HAD CONQUERED SOME of the higher peaks around us by now, and the climbs had become just as enjoyable as the long runs back to Stierva. There still was no way I could make out what people were saying in their dialect, but lately one word had stuck out more than others until it simply dominated every conversation: BIVIO.

"What are you talking about all the time? What's a bivio?" I asked Peter.

"It's a place not too far from here. The starting point for a two-day tour to one of the highest peaks around. Everyone is excited about it, but it's a complicated matter because we can't take all. Only the best skiers with the best equipment can go."

"The best equipment? What does that mean?"

"Steel edges and cable bindings."

"Well, we have that."

"Yes, I know."

"And I think we ski as well as any one here, all except Beat perhaps."

"Yes, I know."

"So is there a problem? I don't understand."

Peter came closer and lowered his voice. "This is Switzerland. Everything has to be discussed and decided on by the group. But I am sure you two will be okay."

"And when is all this happening?"

"Very soon. Don't worry!"

Don't worry! How could one not worry about something that major? I decided not to inform Brigitte as yet, but somehow she had it all figured out already and reacted accordingly. For the first time I fully understood the true meaning of the word "lament." But suddenly she stopped. She wiped her eyes, blew her nose, and looked at me through narrowed eyes. "Wait a minute! Something is wrong here. If we were weak and poor skiers, I could see their point. But we are as fit and good as any one of them. Aren't we part of the group?"

"Yes, we are, but we are also guests and foreigners. I don't understand this either, but perhaps it has to do with their pride in maintaining neutrality and independence for centuries. No outsider can come bursting in and assume anything. It's like that play we all studied, *Wilhelm Tell*. Remember when all the Swiss cantons united in an oath and then drove out the Austrians who were suppressing them? I think the spirit of that event is still in all of them and makes them behave the way they do."

I must admit, I didn't know what the heck I was talking about, linking Wilhelm Tell to Alpine ski adventures, but it must have done the job, because Brigitte's eyes resumed their normal shape.

"I am relieved you were able to make sense of this situation," she said. "It would have been so sad to end up resenting their behavior after all the wonderful times we have had together."

Next day Peter informed us that, of course, we were invited on that overnight tour. He was a little embarrassed about all the fuss, mentioning that his German-raised parents often found it difficult to cope with official matters.

Bivio is a small village, a seemingly endless number of hairpin turns up from Tiefenkastel. Its name dates back to the days when Roman legions marched through the region. It means "two ways" (roads): Latin *bi* and *via*, Bivia, as the legionnaires probably used to say. One of the "ways" leads to the Septimer Pass, the other to the Julier Pass. There also exists a third, less traveled way: straight up from Bivio to the summit of the Piz Turba, a peak of a little over 3,000 meters—3,018 meters, to be exact. Every meter counts.

Among ski mountaineers, reaching anything over 3,000 meters is considered a respectable feat, worthy of a pat on the back. And this would always be one of the first questions after someone's return from a ski tour: "Make it over 3,000?"

"What, the Piz Turba? Yeah, I've heard of that one. Congratulations!" Or—"Oh, that's too bad. A lot of avalanches, you say? A whole village disappeared? Well perhaps next year, then."

That's us tomorrow.

There were eight of us; three were girls. There would have been four girls, but Annelies had allegedly twisted her ankle after the news had reached her that Uli could not join us on account of his truly ancient equipment. "Left behind by Roman legionnaires," he would say with a serious face. "Here, look!" Into one of his skis he had coarsely carved, *Errare Humanum Est,* on the other, *Ulricus Annelisam Amat.*

Almost every night he had to laboriously repair his bindings, which consisted of two leather straps and a few bolts. The prospect of having to stay behind with Annelies somehow did not seem to bother him in the least.

"Well, they both hurt!" Annelies snapped defensively when I

pointed out to her that suddenly she had switched putting the snow pack from the right to the left ankle.

With first daylight we skied down into the valley. From there a bus took us to Bivio. It had been sunny every day so far, and this morning was no exception. The road kept climbing higher and higher until there was nothing surrounding us but white with a few shadows, and above us was that deep blue sky that looked as if someone had stirred some black into it.

Beat, who had made the climb once before, pointed to a distant mountain range. "The highest point in there—that's us tomorrow. Looks further than it is. Some people make it all the way up and back in one day."

The plan for today was that we would climb to the halfway ski shelter. These shelters, called *Hütten,* exist throughout the Alps. They provide unisex dormitories, often consisting of nothing more than straw mattresses with one or two coarse blankets per person. Simple meals are also available.

Even though it had not snowed for quite some time, the old cover was still light and fluffy due to the high altitude and low humidity. This low humidity, incidentally, as I had learned with great interest, was responsible for a famous regional specialty, *Bündner Fleisch* (meat from the Canton of Graubünden). Not that low humidity is a condition particularly conducive to producing superior beef, but it is suitable for air curing chunks of beef which, sliced paper thin, are considered a delicacy by many, even by non-Swiss. Years later, while driving through this region during the summer, I saw balconies laden with beefy slabs suspended from wires or wooden racks. I stopped at a butcher shop and, realizing the per-gram cost of this cold cut, purchased a modest amount. No insult intended, but I don't think I would kill for this meat—not even a cow.

So there we were, filling our lungs with this dry, crystal-clear air, and surveying the distant peaks.

"Have you checked any weather reports lately," I asked Beat. "Do you think it's going to hold?"

He shook his head, showing signs of minor irritation. "No, no. At this time of the year, with the wind coming from the east—nothing to worry about," he said with the authority of the expert that he was not. Neither was I, but I had learned to look at mountains from the distance and to expect changes in the weather when that certain "fair weather haziness" gave way to overly clear and sharp outlines, as had been the case here since yesterday.

I did not feel like being ridiculed by the others, but I shared my concern with Brigitte who suggested that we pack Mo's two featherweight shelter-halves into our rucksacks.

"How about an extra sweater? Think we can carry all that?" I asked.

"Sure," she replied, "we have been carrying heavy packs every day for over a week now."

Adding food and beverage, we ended up with quite a bundle. Never passing up an opportunity for teasing, our friends asked, "Looks like you're carrying enough for a week. Going on to the Matterhorn after this?"

Actually," I answered, "we had the Jungfrau in mind."

Please, let them laugh at this joke, I prayed, because I could see that Brigitte was about to narrow her eyes. No one here knew about her martial arts background. I shuddered to think what damage a kick to the head with a ski boot would do.

We figured a five- to six-hour climb would take us to the Hütte, where we had reserved eight straw mattresses for one night. This was the middle of the week, so we did not anticipate meeting many other skiers.

There is something particularly beautiful about an above-the-timberline climb. When the sun hits the snow at just the right angle, it sparkles in all the colors of the rainbow, and never have I tired of looking at these seemingly endless expanses of white, interrupted here and there by shadows cast by peaks and ridges—and by a single file of skiers. We loved to keep our eyes on the surrounding peaks, because the ever-changing position of the sun created ever-new hues and shadows.

Gradually the peaks in the distance revealed more and more detail. Beat pointed out our destination, the highest visible mountaintop. It looked steep and awe inspiring, clearly standing out among its siblings in the range. We all stopped to gaze, talk, and replace some of our bodily fluids with the inevitable cold cocoa.

By now the sun was just barely above the chain of mountains ahead of us. Soon we would be in the shadow of the Piz Turba. Again, I was struck and alarmed by the unnatural clarity that revealed every little detail on that distant mountain.

"We have about two more hours to reach the Hütte. Better get going."

We were climbing in the tracks of earlier groups. Even in dense fog there would be no danger of getting lost.

The Hütte was a sturdy stone structure, designed to withstand major storms, avalanches, and rockslides. The small windows somehow gave it the appearance of a fortress.

We deposited our skis in the equipment room and entered the guest room: heavy benches and tables, the same heating arrangement as in our house in Stierva. Oil lamps on the tables, some hanging down from beams, Swiss cleanliness wherever you looked. A middle-aged couple welcomed us and showed us everything we needed to know, including the penthouse privy. If ever there would be a competition for rugged simplicity, this place would outclass all competitors.

Our entire group was given one large dormitory: a room with a long wooden bench built into the wall—across, side-by-side, mattresses that smelled like a hay field and rustled and crackled when you touched them. Brigitte and I smiled at each other and claimed two adjacent beds.

Hungry and thirsty, we quickly changed into some dry gear and hung up anything sweaty or damp on wall hooks. Then we all went eagerly into the large guest room where tempting aromas enveloped us. Sautéed onion was the only thing I was able to identify with certainty.

We shared the room with just one other group, four young men whose bearing and appearance were unpleasantly soldierly and who observed us critically and with seeming disapproval.

I could not make out one word they were saying. If not some type of German, French or Italian, what on earth could it be? Asking my friends, I received a rather confusing history lecture, confusing in as much as every one at our table had bits of information that conflicted with his neighbor's. The only thing all agreed upon was the fact the four were conversing in Romansch, which just recently had become Switzerland's fourth official language. At the end of the heated though unresolved debate, I was able to construct some sort of theory.

At one uncertain point in Roman history, probably BC, one or several Roman legions on their march home were cut off from their sunny Italy by inclement winter weather. Huge masses of snow confined them to isolated valleys surrounded by impenetrable mountain ranges. No tale, saga or myth, nor any of the Roman historians mentions these lost legions. No record tells posterity why, after surviving the harsh winter, these battle-hardened men did not continue on their march home, once the snow was gone. Somehow, the Roman legionnaires must have felt that theirs would be a far better lot if they intermarried with the indigenous population, Celtic and Germanic tribes, rather than endlessly fight, fight, fight all these hostile barbarians from Gaul to England. Interesting though, I thought, that it was the language of these Roman legionnaires that had survived and not that of the Celtic or Germanic tribes. If most of what I heard was true, then it could be assumed that this language evolved into its unique, present-day form out of the Latin spoken by Roman legionnaires.

The proprietor was most obliging when I asked him to say a few specific things in his language, for example, "I love your meat with onions and sour cream," and, "Your wife is a beautiful woman." It did not sound like Italian; yet, having studied Latin for several years now, I could make out a few words that sounded familiar. It gave me a queer feeling—as if I had stumbled upon some relics from the days of Caesar.

It was indeed an outstanding meal, especially considering the fact that everything in view, such as the two bottles of wine on the other occupied table, had made it to its destination on someone's back.

Often these Alpine Hütten provide guitars or accordions for guests, and we, enjoying the contentment induced by warmth and a full belly, felt that the time had come for some singing. Perhaps, considering the presence of the neighboring table, we did not gauge the situation accurately, but we were still in the throes of our Texas cowboy period, so we decided on "The Cowboy's Lament," to be followed by "Round-Up Time in Texas," and "Deep in the Heart of Texas." We had sung these songs so many times that we must have sounded like some Western pro group. The proprietor was beside himself with enthusiasm; our four neighbors remained stony faced and kept whispering to each other. Finally, one of them, knocking his chair over while getting up, staggered his way to our table.

Brigitte had accompanied us on the house guitar during the last song; now that young man addressed our entire group and her in particular. "You people are really good, but why do you sing this American crap? It really makes us sick. So we would like you to sing one of our songs for us."

He said this in a threatening tone of voice, but we were so full of kindness and goodwill that we cheerfully asked, "Sure, what are some of your songs? If we know them, we'll sing them for you."

"Oh, you know them, all right. At least these two Germans here who grew up with them, eh?"

He started singing the beginning of that most popular among the countless numbers of German war songs, the "England Song," *Heute wollen wir ein Liedlein singen:*

Let us sing our song and raise our glasses,
Let them ring together loud and clear,
Let us vow our love forever, for the parting time is near.
Let me hold your hand, gentle snow-white hand.
Farewell my love, farewell my love, farewell, fare thee well.
For we're sailing, for we're sailing,
For we're sailing 'gainst the British foe, British foe, ahoy!

We were alarmed. Who were these guys? How could this possibly be happening here in Switzerland? Then I reflected that there was actually nothing specifically Nazi about the song. But when I gave the fellow a closer look, I blinked in disbelief. He was wearing a leather belt with an SS buckle, and dangling from it, there was an HJ dagger, the one with the swastika on the handle. This called for finesse and diplomacy.

"I don't think we know this song. We were in a Danish monastery during the war. We did not know what was going on." I replied.

"Don't make me laugh!" the fellow sneered. "Danish monastery! Is that where you got all that German Army stuff you are wearing? And how did you get into our country, now? I'll tell you how. You come from one of those families who stabbed the German Army in the back. And now the Swiss government is rewarding you. Well, I think, your streak of good luck has just run out. Hey boys!" he called to his buddies at the table. "Come on over, I think we are going to have a little fun here! Or, better, I'll invite this pretty little lady to come over to our table and play for us." As he spoke, he grabbed one of Brigitte's pigtails.

She remained motionless, so it seemed, but any observer of her face would have noticed the narrowing of her eyes.

The other three, perhaps anticipating some resistance, were now coming over, all of them wearing SS buckles and daggers.

"Okay," I tried once more, "if you start singing, we'll help you, and she will play."

"Do you think we really care about that stupid song? We want her at our table—now!" And he gave the pigtail a hefty tug.

As if I had seen it in a movie, I knew exactly what was going to happen. Brigitte's elbow landed in his groin area, and as he was straightening up for the counterattack, she was on her feet, but only for a fraction of a second. Then she was airborne, her feet looking for a landing spot, preferably a face. Her bloodcurdling battle cry accompanied the entire maneuver. All this climbing and skiing must have put a lot of new muscle into her legs, because that thug went down like a sack of potatoes, except that potatoes don't bleed. His buddies appeared to be paralyzed with fear, for the moment at least. I had no idea what they might do—attack or withdraw—but just in case and to discourage them, I placed myself next to Brigitte, imitating her stance and trying to look like an experienced warrior. It worked. They dragged the groaning invalid away and disappeared to their room.

There was total silence now. No one dared to speak or even look at Brigitte. Peter finally broke the spell. "If I touch you now—what will happen to me?"

This was spoken in jest, but there was some real concern in his eyes. "Do you do this often, and where and when did you become such an expert?"

Everyone was fascinated with the story of how her father had turned into a martial arts fanatic while working in Korea, and how he had insisted that she and her brother become experts, as well. "He had me do all sorts of crazy things, even when I was only three years old. But I must say, it has come in handy quite a few times so far."

"Well, do you practice a lot to stay in shape?" Peter enquired.

"Oh yes! My brother and I spar almost every day, and we do certain exercises, too."

"Can you break things just by hitting them?" Sylvia asked.

"Sure—some things. What do you have in mind?"

"Okay," Sylvia looked around, "How about this board here?"

It was a solid piece of wood about six inches wide and one inch thick.

I was fascinated by this turn of events. Never had it occurred to me to challenge Brigitte's prowess.

Brigitte acted as if someone had asked her to swat a fly. She smiled her sweetest smile and asked two of the boys to lay the board across two chairs.

The proprietor, who just a few minutes ago must have had visions of a major battle raging in his dining room, came out of his corner, obviously concerned for the safety of his chairs. "Careful with those," he sternly admonished us.

Brigitte mockingly whirled and took a leap in his direction. That was the last we saw of him that evening.

Now she turned toward the board, facing it silently with closed eyes. She was a beautiful sight. Then she focused on her target, took one step forward; her right arm flashed upward with lightning speed and came crashing down, connecting with the center of the board which snapped in two as if it were a match. We were so impressed we didn't even dare to applaud.

Later, thinking about the evening's events, I could not help but feel grateful that I had never met Brigitte's father. He must have been one scary person, I thought.

"Brigitte," I asked later, "with your father pushing your Karate all the time, how did you have time to study the cello?" I had wondered about this for some time.

"Well," she answered, "both my father and my mother were constantly after me. I guess they were competing with each other. 'If you are turning her into a karate expert', my mother must have said to him or thought, 'by God, then I am going to turn her into a cello expert'. Good thing I was a fast learner in both areas."

Next morning I noticed that the distant mountains had become even clearer than yesterday. There was a ring of haze around the sun, and a bank of clouds was visible above the horizon.

"Let's ask the proprietor what he thinks about the weather. He should know. Perhaps he even heard a weather report on the radio," a voice suggested.

He hadn't been outside yet, but showed no sign of alarm after examining the sky in every direction. "We are heading for a change, that's for sure," he said, "but it will take a while. If you are planning on returning by this evening, you'll be all right."

He sounded convincing, but I could not shake that eerie feeling the sky gave me. "I don't know why I feel this way," I said to Brigitte, "but I can't help it. Let's stick close together and keep our eyes open."

"I know what you mean," she answered. "Feels spooky somehow. Too quiet."

Then we were on our way, following the tracks of our predecessors. Three to four hours of steady climbing, lunch at the summit, and a glorious, endless, powdery descent into the valley. That was the plan. It was hot, climbing in steep serpentines into a sun which seemed to be much more intense than yesterday. The bank of clouds that had been so distant in the morning was now coming within reach, closing in on the sun. A flock of small, crow-like birds that had been following us in hope of lunch morsels suddenly vanished.

We reached the summit just as the clouds reached the sun. Now everything was grey and lacking depth. The light had become so flat that it was impossible to see sudden dips, bumps, or rises. Arriving five minutes later was the first snowflake, soon to be followed by billions of others. A sudden cold blast hit us, triggering a frantic groping for parkas, caps, gloves, and goggles.

"Let's get out of here!" Beat screamed into the wind, by now a full-size storm. "We have to make it back to the Hütte!"

There were three reasons why we were unable to follow his directions: the wind was blowing so hard against us that we could hardly move; the snow was falling so densely that even through goggles we could hardly see the trail, and the light was so flat that it was unsafe to move. Besides all this, there was the danger of getting separated—and then what?

"A rope! Yes, a long rope." Beat carried one in his pack. "We have to tie ourselves together and then keep on groping along, trying to make it." Perhaps conditions would improve a little further on.

Wind drove the snow directly at us, sticking to goggles and making breathing difficult. If someone fell, the rope would pull others down as well. The new snow was already deep, making getting up very difficult.

Suddenly we had to stop. We were up against a cliff which we had not encountered on the way up. Obviously, on top of everything else, we were now lost. It was a desperate situation, one that activated my survival instincts. Our friends may have been more experienced mountaineers, but when it came to coping with life-threatening situations, I knew they were at my mercy.

It was obvious to me that there was no point in going on; there was no "forward," not even a "backward." It was getting dark by now, and if anything, the storm had intensified. Our only chance for survival was to fashion some sort of shelter. We had the cliff protecting us on one side, and if we used our skis, poles, and unused skins, we might be able to construct a low, narrow framework, I thought. I wanted it to support a crude top consisting of our two shelter-halves. The group had no idea that stashed away in our packs we had carried the miracle that would save our lives. "Yeah, yeah, that's what made our packs so big! We lugged all this weight around just so you would not have to die in this damn snow. Now, let's work together and create a cozy little igloo."

Fortunately the new snow was a bit sticky, so we could build a fairly stable base and some low walls.

"Listen!" I shouted, trying to penetrate the howling wind. "Slow down a bit! Don't work up a sweat! You don't want to lie in that icebox all wet and steamy later."

Working in pairs, one holding the tarp in place, the other one tying it to the frame, we managed to end up with something which, by daylight, probably would have made us laugh. Good thing visibility was almost zero, because right then, no one felt much like laughing. On one end of our rectangle we left an opening, just large enough for one person to crawl through.

"Brigitte, please crawl in and check if there are any large gaps where snow and wind could enter," I suggested.

Following her directions, we put some more snow here and there and pulled the straps on the tarps tighter.

"It's nice and comfy inside now," she announced. "I think we can start loading."

"Listen!" I yelled once more. "It's going to be tight as hell in there. So—no dancing! And one more thing—" Do I have to tell them everything? I inwardly groaned. "Everyone to the bathroom once more, and make sure you bring your packs inside. If there is anything extra you could put on, do so. And pass around any food you may have left. Try to find something to put between you and the snow!"

One by one, they crawled through the hole, backwards, so they could pull their packs in after them. Brigitte and I went last. I wanted to be the one to plug up the hole with some snow clumps I had prepared.

"Don't worry," Brigitte whispered as she crouched down to enter the cave. "I'll keep you warm."

Gradually, the initial feeling of coziness and safety gave way to teeth-chattering discomfort. There were tiny air leaks everywhere, stabbing us with icy fingers. Conversation ceased; numbness took over. Brigitte did her best, but I could not stop shaking. Finally she announced loudly, "We have to do something or Horst won't make it. I think every twenty minutes someone new has to take the spot at the entrance. I'll take the first shift."

Having a warm body on either side of me did wonders, and I kept rubbing and massaging Brigitte until her shift ended.

I worried and wondered if my friends knew about the danger of falling asleep in freezing temperatures. Again I raised my voice. "Stay awake and keep checking on your neighbors! Don't let them drop off, or they may never wake up again. And I think the person at the other end should be regularly replaced, too." This way, I thought, everyone will keep moving, thus staying awake.

Suddenly I remembered something—coffee beans! Even though I had bought the small bag to bring back home as a present, there had been more to it—a dim memory of something I had read once, a story in which coffee and survival played a major role. I fished around until my numb fingertips pushed against coffee beans. I opened the bag and put about ten beans into my mouth, chewing them to a fine paste which I swallowed. Then I passed the bag on, asking all to do what I had done. "That will help you a lot," I promised.

It was like putting new batteries into old, limp toys: voices became audible, body parts began to move again, even a little bit of laughter could be heard here and there.

"What time is it, anyway?" a voice sounded.

"Oh, a little after three. A few more hours and it will start getting light," another replied. "Wonder, how cold it is in here?"

"Well, definitely way below freezing. Just touch the ceiling tarp. Solid ice—a lot like my feet."

Thus it continued until daybreak. Then, gradually, the lumps on the ground began to take shape: human bodies that clung tightly to each other.

"Wonder if it's still snowing—," a female voice reached me. "That was one amazing night! Where did you learn all that stuff, Horst? Without you we'd probably all be dead now."

I wondered if there existed a plausible answer. It wasn't as if I had taken a survival course, but then, actually, what I had been through was much more effective than any course I could have taken. So I just condensed the past years into a few simple sentences. "Most of it is common sense and experience. What if we did not have the tarps? Why did we take them? Experience has taught me that you can't be too careful. And the coffee? Well, you've just got to have some plain old luck."

Way back in my mind, it was as if I could hear my mother's voice, "You have to be like Reynard the Fox—smarter than anyone else." Survival course in one sentence.

Suddenly I felt as if I were a hundred years old. That and very, very tired. Time for another coffee boost.

Daylight came and with it some very insistent voices, demanding to be let out to pee.

Okay, let's see what it's doing outside, everyone wondered. It took several minutes to free the entrance. It had stopped snowing, but there must have been about two feet of new snow. Stiff, hungry, shivering, but glad to be alive, we started to retrieve our skis and poles. The tarps were so thickly frozen that we had to free everything by cutting straps and ropes. We left them, hoping that they might be useful to some future party in distress.

Beat was desperately trying to find his bearings. Under the heavy snow nothing looked familiar anymore. The only direction we were sure of was—down.

We were skiing very cautiously.

"If you fall, they may not find you until spring," some comedian commented.

A couple of times we had to backtrack, but after struggling for three hours, we saw smoke rising below us. Not much of the Hütte was visible, but we knew that at the source of the smoke there would be warmth and food.

The proprietor kept shaking his head. "This is a miracle. I knew you were up there, but there was nothing we could do. How did you survive? It was below zero last night."

He crossed himself and went on mumbling in Romansch, but quickly switched to Schweizerdeutsch. "I have radioed the mountain rescue service. They are sending up a team with dogs. There is extreme avalanche danger with all that new snow. Better not go on today."

No need to worry about that. None of us was in any shape to continue.

A huge, steaming kettle appeared on the table. Goulash soup made of pork, potatoes, carrots, tomatoes, and cabbage, spicy with plenty of paprika. Well-being reentered our bodies. With this feeling, fatigue set in. A spoon clanked onto the floor, a head on its way down barely missed a plate. One of us had given up food in favor of sleep. Sleepiness spread like an epidemic. Suddenly I felt that everyone's eyes were on me. What was going on?

"Okay," I murmured, "everyone up and to bed. We won't be leaving until tomorrow."

If there had been any positive side to the night in the igloo, it was that it had led to the discovery of how wondrously blissful it was to spoon up to each other. In remembrance of that event, Brigitte and I pushed our mattresses together as closely as possible and settled into the spoon position.

I didn't exactly know what had awakened me the next morning: was it the sun or something which was, so to speak, in the air? I inhaled deeply, and then I knew. After two days of alternately sweating and freezing, without a chance to change, we all simply reeked. Others soon took note as well.

"Didn't any of you bring any soap?" I asked.

"No! We didn't think we'd be gone that long."

"Well, whoever feels the urge—I have some and a towel, too, and so does Brigitte."

After half an hour we once more dared to inhale.

The *Hüttenvater* served us a hearty breakfast and gave us his best wishes for the trip down. "There are no fresh tracks up or down yet, but the trail is marked with red poles. Be careful not to miss any!"

Many of the slopes we skied would have been magnificent two days ago, but with all that deep snow now, it was an awful lot of work.

In the village a police patrol stopped us. Did we know anything about four young men who had come down from Piz Turba yesterday? They had claimed that one of them had crashed into some rocks and had badly smashed his face. Had to be taken to the hospital—broken nose and jaw. Must have been some fall.

We assured the police that we had seen the group on the mountain, but that there had been no contact.

"Well, thank you," the officer said. "Let us know if you see them again. We think they are the four that have been causing some trouble around here. So be careful."

Wow! Broken nose and jaw! The group regarded Brigitte with a mixture of awe, fear, and admiration.

Brigitte was her own sweetly smiling self again. "Yeah," she grinned, "without me those guys would have eaten you alive for appetizers. Wonder what would have happened if I had worn my boots," she mused.

XXII

A Chinese banquet in Switzerland

WE HAD ONLY TWO skiing days left after our return from the mountain. The prospect of returning to school, starvation, and freezing was depressing. One of the saddest in the group was Uli. During our absence, he and Annelies had become inseparable, capable of facing reality only with their arms around each other. I understood him only too well.

"Uli," I tried to comfort, "I know this is tough, believe me. But consider how you would feel if one of you were moving to America."

He looked at me with disbelief in his eyes. "You are moving to America? Why? When? Does Brigitte know?"

"Nothing is definite, so far. But my mother talks about it all the time. And it's beginning to make sense to me. As for Brigitte? We mention it off and on. She always assumes that we would go together. In a couple of years we would be old enough to get married, but right now?— Only Jews and other Nazi victims are granted immigration visas. Perhaps I can talk my mother into waiting until we are old enough."

"You know," he continued, "I don't understand why you want to leave Germany. Is it the Jewish business? At home we never talk about that. If I am your cousin, am I Jewish, too?"

So I gave him a piece of our family tree and what that meant and had meant. He, of course, was twenty-five percent less Jewish than I, and that had made all the difference. I was surprised how little his family had suffered and how little he knew.

"You are only a second-degree half-breed, you lucky mongrel," I said. "If the war had lasted any longer you too would have been considered racially pure enough to be drafted and killed—like your brother."

"Hmm," was his only response, but I could see that he was moving things around in his head.

"I guess I am glad we have lost the war," he finally said.

For one whole day we cleaned and cleaned, washing, wiping, polishing, and sweeping, until everything looked Swiss-clean. We were singing and joking the entire time, once more enjoying the camaraderie that had solidified our friendship. We three Germans had made some progress at comprehending Schweizerdeutsch—could even say a few basic things. What made this dialect so difficult was the fact that there were quite a few words that had nothing in common with their German equivalents. Take an everyday word like "butter," for instance, which in German too is *Butter*. But in Schweizerdeutsch it is *Anke*. Finally, years later, in the attempt to satisfy my curiosity, I went to the University of Michigan Library, located a Sanskrit dictionary and found the entry: Anke—Indian: burnt fat offering. What could be more logical than the linguistic evolution from fat offering to butter?

Then, one last early morning view of the surrounding peaks, one last earful of cowbells from the barns surrounding us, one last inhalation of the strong but somehow comforting odor surrounding these barns, and one last ski run down into the valley, this time without the hooting and hollering of earlier days. Stepping out of our bindings for the last time was so sad. In need of comfort, Brigitte and I clung to each other as if God had just banned us from paradise.

Chocolate was the substance that turned our thoughts to new challenges. How could we smuggle some of it through the strict customs controls?

"I just can't disappoint my siblings," Brigitte said. "I have promised. Perhaps we could wedge a few bars between our skis, you know, especially if we leave the skins strapped on. The width should be about right. Yeah, wait—if I could sew some kind of pocket to one of the skins, we could just slip the bars in and then bundle the skis together. Should work, don't you think?"

"Brigitte, you are finally beginning to think like a criminal. Congratulations! Yes! I think your idea will work."

The suburbs of Zürich appeared. Time to say goodbye to all our new friends.

"Yes, we'll come again next year, and yes, we'll write, and don't forget Texas and 'The Cowboy's Lament'!"

Onkel Heinrich was waiting for us at the station. He was surprised when Uli, after a brief hello, walked off with Annelies. She had invited him to stay at her house for a few days.

Suddenly I felt a wave of envy welling up in me. Uli would soon be returning to his magnificent ancestral home, he had not missed any time in his schooling, and in a few more years he would be studying pharmacy at the University of Munich, preparing himself to take over his father's two pharmacies. And soon it would become easier to cross the Swiss-German border in case his romance should turn out to be more permanent than the snow on a Swiss pasture in spring.

A few letters were awaiting us: two from my mother and one from Erhard with additions from the girls and Brigitte's mother. Not much had happened back home. Most of the snow in the lower elevations was gone; snowdrops and crocuses were appearing along the southern walls of houses. School was about to start again. "So don't spend too many days in Zürich."

My mother's second letter contained a startling postscript: "Anja sent a note saying that they want to visit us to discuss something important. Any predictions? Are they getting married? Did any of her family turn up? But why would they want to come and tell us in person? Hope it is nothing awful."

I told Brigitte, but she just shook her head. "Can't imagine. But I would enjoy seeing them again."

Somehow I could not shake the feeling that this had to be bad news . . . Kaminska and Gruber?

Kitchen sounds and smells indicated that something on behalf of our stomachs was happening. Tante Charlotte appeared, handing me an apron. "I could really use some help."

Where had I heard that before?

"Do you mind? We had reports that you spoiled all our children with your cooking. Had to think hard to come up with something novel and interesting. This is Italian—saltimbocca?"

"Heard of it, yes, but I have no idea how to make it. Veal?"

"Yes, here. I need you to pound these pieces. Should be about the size of your hand and half a centimeter thick. We'll prepare ten servings, which means that we'll need ten slices of this ham here, prosciutto, also half a centimeter thick and half the size of the veal, because they will be folded into the veal. And onto each slice of prosciutto a sage leaf must be placed. I grow my own herbs in the sunroom.

"I must tell you, it's nice to have someone to cook with and to talk to while working. Both of my men love to eat, but they won't go near a pot."

I did not have to wonder what the others were doing. It was quite audible, and soon my pounding followed the rhythm of whatever the violin and cello were playing in the parlor.

Tante Charlotte smiled at me. "Just listen to it! Isn't it quite remarkable? He has been so looking forward to this. Almost every day he's been after me, When were they coming back? How long would they be staying? And—this has not happened for years—he has been practicing every day. With good results, wouldn't you say? Well—it isn't just anybody he is playing with. Brigitte is such a wonderful, sweet, young woman—and so gifted! Does she know?" She hesitated a few seconds. It was not difficult to guess what was coming: "How shall I put it—about the Jewish blood in our family?"

I had no reason to be on the defensive here, but I just couldn't help it. No matter to whom or under what circumstances I was speaking, whenever the talk turned to this topic, I clammed up. It was as if I could hear my mother's imploring voice: "Don't ever tell anyone!"

Acting very casually, I assured my aunt that Brigitte and her brother were just fine with it.

I was now assembling the veal servings, pinning each portion together with a toothpick.

While the meat was sautéing in a large skillet, Tante Charlotte was busy with the pasta and the preparation of a salad, which was to become and remain my favorite forever. Responsible for this were the little, dark-green rosettes that had tempted a mother into a witch's garden, thus causing the imprisonment of a lovely child who grew up to be a beautiful maiden with long, golden hair: Rapunzel. Back in the days when the brothers Grimm were collecting and recording their fairy tales, many of them centuries old, these crisp, aromatic greens were—and are still—known as "Rapunzel." Among the more modern German names are *Feldsalat, Nisselsalat;* in Switzerland, *Nüsslisalat;* and in France, *mâche.*

Used to her family's addiction to these plants, Tante Charlotte had cleaned a huge bowlful, which she dressed with a vinaigrette mixed with chopped hardboiled eggs and a bit of finely minced onion.

"And now the saltimbocca sauce," she announced. "Here, take this bottle of port—you could also substitute Madeira or Marsala—add three tablespoons plus two tablespoons of butter to the drippings and reduce it for a few minutes. That's all there is to it."

Hollering the word "saltimbocca" repeatedly into the music room finally had the desired effect. The music stopped, and Onkel Heinrich, perspiring but otherwise deliriously happy, appeared. He was virtually speechless, groping for words that would adequately express his feelings.

"This was . . . ach," he paused, shaking his head while we all waited for the rest of his pent-up emotions to emerge.

"Ach, Brigitte, Brigitte! You are making a musician of me, an artist. Ach, if only you lived closer, anywhere but in Germany! Can't we figure something out? How about adoption? Anyway, if ever you need a refuge—look no further. You will be more than welcome anytime."

Brigitte gave me a look which said, "Hm, this offer may come in handy someday."

During dinner Onkel Heinrich was reminiscing about his youth and the summers spent in Oswitz. "In those days your mother and I were a real menace to the community. The things we did! A miracle that no one got hurt.

"What did we do? Let's see. Well, a couple of times we swam across the Oder because there were wild raspberries on the other side. Our parents would have died if they had known. We also spied on local fishermen when they were out placing their traps. Then we'd row out to these places real early in the morning. Got some nice big ones that way—pike and catfish.

"Then—I remember how hot it was that summer—we packed a few things together, took some food and some water and snuck over to the stable, saddled up our favorite horses and just took off. Had no idea where we were heading, but those were the days when we went wild, reading all those Indian stories. We had that romantic yearning for endless forests and cozy campfires at night, maybe finding some nuggets in some creek. Did we find our way back? Not a chance. They all went crazy when we did not show up in the evening. Feared that we might have been abducted by Gypsies or barge people. Had the police, the foresters, and an army unit out looking for us. How embarrassing, riding home escorted by cavalry!

"Oh, and this! Wait till you hear this! I believe it was just before your grandmother's birthday, when we snuck into the pantry and ate all the streusel off the Streuselkuchen."

He chuckled at the memory, but I could not believe what I had just heard. That was my mother he was talking about? She had done all those things?

"You know what I really crave sometimes?" he continued. "Comes right after wanting to be able to play like Jascha Heifetz—Streuselkuchen! The real Silesian kind, like your grandmother used to make, not what they try to pass off as such around here or in southern Germany. Did you ever help with the baking back home? Think you could make one for us? I often talk about it, and we have tried several times. It's always good, but not one hundred percent authentic. Or perhaps it's just that one can never do justice to childhood memories."

What could possibly have evoked greater enthusiasm in me than this request? How long had it been? Would I remember everything correctly? How much yeast to a pound of flour, and what were the proportions of flour to butter and sugar for the streusel? Somehow I knew that my grandmother's spirit and my culinary instincts would not forsake me.

That night I prayed for a little help from above, hoping Oma would somehow be able to slip a message to me.

It was Saturday, so there was no need to hurry with breakfast. The only shopping requirements were yeast and butter. So we sat and enjoyed something I had not experienced since the beginning of the war: a real breakfast with soft-boiled eggs eaten from real eggcups, assorted cheeses, smoked meats, and delicious coffee—unlike the black brew they had served in the army mess halls, or our home brew, made of roasted ground barley.

Onkel Heinrich carried a small box when he appeared, obviously something of interest, if not importance.

"Last night," he began, "after all that talk about Oswitz and my visits there, I went to the chest where I keep old pictures and letters. Thought I might find something of interest to you, Horst—well, to all of us. I started going through some of the bundles, letters from old friends and relatives, including your grandmother, and there was one from her—from your grandmother, who is my Tante Elli. It was addressed to me, but I had never opened it. A letter from an old aunt? How interesting could that be to a young boy? You may not believe it, but here it is—she sent me her recipe for Streuselkuchen. Not very precise, but you experts can surely fill in the gaps. Oh yes, and there is a note in addition: "I hope this will help you to get your cravings under control, so you won't embarrass me on my next birthday. Tante Elli."

As he handed me the yellow, somewhat brittle paper with Oma's familiar handwriting, a chill ran down my spine. Holding the paper, I closed my eyes and whispered, "Thank you."

"Oh, you are welcome!" Onkel Heinrich was obviously startled, somewhat taken aback by the fervor in my voice.

The recipe began as follows: "Unfortunately I always bake entirely by instinct. For the yeast dough, take about one pound of flour, one egg, one stick of butter, some vanilla, a pinch of salt." No mention of yeast, sugar, or any liquids. We decided on one package of active yeast sprinkled into a bowl with one-quarter cup of lukewarm water and a pinch of sugar. We combined and stirred these ingredients and let the mixture double in volume; then we stirred in three-quarters of a cup of lukewarm milk and one-half teaspoon of finely grated lemon peel. Next, we beat one-third cup of sugar and the egg and stirred in the yeast mixture. We added the flour one cup at a time. When smooth, we added the soft butter. We kept kneading the dough until it was elastic. This was left to rise in a warm place for about forty minutes. After that we spread it about half an inch thick onto a buttered cookie sheet. By that time the streusel mix should be ready.

In regard to the streusel, Oma's letter said, "Combine one-half pound of very soft butter with four to five tablespoons of sugar and enough flour to make the mixture thick but not dense. This requires finely tuned fingertips. If the mixture is too soft, the streusel will melt into mushy blobs. If it is too dense the streusel will be too hard. Some people use melted butter, which will produce hard streusel which is not so nice. Form the streusel into a generously large but no more than a little over one-half inch thick pieces. I like to brush the dough with milk first, so that the streusel will adhere better. Bake at a high temperature (375 degrees F) until the streusel are golden yellow, about 25–30 minutes."

We followed these general guidelines, using two cups of flour. Judging by the appearance and the smell, we had been on the right track.

"Aha," Onkel Heinrich proclaimed, "lemon rind! That's what was missing all these years, and we always used melted butter which is 'not so nice,' as Tante Elli put it."

It was an agonizing wait. When would we find out whether we had reached perfection or once more had scored a disappointing "pretty close"? We kept hovering around the pantry, which did not yield any clues.

Tante Charlotte caught Onkel Heinrich trying to sniff out something through the keyhole. "At four o'clock Stephanie and her parents are coming for coffee," she scolded. "Until then—forget it!"

But who can endure for long the sight of grown men tormented by irresistible cravings? Petitions for a reduced waiting period were granted, and at three o'clock the unveiling of the Streuselkuchen took place. We, the experts, looked at it critically: golden yellow, nice and level on top, no lumpy peaks as sometimes happens with yeast, and that inimitable yeast-butter aroma with just a hint of lemon.

Without crumbling the streusel, the knife slid smoothly along the cake, severing a one-inch strip. Putting an end to the torturous uncertainty, Tante Charlotte cut it into five pieces. Brigitte, Charlotte, and Peter gulped their pieces down without notable indications of pleasure. For them it was just another good cake. But for Onkel Heinrich and me, it was a mystical experience, a return to the womb. We slowly took a bite, checking the consistency, the sweetness and butteriness of the streusel; then we chewed, leisurely and pleasurably, not greedily swallowing, but shifting the substance from side to side and turning it over from time to time. Thus, acting as a skillful wine taster would, every subtle nuance of flavor was revealed. I was relieved to see Onkel Heinrich's expression changing from neutral to unmitigated bliss. He

came over and hugged me. "This is exactly the way I remember it. And to think that this perfection was brought about by a miracle, no, a double miracle: first, finding the recipe, then realizing that it is incomplete, and you and Charlotte filling in the gaps to make it come out perfectly."

Visits from friends or relatives on a Saturday or Sunday or, for that matter, on any afternoon, are common practice in German-speaking countries. "Coffee" or "tea" is, of course, merely the code name for platters filled with pastries, homemade or quickly purchased at the corner bakery or *Konditorei*. In Germany this lovely custom had all but vanished in the course of the war, except perhaps in the summer when the availability of cherries and diverse berries inspired the Hausfrau to dream up some no-sugar, no-fat Kuchen or Torte. In Switzerland, however, there was no need to abandon the dear old tradition. Phone calls back and forth had established all the details for the Höhnes's visit, and, as additional calls revealed, some bigger party was being organized for the following day. Brigitte and I were looking forward to seeing everyone, as well as to spoiling our taste buds once more before returning to starvation.

Precisely at four, the Höhnes appeared. I could tell that Steffi's mother was somehow totally out of control. No sooner had she slipped out of her fur coat than she rushed toward me, threw her arms around me and, mumbling my name and some incomprehensibles in Schweizerdeutsch, applied pressure. She was a strong, ample woman, and while I was gasping for breath, tears were running down her cheeks. For one brief moment I caught a glimpse of Steffi. The expression on her face said, "I am sorry." I realized then what was going on. On our return trip from the mountains, I had asked everyone to keep me out of accounts of our blizzard night on Piz Turba. Obviously my wishes had not been respected. Actually, who could blame these kids for sharing some real adventures with their parents? That was Brigitte's opinion. "You didn't really believe they wouldn't share an event of such magnitude with their parents, did you? Besides, why shouldn't you get credit for what you have done? They would have all died up there! I just hope they didn't talk about me! Makes me look like a freak."

"Well, without you some of them might have ended up in a hospital with broken bones and missing teeth," I replied. "So there!"

The whole scene was a little awkward, especially since my relatives had no idea what was going on. In speechless amazement they beheld what took place before their eyes. I liberated myself from Frau Höhne's emotional embrace and surveyed the situation. Free once more, I looked at her. Tears had left marks on her cheeks that brought back memories of skiing through deep powder. Giving me one last heart-rending, teary glance she disappeared into the bathroom.

After a quick update, and now fearing the same treatment from Peter's mother, I held on tightly to Brigitte. No escaping Tante Charlotte's words, though. "Oh Horst, what a fateful turn of events! How marvelous the ways of Providence. If we had not invited you, our children would be dead now."

She tried to get to me past Brigitte, but we withstood the attempt. Just one of her hands broke through the defenses to stroke my cheek.

"Heinrich!" she called out. "Why don't you go down to the basement to fetch us a bottle of champagne—better make that two."

While the two mothers were heaping their attention upon me, interrogating me on every aspect of that night—why I had done something one way and not another and whether I would do anything differently if I had to do it over again—the two fathers were beleaguering Brigitte. Soon after the second glass of champagne, they simply paid no attention to anything else. Brigitte and Karate had captured them, minds and bodies. Had it been up to them, they would have asked her to reduce one of the Biedermeier chairs to kindling. A beautiful young woman endowed with deadly powers was something that sparked their imagination. Brigitte, as her flushed cheeks revealed, did not mind at all until, after some hesitation, Herr Höhne asked if he could feel the muscles in her arm. The two mothers, though they had carefully avoided any overt interest in their husbands' behavior, suddenly, as on cue, showed no further interest in me, instead pelting their men with looks brimming with anger and apprehension.

Had Herr Höhne overstepped his boundaries? Fearing the worst, I stared at the mood indicator in Brigitte's face—her eyes. For a moment there was a little twitch around her lids, but Onkel Heinrich's voice defused any imminent outburst.

"Brigitte," he said, "I promised our guests to treat them to some fine music—at least, as far as the cello goes. Why don't we play the piece we did last evening?"

Smiling gratefully, Brigitte followed Onkel Heinrich and slipped into the music room to tune up. She would have been amused to witness what happened to poor Herrn Höhne as soon as she had left the room. Unfortunately, the tongue-lashing he received from both ladies was delivered in Schweizerdeutsch. I could only guess at what he had to endure by the way he slowly disappeared deeper and deeper into the leathery depth of the armchair.

Perhaps it was a somewhat guilty conscience that empowered Brigitte to produce sounds so tender and melodious that all strife succumbed to her playing. Overcome by emotion, Frau Höhne inched closer and closer toward me until she had me once more cornered against the end of the sofa.

"My dear, brave boy," she kept whispering, always waiting for a *forte* passage that would drown out her voice. Tante Charlotte observed my predicament and later warned me to be prepared for more of the same treatment the following day, Sunday. Beat's parents had issued an invitation to all for a "light supper" at their house.

"For all of us, including parents? That's going to be a lot of people."

"Don't worry about that, Horst. Herr Stucke is a high government official and also owns a couple of factories. Their house is big enough for five groups like ours. But don't be shocked if they all, the women in particular, treat you like Frau Höhne. As for you, Brigitte," and she sighed, "I am afraid you will receive a lot of attention, too—mostly from the male contingent. Oh, by the way, Heinrich, should you and Brigitte take the instruments? What else would we have to offer? Otherwise their view of Brigitte might be a bit one-sided. I don't want them to think of her as a battle maiden."

"Personally," Onkel Heinrich answered in his wry manner, "I suggest we take a few two-by-fours. That would really make a hit—with the men, anyway; I being one of them, I must admit. I just can't imagine . . ." Shaking his head he looked at Brigitte.

"May I touch?—" Doubling over with laughter he parried a slap from his wife, aimed at his arm. "But that is a good idea—I mean the instruments, of course."

I was beginning to feel less and less enthusiastic about the whole idea of going over there to be celebrated like some hero, though the prospect of one last chow fest was enticing.

"What about dressing up? Can we go like this?"

Except for my ski pants—part of a German combat uniform—I had with me some virtually indestructible German infantry officer's trousers, appropriated by me during the early days of the siege. At the time it had seemed unreasonable, if not cruel, to separate the officer's high-shaft riding boots from their lifelong companion, the pants, so ever since, except during the summer, this was what I had worn every day. With a good brushing and a polish, everything looked almost like new. Both pieces were still about two sizes beyond mine, but I was gaining on them. In Germany, among my peers, I was one of the most elegant, so I thought. I could tell that my relatives were not sharing my optimistic opinion.

"Yes, well, everything is in excellent condition and looks great on you, Horst, but a replica of a German officer is not the image you want to create. Perhaps Peter can find something suitable for you. True, he is a bit bigger than you, but bigger does not appear to bother you, anyway; in fact, you look good in bigger." Another wonderful joke which made Onkel Heinrich roar with laughter, while his wife just shook her head.

"Don't worry, we'll find something," she said. The same goes for Brigitte. Think she could get something from Steffi, Peter?"

"Sure, why not. I'll call a little later."

"Yeah, and mention it should be something compatible with acrobatic movements," Onkel Heinrich quipped.

With mixed feelings I awaited our entry into Swiss society. Would I be treated as their children's friend or celebrated as their savior? Would they conceive of me as a German or as the victim of Germans? This possibility raised another issue in my mind. It was a well-known fact that the Swiss government had displayed very little sympathy for Jews who came asking for help.

"By the way," I asked, "do they know or suspect?"

"Hm," Onkel Heinrich pondered this question for a few minutes. "I doubt it. They probably don't know about me, and they are not preoccupied with Jewishness like the Germans. I would not worry about it."

We ascended a driveway through a park with orchards and greenhouses until we reached a house, a mansion, three times the size of the Hopf villa, with turrets, balconies, and wrought iron all over the place. Several cars were already parked in front of the entrance. A butler came to direct us and take our coats. Mine was an old German Air Force coat, which he carried with two fingers and as far from his body as possible, audibly sniffing it as if I had rolled in manure in it—and I probably had. Underneath, I presented a fairly decent picture, though. Brigitte, looking very smart in Steffi's clothes, received a princess's welcome, as always.

It was as Tante Charlotte had predicted. All the gentlemen gathered around Brigitte, trying to outdo each other in showering her with compliments, clever comments, jokes, and champagne, while I was besieged by a horde of aggressive mothers. Many had tears in their eyes, asking me the same questions over and over: "How did you, a flatlander, know so much about mountain survival?"

"Hey, there are mountains where I come from, too. And it gets a lot colder there."

"Would you ever want to come back?"

"If you can arrange it—we'll be glad to."

"Is Brigitte your girlfriend?"

"Definitely!"

"How and where did you learn to cook all those wonderful things?

"From my grandmother, my mother, our maids, some friends, books."

"Are you going to pursue a career in culinary arts? Switzerland is famous for its hotels, you know."

"Hm."

"Oh, just one more thing. We are all wondering about this. How did you ever get that coffee idea? Would you have made it without it? And to take some along on a ski tour like this—isn't that a bit unusual?"

These were three questions I had asked myself repeatedly. Here is what I was able to reconstruct.

"I think it was something we had read in German class," I said. "Do you read Stifter here in Switzerland? He wrote a very famous novella, *Bergkristall*. The story goes that these two children get lost in a snowstorm. It's Christmas Eve, and they are on their way home across a high mountain pass. In his pack, the boy carries presents for his parents, among them a container with some sort of coffee concentrate or extract. After the storm subsides, the children see the most beautiful northern lights. It is bitter cold, and they keep drinking this coffee. In the morning, the village people find them unharmed. I always thought that it was the coffee that saved their lives. Couldn't hurt to carry some coffee along when you are on a long tour in the mountains, I must have thought when I bought it and stuck it in my pack."

The ladies looked at each other and kept shaking their heads.

I was bracing myself for a continued interrogation, but Onkel Heinrich intervened, announcing that Brigitte and he had prepared a wonderful treat for all. "I realize Brigitte has already a considerable reputation for one rather unusual ability, but it would not surprise me a bit if her musical talent and expertise outshine it. And please be tolerant of my modest contribution."

Observing the men during the performance, I noticed how a change came over them. Their excitement subsided, their movements became relaxed, their faces assumed expressions of tranquility—all signs that their minds had become receptive to beauty that was not feminine alone.

There was warm applause at the end, and just when I thought that I could sneak over to the buffet table where steaming platters and bowls were beckoning me, tempting me with indescribable delights, one of the mothers stepped forward, tapping on her champagne glass, "This was a truly memorable performance, and nothing will be able to detract from its beauty, but we have heard so much talk about the music, playing and singing that went on up there in the mountains that we are all eager to hear a sample. Might I persuade you to humor us?"

The skiers looked at each other. Some of them were already munching on exotic nuts and fruit. Their expressions told me that this request better not be ignored. No one would dare to refuse Frau Doktor Franzen, Herrn Direktor Franzen's wife.

Quickly remnants of food were washed down with champagne. This was done with such haste that the champagne bubbles had no other choice but to escape noisily the same way they had entered. Some of the guests applauded vigorously. It was the perfect introduction to our performance. "Thank you for your kind response," I said. "Our next number will be a song a good friend of mine, a black captain from Texas, taught me, "The Cowboy's Lament."

When Urs had found out that Brigitte was bringing a cello, he brought his guitar, "Just in case," as he said.

I thought we sounded great. With all that champagne it was easy to put a lot of expression into our lamentations. We did a few more of our cowboy repertoire, ending with the woodchuck jingle. Any woodchuck would have been proud to have his species mentioned so elaborately in this mansion.

How much wood would a woodchuck chuck
If a woodchuck could chuck wood?
A woodchuck would chuck all the wood he could chuck
If a woodchuck could chuck wood.

All the parents had studied years of English, but that was beyond their ability. Upon request we did it twice more—in slow motion— and even then I had to explain words like "woodchuck" and answer questions like "How do you chuck wood?" and "Can a woodchuck really do that?"

"Only the ones from Texas," was my reply.

While all this was happening, a dreadful thought kept plaguing me. What if?—

So I went directly to the highest authority I could think of. Oh, please, God, don't let this lady make me sing!

But there was no merciful God looking out for me that evening, and my grandmother's spirit had abandoned me. No sooner had we ended our concert than this mother approached me, giving me her most irresistible smile. "Oh, Horsti!" How dare she call me that! "We have heard so much of your own singing. Just one song? Please?"

Her husband stood next to her, staring at me seriously, if not threateningly, raising his head in anticipation of my affirmative answer, "And Brigitte, you will accompany him, won't you?"

There was no escape here, no shelter-half to hide under. So I decided to do the Innsbruck song, one of our favorites, that famous fifteenth-century song by Heinrich Isaak. It is a song full of sadness and fear of the unknown and a farewell to Innsbruck and a ladylove. Following a sudden impulse, I substituted Zürich for Innsbruck. We were, after all, leaving the next day. All of our friends understood what I was doing, and so it was kind of quiet for a while afterwards.

This, however, did not dampen our appetite. The buffet table looked and smelled unlike anything I had ever experienced. The hostess, who kept calling me Horsti all the time now, educated me—Chinese food, virtually unknown in Europe back then. I was introduced to things I had never even heard of before, prepared in new and wonderful ways. Everything fried, sautéed, steamed: water chestnuts, bamboo, bean sprouts, ginger, garlic and sesame seeds; fish sweet and sour, shrimp and chicken encrusted in deep-fried batter, bright red slivers of pork with chunks of pineapple and nuts—all of these and more, delivered from the only Chinese restaurant in Zürich. Fortunately none of these dishes had anything in common with the American chop suey we had tried in the U.S. Army mess hall in Garmisch.

I don't know how many times I went to the buffet table for refills. Besides being exotically delicious, it is another characteristic of Chinese food that it does not fill you up. No matter how much you have eaten, after a brief pause you feel like starting all over again. Only the Chinese restaurant staff, clearing away platters and plates in ghostlike silence, saved me from becoming a Zürich legend.

I was the only one still chewing when Herr Doktor Franzen strode to the center of the room. No need for him to tap on a glass. A casual glance around sufficed to create a churchlike silence. "Dear friends, we don't usually celebrate the return from a ski trip with a big party. What we are celebrating here tonight is the *safe* return from a ski trip, a safe return made possible by the experience and circumspection of one of the members of the group, Horst, a boy from our neighbor, Germany. Without him we would be mourning the loss of our children tonight and for as long as we live. We want him to know that we shall be forever grateful to him and that he and his friend Brigitte will always be welcome here. Let us drink to them, to a speedy recovery of their homeland, to their future in that country, and may they come back to Switzerland soon."

Tear ducts were straining to meet the demand. After the applause and discreet nose blowing had subsided, Doktor Franzen took me aside. "Listen, Horst, you know how we feel, and we know what your situation is in Germany. So we have prepared a few things for you to take back to Germany. Black-market merchandise to the Germans. Don't worry! I know what you are going to say. Customs regulations! Well, I am in charge of many things here. I have an official authorization for you to bring otherwise illegal goods into Germany. And," his voice turned into a near whisper now, "if you and/or Brigitte want or need to come to Switzerland—and not just for a ski trip—inform me at my office." He handed me his card. "Keep it in a safe place. You never know. But I don't need to point that out to you, the champion of 'you never know', as I understand."

XXIII

How we got our contraband through customs, and Misha's revelation

I T WAS NO MYSTERY what the pack in the hallway contained. Any customs official could have told you. Roasted coffee beans carry a powerful aroma. That's why it is almost impossible to get it undetected across the border. Doktor Franzen handed me an envelope. "Here, guard it well. With it you will not have any difficulties on either side of the border."

Christ, I thought, as I strapped the package on my back a little later, this weighs at least thirty pounds.

"Write us if you need anything."

One last handshake, one last hug from THE mother, and we were gone.

Brigitte was jubilant. "Now I won't have to sew pockets into the skins. Would have taken me all night."

"What on earth are you talking about?" Tante Charlotte inquired, shaking her head when we told her.

"I guess, here in our little world we just don't have any idea what it's like over there," she mused.

The following morning we encountered two very unhappy humans at the Bahnhof: Uli and Annelies. They swore they would write each other every day, and Annelies had already made plans to visit during Easter vacation. But still—who would have ever guessed that parting could be so devastating.

"What's in that bag?" Uli asked. "You smell like a grocery store."

"That's my bounty for saving all you sorry civilians."

"Too bad they'll confiscate it at the border. Let's be practical and eat as much chocolate as we can," Uli suggested.

"Do you really think I'm so stupid as to think I could get through customs with that much?"

His eyes went back and forth between me and the enormous pack. Finally he shook his head. "You're right. Nobody could be that stupid. So what's your plan?"

"Well, when we get close to the border, we'll first help you get up on the roof; then you'll hoist up the pack with a rope."

Uli's brow furrowed. "You mean . . . while the train is moving?"

Brigitte could not control herself any longer. "Here, Uli, have some chocolate and don't worry."

"Oh, I should have known better," Uli pouted. "You always pull those jokes on me. That will cost you another chocolate bar."

Other travelers were entering our compartment. An older, portly gentleman inhaled repeatedly and noisily through his nostrils, shaking his head in disbelief. "Are you kids nuts? Any blind man could feel it with his cane that there is coffee in that pack. How about selling some to me—if you make it?"

The train ride from Zürich to the German border takes just a little over an hour—plenty of time for me to let my imagination run amok. By the time the train stopped, my stomach was in knots, sweat was oozing through my pores.

"And what have we got here? Do I have to empty every piece of luggage or wouldn't you rather just tell me where it is?" It was the German custom's officer addressing me.

"Yes sir, up there, sir. And here is a list of what's in that pack—and there is a letter in there, too."

"Yeah, yeah. That's what they all say. Let's have a look."

First the Swiss read it, then the German.

"Looks official, I must say, but I better have the duty officer check it out."

The Swiss left, the German stayed. After about ten minutes the guard returned with an officer, a captain. "Which one of you is Horst Küter?" he asked. He handed me the papers and smiled at us. "All clear. I talked with Zürich. That's a fine job you did at the Piz Turba. Have a good trip home."

I wiped my forehead and passed the chocolate around.

The older gentleman was all smiles. "Man, what a lucky day!" he said. "Couldn't have made it without you guys. What? Well, you didn't really think that bulge under my coat is all fat, did you?"

He was truly enormous around the middle. His face and neck looked almost emaciated in comparison.

"Let me show you what I mean." He rose, unbuttoned his overcoat and proceeded to tenderly pat his midriff. There, strapped ingeniously around his waist and hanging from suspenders as well, was a broad belt with deep pockets. From each one a smooth leather pouch protruded. We knew instantly what they held.

"It's almost impossible to completely hide the coffee smell," he explained, "so without you, I might have been caught. But with your ten or twenty pounds up there, making the compartment smell like a Sunday afternoon *Kaffeeklatsch*—what did I have to worry about? Thank you very much!"

We got off in Konstanz and said farewell to Uli. He was pursuing a long and difficult route that would eventually land him in Munich. Brigitte and I took a bus that brought us to the shores of Lake Constance. From there we took the ferry across to Meersburg, continuing the way we had come. Traveling on by bus and train was quite an experience. As soon as fellow travelers had figured out that the coffee vapor trail was coming from my pack, they lost interest in any other activity, made an about face and followed it. Somehow they could not figure out why we were carrying such a precious cargo as well as skis, not to mention our tans. Finally we came up with a scenario that would reconcile all theories.

"Been to Switzerland?" people would ask.

"Yup."

"Skiing?"

"Yup."

"How did you manage to get in? No Germans allowed over there, as far as we know."

"Didn't ask."

"You mean?—"

"Yup. If you have skis—and if you are good—there are ways."

"Wow! And you came back the same way?"

"How else?"

"And you bought all that stuff over there? The coffee and whatever else?"

"You bet!"

"Wow! And how did you get the Swiss money for all that?"

That was the point where I suddenly discovered that we had to hurry on for our next connection. By the time we were approaching

Kempten, we had added so many new elements to the story that we had come darn close to the truth.

"Why didn't we tell everything the way it really happened?" we wondered.

"Yeah! But how much fun would that have been after the fifth time?"

Journal entry, February 1946: Thank God they are coming back finally. I really was worried when I read about the record snow in Switzerland and all the skiers cut off in the mountains. Five deaths from avalanches! Heinrich told me the story of the night on the Piz Turba. Now they treat him like a little hero. Well, he certainly is. Hope he adjusts as easily to America as he did to Switzerland.

Antek was awaiting us at the Kempten station. He looked different, downright prosperous in elegant leather boots and a long loden overcoat, his head covered by one of those Tyrolean hats. Thumbs up and winks assured me that it was really he. "Wait, till you see what I've got outside," he said.

Antek bragging? That had to be something extraordinary. We followed him outside and looked around. Nothing new, just a lot of GIs with their *Bahnhof-Liebchen*.* Across the street a car was parked, one I had always liked—a 1936 Ford Eifel convertible, light blue with a black top. Antek was heading for it.

"Well, do you think this will get us home?" he asked with the biggest grin I had ever seen on him.

"That yours, Antek?" I gasped. "What did you do, rob a money train?"

"No. Found a safer method: work like hell plus a bit of good luck. But come on. Let's get your gear loaded up and drive over to my place for a little snack."

Loading skis into a Ford Eifel is no simple matter. But it was warm enough, so he just put the top down and stuck the skis in.

"And this?" he asked, sniffing all over our pack. How did you manage that?"

"Same way you got your car—worked like hell and a bit of good luck. Mama hasn't told you? Well, that can wait."

*Bahnhof sweethearts

Our next surprise came twenty minutes later. Antek stopped in front of a nice, modern-looking house. It was nestled into a hillside facing south, one of those Bavarian-style houses with balcony and garden. Every Upper Silesian refugee's dream.

"Nice house, nice neighborhood! I'll bet that on a clear day you can see mountains from here."

Antek nodded affirmatively as we were walking over crushed rock toward the entrance. He unlocked the door and gestured invitingly to enter.

I had expected the customary regional furniture, complete with mounted antlers, but there was none of that. In fact, there wasn't any furniture at all—almost. Just one chair and a folding table.

"Don't rental houses usually come with furniture?" I asked.

"Not this one," he answered, again with that grin. "Want to know why not? Because it's not a rental. It's mine! Been mine for three days now. Make yourselves at home, or come with me to the kitchen. But bring that chair. I'll tell you all about it."

If I had expected to hear tales of daring feats involving illegal activities, I was disappointed.

"You remember the little shack I had," he began. "Way back you helped me with all those gadgets, baubles and household goods we made from leftover war materials. Very popular. Huge demand. People came from all over to buy things they couldn't find anywhere else. I had to get more and more help to keep up, meaning that we had to have more space. So soon there were two, three little shacks, then one big one. A real building with brick walls and a toilet."

Many an afternoon Erhard, Brigitte and I had helped him make simple but tasteful pieces of jewelry out of ammunition parts: decorated buttons, broaches, necklaces. We had filed, polished, soldered and painted, in no way suspecting that this was gradually turning into a real industry.

"Then," he continued, "quite recently we started on bigger things: cookware, kitchen utensils, garden implements, like shovels, spades, rakes and hoes. People just went crazy. Ours was the only place where they could get anything decent. Now, once more I couldn't keep up with the demand. Trucks came from all over the place, even from some of our neighbors like Austria, Holland, Denmark, Belgium, even France.

"When I was looking at a building for an additional production hall, the owner mentioned that he was also selling a private home. Said he would give me a real good package deal if I took both. So I did. Perhaps your mother can help me find nice furniture. She knows my taste. May have to go to Munich and shop around."

And they say America is the land of unlimited possibilities? What Antek had told us was the most fantastic success story I had ever heard, never mind witnessed. I realized that the key to everything was not the *where* but the *how*. Antek had summarized it correctly when he said, "Work like hell and a bit of luck." So maybe there was no need to go to America, after all? If the formula had worked for Antek, why shouldn't it work for me, too? Didn't I have the same formula to work with? I knew I could work like hell and that my luck had occasionally bordered the miraculous. Then, like a lightening flash, it shot through my brain: Antek had failed to mention one other factor, one that was so ordinary that it was hardly worth mentioning. It was a factor he shared with millions of Germans but of which I was deprived by birth—that damn blood thing!

Antek's voice tore into my brooding.

"Horst, what's gotten into you? Are you seeing a ghost?"

"Yeah, sort of, but I am okay. Man, you have really done it! Without treasure or coal train! Just you! Congratulations! By the way—what did you do with your BMW?"

"Oh, don't you worry. I'll never part with that baby. It's in the garage. But you know," he mused, "without it I might have never made it out of Breslau."

Antek put some bread, butter, cheese, meats, and pickles on the table. "We better hurry because it's getting late, and you have been traveling all day."

We reached home just in time to see my mother stride through the garden gate. When she heard a car stop she turned around. Cars were a rare occurrence in our neighborhood, especially convertibles with skis sticking out. When she realized who it was she came running. "Oh, I was hoping you would come today! Wow! What a car! Business that good, eh? What? A house, too? And all within one week? Perhaps I should reconsider your offer, Antek. Let's see what's going to happen in two days. I'll know more then."

In two days? What's happening in two days? I wondered. Can't say I like the sound of it.

"Let's get everything out of the car and go upstairs," she added. "Let me take the pack. I haven't smelled anything that good in a long time. I'll bet this is Horst's reward."

"For what?"

"Don't you know? Horst has become a Swiss hero, Antek. He didn't mention it? Well, I'm sure you'll find out sooner or later."

My mother tore into the pack and hauled out a huge Lindt chocolate bar—half bitter—her favorite. Something had come unleashed in her. She just heaped everything on the table and kept fondling it, groveling in it, pawing, running her fingers over and through it, just the way she had behaved when we had examined our treasure in Breslau.

"I know it's getting late," she said, "but by God, let's make some coffee. And then I'll tell you what's happening."

"In two days?" I asked.

"Yeah. How do you know?"

"You just told us, Mama."

"I did? Must be losing my mind. No wonder."

There is nothing like the aroma of freshly brewed coffee. You inhale deeply through your nostrils, and you know everything is going to be all right. It is a civilized smell, implying the existence of a civilized world, and in a civilized world nothing goes wrong, right? At any rate, that was what that Kaffeeklatsch did for me—not for very long, though. It was like waiting for some kind of verdict or the feeling you have before the teacher is returns the exams.

After the first couple of sips, I could not stand it any longer. "Okay, Mama. So what is happening in two days?"

"You know, Misha and Anja are coming to tell us something important. I thought I had written you about that."

"No, you only wrote that they want to come and visit and talk to us. Not when or what. And you have no idea what this is all about?"

"No. But it must surely be something important. Why else would they drive all that distance?"

Two days later, around noon, the Mercedes stopped in front of our house. I was so tense that not even Anja or the huge Black Forest ham could hold my interest for long. Misha appeared unchanged. There was the hug, the customary reference to the "big boom," then the ritual of a round of vodka, accompanied by ham and smoked sturgeon. Obviously, he was not suffering any hardships. "What's the matter, Horst? I have never seen you like this. Trouble with Brigitte? Why isn't she here? We've brought her something. Anja saw it at the black market and said, 'That blouse is Brigitte'. I hope she'll come, so I can see her in it."

By now my stomach had turned into a mass of knots. Mama gave me a worried look. "You don't look well, Horst. Perhaps you should lie down for a while? And don't have any more of that vodka!"

It wasn't just my lack of patience, but a feeling of intense apprehension that made me blurt out, "You wrote that you had something important to tell us. Do you? What is it? Is it something that concerns us?"

Misha tossed down one more glass of vodka, then, as though he had changed masks, his face was serious, businesslike. He glanced at Anja, sighed, groaned, fiddled with his mustache, and tossed down one more shot.

"Yes, might as well get it over with," he began. "So, where were we? Ah yes, at the beginning. Well, the work we, the Allies, do, covers a lot of ground. My section has mostly to do with war crimes. There is a lot of undercover work—like that business with Kaminska and his gang. By the way, Horst, that was some coup! Large part of our work has to do with tracking down stolen artwork. On their way, the Nazis packed up entire houses, museums, and art galleries and shipped them to Germany. You wouldn't believe the things people like Göring, Himmler, and countless others accumulated. And then there is all the stuff some of the smaller fish, colonels and generals, collected. They just picked up whatever they could find and shipped it home. You have seen one of these collections in Breslau. We would not be here, perhaps, if Horst had not remembered the burial spot. Financing our trip to the West was not quite what the good general had in mind, I am sure. At any rate, there are long lists, descriptions, locations, names of possible owners—volumes. And then there are lists, compiled from the letters of former owners: descriptions, value, when and where lost. We coordinate all the information, make more lists and see if any items can be matched with owner claims. Of course, there is a lot of undercover work, too."

I was getting a little impatient at this point. Granted, it was fairly interesting to learn about the process of finding and returning artwork to rightful owners, but what did all this have to do with us? I was about to find out.

Misha continued, "Some time ago I came across something that looked very familiar: straight lines, triangles, cockeyed, purple hat—I think you all recognize her. The owner— a rich Dutchman living outside of Amsterdam. When the German Army came to occupy Holland in 1940, one of the generals went through his house, took everything of value, packed it into crates and shipped it to Germany, including our lady, of course. And now I knew her present whereabouts. What a dilemma! What was I to do? Keep quiet to be loyal to my friends or speak up and be loyal to my job and my country? As it turned out, I was spared this decision. A few weeks after my discovery, a memo came from our central office. The owner of our lady had notified them that this painting had been the result of an elaborate wedding gift prank that one of his friends had pulled on him. He apologized for any trouble he may have caused and assured us that our lady had no more value than that of a cheap imitation."

Misha took a deep breath, sighed deeply, wiped sweat from his forehead, and gulped down two shots in rapid succession. "I am so sorry, Käte. I knew what that picture meant to you."

My mother sat there rigidly, staring into space. Just her head moved. Every few seconds she shook it as if chasing away a fly that had landed on her face.

What could I say or do to help her? Trouble was, whatever I might say to her would have to ring insincere. She knew how sick I was of hearing the phrase, "our ticket to America."

"Ach, Mama," I finally managed to come up with, "we'll be all right. It wouldn't have been rightfully ours anyway. Antek will help us. We'll get rich together."

At least, this brought her back to life. "Not rightfully ours?" she said, a little louder than necessary. "Perhaps not in a legal sense—although there too wasn't it a finders-keepers situation? But emotionally, morally, I surely felt entitled to it. Aren't you the one who always justifies everything from the Robin Hood point of view? Justice for all? Well, I thought that I deserved that picture to make up for all the abuse we had to endure over the years and for all of our losses. No, whoever thinks he is Robin Hood up there—," and she pointed at the ceiling and beyond, "this is not my idea of justice. And now to learn that it has all been a joke!

"As for the ticket to America, my dear son, there are other possibilities. Sponsors and affidavits, the way Bastel and Werner are going. It just takes a little longer. Pour me another one, Misha! Better make that a double."

I did not exactly know how involved affidavits were and how long it might take, but I figured that it was not something that could happen overnight.

Journal entry, February 1946: The Picasso a hoax! What a cruel awakening. After hiding it so carefully and fretting over it and building our future around it. This definitely has the makings of a comedy. Almost got us killed!—Kaminska was caught due to it. Strange though. It's a shock, but somehow I had a premonition something like that was going to happen. Now we'll have to struggle like all the others to make it in America. If nothing else, it will build character, as they say. But who needs that? From now on it will be, as Horst puts it: work like hell and a bit of luck. Haven't we had enough hell already? I am tired of hell.

XXIV

How I learned to define a fanatic, how our idyllic existence was terminated, and how I dealt with my anger

S PRING WAS DEFINITELY IN the air—in more ways than one. Yes, crocuses and snowdrops were appearing; yes, sparrows were enjoying warm sand-and-dust baths in public places; yes, the chickens were stepping up their egg production, and yes, pastures were making a modest attempt to change from grey to green. But beyond all this, an annual springtime rite had descended upon the peaceful, awakening countryside. No longer was it safe to duck under a fence to find a cozy, sunny spot in the grass. An unpleasant, indeed sickening, odor weighed heavily upon the area, as oxen-drawn carts with tub-like structures on top were making their way across hill and dale. It was the content of these tubs which turned pastures the brilliant green that put a smile on every cow's face.

The content in question was a liquid mixture indescribably vile yet so powerfully nutritious that it conjured luxurious plant life out of the ground. After the winter's monotonous diet, cows now expected to find exciting flavors in their food: dandelions, sorrel, daisies, violets, yarrow, and cowslip. The powerful substance behind all this growth was known as *Jauche* (liquid manure). Animal and other organic waste, collected and jealously guarded during the rest of the year, made up the thick and sickening liquid that was dispensed wherever cows were expected to tread. The carts used for this operation were referred to as "honey wagons," in German, *Jauchewagen*. They left their mark everywhere.

Once there occurred an unfortunate accident involving one of them and a Sherman tank on maneuvers. The collision rendered the tank, though barely scratched, utterly useless. Neither direct orders, nor the threat of courts-martial, nor offers of promotion could persuade anyone to enter the innards of the defiled vehicle. It was scrubbed, hosed down, pushed into the river, and finally doused with gasoline and set ablaze. All to no avail. It can still be seen at a secluded hillside in the woods, shunned by humans and animals alike.

With the onset of warmer weather, the Gasthaus Schwan had become habitable again. We often ate and studied there. It was nice to be surrounded by familiar furniture. Antek's transformation was still a topic of undiminished interest. Erhard, Brigitte and I were earning good wages during our occasional afternoons at one of his plants. He had offered a permanent position to my mother. She never gave me any precise reason why she did not accept. I sensed that it had to do with America and her resolve to get me there, no matter what.

As far as I was concerned, except for food, wood, clothing, and prospects for a promising future, life could not have been better. But once more an old saying about trees and the sky struck me down with its ageless truth and wisdom: *Es ist dafür gesorgt, dass die Bäume nicht in den Himmel wachsen,* "Life sees to it that trees don't grow into the sky"—or into heaven? "Himmel" being the word for both "heaven" and "sky" in German.

Late one afternoon there was a knock at the door. It was Frau Hilgendorf. That alone was enough to alarm us, especially my mother. Beyond this it was her appearance that led us to believe that something horrible had happened. Her eyes, red in a white face, looked at us in shock. Her hands were shaking; her lips were forming words that bore no sound.

"One of your children?" my mother asked. "Can we help, shall we call someone?"

Frau Hilgendorf kept shaking her head, finally handing my mother a letter, one of those official Red Cross letters. My mother, too, read it. Without uttering a word she passed it on to Brigitte and me. Brigitte didn't have to read it. She knew. "It's about him, isn't it?" she asked in a whisper. "He isn't dead at all, is he? How much time do we have left?"

Thoughts raced through my mind, trying to make sense of Frau Hilgendorf's past and present behavior in the light of my mother's repeated warnings. Why did this Red Cross letter have such an impact on mother and daughter? Was I going to be affected by the information it contained? Had my mother's instincts been right? Had all this once more to do with our Semitic blood?—well, what else could it be?

"How much time do we have left?" I heard Brigitte repeat her question.

Her mother first nodded then shrugged her shoulders, "A few weeks . . . perhaps? He is still in a French hospital."

Did I hear this correctly? How much time do we have left? Left? Like a terminally ill person asking his doctor? Or, when is this epidemic scheduled to strike our neighborhood? Or, so when am I going to be executed for—what was it again? Was doomsday descending on us, mostly on Brigitte and me?

My mother was remarkably calm. She gave Frau Hilgendorf, who was quietly sobbing now, a comforting hug, poured two glasses of brandy, one for herself and one for Brigitte's mother, and announced that she would make some coffee to go with the Käsestrudel we had made two days ago.

"You just can't think rationally on an empty stomach," she said.

Indeed, the sobbing stopped and words began to pour out. "Oh, you can't imagine how many times I was about to come over and talk to you. I just didn't have the nerve. All the time I had a feeling that he would come back; he is the type that always finds ways to survive. If I befriended a Jew—he would do horrible things to all of us. But I did not have the heart to interfere with the children. I have never seen Brigitte so happy—the music, the skiing, her schoolwork—she has made such wonderful progress. And Horst is such a good friend to all of us."

She was on the brink of renewed tears, so Mama quickly slid another piece of strudel onto her plate.

"Please eat and have some more coffee, Irmgard. May I call you that? Yes, I knew it had to be something like that, and I tried to warn Horst. But what good does that do when you are—well, you know the way they are with each other.

"And you don't think that now, after the truth about so many things is known, your husband may think differently? After all, he must be an educated, intelligent man."

Irmgard sighed and shook her head. "Yes, that's what I kept telling myself, too, but . . . Do you know what the definition is for a fanatic? Someone who believes something zealously and unreasonably with uncompromising insistence. Yes, I did look this one up, and it describes Detlev to a T. Oh yeah! Except they forgot to list *brutal* and *ruthless*. You wonder how I ever got involved with someone like that? Well, we were still at the university, he in architecture, I in music. Everything seemed fine, but then he started to sit in on lectures on biology, philosophy, and history. He read Nietzsche with his superman ideas, works by Haeckel,* even by Darwin who certainly was not a racist. But it was his theory of evolution that worked well for the racists. So Detlev became a fanatical believer in the superiority of the Aryan race, and after he had read and studied Hitler's *Mein Kampf,* he was convinced that the Aryans, in order to become a race of supermen, had to be protected from any contamination from inferior blood. He thought the Nuremberg Laws were too lenient, if you can imagine that."

While her mother was speaking, Brigitte had risen. She was now standing behind me; I could feel both of her arms on my shoulders, her hands taking turns squeezing my arms and touching my cheeks.

I tried to make sense of what I had just heard and what it might mean for Brigitte and myself. Was our relationship endangered? A father and husband was a powerful figure, endowed with awesome moral and legal rights. I knew Brigitte would not cave in to any demands. But what about her mother?

"Have you considered talking to a lawyer?" my mother suggested. "Legal separation—divorce?"

Irmgard shook her head.

"That's the crazy thing about him, a real paradox. You'd think he would be an atheist. But no! He comes from a very strict Catholic family, and he is just as fanatical about the sanctity of marriage as he is about his racism. Pack up and leave? Join the thousands of refugees on the march everywhere? But with four children?"

"Three," Brigitte snapped. "I am not going anywhere."

Journal entry, early June 1946: So my hunch had been right— there is a Nazi connection. Now what? Aren't we ever going to be free of this curse that keeps haunting and following us? I feel so sorry for Horst, for Brigitte, too. What sort of chance do they have now? Will this monstrous obsession follow us across the Atlantic? Trouble is, whether it does or not, what we have experienced and what we are experiencing now will be our baggage forever.

*Ernst Haeckel: 1834-1919 German biologist and philosopher, provided a scientific framework for the Nazis with his justification for racism.

For the moment I could not imagine how this was going to end. Days went by. There was no follow-up. Gradually the sense of imminent disaster diminished, but the feeling that somewhere a deadly disease was threatening us never quite left me. Now and then we pondered possible courses of action, should circumstances warrant incisive action.

"What about that offer from Doktor Franzen? Do you think he was serious? Do you think he would arrange it for both of us to live in Switzerland?"

"Perhaps for a month or so. But to really live there, going to school and all that? I think it would be too much to ask."

It really made me angry that once more I had been victimized by my background, even now, after the so-called liberation. Suddenly I perceived the loss of the Picasso no longer merely as stroke of bad luck but as an act of malice by some pagan deity against my mother and me. Perhaps a ticket to America wouldn't be such a bad thing after all, right now, or, if we had a pile of money, dollars of course, we could disappear to some remote location, taking Brigitte along. With enough dollars, anything is possible—thus I went on fantasizing, knowing full well that there was no substance to my dreams.

School had become a terrible chore; my grades in all subjects were taking a nosedive. Doktor Schweitzer, my faculty advisor, called me to his office. I had always liked him, and it felt good to confide in him. He was shocked at what I told him and pleaded with me to improve my standing, otherwise I might not make it to the next grade.

Adding to my anguish was the food situation. It was as dismal as ever. Inadequate rations and infrequent packages from America barely kept us alive. I had tried fishing for trout, but without Mo, the conqueror, I was nothing but an unwanted refugee boy and quickly driven away by a very watchful game warden. My anger mounted, and I was getting desperate.

Journal entry, late June 1946: It is very painful to see how the news about Brigitte's father has affected Horst. I can understand his feelings, but I don't know what to do about them. He is so angry all the time: against me, Germany, the hunger, Brigitte's family, school, fate, God, the weather. I think he has developed a persecution complex—that everyone is out to get him. Blames me for having brought him into this world. Even Brigitte suffers. Came to me in tears the other day. America might be the answer, perhaps the only answer. He is still unwilling to talk about it, but I think his head is working on trying to persuade his heart.

"Brigitte," I said, "we've got to find that little trout pond that is supposed to be hidden somewhere in the woods. Any idea where that might be?"

"Well, if it is a pond, then there must be a source of water, a brook or spring or something heading downhill. We have been through most of the woods around here, so let's look in a different direction."

I put together some basic equipment, dug up a few worms, and on a Sunday morning we left to look for new territory. We were very fortunate. Hiking up along a small brook, we came to a crystal clear pond surrounded by dense forest. On one side, there was a structure in the water: four posts with a platform on which, about a foot above water, there was a box. Its bottom was nothing but a few metal bars, and on it a big hare was lying. Our noses told us that it had been dead for some time. Inspecting it more closely we noticed that it was crawling with big, white maggots. Every few seconds one or more of these would drop into the water where they were eagerly snapped up by fat trout.

Perhaps a change in diet will be welcome to these creatures, was my hope. I attached a lively wiggler to my hook and cast the line right into the maggot-drop area. The result reminded me of carp pond exploits. As soon as the worm hit the water, about five trout raced for it. Five seconds later the winner of that race was in my hand. Some of my vanished enthusiasm returned as I pulled in one fish after another.

Brigitte quickly caught on, but when she held one of these elegant, beautifully speckled fish, she sadly shook her head. "Can't do it, Horst," she said, and gently let it slip back into the water. "I think we have enough, anyway."

That evening, many of us assembled once again around the family table. Frau Hilgendorf was among the diners, fearfully looking over her shoulder every time she heard the door or footsteps in the hall.

It was like old times—almost. Back then providing food for everyone had always been an immensely satisfying experience for me. There still was a lot of that left, but in addition I knew that I had caught these fish to vent my anger. It felt good knowing that I had done something illegal. If I had liked alcohol, I might have been inclined to do some experimenting in that direction.

"Let's explore the woods some more, look for places we have not seen yet," I said to Brigitte. "Perhaps there are some pheasant or deer preserves somewhere."

The following day we skipped school so we would have plenty of time. We had packed a lunch. It was a sunny day, perfect for a pleasurable bike ride through the woods and meadows.

But I was driven. I pushed on and on. Brigitte was getting tired and started to complain. "Where are you going, and what do you hope to find when you get there?"

She was right, of course. We had passed the last farm half an hour ago. There weren't even any cows around anymore. Had there been, God knows what I might have done.

"Come on, Horst! To the end of this forest, and then let's turn around."

Just then we came to a narrow, grassy path to the right.

"Oh no! You aren't going in there?" Brigitte groaned. "What for?"

"I just want to see. If someone took the trouble of clearing a path here, there must be a reason for doing so, don't you think?"

After a few hundred feet, we came to a clearing with a small, strange-looking cabin. It had a door and one small window, and all along the walls there were little openings like tiny windows or doors.

"See?" I said triumphantly, "I knew what I was doing."

There was a smirk on Brigitte's face. "What is it, a doll house?"

"Well, I wouldn't want to play with the inhabitants of this house. Don't you know what this is? Go a little closer, but not too close, and check those little holes. What do you see?"

"Wow! Bees! Thousands of them. That is so cute, how they bunch up in front of their entrances and crawl over and around each other. And some of them seem to carry little bundles, brownish bundles. I think I could just watch for hours."

"Those little bundles—that's pollen. They need it inside to feed their young and their queen. This is a bee house, and there may be millions of them living in there."

"How do you know so much about bees? You never told me."

"Those books I told you about, *Brehms Tierleben*. Anyway, where there are bees, there is honey, I read. So, let's see if there may be any for us. But move slowly. We don't want to alarm them."

Of course, I had no idea what to do. Trying to get inside the building seemed like a reasonable first step to me. There had to be honey in there, because there were blossoms everywhere. But beyond that? I tried the door. Locked. The window? Very sturdy. "Let's try our house and apartment keys."

Brigitte had that smirk on her face again. "Hope you didn't forget to bring the right keys," she teased.

She could be so sarcastic sometimes. I shrugged my shoulders, inserted the first key and tried to turn it. As in a well-oiled machine there was absolutely no resistance, the door opened, and we stepped into a neat little room with benches, shelves, and buckets. And there was such a wonderful smell! A mixture of beeswax, honey and flowers. Some of the buckets were filled with honeycomb, each hexagonal little chamber still sealed; others were filled with pure honey. A truck would have come in handy.

I was anxious not to get caught inside, so both of us grabbed two honey buckets, about five-pounders, and attached them to our handlebars. Then we locked the door conscientiously and left, praying we would not meet anyone on that narrow path.

Twenty pounds of honey! Wow! All the way back, over and over, we dipped fingers into the buckets and licked them.

At home, most of our friends and relatives had not seen real honey in years. Erhard, after several spoonfuls, announced earnestly, "This is amazing. I can already feel my teeth tightening in my gums."

"Is there going to be any more at some later date?" some inquired.

"I'll do my best," I answered grimly, somehow feeling that we were entitled to that honey.

As soon as everybody had left, that restless feeling of anxiety and anger returned, and I racked my brain as to what to do next. It was almost as if I was hoping to get caught at something outrageously illegal. Then at least they would have a reason for punishing me. Because that's what I felt—that I was being punished for something that was not my fault.

After a couple of days I couldn't stand it any longer. "Okay, Brigitte, time for another visit to the bee house."

She was not happy to hear this. "I don't know, Horst. I think it's too dangerous. If you were the beekeeper, wouldn't you really guard the honey now?"

True. And why should I endanger Brigitte? So the following morning, instead of going to school, I biked toward the bee house. All the way out I didn't meet a single soul, and except for the bees doing their work, nothing was stirring. I hid the bike behind some bushes and proceeded cautiously toward the cabin. No unusual activity there, just busy little creatures darting back and forth. It was mesmerizing to watch. To keep your eyes on one particular bee was like focusing on one flake in a snowstorm. Brigitte had been right. One could just watch them for hours—hours I did not have. I had no idea what lay ahead of me, but I foresaw three possibilities: there might be someone, the owner for example, inside the house, or he might be somewhere watching from behind a tree, or he had changed the lock.

That's what I felt.

Keys in hand, I approached the door. There were some fresh scratch marks around the lock and wood shavings on the ground. Darn! But what had I expected, anyway? No one is that stupid. Trying to insert our house key confirmed the third possibility. It didn't even fit into the hole anymore. Any point in trying other keys? I chose a smaller one, our apartment key. Out of morbid curiosity and totally perfunctorily, I stuck it into the keyhole. No resistance! I twisted it counterclockwise, and it opened the door as smoothly as if lock and key had been manufactured for each other. Could that happen twice in a row? What were the odds? I almost felt a little bit sorry for the beekeeper. He would have to think that some real pros or supernatural powers were at work here.

Inside nothing had changed, except that there was more honey now, buckets of it lined up along the wall. Were they waiting for an imminent pickup? No time to enjoy the clear, amber-colored treasure now, or the wonderful smell. I quickly grabbed two buckets and a chunk of honeycomb, locked the door carefully behind me, and fetched my bike.

After pedaling for about ten minutes, I stopped. Something was wrong. Despite the full buckets, a feeling of emptiness overcame me. This had been too easy. I was close to turning around to put the buckets back, but that would have been dangerous as well as silly. In those days you just didn't surrender vital food for personal reasons. So, amidst fragrant wildflowers, soft grasses and moss, I decided to contemplate my dilemma. I had taken some bread along, which tasted wonderful when dipped into honey. I watched with fascination how bees were working around me. Occasionally some would come and check out the contents of the buckets.

"Yeah," I said to them, "that's your honey. Recognize it? Thank you very much for all your work."

A few more bees were buzzing around the bucket now. "Well, go ahead and have some," I said to them. "After all, it's yours."

The sun was shining on me, inducing sleepiness. No longer could I resist the urge to stretch out. It was so peaceful and warm and cozy that I fell asleep.

I knew I had not slept very long, because the sun was still on me when I awoke at an unusual noise. It was a loud humming and buzzing, like a droning produced by hundreds of cellos, I imagined, all playing the same low-pitched notes. I looked for the players, and there they were, tens of thousands of them, clouds of bees swarming around my buckets, clinging to the sides, crawling up and down on the inside, reclaiming what was rightfully theirs. Half the honey was gone already, and there was nothing I could do. I had to laugh at the irony of it all. Leaving the buckets to their fate, I took my bike and rode home, feeling strangely relieved.

When I arrived at the Schwan, Onkel Pippi was there. He looked ill at ease.

"This is rather awkward," he began. "You know how we all appreciate and need your wonderful talent for conjuring up food for us. Well," he paused, looking for the right words, "have you ever met my friend, the grade-school teacher? Such a sweet, humane fellow! He came to me, just heartbroken. Someone had broken into his bee house and made off with a lot of honey. It was very embarrassing. Of course, I did not say anything, but I implore you not to do it again."

The teacher's dismay as well as my uncle's request were certainly justified. Still, they angered me. "You saw how much honey we had," I answered. "About twenty pounds. There are roughly twenty-five hives in that bee house. Do you have any idea how many pounds of honey one hive produces in one season? About eighty to a hundred pounds. That comes to a total of at least two thousand pounds a year, altogether."

"That is absolutely astounding. I had no idea," he marveled.

"Has your good and humane friend ever given you any honey when things were rough? What do you think he does with all that honey?"

"Was this another one of your Robin Hood actions?"

"No. I had not really thought much about him for a while. But now that you mention it—and don't worry. I am all through there."

I finished the interview by telling him the story of the keys and of the bees getting their honey back.

"Isn't nature just amazing and miraculous in its workings?" he said, shaking his head.

Journal entry, July 1946: That honey incident! What else will that boy do in his anger? He needs something new to focus on— America! Otherwise, God knows what he will turn into. Pippi doesn't quite see it that way. He uses the incident to convince me that what the boy needs is a strong father figure—him. He is nice to Horst, I admit, but isn't he just trying to win him over? And as my sister's widower? Almost smacks of incest to me. It is very uncomfortable to have him badger me all the time. If for no other reason—escape to America!

XXV

How Brigitte honored the fourth commandment, why we had to run, and how Anja helped us

THOUGH EXPECTING SOMETHING ANY day, there still had been no further indication as to Herrn Hilgendorf's whereabouts or intentions. We began to rationalize: What can he do? We are almost adults, after all. Nazi Germany and the obsession with a master race no longer exist. And how would he even know about my Jewish blood? We did not consider the fact that fanatics cannot be influenced, stopped, swayed, or reprogrammed by rational thinking and that there was probably not a soul in the whole village who did not know of my background.

We were not exactly rolling around on the couch that afternoon in the Schwan, but neither were we sitting at opposite sides of the table, when, without a knock, the door flew open. Both of us jumped up. One look at Brigitte and I knew. There were white and red blotches on her face; her eyes said it all. I thought she was going to scream, but just one short, tiny word came out of her mouth. "Him!" It was laden with contempt, disgust, fear, loathing and hatred.

"Get outside, and wait for me there," he snapped at his daughter.

"Remember the fourth commandment, and do as I tell you!" he growled when Brigitte remained motionless.

"And you the fifth," she spat at him. "Or did God make no provision for Jews?"

But he was not inclined to get bogged down in religious polemics. "All right then, we'll settle this right here and now. It should not take very long," he added contemptuously.

I was still standing at the table where Brigitte and I had been holding hands less than thirty seconds ago. Thoughts were racing through my mind: "Should I place myself protectively in front of Brigitte? Should I address him in a polite, rational, reconciliatory manner?" One glance at this man convinced me that any discourse would be futile. His face was distorted with hatred and rage; there was no provision made in his eyes for warmth or understanding. Like two lifeless devices made of blue steel, they drilled their message into me, the message of a maniac, totally insane, but murderously real. "How interesting," I somehow managed to think, "his face turns dark red in anger—just like his son's."

Only now did I register that Herr Hilgendorf was carrying a large, heavy walking stick, oak or hazelnut. He was flipping it from hand to hand. Many returning soldiers carried them.

Had they been created during rest periods or between battles or in a peaceful village in Norway or Greece? Perhaps in a POW camp? But were knives allowed on POWs? Among the sticks I had seen, there were some of truly astounding artistry—religious motifs, flowers, parts of the female anatomy, and geometric designs. Herrn Hilgendorf's walking stick was a little heftier than the norm and shockingly bare. It was not difficult to guess that he had no ambitions for it other than to test its sturdiness on some human body, preferably mine.

Brigitte and I were now standing side by side, but suddenly she placed herself between me and her father, watching his every move.

I did not know how long it had been since father and daughter had seen each other last, but it was obvious that the father was not fully aware of his daughter's reactions to danger or insult, otherwise he would have kept his eyes on hers. I did, and what I saw almost made me want to shout, "Hey, watch out!" Because by now they were merely narrow slits.

When Herr Hilgendorf raised his weapon, ready to push Brigitte out of his way and to deliver his blow, it was all over for him. Precisely as he must have taught her years ago, she catapulted into the air, spun around and landed a kick to the side of his face. I must say, I had seen her administer more forceful kicks before. Her concession to the fourth commandment? I wondered.

Still, after this, Herr Hilgendorf was disinclined or unable to get up. He was groaning softly, his eyes were closed, a thin thread of blood ran out of the corner of his mouth.

"We'll get help," Brigitte said. "Now hurry, Horst! I have things to do."

Things like what? I wondered, as Brigitte dragged me past her father and out the door.

"The bikes, Horst! Quickly to my house first."

She stormed into her kitchen, motioning me to wait there while she raced on to her room. After two minutes, she returned with her full pack and the cello. "Erhard," she said to her alarmed brother, "go to the Schwan. Your father needs some help. Try to delay him. Mother, I have to leave. Don't worry, I'll be in touch. Let's hurry, Horst. We don't want to get caught again."

She gave her speechless mother an embrace and handed me the cello. "Go!" she ordered.

She had never said anything to me about her preparations, but it was obvious that she had planned and rehearsed this scene many times.

"We'll drop off the cello at your place, then we'll bike to Günzach and take the next train to Kempten. We can stay with Antek a couple of days. Then we'll go to Munich. Anja is sort of expecting us."

"Anja? You have spoken with her? Why have you never mentioned it to me?"

"Did not want to worry you, and yes, I called her from the post office the other day. I also have quite a bit of money saved up from work."

I was stunned. She had thought of everything, so there was not much to say. As for long-range plans? Had she already figured that out, too? All of a sudden she had become an adult, I felt.

My mother did not know what was happening. It all seemed confusing and threatening to her, I am sure.

"What's going on?" she wailed. "What happened? Why are you bringing the cello here? Why is Brigitte carrying a full pack?" She looked as she had on the day when the Gestapo informed her that we had lost our home to them. "And why are you going to your room to pack and asking me to make sandwiches?"

Brigitte must have done some explaining while I was packing, because mother was somewhat composed when I came back.

"Don't worry, Mama. You can come to visit us at Antek's if you like. And don't tell anyone what our plans are. Hide the cello somewhere. We'll take the bikes on the train, and then we'll leave them at Antek's."

Mama's tears were flowing when she kissed us goodbye. "This is too sudden," she sobbed. "Are you sure this is necessary?"

"Yes, it is," Brigitte answered. "I have thought about it for a long time, because I knew there wouldn't be any other way out."

Journal entry, July 1946: So the fight is on—Nazi against Horst. No score so far. The Nazi has been temporarily knocked out, but Horst is gone. Any prediction for the outcome? One loser for sure: me. Who will get to the children first? Herr Hilgendorf or the tall lady with the torch? This is the worst thing that has ever happened to me. They got my house, and now they've driven Horst to abandon me? America was already so close. Now it is—indefinitely postponed? But I know Horst is a good and reliable son. I must have faith. But what weighs heavier? Me or Brigitte?

So many questions kept racing through my head, all of them coming to an inevitable stop at the only destination Brigitte knew—Luisenstrasse 56. Was there anything in Brigitte's plans beyond that? Was she, or were we, to be there forever?

When we discussed this issue on the train to Kempten, she was amazingly indefinite and nonchalant about the future. "Oh, don't worry so much. For now we are safe and still together. Isn't that enough? As for the future—," and she gave me that old familiar saying of dubious comfort and credibility, *"Kommt Zeit, kommt Rat."*

From experience I knew that there was not much that could upset Antek's emotional equilibrium. But when he saw us move in with bikes and luggage, he felt compelled to inquire. "Do you mind telling me what is going on? Are they after you again? What have you done this time? Or—," and he winked vehemently, as if he had a nervous tic, "did you elope?"

I had seen him angry before, but nothing compared to now. After he had heard our story, he kept shaking his head, muttering words of Slavic origin. It took all of Brigitte's sweetness to make him abandon his plans for the re-education of Herrn Hilgendorf, designed to make him a cooperative member of society. Several times he referred vaguely to "persuasive measures" he had in mind.

"No, no, Antek. Very kind of you to offer your help. But I am not the only person to think about here. Think of my mother, my brother, my sisters!"

"Well, all right," he grumbled. "You just say the word if you want anything done. Seems to me, some disciplinary action is in order here."

The following morning Brigitte called Anja. It was not difficult to reconstruct Anja's part of the conversation.

"Hello! Brigitte here . . . No, we are staying with Antek . . . Yes, yesterday he suddenly burst into the Schwan . . . Yes, Horst was with me. We were just reading something. No, no. Horst tried to say something, but no use. He sort of went berserk and tried to hit Horst with a big stick . . . No, nothing happened to Horst . . . To my father? I don't think anything serious. I was gentle, but he was flat on the floor as we left . . . . Yes. I had everything packed. It was exactly as we had discussed, and we left the cello at Horst's apartment . . . Yes. She was really shocked and cried . . . No. She is okay now. I told her what our plans were. I hope she'll have a chance to talk to my mother, but my father will be watching her like a hawk now . . . I am not sure, but I think we'll come day after tomorrow. We are really looking forward to being with you. Give our regards to Misha . . . Oh? But he'll be back next week? Do you really think I should? We'll try. Depends on if we can get Antek to make the trip to Obergünzburg tomorrow . . . No. We just have one backpack each . . . Are you kidding? That's all we own . . . That would be wonderful. Horst could use some new stuff, too. I think he's been wearing the same pair of boots for two years now. One more year and they'll fit . . . Oh, I'm sure he'd love that. So thanks again—until the day after tomorrow."

I had no idea how often Brigitte had talked to Anja in the past, but they sure sounded like old friends to me. Gave me a warm feeling all over. And had I understood that correctly? I would be alone there with Brigitte and Anja? Gave me hot flashes all over.

"Just one question, Brigitte—or make that two," I said. "What is it we don't know if we should, but we'll try?"

"Oh, bring the cello. Anja plays the flute. Did you know that?"

"No, I didn't. And what is it I would love?"

"Oh, if the two of us take you shopping to the black market."

We asked Antek what the chances were for the cello pickup.

"Well, if I can work it in tomorrow, I'll make the trip. We are kind of busy right now. Huge order from Italy. Could really use you two. Perhaps I can get Erhard and your mother to come and help, Horst."

So, next day, Brigitte got her cello, Antek got his extra helpers, and my mother got some more time with me.

Two days later we were on the train to Munich. Refugees with bundles and trunks were still on the march, but some of the frenzied confusion of former days had subsided. So there was progress, be it ever so slow—an evaluation I unfortunately was not able to apply to my own situation. For a while I had been quite content and optimistic; now everything was once more a big question mark. Brigitte appeared strangely confident in view of what had happened, relieved now that we were taking some decisive action.

What about my own progress? Slow? Was there any? Or had fate shifted me into reverse? What was I doing on this train? Why was Brigitte on this train? Were we running away? Would we be sitting here if I were a nice Aryan boy with an illustrious past in the German Youth? Somehow the rhythmic pounding of the wheels below me forged my thoughts into a monotonous litany in which the theme of running made up the refrain. Soon all there was left in my head was an endlessly repeated run-run-run-run-run which finally lulled me to sleep.

I awoke feeling refreshed, hungry, and optimistic. Outside, a familiar landscape welcomed me: streets truncated by bomb craters, piles of brick adorned with occasional bathtubs. Just like home, I thought, touched by a nostalgic longing for the rubble piles of Breslau. Here and there a speck of vegetation was attempting a modest comeback; children were playing their games, and teams of adults were collecting and cleaning bricks for recycling. A gigantic bomb crater caught my attention. Some enterprising or desperate soul had turned it into a lush garden. Ingeniously and with artistic flair, that person had made use of thousands of pieces of broken brick to build narrow terraces into the fairly steep bank of the crater. I recognized trellises with beans and peas, rows with salad greens, and a jungle of tomato plants. It was uplifting to see new life sprouting from the depth of death and destruction, and I interpreted this miracle, performed by the human spirit, as a favorable omen for our future.

We ate some of the sandwiches my mother had prepared from Antek's pantry. Brigitte was in good spirits. She was very much looking forward to seeing Anja again. "I told her when we would be arriving," she said. "Think she'll be there? Perhaps even with the car? I'd hate to lug my cello through half of Munich."

That, of course, was an exaggeration. Luisenstrasse is no more than a twenty-minute walk from the Bahnhof. But Anja was there anyway—with the Mercedes.

"Can't wait to play with you," she said when she saw the cello. "Horst can sing."

There hadn't been much cause for hugging lately, but that brought it on. Easy, because we were all sitting in the front seat.

"Any objections if I put you two in the guestroom?" Anja asked. "Your mothers would probably kill me for even suggesting this, but in this case, where I sense that there is a lasting bond between two young people—why not?"

A lasting bond—expressed my sentiments exactly. Brigitte, too, nodded approvingly. Then she hugged me.

The next few days were so wonderful it was difficult to remember why we had come.

We went shopping, ate well; some evenings we visited one of the little dance bars that were popping up everywhere, especially in Schwabing. Schwabing, home of the university, was the old artists' section of Munich, and now the place where students would get together in the evening. It was difficult to find a table, more difficult to squeeze onto the dance floor, and impossible to pull off any acrobatic dance maneuvers. We told Anja the story of the Goldene Engel jitterbug contest, about Mo, about the deer, the trout, the coal train, everything, right through Brigitte's fight with her father. Brigitte and I danced a lot, and occasionally I asked Anja, but I knew better than to stay on the dance floor with her when the band played one of those slow tunes.

Journal entry, August 1946: Notification from the immigration service that our papers are in order and have been processed. Feel a little guilty that I had not informed Horst of my initiative. I just could not have endured another fight. Now I'll just wait and see what happens. I think the earlier we get there the better. The older Horst is, the harder it will be for him to adjust. And all the relatives are very encouraging, saying that good jobs are easy to find; in fact they wrote that there is one rich family that is just dying to have a German cook. How ironic! Suddenly I am a German cook! I can almost hear what my mother would say.

It was obvious that we took pains to avoid any opportunity to talk about our options for the future. If my life were to continue like this for a few more weeks, years—decades—who was I to complain? Anja saw our life from a more realistic point of view. Finally she could not take this silence any longer.

"Not that I wouldn't love to go on like this forever," she said, "but you have to think about your future: school, jobs, family and all that. Don't you have any thoughts about the next weeks, months, years? Your mother has called almost every day, so far. What does she think, Horst?"

"She just wants to go to America, the way we have been planning for a long time—as if life would be any easier for us over there! And without Brigitte? If only we could find a way for her to go, too. Of course now, after that encounter with her father, it would be madness for us to stay in Germany. I think if I told my mother to go ahead with our plans, we could be out of here in about two months."

"Two months? What about me? Us?" Brigitte asked with a shaky voice.

"Well, yes. That precisely is the problem and the reason why we are still here. How could it be arranged and under what circumstances would Immigration admit you?"

I addressed Anja, "Do you think Misha might have any ideas or contacts?"

She had listened with great interest, looking from one to the other as we spoke. Something seemed to be working through her head. She was now focusing on Brigitte with a look so intense, that Brigitte averted her eyes and blushed. After several minutes, Anja slowly relaxed and nodded affirmatively. "This may be an outrageous idea, but it might stand a chance. How old are you, Brigitte? Sixteen? Wait a minute while I get something from my room."

Brigitte and I exchanged questioning looks and shrugged our shoulders.

Anja returned with a little folder from which she took an official looking document.

"This," she said with a sigh, "is my sister's birth certificate. My mother had insisted that I have copies for all of us in my possession. Marlies was also born in 1929. As you know, I have not found her or my mother. The trail, as far as I could find out, led to Dresden. There is nothing after that. How many perished there on February 13 and 14, 1945? Some forty thousand? People vanished without a trace, but not necessarily due to death. Some were merely sucked into the incredible turmoil that took place after these attacks and during the final months of the war. They were swept along by the current and finally spit ashore somewhere miles and miles away from where they belonged or wanted to be. I hear stories like that all the time.

"There are those who take advantage of this situation. It's so easy to assume a new identity nowadays. Practically all you have to do is mention the word *Dresden,* and if you tell the authorities you are Stalin's illegitimate daughter, they'll give you a new ID to that effect. Misha has told me some incredible stories. Well, I have given up any hope by now. But there is something I want to do now, sort of in memory of my sister. I want to do it for her, for myself, and for you."

We—at least I—had no idea what Anja had in mind. Whatever it was had to be something major, judging by her face. Brigitte observed her with moist, wide-open eyes. She sensed something I could not. Women are way ahead of men when it comes to intuition.

"This idea is not something that popped into my head just this evening," Anja continued. "It's been on my mind for a few days, and I think it might be the answer to your problems. A bit overwhelming, no doubt, but here it is—Brigitte, how would you like to become my sister Marlies? All we would have to do is declare that you turned up. I have your birth certificate, and I can identify you as my sister. I'll bet they won't even ask much about your temporary disappearance. If they do—nervous shock after Dresden—amnesia! Happens all the time."

At this point I thought it might be discreet to leave the room for a while, but Anja motioned me to stay. I wondered why. Then it came to me. That's right, I thought, she hasn't told us how her little scheme is going to solve our problem.

Anja did not keep us waiting for long. "This is not generally known and is kept kind of secret, but the U.S. is extending special immigration privileges to dependents of victims of the July 20 assassination attempt on Hitler. Misha has all the details on that. He said it may affect us someday.

While Anja was filling her new sister in on family history, I had time to contemplate this turn of events. On the one hand, I naturally was relieved and delighted by this totally unexpected development; on the other, it made me feel a little uncomfortable. How would Brigitte present and justify a change of identity to her family? The reason for such action was quite obvious, I thought. If she wanted to maintain any control over her life, then, given the nature of her father, she really did not have any other choice but to disappear. But still—

When Brigitte returned from talking with Anja, she looked at me with a thin, uneasy smile. Was that an indication of her acceptance or her refusal of Anja's offer? I wondered.

"Well," I finally broke the silence, "do I call you Brigitte or Marlies?"

"It does not matter, because for you I'll always be the same one, no matter what the name," she replied.

"Yes," I reasoned, "but Marlies would give up her family to go to America, and Brigitte would—I don't know what—would face a very uncertain future of constant oppression here."

"And that is why Brigitte must become Marlies," she continued my thoughts, "at least temporarily. If Brigitte's father had not returned, she and Horst would have made it here. But that hope is gone. It will be tough as Marlies—probably most so for my mother, having to put up with him and not being sure of what is happening to me. But in a couple of years we'll be legal, and there will be nothing he can do about that."

I had to agree. It all sounded ethical, logical, and reasonable—under the circumstances. Kommt Zeit, kommt Rat, I thought over and over. How true, how true!

"So, what do you think the next—or first—step in that direction should be?" I asked Brigitte.

"Okay. Next time your mother calls, which should be in about ten minutes, tell her to take the necessary steps to initiate your immigration procedure. Then tell her to come and visit and to bring Erhard. But tell her to be extremely cautious. Perhaps Antek could contact him."

Indeed, with German-Jewish precision the phone rang after ten minutes. I went to get it.

"Hello, Mama. Yes . . . Yes. No, not yet . . . Yes, I'll try again. May I say something now? No, no—nothing terrible. To the contrary. Guess what! You can start the immigration process. No! We did not break up. It's too complicated to explain. We'll tell you when you get here. What? Yes, we want you to come. And bring Erhard. But make sure you-know-who doesn't suspect anything. No. Better not say anything to Frau Hilgendorf. Tell us when you'll arrive, and we'll pick you up. Yes, in the Mercedes. Bye, Mama."

There was one thing I really wanted to do while in Munich—visit

Planegg. I just craved to see Uli's eyes pop out of his head when I showed up with Brigitte and Anja. Lindhilda was also high up on the list. Uli answered the phone when I called.

"What? You are in Munich, and you are not staying with us? Is Brigitte with you? When can you come? Oh, you have to meet my girlfriend, Margot. She is sooo hot! Who? Oh, Annelies! No. Never heard from her again. Say, when you come, could you bring some food? Something to cook? My older sister is home now. Ursi. She is a marvelous cook. Between the two of you, I expect great things. But no Texas omelet, please! Yeah, yeah. Day after tomorrow will be fine. Try to come early so we can visit Lindhilda. She keeps asking me about you. See you soon, Tex."

"Okay, what should we bring? Shopping trip to the black market?" I asked Anja.

"Yes, we could," she answered. "But I have a better idea. Misha got us a pass for the U.S. commissary. You can buy almost anything there— for practically nothing. How about if I get three or four chickens, plus whatever else looks good? To ordinary Germans, everything looks good these days. Whatever we get will be a treat."

On our way, we stopped at the commissary. Anja went in alone and returned, pushing one of those funny little carts. Seemed to me she had bought one of everything, not just food items, but soap, a toilet brush, kitchen cleanser, and toilet paper. Women just have different priorities—as if I didn't already know.

As I remembered, Uli had not been present when the Mercedes with the two officers, Anja and us—almost a year ago—had come through. Uli took one look at Anja now, and I could tell it was goodbye, Margot, at least for the moment.

After gaping at her in speechless adoration, he closed his mouth and ushered us into the house. Evi was still in school. Tante Angelina greeted us and then introduced us to Ursi, her older daughter. Ursi was a little taller than her siblings. She had sparkling eyes, and when she smiled, dimples appeared on her cheeks. After the first ten minutes she had already told us three jokes, good ones, too.

"What about dinner?" she asked later. "They told me that I am to prepare a gourmet dinner for you. What do I have to work with?"

"We brought four small chickens and a variety of other stuff," Anja reported. "Of course, we'll all help when the time comes."

"Chickens, eh? Let me think. This is a good mushroom year, so I gathered some yesterday. Do you like Italian? Great! Then how about *pollo alla cacciatora?* That is simple, fast and delicious."

A fellow mushroomer? I thought. Finally there is one in the family besides me. "May I see what you've found?" I asked.

"Are you checking up on me? Are you afraid I am going to poison you? I've heard you are quite the expert. Well, so am I," she informed me. "Here. Have a look." She proudly put a large basket on the table.

I instinctively took one step backwards. What I saw was not yellow or brown, but bluish, red, pink, and purple, with some yellow and brown strewn in. There must have been about eight varieties in there, none of which I would have wanted to touch with a ten-foot pole.

She registered my reaction with amusement.

"I know," she said. "You are strictly a chanterelle and boletus man, but if you enjoy more complex flavors, you have to have a variety of mushrooms."

She selected a few out of the basket, gave their names and pointed out their characteristics. I was relieved to notice that there was nothing all white in the bunch.

"If you'd like, I can teach you more and better in the woods tomorrow," she said.

Uli was getting a bit itchy from all this discussion. "How about riding over to the Moosbacher farm now? Lindhilda is expecting us."

"Can I come?" Ursi asked. "I've heard so much about her, the pig and the Blutwurst orgy. I'd love to try some of that. How about you, Uli? For old times' sake?"

But Uli had grown up. "Sure, why not?" he answered with a grin. "After a couple liters of beer there is nothing I wouldn't eat."

Lindhilda must have been watching the road, because she came rushing out as we approached.

"Better stop out here," I cautioned Anja. "You don't want to get mired down in cow manure."

Lindhilda was wearing something ethnic and looked downright regal.

"Doesn't she remind you of that statue of Bavaria that overlooks the Oktoberfest?" I whispered to Ursi.

She nodded with a grin. "Remind me later to tell you the Bavaria joke. It's great."

Unfortunately I forgot to do that, so I never heard it.

There was heavy hugging all around when we faced each other.

"So which one is Brigitte?" Lindhilda asked. "From what Uli told me, I'll bet it's this one," she said, pointing at Brigitte.

Sigi, the German police dog, came to see what the commotion was all about. He sniffed around and dedicated the next five wags to me.

"What happened to your lederhosen, Horst? Almost didn't recognize you without them. You are so much taller and look so much older than last time. But do come on in. Too early for plums, but I baked a strawberry torte—with whipped cream, of course."

We sat, ate and talked, told stories of our adventures and exploits. Lindhilda raised one question that made me wonder why I had never asked it: "What did finally happen to those men from the black market, and why was Misha so vehement in his pursuit of them?"

Anja was the only one who knew the answer, and after some hesitation she gave us the facts. "They had been responsible for the massacre of a large group of captured Russian officers, among them Misha's brother. Misha had witnessed the incident, testified, and saw to it that the guilty received the maximum punishment."

I had suspected something like that.

To reestablish emotional equilibrium, Lindhilda resorted to the regional, time-tested cure-all: Obstler. After two rounds, jokes and laughter emerged once more. Several times by now we had complied with Lindhilda's request for ever more details of Brigitte's martial arts encounters. She just couldn't get enough of it. "How high can you kick? What is the most effective attack? Have you ever killed anyone? Could you, if you had to? If I found a teacher, could I still become good?"

There just was no way to satisfy her yearning for more knowledge about this exotic, deadly, and ancient form of combat. Over and over she looked at Brigitte, as if she couldn't fathom it. Something more than mere curiosity had seized her. She was fidgeting with her glass and kept shifting around on her chair. What is she after? I asked myself. Yes! That has to be it—a demonstration. "Okay, Lindhilda, don't be bashful. Where is the board?"

She turned bright red. "The board? What board? What are you talking about?"

"Oh, come on. You know there is a board somewhere, a board with Brigitte's name on it."

"Really?" Lindhilda beamed. "You mean it? Will you do it, Brigitte? Just the way you did on that ski trip?"

Brigitte giggled and nodded. After two Obstler there was no stopping her.

We placed the oak board across two chairs, and then Brigitte did what looked like magic: one blow, swift and powerful as a cobra's strike, and two pieces of wood tumbled to the floor.

Lindhilda shrieked with amazed delight, and Anja said proudly, "That's my sister!"

"Your—what? You two are sisters?" a chorus of three inquired.

"That's a long story," I said. "You'll hear it someday."

It was now getting late, and Ursi reminded us that we should get back if there was to be any dinner tonight. Lindhilda was disappointed. "I thought, you would stay here for some beer and sausage. Now you'll just have to take a package home with you. It will remind you of the slaughter feast, Uli. Oh yeah, now I remember. You were sick that day."

Outside, Uli sighed with relief. "Wow! That was close."

Pollo alla cacciatora had such an elegant and exotic ring to it. When I assisted Ursi, I found out that it sounded more promising than it was. You cut up the chicken, take some carrots, celeriac, garlic, chop them coarsely, sauté all this with a bit of bay leaf and rosemary in olive oil, and add the chicken pieces and a few cut-up tomatoes. When the chicken is browned, add a glass of white wine and simmer all for about thirty minutes. Sauté the mushrooms separately and add them to the chicken. This we served with noodles. I mean, it was really good but not fantastic. Or perhaps my mind was too preoccupied with the latest events, thus incapable of fully appreciating what everyone else was raving about.

Uli appeared to have completely recovered from having been struck down by Anja's presence. Margot had not wasted any time reviving him. She was very pretty and very sweet. Her father owned the local brewery, and all of us partook of his bottled product. Not quite appropriate with Italian, but, as Uli put it, "Good beer goes with anything." How could Annelies compete with that! Poor Annelies!

Late in the evening we drove home. My mother was due the next day at fifteen thirty.

Punctually the train pulled in; my mother and Erhard emerged.

"Why are there so many girls swarming all over the Bahnhof!" my mother complained. "Terrible! They look like prostitutes."

"That's what they are, Mama. You have a good eye. For a carton of cigarettes you can rent a genuine Bavarian for a week. Of course, you'd have to feed her, too. That's how they survive."

My mother clutched her little bag tightly and accelerated her pace. She was very businesslike. She had brought all the papers and planned to arrange for a visit at the U.S. Consulate. It was difficult for her to accept Brigitte's new identity and to comprehend the motivation behind her action. How could someone's child suddenly decide he or she wanted to be somebody else's child? She beheld me with an expression which betrayed fear and curiosity: would I be capable of behavior like that?

Erhard pierced his sister with his looks, as if he was trying to read between the lines. "Von—what?" he kept asking belligerently, "Woltershaag? Hilgendorf isn't good enough for you anymore? Is it the *von* that is so irresistible to you?

"I am sorry," he apologized after a brief pause. "That was dumb and mean of me. But you can't imagine what it's like at home now. Our father is absolutely insane! Demands that I go with him to Brazil to help build up some Aryan supremacy force. I have asked Antek if I could move in with him. He has no objections—hopes I would help out more if I lived there. But mother? I think it would be too much for her if I left now. Yeah, I guess I can see why you did it," he paused. "I wish I could vanish the way you did. And what's that about America?"

"Yes," Brigitte answered, "that's the other huge factor here, really *the* decisive motivation. With that name, as the daughter of one of the victims of July 20, I will be able to emigrate to the U.S. So you see, in a couple of years, when I am married to Horst, that *von* and any name attached to it will be gone. Doesn't mean anything anyway in America."

"That's right!" came my mother's emphatic contribution. "That's right! America! Herr Hilgendorf—no offense, Brigitte and Erhard—is the ultimate proof of my theory that Germany is no place for us. As we have seen, it takes only one crazy fanatic to hurl an entire nation into a frenzy of hatred. What we have learned and continue to learn about the fate of European Jews during the past ten years, well—the next round, please, without us, thank you very much. And thank you too, Brigitte, Erhard, and Anja for giving us hope.

"I once did not believe the people who predicted our doom. I had to learn the hard way and, as always, there is an old proverb for every situation. This one describes my current fear and my behavior very well: *Gebranntes Kind scheut das Feuer"* (it's the burned child that shies away from the fire).

It did not happen very often that my mother got up enough steam to speak out, but when she did, people generally paid attention.

The morning after the interview my mother started her return trip with the assurance that all our immigration papers were in order, that the consulate had received from America all the affidavits, and that we could expect to be notified in six to eight weeks. Then there would be a few weeks in a camp in Munich, followed by a train ride to Bremen. From there, after another week or so in a camp, a train would take us to a U.S. Navy troop ship for the rest of the way.

"What's the matter," my mother asked me before she left. "You are making a face like *sieben Tage Regenwetter"* (seven days of rain).

"Yeah, I know. I'm sorry."

Journal entry, July 1946: What a visit! My head is still spinning. It all seems a bit too artificial, too contrived. But I did not want to spoil their "victory." Horst is so mixed up and torn as it is. There are so many things that can go wrong now. What if her father somehow finds them? What if the real sister suddenly turns up, after all? I wish I could do something to shorten the waiting period. Pippi's insistence is really beginning to bother me. I don't dare tell Horst about his Onkel Paul's offer to take us in. He could work with him and later take over his office. Horst as a public accountant! He would just die—both of them would. Of course Paul is looking for a replacement for his fallen son.

In the afternoon Misha returned from his trip. He appeared underslept, exhausted and grumpy. When he saw Brigitte, he cheered up.

"Better be nice to her," Anja warned him. "She is family now, you know. Go ahead and show him your new ID, Marlies."

"You do know what we do in Russia to welcome a new family member, don't you?" Misha asked.

There was no disagreement because there was no chance of getting this one wrong.

Besides, the vodka bottle was already on the table.

Life definitely had taken a turn for me. Trouble was, I couldn't determine if it was for the better or for the worse. There was food, at least for us in Munich; there was Brigitte; there was the certainty of America, but I felt like a car in neutral, just sitting there, idling time away. I dreaded leaving Brigitte behind, even for a short time. And how was life to work out for us in America? Here at least everyone was more or less in the same boat. Aside from the Jewish business, we were one handful of people among millions of other refugees. Over there, we would be just one lonely handful. Period! Now I wished that the Picasso had not turned sour on us.

Salvation, solace, stimulation—even optimism—reached me in the form of a letter. My mother certainly knew what she was doing when she forwarded that letter to me. It was exactly the right prescription and the correct dosage: two tightly filled pages from two cousins I had never met, but their mother was my mother's first cousin, a lawyer with a doctorate from the University of Berlin. Her husband was an MD. Between the two of them they must have had just the right amount of grey matter to figure out the proper timing for bailing out of Germany before the war. Now they were in Chicago, where their identical twin sons, Fred and Ernie, same age as I, went to school. Their letter to me was a German-English mix. Their handwriting, their grammatical errors, and their spelling mistakes were identical, as well as hilarious. But their message to me was exhilarating. They talked about school, sports I had barely heard of, like baseball, basketball, football, and badminton. During their three months of summer vacation—compared to our five or six weeks—they both worked at a resort in Colorado, making fantastic sums of money in tips. They expressed the hope that next summer I would be working with them. And in the fall, if I lived in the right place, I could make good money working in orchards. And in the winter there was always snow shoveling or, if I was good, I could get a great—everything was either "great" or "fantastic"—after-school job in one of those little restaurants they called "diners." As a matter of fact, over the last two years they had saved up so much money that now they both owned cars—"jalopies," as they called them. A car! Wow! Once more, America started to sound like a dream to me, and I remembered what had really enticed me some time ago, "America, the land of unlimited possibilities or opportunities." If sixteen-year-olds could buy cars just by working after school, it had to be true.

Speaking of unlimited possibilities—not exactly our situation here, for the moment. What were we supposed to do for the next eight weeks? Stay here? I thought I had noticed something in Misha's behavior which might qualify as a mild form of irritation. Perhaps Brigitte would be acceptable by herself. But both of us? Not for eight weeks. Obergünzburg was out of the question.

"What about Kempten?" Brigitte inquired. "Antek's house is big enough and out of the way. I'd bet he would love to help us."

I had to agree. Antek was the most obvious and rational solution. But it would be very difficult and embarrassing to explain Brigitte's name change to other people. Well, how about Planegg? They already knew, anyway. But in Kempten Brigitte would have a chance to see her mother. And mine, I was sure, would be happy to have me around to help her get ready for the big journey. Besides, there were a few good friends I wanted to bid farewell to.

Antek didn't just say okay, he was overjoyed and immediately set out to furnish the upstairs apartment in his house.

"Listen," he said, "I am so glad this is happening. Now I have a reason to call that interior decorator again. Such wonderful taste! Of course, I may have to fly to Spain or Norway, but so what? Then you can have the whole house to yourselves. Oh, great idea! Perhaps I can take that decorator along, so we can pick things out together."

"That decorator—sounds like he is a good friend. Someone we know from the old days?"

"No, no." Antek chuckled and cleared his throat a few times.

"It's a lady—Marianna. Well, you just have to meet her. Does some designing for me, too. Very talented. I have been invited to display at that huge winter fair in Paris. That's first. After that—who knows?"

Clearly, Antek was no longer the old Antek on the motorcycle, the cool coal robber, MP impersonator, and dairy thief.

"So," Antek addressed us, "when you come and I am not in, the key is under the flower box, food is in the refrigerator. Got to run! Negotiating to buy a factory."

Like snakes slithering through lush vegetation, disturbing thoughts and doubts tunneled their way into my mind. Why make it difficult for myself, if here I could work with Antek, become his right hand, have a villa with a garden, a yacht in San Tropez, and a ski chalet in the Alps? Dream on! In the newspaper there were reports of pro-Nazi student demonstrations, and on the way to the Bahnhof we encountered anti-Semitic slogans on walls and billboards.

"Your mother is right," Brigitte said. "America is the only safe place where Jews can hope to live without constant fear. So cheer up! Together we'll make it."

"Yeah. You are right. You and my mother. And think of all those places from my cousins' pictures. Colorado must be just like the Alps, and then those shots of Maine? The crashing surf on the coast, the fall colors in the mountains? And lobsters—all you can eat for practically nothing."

We were stacking up the merits of one country against those of the other. I don't remember which one won, but that didn't really matter because safety was the one factor which outweighed all others.

We had hoped that Antek would be there to pick us up at the station, but when we emerged from the building and looked around, no little Ford Eifel was in sight. Not that we would be unable to make it by foot, but we were carrying quite a load of groceries, and perhaps we had become a little spoiled.

Across the street a big American car was parked, a 1941 DeSoto, if I was not mistaken. Learning to identify American cars by make and year had become a major pastime for us boys. These monstrous machines, much too large for narrow German city streets, were beginning to inundate the landscape. GIs were having their cars from home shipped over—free of charge.

A well-dressed man climbed out of the car and, waving his arms, headed in our direction. Only when he flashed his thumbs at us did I realize that this was the outwardly transformed Antek. Inwardly he seemed undamaged by his sudden success.

"I am sorry," he greeted us. "I have to do so much traveling now, often with others, that I just had to have a bigger car. And often I carry some of my products to potential customers. But it is a lot of fun. Especially when you are successful. It makes a great impression when they see me coming in one of these. Well, let's get going. Your mothers are already going crazy."

Brigitte and I exchanged alarmed looks. Mothers? As in plural? Was that prudent?

"Oh my God," Brigitte groaned. "What am I going to say to her? Worse, what is she going to say to me?"

"Just tell her the truth," I advised. "There just was no other way of escaping your father. But make sure she understands that it's only temporary. And don't get angry."

I had always thought that Frau Hilgendorf was an unemotional, rational woman. I couldn't have been more mistaken. The way she cried and hugged her daughter—it was the most piteous scene I had ever witnessed.

"Let's leave them alone for a while," my mother addressed Antek and me. "And let me make some coffee. The aroma! Know what I mean?"

She brewed a large pot and let the fragrance waft through the house before she took it with two cups, sugar and cream, into the living room, yes, including a few unearthly delicious *petit fours* we had brought from Munich, and withdrew. Soon thereafter the sobs and lamentations subsided. My mother nodded knowingly. "Works every time," she beamed.

But we waited a long time before we asked if it was all right to join them.

When we peeked into the room, they were sitting close together on the couch, holding hands, smiling at us. What a relief!

For a while we tiptoed around the subject. Finally, Frau Hilgendorf could not stand it any longer. "I know you are anxious to hear something about our private conference. Well, I feel so much better now that I understand everything and know what is going to happen. I had really thought I had lost her forever."

"Quickly Horst," my mother whispered, "pour her some more coffee!"

Then we showed her the letters and pictures we had received. "And what about your husband?" my mother inquired. "Is he getting the police involved in trying to find Brigitte?"

"I don't think so," she replied. "But I really don't know. We don't speak anymore. He has not said a word to me since the incident. Erhard has complained that he is being pressured to participate in some Nazi activities. That's all I know. Perhaps now he'll agree to a divorce. But tell me, how long do they think it will take until Brigitte is granted her immigration permit, and after that, until she is actually on a ship?"

"Misha said it will take eight to ten weeks. There is an organization that helps the victims of Nazi atrocities. They are taking care of everything," I explained.

The next day a fairly content Frau Hilgendorf took the train back to Günzach. My mother stayed in Kempten, partly because of us and partly because she was now working for Antek. Proudly she showed us some of the pieces she had designed: brooches, cups, mugs, plates, and small decorative figurines.

XXVI

How we celebrated what my mother called "Horst's last hurrah," and how Antek's neighbor was cured of his belief in fences

LATER THAT DAY I approached Antek with a request. "Antek, would it be okay if I invited some of my best friends for a party here? And, with your permission, I would like to treat them to a real all-you-can eat dinner."

"Only if I can come too," he answered.

"And, for that occasion," he continued, "might there possibly be something you would like me to get? Meat, for example?"

"Yeah, right. I don't know if you have any connections, but what I am hoping for is a big piece of beef—or a couple of smaller ones. Like the ones that went into making that horseradish dinner. Remember?"

"Sure do. Still get tears in my eyes when I think of it. Is that what you are planning?"

"No. It's something I haven't made or eaten in a long time. Sauerbraten with dumplings and red cabbage."

"Sauerbraten? I have not had that since my mother made it at home. Meat? No problem, and if I have to run down a cow with the jeep—and I know where to get cabbage, too. The rest should be easy. So how many pounds of beef are we talking here? Ten pounds about? And how many days does it have to marinate? Four to five days? Better get some large pots and a roasting pan, too, right? What about spices, or do you use ginger snaps in the gravy? No? Just the spices? So that would be cloves, cinnamon, and ginger, right?"

I had not seen Antek that happy and excited since the day of the big train robbery.

There is something very satisfying and exhilarating about preparing food for a group of friends. I had always felt that way, in Switzerland too, but there it had been more like a job, an obligation. This here was altogether different—a feast for my friends, heaps of deliciously prepared meat at a time when ration cards allowed for 100 grams of meat per week per person. And for dessert? Why not Streuselkuchen? Might as well go all out. Give them something they would tell their friends and parents about. Streuselkuchen? I had not mentioned butter to Antek. How much? About two pounds.

The next two days Brigitte and I were busy with preparations. We got our bikes out and made the rounds. Summer vacation had just begun, but vacation trips did not exist in those days.

My friends had wondered about my premature disappearance from school. Someone had even started the rumor that I had already gone to America. "I knew it couldn't be true," so some comments went. "You wouldn't have left without saying goodbye. But now it's really getting serious? God, how I envy you! A big feast next Saturday? Sure. Haven't had a full stomach in a long time. What's that address again? Lessingstrasse 24? Isn't that out there where all the fancy villas are? A friend of yours? Sure! Three o'clock."

With some alarm I noticed that Brigitte was not her usual enthusiastic self. From time to time I noticed an ever-so-slight narrowing of her eyes. "How many of your friends are you inviting?" she inquired.

"Six, if they all show up."

"And you and Antek?"

"Sure. You too, of course."

"I? Don't you think it would be a bit awkward for me? The only girl with eight guys? You know—," and her voice was quivering, "you might have considered the possibility that I have friends too, whom I would like to invite and say goodbye to."

Aha! That's what was bothering her! No wonder she was a bit miffed. The klutz of the month award was mine, for sure. When would I ever learn?

The young ladies were delighted to receive our invitation and promised not to disappoint us.

"Oh! Boys from your school are also invited, Horst?" they giggled. "Oh!"

Later, when I informed my friends of the increased numbers, they addressed Brigitte with identical sentiments. "Oh! Girls from your school are also invited, Brigitte? Oh!"

Antek, on the other hand, scratched behind his right ear. "So there are going to be fourteen of us now? Well, I guess I needed more chairs, plates, glasses, and silverware, anyway. Speaking of glasses, what do you think we should drink? Wine, I think, might be too strong, but beer sounds great with Sauerbraten."

"Sure," I said. "Fine with me. Okay with you, Brigitte?"

So everything was set and agreed upon; work was about to commence.

Punctually five days before the target date, Antek delivered two lovely pieces of beef, top or bottom round, each one weighing five to six pounds. A large porcelain washbowl from some hotel, elegantly decorated with flowery designs, appeared to be just the right size for accommodating meat and marinade.

I had never made sauerbraten by myself before, but I remembered Emma's advice: "Don't go crazy trying to find a good recipe, because there are as many different ways as there are regions, if not families within Germany. So, keep it simple. First, make the marinade. Use enough water to just cover the meat; then add a good shot of red wine, a few slices of onion and a few bay leaves and enough sugar and vinegar to make it good and sour and good and sweet."

This I did, dissolving the sugar with my fingers the way I had dissolved clots in that bucket of pig's blood. Licking liquid off my hand, I found it necessary to add more vinegar and sugar. Then it all went into the cool basement.

Nothing I had ever read said that Streuselkuchen is best when eaten fresh. In fact, my experience was that after a few days the buttery sweetness of the streusel on top seeps into the yeast foundation, thereby creating a most fortunate union.

So, after we had come into possession of butter, Brigitte and I tripled my grandmother's incomplete recipe. This was not an easy task, because, after all, what do you get when you multiply uncertainty by three? But, as in Zürich, we were successful, as a strip cut off the finished product told us.

When the red cabbage and some apples arrived, we immediately set out to convert it all into the moist, purple, sweet-sour mélange that had delighted diners at the goose dinner two Christmases ago. And red cabbage, as any connoisseur would swear to on a Bible, does improve with each reheating.

I had no idea, nor was I curious, how Antek had tracked down and secured everything we needed. Bread, eggs, milk, parsley, onion, and butter—all the components for the dumplings—suddenly appeared. At the end, there was only one thing still missing: the beer. My mother tried her best to steer us in the direction of lemonade; this, however, met with stiff opposition.

"Mama! Lemonade? Are you crazy? Do you think I want to be remembered as the one who served lemonade with Sauerbraten? Beer is good for you! It's actually more like food. Remember Lindhilda Moosbacher? That's what she said: like food."

"Yes, sir!" Antek agreed. "Like food—good food. Some doctors even prescribe it for certain illnesses."

"Yeah," my mother mumbled, "alcoholism."

So, outvoted, outnumbered, outmaneuvered, she withdrew to her room and announced that she was washing her hands of the whole affair. "And I am not cleaning up any vomit!" were her final words that evening. After that, whenever she mentioned the impending feast, she referred to it as "Horst's last hurrah," not without a trace of loathing in her voice.

I actually liked the phrase. In the *hurrah* there was that element of something jubilant, celebratory. You shout or think it when you have succeeded at something. *Last* implies that this is not an isolated occasion. Others must have preceded it. Therefore, it was one of several. Thinking back, I was able to come up with quite a few hurrah-worthy situations here in the Allgäu. They sort of accented my time here: the jitterbug contest, the deer, the dairy truck, the Zorn episode, the Swiss adventure, the sting operation, and the *last* one, coming right up. Looking at it from this perspective, the phrase suddenly had acquired a sad note. If this was the last one, what then about the future?

Judging by the amount of beer Antek had delivered, this feast was bound to earn major hurrahs from all the guests.

On Friday we shifted into high gear. I wanted everything as ready as possible. Early in the afternoon I browned the meat on all sides on top of the stove. Then I transferred it into a huge roasting pan and added enough of the marinade to half cover it. I selected a slow roasting temperature and pushed the whole thing into the oven. As the liquid began to boil down, the meat turned a beautiful shade of brown. After about an hour I turned the meat over. One more hour and the liquid had turned into a dark brown substance at the bottom of the pan. That's what I had been waiting for: a concentration of roasting flavors, which would give the gravy its wonderful taste. It was one of the tricks I had learned from Emma, who had inherited it from her ancestors.

With the roasting pan on one of the stovetop burners now, I transferred the meat onto a platter and poured some of the leftover marinade into the roasting pan to loosen and dissolve any crusty layers on the bottom and the sides. Next I stirred about one cup of flour into a quart of the cold marinade, added some salt, and a good pinch each of clove, cinnamon, and ginger. All this made up a smooth, thick liquid which I poured into the roasting pan. Constantly stirring, I waited until it had bubbled itself into a brown gravy, which I checked for sweetness, acidity and spices.

Now came the part which made our way so different from all the others I knew. I sliced the meat into thick, half-inch slices, which I layered into the gravy so that all of it was submerged. Lid in place, I shoved it back into the slow oven to simmer for another hour. Tomorrow I would repeat the simmering process, roasting it on "very slow" for another one to two hours until the gravy would be thick and of the darkest brown and the meat fork tender. So, except for the dumplings, everything was ready.

Some came by bike, some by foot. By 15:01 everyone invited had arrived. It was a warm, sunny day. On the lawn, tables and chairs were set up. In the shade of the old chestnut tree, several cases of beer were awaiting their predictable end. "No, this is necessary," Antek had once more overpowered my mother's objections. "These are shy, young ladies and gentlemen," he enlightened her. "They need to learn how to act in each other's presence. Beer will save them hours of awkward attempts at conversation."

Full glasses in one hand, the other dipping into huge bowls of unfamiliar but pleasingly crunchy-salty things, small groups of mixed-gender participants began to form. Shred by shred, boys and girls began to lose the armor that protected their fragile psyches. Masculine laughter and feminine giggles filled the air. Antek must have activated his GI supply lines for the contents of the bowls: potato chips and popcorn, hitherto unknown to German palates.

Panic seized me. If this kept going at the present pace, everyone would be full and/or drunk by dinnertime, and all that delicious food would go unnoticed.

"Okay," Antek agreed, "hadn't anticipated this. Let's save the beer for dinner and get rid of the snacks for now. We'll wait a bit, and then we'll eat. Afterwards—who knows? I might bring the record player out. Got some incredible new records. Glenn Miller, Tommy Dorsey, Benny Goodman, Bing Crosby—well, you'll see."

A huge platter of dumplings, stacked like cannonballs, disappeared at a staggering pace. Was that a dumpling contest going on over there between two of my friends? Was it possible to down a dumpling without chewing?

"Well, if you have enough gravy in your mouth, they slide right down real smooth."

Similar feats were performed at every table. Even some of the ladies accomplished astonishing things. My mother watched with renewed anguish as empty beer bottles began to outnumber the full ones. "Don't serve the Streuselkuchen for a while," she implored me. "You know what they say, don't you? 'Streuselkuchen on beer makes the stomach act queer'."

"You just made that up, didn't you?" I asked with admiration. There were still sides to my mother that had eluded me for sixteen years. She just smiled.

It was getting dark; evening breezes carried cool air from the not-too-distant mountains. Some of the girls in sleeveless summer dresses sought the warmth of nearby manly bodies. Suddenly, as though planted into our brains by alien forces, the word "campfire" slipped into the conversation. It was the perfect setting for it. As cave dwellers thousands of years ago may have craved the warming glow of the divine gift to man, so my friends and I succumbed to this desire. It was a primeval force within us that drove us into the dark in search of firewood. For once Antek was at a loss. No wood anywhere. At that moment, some of my friends, grinning slyly, appeared with large sticks of—dry wood? It was milled wood, grey with age and ready to burst into flame on command.

"Careful with the nails," someone shouted.

More and more of my friends, all carrying armfuls of these sticks, emerged from the dark. Within minutes a respectable woodpile was rising on the lawn, and two boys were constructing an artistic structure resembling a funeral pyre.

Puzzled and alarmed Antek followed one of the gatherers into the darkness. He was visibly shaken when he returned. "Unbelievable," he groaned over and over.

"What is it, Antek? What's the matter? Anything wrong?" I asked.

Antek nodded gloomily, "I just can't comprehend it. The entire fence, my neighbor's fence, it's gone—no!" And he pointed in the direction of the woodpile. "Actually, it's here now. At least the wood is."

"Antek," I whispered, "hey, Antek! I think we have company."

A tall, thin male figure had emerged from the darkness and was heading toward us. Continuously shaking his head, the man stopped in front of Antek. He was quite old and at the moment seemingly incapable of speech. Several times he inhaled deeply, but no sound came out. That was Antek's chance.

"My dear Herr Richter! What a terrible mistake! Those boys! Give them a beer and there is no telling what they will do."

Now Herr Richter was ready to speak. "Well, this may be so, but I sure know what I will do: there are legal terms for incidents of this nature. You will hear from my lawyer, I can assure you."

"But my dear Herr Richter! We are good neighbors. No need to let this fence stand between us—in the legal sense, I mean. After all the things that went kaput in the last six years, isn't it refreshing: finally there is something that can rapidly and easily be replaced. No need to involve the authorities. I promise you, I'll hold these boys responsible for having a replacement fence put up for you by Monday evening. Just like the old one, only newer."

Once more the old gentleman shook his head. "But it is so outrageous! I feel so violated!"

"My dear Herr Richter," Antek said with his sweetest, warmest smile, "I am so terribly sorry. How can I make it up to you? I don't know—this sounds so crude. Please don't be offended, but—as a token of my deep regret over this—may I drop off a ham at your door? Perhaps some butter and some coffee?"

Herrn Richter's head went from shake into neutral; then he shifted into nod. He appeared a little embarrassed but quickly recovered from this decadent notion. "And some cigarettes, too, please? Chesterfield, if possible?"

"Of course, my dear Herr Richter. It's the least I can do. And now, how about a beer and some Streuselkuchen?"

"Beer with Streuselkuchen? Oh, what the heck."

The party went on quite a bit longer after this. There was more drinking and eating, even some singing and dancing, until the last stick of Herrn Richter's fence was gone—and no one got sick.

A chilly wind was rustling through the chestnut trees, countless stars were above us in a cloudless sky. In little groups and arm in arm our guests left.

"Better pour some water on what's left of the fire," Antek said.

Thus ended the feast my mother had named, "Horst's last hurrah."

As it turned out, Herr Richter was a long-retired teacher of Latin and Greek. He took it upon himself to supervise the resurrection of his fence. Joyously he shouted directions in classical languages at us, lecturing us on what differentiated Roman from Greek architecture, and finally treating us to the story of the legendary Egyptian bird, the Phoenix, rising rejuvenated from its own ashes. He was a fine old gentleman.

"If you ever again need wood for a fire," he said, "help yourself. Who needs fences anyway? Remember the *Limes Britannicus,* kids? Didn't do the Romans one bit of good."

Limes? Ah yes! That fortified wall the Romans had constructed through parts of England and Germany!

XXVII

How Antek replaced our "ticket to America," and how Brigitte became Anja's sister

ALL DAY, IN FACT all weekend, something had been festering in Antek. A few times I thought he was about to speak up, but then he'd shut his mouth, shake his head, and walk away with an unhappy expression on his face.

This time he is going to say something, I thought—but no! Once more he walked away. My mother, too, had caught on to his strange behavior and was shooting question mark faces in my direction.

I answered by gesturing, "So what do you want me to do about this?"

She gestured back, tapping her forehead repeatedly with her index finger, sign language for, "Talk to him, dummy, say something!"

In the kitchen I caught up with him. I didn't really confront him; I rather nudged him gently. "Antek, something is troubling you, isn't it? You know, you can tell us. If not us, whom can you?—"

He sounded relieved. "You are right. It's been going around in my head for some time now. I guess I have to talk to you and to your mother. It's sort of on my conscience.

"You know," he began after my mother had joined us, "ever since the fake Picasso incident, I have felt that I cheated you. No, no! Please, let me continue. We shook on it back then in Breslau. I am sure you'll remember: the pearls for the Picasso. Both of us thought we had pulled off a great deal. For you it was your ticket to America; for me—I guess I had no definite plans, but it sure helped me in getting a good start here. Now it looks as if you are making it to America even without the Picasso, and that is wonderful. But the fact remains that you were cheated. I got what I wanted, but you got nothing. So my conscience tells me you should be compensated. It's not a matter of a certain amount of money, but a matter of giving back to you what you had when you thought you owned a genuine Picasso: a feeling of security and something to help you on the other side. It won't be easy, no matter what, so take all the help you can get. Business is going well and better every day, so why shouldn't I help the dearest friends I have? We have shared so many things in the past months. Now I am asking you to share one more with me: my good fortune."

My mother was visibly touched, if not shaken.

"Ach, Antek, Antek! What a human being and friend you are! People like you make me want to stay here. I don't know what so say. I certainly don't feel cheated. It is a most generous offer, and true, I have been worried about starting from scratch over there with nothing. So—yes, but whatever you give us, please consider it a loan. You have done so much for us already! And now this. Thank you!"

It was a very emotional scene. Antek looked relieved and mumbled, "Good!" Then everyone tiptoed out of the room.

Journal entry, August 1946: What a weight off my chest! The biggest surprise of my life! Antek is giving us $5,000 as compensation for the loss of the Picasso. This is the most overwhelming example of friendship I've ever heard of. I certainly did not feel cheated in any way. But now I am so relieved that we won't be arriving like paupers. I'll still take that job, but now I won't have to panic every time we have an unexpected expense, and perhaps I can save something to help Horst with his education.

Brigitte and I could have stayed with Antek a while longer, but we felt that this might be too risky. How easily Herr Hilgendorf could pick up our tracks here! Time was rushing on, and we began to feel excitement mounting in us. What an enormous undertaking: Wasn't starting a new life like being reborn, reborn like a phoenix, out of what the Nazis and their war had reduced to ashes? Which of my belongings should I take? What made sense, what not? Skis, skins, bike, fishing gear?

"Don't be silly," my mother said. "How would you transport all that, and how would it look? There come the poor refugees—skis, bike, and fishing pole! This is not like going on vacation, you know."

True enough! It was the first time Erhard was not entirely unhappy with our decision to go to America. "All this for me?" he asked. "Will you teach me fly-fishing before you leave?"

"The only item I am concerned about is the cello," Brigitte said. "Do you think they will allow me to take it? How much luggage can we take, anyway?"

None of us knew, but it said somewhere that we would receive detailed instructions.

Back to Munich we went. The little tower room apartment in Planegg was vacant, so sure, why not live up there?

"What?" Tante Angelina was horrified. "Brigitte living with you up there? Your mother would never forgive me. In our family there never was—"

"But we go camping together—one tent, you know? What would be the difference here?"

"Camping, that's a different story. Out in nature and all that. But here? Under my roof?"

She seemed to weaken. Trying to figure out what the moral differences were between sleeping in a tent and sleeping in a room left her speechless for a few minutes. Her sighs betrayed her torment.

"Well, I guess, occasionally I'll allow it. But don't tell your mother."

Brigitte and I thought it would be best if she stayed with Anja most of the time. After all, she was her sister. In order not to stress Misha's hospitality, I would stay there only occasionally. But somehow I still felt that he owed me; if it had not been for me, he might not be here at all, and certainly not surrounded by such affluence.

When we checked in at the Luisenstrasse apartment a few days later, an excitingly scary letter was awaiting us. It was addressed to Marlies von Woltershaag and requested that she appear at the U.S. Consulate for an interview—on Wednesday. This was Monday.

"Wonder what they want?" I asked.

Misha knew. "That's standard procedure for applicants in this category, but one never knows. So you'd better be prepared. There are so many imposters. In this great upheaval it's so easy to disappear and then surface again as someone else. At least we have one irrefutable player—Anja. And then there is the birth certificate for her sister. Their father's participation in the July 20 event is well documented, as well as his subsequent execution. It all seems very legitimate, except for that one factor: why did it take such a long time for her to show up?"

The way in which Misha spoke made it clear that he was a skilled interrogator. I surely would not have wanted to face him if I had something to hide.

"I have an idea," Misha continued. "Why don't you work out every angle in your disappearing and reappearing act, and tomorrow we'll have a dress rehearsal. You know what part I'll be playing. By the way, what did you tell the German authorities when you went to get your new German ID? No questions? No arguments? No skepticism?

"Well, that confirms my old suspicion: when there is a 'von' in front of your name, they still bow down and lick your boots." He laughed contemptuously. "Don't count on that kind of treatment from me—not from the Americans, either, because they generally don't even know what it implies. Seriously though—don't take this appointment lightly. They are really strict about whom they admit."

He cleared his throat suggestively, and his eyes wandered between Anja and Marlies. "So you'd better do some serious rehearsing between now and then, and you, Anja, better go in together with Brigitte—or whoever she is—because now you are actually the legal guardian of a legal minor." He cleared his throat once more and left the room.

"Yeah," I said when the three of us were alone. "Yeah, so tell us, where the hell were you for a year and a half when everyone was going crazy looking for you? What would you have said if the Germans had asked you that question? How are you going to answer when Misha asks you a whole bunch of questions tomorrow? He is right, you know. For example, how come you didn't turn up until now? Where were you? What were you doing? How come no one could find you? How come you disappeared in Dresden without a trace, and how come you turned up but your mother did not?"

Brigitte put on a confused, innocent little girl's look and spoke haltingly in an infantile whisper. "I am sorry. I wish I could answer all your questions. My mother and I had come from Breslau, you know. There were thousands of refugees around us when they sounded the air raid alarm. We tried to run to a shelter, but it was overcrowded already. When the bombs came, we were swept along by a stream of screaming people. Didn't know where we were and where we were running. More people were fleeing out of burning houses. It became unbearably hot. You could not touch the pavement anymore. I saw people burning like torches. Mother could not keep up anymore and collapsed in front of a burning house. She yelled I should keep running toward the park. That's the last thing I remember."

We were not prepared for that kind of realism. Anja looked as if she had just witnessed her mother's and her sister's death. She was trembling; there were tears.

"And when and where did you get your memory back?" I asked gently. I was completely caught up in her story; she had cast a spell on me.

"Oh," she replied as though in a trance, "the only thing I remember now was hearing a cello. Mozart. A piece I knew. I wanted to hear more and the nurses, nuns, must have noticed that I was responding to music. So every day one of them, and she was very good, played for me, and every day some more of my past came back. That nun, Sister Anna, asked me if I wanted to play. 'Play? Play? Play?' she kept repeating, and when I finally did, it was as if I had never stopped playing. I remembered all the pieces I had studied at home. Now I played every day. I grew stronger, I spoke again, and I asked what had happened. But it was a very slow, step-by-step recovery. It took more than a year before I remembered my name."

"And what is your name?" I asked.

"Marlies von Woltershaag," she replied with such conviction in her voice that I felt ashamed for having asked.

"And then, what happened then? How did you finally find me?" Anja asked.

"Well, they found my name on the missing persons list, notified you, and the Red Cross arranged for my trip to Munich. And here I am." She went over and hugged Anja.

"I am sorry, but I have one more question," I interrupted. "Where is that nunnery or cloister where you were?"

"Oh, the Sankt Katharinen Kloster? Well, you know how the Russians are with Christianity. The nuns had to leave, and the buildings were turned into army barracks. I think they burned all the records. It was near Dresden, I believe.

"How did I do?" Brigitte inquired after a brief pause. She was wearing her sweetest smile now and spoke in a tone of voice that reminded me of how she sounded when she informed Mo, "We are going to win that contest."

"Marlies," I said, and I could not have called her anything else after this performance, "I don't think you have anything to worry about. Where and how did you get all that?"

"Aren't there stories like this going around all over the place?" she asked. "And doesn't everyone know exactly how it was in Dresden? Anja and I have talked about this a lot. It's so vivid in my mind that it felt as if I were retelling what actually happened to me. Of course," and she put on a guilty smile, "I may have been overacting a bit."

The next day, Misha, looking very stern and official, closed the door behind himself and Brigitte as he proceeded to conduct his interrogation. After ten minutes he came out again, appearing shocked. "I had no idea about all those horrible things that happened to her," he said very softly.

We explained.

"You mean she was acting in there? I could hear the bombs whistling, I could feel the heat, I could hear people screaming. If she repeats this performance at the consulate, they might fly her over. They are very sensitive and accommodating when Dresden gets into the act."

I was not present during the consulate interview, but Anja indicated that it was an overpowering performance.

"We were in there for over an hour," Anja continued her account, "but all that interviewer wanted to talk about was Marlies's cello and the healing power of music. He hopes that he will be able to arrange some kind of audition for her. His wife is a professor of music at some famous university in New York. Can't remember the name. What was it, Marlies? You knew about it. Juilliard? And there are many stipend opportunities for gifted musicians in the States, he told us."

Brigitte was excited that she would be playing for someone—playing for her future, as it were. She immediately got out some music and started to practice.

I, on the other hand, grew impatient. Waiting had never been my thing. We should have heard something definite by now, I felt. People we knew were already in the last stage camp in Bremen, awaiting transport to their ship. Almost daily I was in telephone contact with my mother. She begged me to come and help her get ready. So I spent a couple of days in Kempten.

Journal entry, August 1946: One question keeps me awake at night—is it fair or prudent to separate Horst and Brigitte? They seem so made for each other. But at that young age—can one really evaluate a relationship? Perhaps this separation is a good test of the depth and maturity of their relationship. I guess they are like husband and wife now. Never did have that "talk" with him or her. Just hope they are careful.

XXVIII

How my mother packed up her past

WHEN I ARRIVED IN Kempten, mother was preparing to pack up a large crate with everything she thought we could not live without, things we had hand carried from burning house to burning house in Breslau, all the way to Obergünzburg: my down comforter, linen towels and sheets, still from her mother's household, all the old family photos, my father's Iron Cross from the First World War, a couple of her favorite books, even some pots and kitchen utensils. It was like entering a museum commemorating our existence. I realized that many of the items were there, not because they would be useful in the new world, but because they represented part of our heritage.

"These things are like old friends," my mother mused. "They have often comforted me, and I know I'll need them in the future." She had, consciously or subconsciously, arranged all these items around her now, as though to shield herself from any new and alien environment.

How will she ever be able to feel at home in America? I wondered. "We don't have to go, you know," I said.

Sadly she shook her head. "I am afraid we do. I have made the wrong decision once, and it nearly killed us. In America we can live without fear. That's the primary consideration here."

"You mean, once we are there I can tell people I am part Jewish?"

I knew that remark would snap her out of the spell she was under.

"Don't you dare!" she scolded. "We are branded, even in America! Don't ever forget that—or Reynard the Fox."

But she was not ready yet to return to a world of practical considerations. She handed me a postcard-size charcoal drawing. It showed one of our family houses. "My brother drew this, age fifteen, shortly before he died.

"And here, your first stuffed animal. Remember Pümmi the monkey? You wouldn't go to sleep without it. Oh, and here! Oma's favorite paring knife."

I didn't know if it was coincidence or intentionally placed there to underscore the absurdity of it all, but next to my father's Iron Cross there was a little box with that hated yellow star in it. Pinned to it was Oma's pride and joy—her little medallion inscribed with GOLD GAB ICH FÜR EISEN (Gold I gave for iron), from the German emperor, Wilhelm II.

My mother noticed my look. "Yes," she said, "that, in a nutshell, is why we have to leave Germany. Both medals are symbols of sacrifice and love of country, but," and she pointed at the star, "they are rendered meaningless by this. For a long time I wondered if I should take it. Now I think this trio is a significant capsule of our past, a reminder of why we are leaving Germany behind. Well, enough of this. Let's clear off the bed, so I can get some sleep."

When our notification came, we were not ready. I mean, we were all packed, had said our goodbyes and had our transportation all arranged, but why did it have to be such beautiful, late-summer weather? Why couldn't it be chilly and rainy? Brigitte and I had planned a short trip to Salzburg, and now this? Can we still make it to Salzburg? How many days until we have to report to that place—what's the name of it? Funk Kaserne?

Predictably, Mama was horrified. "To Salzburg? Hiking in the mountains? What if you break something?"

But we went. Took our tent, climbed mountains and felt closer than ever before. We speculated endlessly how long it might be until we would be together again and listed all the things we would do and see together. Did we have any doubts? I don't think so, but all the way back to Munich we were very silent, just sitting very close together, holding hands.

Originally we had planned that I would go back to Planegg, while Brigitte would stay with Anja and Misha. Brigitte would not hear of it. "I have to come to Planegg with you," she said. "I don't think I could bear being alone tonight."

Next morning I took the train to Kempten to help my mother with last-minute tasks. Antek had insisted on driving us to our Munich destination. Even though it was out of the way, we stopped briefly in Obergünzburg for the final farewell. Onkel Pippi was very solemn. He and I had become very good friends, and he seemed to be very fond of my mother. It was hard for him to see us go. Soon his youngest son, Werner and wife, Gaby, would be following us. He stood there in the middle of the road, a white-haired figure, bent forward slightly and waving sadly with his right hand.

The Funk Kaserne, former German army barracks, was a depressing looking cluster of grey buildings. A high brick wall surrounded the entire area. At the gate, a sentry of unidentifiable nationality checked our papers. And then we saw them: the tired, the poor, the huddled masses yearning to breathe free. I believe every possible European language was represented. Russian, Polish, Czech, Italian, and French I managed to identify. That's as far as my linguistic experiences had taken me. Using a little bit of English and German for questioning, I became acquainted with Rumanian, Greek, Hungarian, Lithuanian, Estonian, Finnish, Turkish, and Albanian. From wherever these humans had been swept in the wake of invading armies, Funk Kaserne was the point where they surfaced again—if they had been lucky.

"My brother drew this, age fifteen . . ."

Viewed in this light, the message of the lady at the entrance to New York Harbor became a significant and comforting promise to me—as if it had been tailor made for the inmates of the Funk Kaserne.

Thus, a feeling of compassionate camaraderie with these survivors sprouted within me, and when I read on the camp bulletin board that there was a demand for English teachers, I volunteered. Not that I considered myself an authority on this subject, but my contact with Mo and a few other GIs, plus schoolwork, had combined to turn me into a fairly competent speaker of that language. My strong point, so I had been told, was pronunciation. Mo had seen to that. He spent many a frustrating hour with me. Nothing but perfection would do for him.

"But Mo," I would groan, "that was exactly the way you said it."

"That's a *th* here," he would say. "The tip of your tongue has to be touching your upper front teeth. But very lightly. The way you do it, it sounds like a lisp."

So we went over it again and again—fast, slow, loud, low: "There are the thousand thorny thistles, a thorough thrashing, through thick and thin." For a German, plain *th* is difficult enough. When followed by an *r*, it may lead to serious psychological damage—for the teacher as well as for the student.

My class was composed of children between the ages of five and twelve. I didn't know about my pupils, but I sure had a lot of fun there. We sang many of my old cowboy songs, and it did not take them long until they could rattle off the woodchuck jingle. If they knew that, I figured they would be off to a good start in the States.

Four weeks we spent in that place. We shared one room with ten other humans of assorted ages and genders, as well as with innumerable bedbugs which came out of the woodwork at night, crawled up the walls and bombarded us like kamikaze planes from the ceiling.

Food was provided in ample portions, making up in quantity what it lacked in quality. Even the neediest among us soon realized that it was not worth the effort to fight for a front place in the chow line. Everything served consisted of dehydrated or canned leftover U.S. Army supplies: powdered eggs, powdered milk, instant mashed potatoes, canned beef, beans, corn, and peas. To be a cook here, all you had to be able to do was to follow the instructions for adding water and know how to operate a can opener. Surely, it was a reasonable endeavor for the army to try to reduce their war surplus; our question however, was, which war are we talking about here? There were some historians among us who treated us to ever new food accounts of certain campaigns in wars dating back all the way to the American Revolutionary War, in which, as these comedians claimed they could prove, the egg powder for today's breakfast had been used. I learned a lot of history this way.

Monday mornings were always stressful. That's when the list of names for the next transport to Bremen went up on a bulletin board. Our hearts always picked up a few beats per minute as our eyes wandered down the columns. For me, failure to find our names resulted in a mixture of disappointment and relief. Their appearance would signal the termination of our Munich-Germany-European days and the approach of the time for my date with the formidable lady with the torch. I was afraid of what I would feel at the sight of our names, but when they finally did show up, I pleasantly surprised myself: no despair, no panic, no fear, no regrets, no rage against my mother. What was about to happen, I realized, was merely a calm, rational, logical affirmation of our fate, the fulfillment of a long-harbored dream. Perhaps it was happening about ten years too late; nevertheless, here it was, and by God I was going to make the most of it. I felt energized and focused, the way I always felt when there was a definite objective coming within reach, be it goose, fish, coal, cheese, or honey. But all of these had been just little warm-up exercises compared to what I imagined lay ahead.

As I climbed the stairs to Misha's apartment I prayed for the power to instill the same positive attitude in Brigitte. Half way up I could hear her practicing a complicated passage over and over. Hoping she would be receptive to my mood if I presented myself as the harbinger of joyous news, I beamed at her, hugged her, and was about to open my big mouth when she looked up at me, uttering just one word: "When?"

Didn't she always know everything before anybody had said anything? So instead of infecting her with my idiotic enthusiasm, I just held her, stroking her back and head, trying to steady her shaking shoulders. Gradually she calmed down.

Perhaps now I could venture to say a few things. Still holding her, I tried to sound as soothing as possible. "Just think of all the places we talked about. The oceans and the mountains and that famous music school you'll be attending? And I'll be nearby so we can see each other all the time. You know what they say, and I believe it! In America, if you work and try hard enough, you can achieve anything."

As I said all this, as I talked on and on, one of Mo's favorite words seeped into my brain: bullshit! What a bunch of bullshit I was telling her—no, not telling—"telling" wasn't the word Mo used—"feeding," yes, *feeding* was the word Mo would have used to describe what I was doing here. "Stop feeding her all that bullshit," he would have said. So I stopped.

"And when do you have to leave?" she asked once more after she had blown her nose and, "How many days do we have left?"

Where and when had I endured that question before? Ah yes! Brigitte's father. As it had turned out, he had been the catalyst which had set our wheels in motion. Shouldn't we be grateful to him for providing the decisive impetus?

I quickly realized that once more I was getting bogged down in the realm of bullshit, while Brigitte was looking at me, expecting my answer.

"Three days," I said, "but don't make it sound as if this is going to end our lives. Well, our lives in Germany, yes, but soon they will continue on the other side of the Atlantic."

And then—even while the words were still in my mouth, I regretted using them, but too late—I said, "It will be like a rebirth—another Phoenix."

One look at the expression on her face said it all: still on the bullshit track.

Hundreds of times we had gone over it. We had discussed it calmly, rationally, and optimistically. It would be a separation of one to two months. I tried to remind her of these talks: summer jobs, trips, that famous music school. But strange. Now, in the face of reality, all this suddenly had lost its adventurous appeal. What remained was fear. Fear of the unknown, fear of something going wrong, fear of situations which would be too overwhelming to handle for one without the support of the other. Now it was I who needed to be comforted.

"No," she said, "don't do this; one of us falling apart is enough."

I could hear it in her voice that with every word her courage was returning.

"Remember when both of us were discouraged?" she asked. "We were surrounded by all those Amis in Garmisch and couldn't understand a word they were saying? And I said to you, 'Don't worry, together we'll make it. I know we can handle a short separation'."

I nodded and took a deep breath. It came out like a sigh from a bottomless well.

"Good!" she continued. Apparently my anxiety had relieved hers. "Now I'll tell you my success story. I had my audition yesterday, remember? That music professor from Juilliard was wonderful. Frau Doktor Bromberger. Yes, of course a Jewish lady. Went over before the war. What a musician! First she had me play what I had prepared; then I had to accompany her. She played the piano, then the violin. I had to improvise. No problem there, as you know."

The more Brigitte spoke, the stronger and more excited her voice grew. "The last part was talking about music, musicians and music theory—family stuff, too. I think she really liked me. She practically guaranteed me a full scholarship. Here," Brigitte pointed at a folder, "she gave me the application forms right then and there. Anja, as my legal guardian, will have to fill out parts of it."

"So, with all this great news—what were you so upset about?"

"Well, I think you know how it works," she answered haltingly. "You wait for it, you expect it, you know it will happen, but when it finally does—and you know it's going to be the end of everything you have ever done and known—yeah, I agree. One will still be the same—more or less. But I think you know what I mean."

I did. And by the looks of it, all her problems would be over as soon as she set foot on American soil. Even sounded a little worrisome to me. Would I be able to fit into this picture? But I kept my mouth shut, for once. At least for now, she was optimistic about the future, and that's what counted.

Journal entry, September 1946: This is turning out to be more difficult than I had thought—emotionally, that is. The German-European roots run deep—many questions deep—no matter what. I only hope that Horst is still young enough to set roots in the new soil. I keep telling myself that I am doing this for him. I hope it's the right choice. And I can't help worrying about Brigitte—about Horst, for that matter. Are they mature enough to endure a separation? This will be the test.

It would be pointless trying to recall those last three days. Getting our stuff together took about one hour. Then there were some official tasks we had to endure, endlessly waiting in lines, pushed around by Ukrainian guards. The rest of the time it was like waiting for time to pass while continually staring at a clock. These guards had turned our stay into more of a concentration camp scenario than an introduction to the Land of the Free. One old Jewish couple had scornfully gathered up their belongings and left the camp in protest.

My mother tried to rationalize, "Think how difficult it must be to keep order among all these nationalities, most of whom can't understand what they are being told. And I'll guarantee it—once we are with our relatives, you'll be glad we came."

But I could read in her eyes that she had her doubts. "Still time to go back home," I said in a half-teasing way. It shocked me when she just turned her back without answering.

Buses came and took us to the Bahnhof. Once more, endless waits until our names were called. They had shipped the crate ahead of us, so we carried just two pieces of luggage each, pieces that had been with us since Breslau. One of mine was an ancient contraption, the kind one sometimes finds in antique stores. Made of raffia or similar reed-like material, they are very flexible and can be stuffed to the bursting point, a feat which I had more than accomplished. Brigitte, Anja, Misha, and Uli were present on the platform when it spilled its contents. It was precisely the event necessary to diffuse the emotional atmosphere which likewise had reached the bursting point.

All present welcomed the comic relief. People sobbing in each others arms were suddenly doubling over with laughter when I began to scoop up my ancient socks and underwear, my lederhosen, the old army pants, and my ski boots. Men with alleged suitcase-disaster experience gathered round, advising me gravely on the seriousness of the mishap, as well as of the situation—only fifteen minutes to departure time.

If Misha had still carried his gun, he would have fired into the air to achieve order. Now he merely shouted, "Quiet! Away!"

Misha, the victor of Stalingrad, the navigator of T-34 tanks, the capturer of war criminals, the mighty blaster of fish, dispenser of depth charges, and above all, the world-class vodka guzzler—undisputed, unchallenged champion in this category—Misha kneeled down and examined the damage. The old, brittle leather straps holding the two halves together had snapped. Without a second's hesitation, he ripped the belt out of his trousers, motioning me to do the same. Someone volunteered a pair of yellow suspenders to complete the restoration. All bystanders applauded.

"Good work!" he said, admiring his repair job. "The Americans will be so jealous when they see you with it."

I had wondered why Misha had brought his briefcase. Now I found out: ancient Russian custom—Vodka brings good fortune to departing dear ones, also to arriving dear ones or visiting dear ones. Obviously everyone present on the platform was dear to him. Several full bottles made the rounds. No one wanted to miss the chance for good fortune. Tears dried up, voices grew louder, then there was laughter, someone started singing the "Star Spangled Banner," others joined in, and soon the entire platform, vodka or not, was singing. Yes, in addition to everything else, Misha knew how to ease the pain of parting in man's fragile breast.

Once inside the train, I felt kind of numb, grateful for the seat next to my mother, who had put on her tight-lipped face, occasionally giving me a sorrowful, apologetic look. Closing my eyes, the picture of a fox appeared before me. It was circling a huge, high-rising, stony-faced shape. The fox looked lost, occasionally stopping, lifting one of its front paws while sniffing the air. After about ten minutes I opened my eyes again, just as we were passing that terraced, bomb-crater garden. Red, red tomatoes everywhere. That's when I could not hold back any longer.

Hubert C. Kueter, born 1930 in Breslau, Germany, received his PhD in Germanic languages and literature at the University of Michigan. He taught German language and literature at Colby College from 1965 to 1997. During the first ten years at Colby, he enjoyed working part time as a certified ski instructor at Sugarloaf USA.

Following a lifelong interest in good cuisine, he opened the Johann Sebastian B Restaurant in Oakland, Maine, of which he was the owner/manager/chef from 1975 to 2003.